THE SAGA OF A SHIP
THE EARL OF ZETLAND

THE SAGA
OF A SHIP
THE EARL OF ZETLAND

ADAM ROBSON

THE SHETLAND TIMES LIMITED
LERWICK, 1982

First published August, 1982

©Adam Robson, 1981

I.S.B.N. 0 900662 37 9

Illustrated by the Author

Printed and published by
The Shetland Times Ltd.,
Prince Alfred Street, Lerwick, Shetland

CONTENTS

LIST OF ILLUSTRATIONS

To My Shetland Forebears

ACKNOWLEDGMENTS

Firstly, I owe a very considerable debt of gratitude to many people without whom the task of gathering information would have been difficult, if not impossible. Inevitably the *Earl of Zetland* wove an intricate web of human relationships during her 73-year career, and the esteem in which she was held in Shetland emerged even during conversation and correspondence in preliminary investigations.

Those who follow evinced this high regard, and I am most grateful to: Gordon Donaldson, Professor Emeritus of Scottish History, University of Edinburgh, who first saw the possibilities of a book and has been a patient mentor with counsel and encouragement at every stage; William Lind of Bridge of Weir whose correspondence and important historical documents provided valuable data about the ship herself and shipbuilding by the River Cart, Paisley; the late Captain William (Willie) Inkster, formerly harbourmaster, Lerwick Harbour Trust, a veritable mine of information about Shetland shipping and people, who offered many an evening of yarning and a flow of vital evidence in letters; and Captain Adam Tait, Master, *Earl of Zetland* during most of World War II, whose invaluable contribution in tape recordings, letters and documents brought the war years colourfully alive. Captain William (Willie) Sinclair served on the old and new *Earl,* and was skipper of the latter vessel for seven years until his retiral in 1972. His assistance in providing research background and checking writing proved of great worth, as did the provision of accurate material and a wide variety of facts by Alastair McRobb of Glasgow, whose extensive records of the North Company are unsurpassed. Anderson Manson, originally from Maryfield, Bressay, was kind enough to contribute useful reference books as well as a selection of stories and anecdotes from his experience of the old ship. I am in debt to John Manson, depute director of design and technical services, Shetland Islands Council, whose ready work in checking newspaper files and general advice have been a great aid in filling numerous gaps. Also, Captain David (Davie) Henry, skipper of the *Earl* for a time, Laurence (Lowrie) Gifford, former crew member, and Freddie Pottinger, at one time cabin boy, and latterly catering manager of the North Company, all willingly brought authenticity to many aspects of life aboard. Andy Irvine, former

Shetland county councillor, knew the *Earl* well and ultimately put into rhyme what was a summing up of the feelings of people in the North Isles of Shetland. His talent immortalised the ship in verse. The magnificent photographic collection in the Shetland Museum provided numerous prints of yesteryear on the *Earl* and I am grateful to Tom Henderson, formerly curator, for permission to have these. Several other notable photographs are included through the co-operation of Mrs Derek Mann, Lerwick (grand-daughter of the famous Captain William Spence) and Mrs Agnes Gifford. If those named above played a very important role in the Shetland aspect of this book, I am no less grateful to many others who gave generously of time in many ways and they are included in an acknowledgement list at the end.

Secondly, I am greatly obliged to a group in Britain, Norway and Israel who have contributed in writing to me concerning other features of the steamer's involvement with people. For war-time aspects and references to the fight of the Norwegians against the German invaders I acknowledge the help of Andreas Alveberg, Stavanger, Martin Bjorlo, Alesund, Mathias H. Myklebust, Fosnavag, Peter Sperre, Alesund, J. Chr. per Sundt, Bergen, and Ragnar Ulstein, Alesund. Although the old ship had only an insignificant and peripheral role in the vast movement of the Jewish people to their Promised Land, she was, nevertheless, the vehicle for hundreds of impassioned immigrants to seek their Utopia. Their experiences in adventure and privation are an embodiment of sacrifice and I hope that this may in some way be conveyed in what could only be a sketch of an involved, intricate and emotional human situation.

There are many people whose understanding brought response to my initial letters to "Davar", the Hebrew language newspaper in Tel Aviv, and "Jerusalem Post", the English language publication in Jerusalem. To Peggy Priscilla Fuchs I owe special appreciation for the series of informative letters which led to full data about Yehuda Halevi, Hebrew poet and philosopher whose name was chosen by the immigrants to grace their ship, and the commander Israel Kharkovsky (now Horev). His assistance in describing the epic voyage from North Africa to Palestine was the key factor in researching the actual passage. In turn it was Israel Horev who mentioned the name of a courageous and resourceful girl, Nadia Franco, who was closely involved in organising the immigrants ashore. To her I offer my sincere thanks. Clearly she was dedicated to her mission. Jacob Melnitzer (now Metzer), radio operator on the ship, and Shimshon Sarfati, immigrant, have presented significant viewpoints in their experiences of 35 years ago. I sincerely thank them for correspondence. V. N. Malinov supplied eye witness accounts of the *Earl of Zetland* as she lay at Aberdeen in July, 1946, when he coincidentally inspected her as a possible purchase for the Palestine Marine and Commercial Agency, a strictly commercial proposition and unrelated to illegal immigration, also of the *Anal* or *Yehuda Halevy* (alternative spelling of Halevi, "y" instead of "i") when she was moored amid a "ghost fleet" of immigrant ships at Haifa breakwater. His information has been invaluable, as was the boost provided by the adventures of another Jewish girl, Ruth Kluger (now Aliav), as described in the book "The Last Escape". I was privileged to have the help of Norman H. Morris, executive secretary of the Zionist Federation, who, along with many others, assisted in a variety of ways. They are also listed at the end.

If those named above offered the evidence from a Jewish viewpoint there were the Royal Navy seamen who had the unenviable task of ensuring that vessel like the *Yehuda Halevy* alias *Anal* were intercepted before reaching the shores of Palestine. In describing the events leading up to and the remarkable encounter between *Yehuda Halevy* and His Majesty's Ships *Whitesand Bay*, *Peacock*, *Talybont* and *Skipjack* I had the inestimable help of Lieutenant Commander D. L. Satterford, D.S.C., Commanding Officer, HMS *Peacock*, and Petty Officer (Electrician) H. G. Fuller, Chief Petty Officer, Torpedo Coxswain (T.B.D.) C. T. Martin and Torpedo Electrician R. C. Mellor, all HMS *Peacock;* Petty Officer (Q.R. Rating) G. A. Neale, HMS *Talybont*, and Petty Officer (Shipwright) C. A. Thompson, HMS *Skipjack.* I also heard from Signalman (Bunting) J. Reed who crewed on HMS *Whitesand Bay.* I am especially in debt to Mr Fuller and Mr Thompson who came up with the splendid collection of action photographs of the interception and aftermath, also to a nephew of Captain Adam Tait, *Earl of Zetland,* the late Tom Anderson, who coincidentally was serving with the 6th Airborne Division in Palestine. He chanced to be at Haifa when the ship was towed into harbour, was astounded to be confronted by the profile of the *Earl of Zetland* so familiar from his life in Shetland, and took a number of historic photographs.

THE SAGA OF A SHIP
THE "EARL OF ZETLAND"

The story of the *Earl of Zetland* in northern waters is an historical fact. Her subsequent final voyage in the Mediterranean as a Jewish immigrant ship and her demolition, cast away and seemingly forgotten, a gaunt hulk in shallow water at the Shemen beach, Haifa, is also fact. Undeniably, however, a ship and her voyages never end as long as we remember. And such memories can be vivid. These events live on in our minds, their significance in proportion to what we have experienced or have heard. Thus the old *Earl* survives. It is further fact that generations who have passed on, and who knew her particularly well, can no longer reflect on her saga, but those of us who remain, and who experienced her atmosphere, live to tell the tale and now record it for posterity.

While there was the literal evidence gleaned from a variety of sources, it seemed appropriate to develop free paraphrases to lend individuality and colour to situations. Therefore, certain liberties have been taken in description. Inevitably in the complexity of research there was much detail and, in consequence, risk of omission or error. For any fault I apologise. Also in such involved human experience there must remain untapped sources of information, and doubtless there will be those who read this book who know yet another tale or anecdote about "da auld Earl", *Anal* or *Yehuda Halevy*, as inter-island steamer or illegal immigrant ship. It is hoped, however, that as her story unfolds in these pages, what emerges will sufficiently illustrate the many splendoured facets of life centred around this steamer. If this be so then I will rest content.

ADAM ROBSON

Dollar, 1981.

1

Beginnings

George Hay of Hayfield, the big house overlooking Clickimin Loch
outside Lerwick, Director of the trading firm of Hay & Company,
was in a contemplative frame of mind. It was time for a consultation
with the past and a careful assessment of the future. He passed the
Mercat Cross and greeted inhabitants of the island capital to whom
he was a well acknowledged personality, a figure of authority
tempered by tolerance and humility, interested in the affairs of men
and public spirited. His fellow citizens knew about the meeting to
which he was going and they reckoned that he would be called upon

A Shetland trading ketch under full sail.

to chair it. The 25th February, 1876, was to be a significant day.

Hay's thoughts were of Shetland; its isolation as a group of 100 islands — 17 inhabited — set in the turmoil of the northern seas; its seventy mile length extending from Sumburgh Head thrusting out into the notorious tide-riven Sumburgh Roost, a perpetual risk for sailing craft, to Muckle Flugga, the outermost projection of rock to the north, nothing but vast tracts of ocean between it and the Arctic ice cap 800 miles beyond; its 35 mile expanse from Ve Skerries pounded by the mighty Atlantic Ocean in the west, to Out Skerries, remote and frequently inaccessible, in the east.

He reflected on the practical difficulties of communication, with a population of over 29,000 souls to consider, and the sparse and inadequate liaison by sea between one island community and another, of how in the early part of the 19th century, not many years ago, the major town of Lerwick was a world apart for the great majority of those who gleaned a living in the North Isles. Inevitably the sea imposed severe limitations on any form of regular transport,

whilst on land a man and his family were confined to foot traffic over often saturated and trackless moor and bog. Indeed it was true to say that from the eighth century AD when the Norsemen were finding their way to Ultima Thule, there had been little change or development in the method men, women and children could contact their brethren elsewhere in Shetland. Sea distance between one island and another was, admittedly, relatively short and boats were in abundant supply, yet the risks brought their toll of life over the years, through swampings and capsizes — there was the unheralded squall or unexpected gale.

Hay kept left across the square towards Commercial Street and the new office of the North of Scotland and Orkney and Shetland Steam Navigation Company, his head tilted, countering the chill east wind. Momentarily he paused and glanced back over his shoulder to scan the white-punctuated lead-coloured water, with the sheltering island of Bressay a mile away. The old phrase "so near and yet so far" occurred to him. Maybe today the strong breeze stirring the harbour waters was not enough to prevent the sixern (a six-oared open boat) ferry, under sail or oars, making the passage from Lerwick to Mail on Bressay, but he thought of the relentless pressures of the sea and of the innumerable occasions over the decades when such a passage was utterly remote — much too risky to consider, especially in winter. And inevitably this problem prevailed in the country districts.

His train of thought was broken by the appearance of several more men. Alexander Mitchell, solicitor, Charles Robertson, partner in the grocery firm of R. & C. Robertson, also serving on the town council as a bailie, and William Sievwright, another solicitor, all arrived. They were from Lerwick, although Robertson had a strong kinship with the North Isles, having been born in Unst. George Hay was greeted warmly and together they entered the office of the company. The atmosphere of the room belied the chill February blast outside. Three more times the glass panelled door opened. It was embellished by the company's crest, showing a steamer with a flurry of smoke about her funnel, confirming the developing age of steam propulsion, and with the name of the firm encircling it. John Robertson and Charles Merrylees came together. The former was nicknamed "Robertson of the Trance" — not to be taken literally, because he was a man who wielded considerable influence on community activities — and the latter was already agent of the North of Scotland and Orkney and Shetland Steam Navigation Company, known locally as the North Company. William Irvine, a director in the firm of Hay & Company, was followed by Arthur Laurenson, partner in the hosiery firm of Laurenson & Company, also a distinguished Shetlander. They formed an intelligent, practical group. Little time was wasted. After a brief discussion George Hay was appointed to the chair. Charles Merrylees took the minute book as secretary. As the others talked informally, he made the first entry: "25th February, 1876. Lerwick. A meeting of gentlemen interested in the formation and promotion of a new steam company for the North Isles trade was held in the North of Scotland and Orkney and Shetland Steam Navigation Company's office this day."

The chairman opened the meeting formally, and the eight Shetlanders thus began to pave the way for a new era of sea transport amongst the islands. A wide ranging discussion was summed up later in the minute book by Merrylees in his contemporary stylish and regular copperplate writing. "It was resolved in view of the s.s. *Chieftain's Bride* being about to be withdrawn for sale from the North Isles trade and the consequent inconvenience upon the isles, that those now present form themselves with any other persons who may be disposed to join them into a company for continuing communication by a steam vessel among the islands." He added ". . . improving communication between Lerwick and the North Isles on the dissolution of the Shetland Steam Shipping Company Limited, whose vessel the *Chieftain's Bride* has for seven years carried on the trade. Owing to the unsuitability of that vessel and the heavy annual outlay required to keep it in repair as a certified passenger ship, the Company decided on winding up. With a view to meet the largely increasing trade of the islands the promoters consider themselves warranted in starting a new company."

Unanimously the group of islanders decided to name the new organisation "The Shetland Islands' Steam Navigation Company (Limited)". Half the share stock would be subscribed by the North Company, in whose offices the meeting was held, with the remaining half being taken up by interested persons in Shetland.

To ensure a balance, further directors were proposed. Joseph Leask of Sand would represent the country districts, whilst Lord Provost Jamieson, Simpson Shepherd and Alexander Webster would be delegates from Aberdeen. A prospectus would be submitted for public scrutiny and advertising done in "The Shetland Times". The capital would be £6,000 divided into 1,200 shares of £5 each, to be called up as the directors saw fit. Hay was well satisfied with the outcome of what was to be an historically meaningful meeting.

Conversation became general after the customary vote of thanks to the chair, but tended to dwell on aspects of travel in the islands. The immediate past had not been satisfactory. In the mid-nineteenth

B

century the Unst Shipping Company owned two smacks, the *Imogen*
and *Matilda,* which traded between the island and Lerwick, subject, of
course, to the vagaries of the northern seas with their fickle tide runs
in narrow sounds between the rock-girt shores. Alexander Sandison
of Unst was their agent. The skippers of these vessels did everything
humanly possible to maintain a respectable timetable, but limitations
were obvious. In the early 1860s a group attempted to introduce
steam and in May, 1863 the erstwhile newspaper the "Shetland
Advertiser" had carried the statement: "We learn with much
pleasure that a meeting was held in Unst on the 17th instant to
consider the propriety of putting a steamer on the North Isles trade,
when it was agreed to form a company with limited liability, capital
£4,000 to be called the Shetland Isles Steam Navigation Company.
The prospectus is in preparation and will shortly be laid before the
public." An imaginative and far-sighted idea never reached fruition
since it was not possible to obtain a ship.

In mid-1868, however, the Shetland Steam Shipping Company
Limited had been founded in Lerwick. On 1st September Alexander
Sandison received a letter from their secretary with the suggestion
that the two small 10-15 ton vessels should be sold and that the Unst
company should invest in the new firm. This was agreed.

Meanwhile, the Lerwick company had been searching for a
suitable steamship to serve the islands. They discovered the
attractively named *Chieftain's Bride* lying at Glasgow and bought her
for £2,100. She had been built by Kirkpatrick, McIntyre in 1866 and
was owned originally by Hugh McLean of Tobermory and Archibald
Murray of Glasgow. In June, 1868 she passed on to John Steel who
released her for sale on 24th December, 1868. Sandison had had
information about this vessel and, in writing to the manager of the
Shetland Steam Shipping Company accepting their proposal about a
merger, he expressed a prophetic opinion, "You must not think that
any of us are against Steam, but at the same time I wish hereby to
record to you by this letter, my firm belief that the *Chieftain's Bride* is
unsuitable for the trade. A vessel of 94 tons burden with a 25 horse
power, she is a trash and would be thrown aside where either speed or
power is required. Her class for purposes like ours is fast going out of
use . . ." The underpowered ship proved to be inadequate as
expected. If she could work in the sheltered stretches of the Firth of
Clyde, the east side of Shetland was a different proposition. These
were testing waters for any type of small vessel and the ferocity of
numerous storms, fast moving ebb and flow, the demands of
incessant work and the vessel's failure to cope led to criticism which
grew in volume. Although she held the distinction of pioneering

regular steam travel in the North Isles of Shetland, the travelling public had no illusions about her inadequacy for passenger and cargo work in the conditions, and locally she was dubbed *The Crab*. Her reputation was discussed in the local press. One correspondent had strong views: " . . . I am quite sure that very few people indeed take the trouble to consider how much of the *Bride's* success is due to the incredible amount of exertion and labour of her captain and crew. Leaving the regular days of work out of the question, the amount of night work is excessive. Night after night without sleep or rest these great fellows endure without a grumble, and all this for a pittance in wages. Why, I understand the captain gets no more, and in some cases even less, than an ordinary seaman on a trader. As regards his capabilities as a captain or his manners as a gentleman let those who have had the pleasure of sailing with him testify, as that is not my object in writing. The crew, I may mention in passing, are well known to be as civil and good a set of men as ever sailed in a ship.

"Is it not a downright shame now to allow these men to slave and toil like this in that rubbish of a thing that is not worthy of the name of a steamer, which can't and won't be made to move, taking twenty-four hours to do the work of twelve, thereby depriving the crew of their needed rest, and all because we do not have the pluck and spirit to get the right vessel for the growing trade.

"I, for one, would cheerfully enter into the speculation of a new boat to do the whole trade for the country twice a week, of sufficient power and capacity for the daily growing trade, and I am certain that influential men, who would have nothing to do with this boat, would come forward and may support the scheme. Only try it and see. The result would be a new and commodious vessel commanded by the present captain, if he has not by that time left in despair, giving the shareholders a reasonable dividend and the feeling that we have at least done our duty to ourselves and the country while at the same time we have laid off the yoke on the truly hard wrought slaves on board the *Chiefain's Bride* . . ."

The letter was a condemnation of the ship, but a testimonial to captain and crew. William Nicolson, her skipper, had the character to endure because he had been brought up in a hard school. He was born in the district of Whiteness during the autumn of 1838 and, in keeping with the Shetland tradition, went to sea. His first voyage as a cabin boy on a Leith ship employed in the Faroe and Iceland cod fishing, tested his resilience and resourcefulness. Life was tough for a young teenager and his reward of 6/8d a week must have seemed a pittance, yet he stayed with the fishing for 11 years and thrice survived from vessels which were a total loss. His perseverance benefited him because in 1864, aged 26, he became chief officer of the sailing packet *Queen of the Isles,* trading goods, passengers and occasional mails between Leith and the west side of Shetland. Quietly yet determinedly ambitious, he took navigation classes in Leith which enabled him to apply to the Aberdeen, Leith, Clyde and Tay Shipping Company and in 1872, through that contact, he was given the *Chieftain's Bride.* This firm became the North of Scotland and Orkney and Shetland Steam Navigation Company in June, 1873.

If the conversation of the new directors had centred on the unfortunate trends in transport during the seven years of the reign of the *Chieftain's Bride,* subsequent opinion was full of optimism for an era of progressive development. The eight Shetlanders had reached a momentous decision. Now it was a matter of discovering the best kind of ship to cater for the extending needs of people and trade in Shetland's temperamental climate. They could not then anticipate the remarkable success stemming from their inaugural meeting and subsequent decisions. In any event they ventured into the windswept dusk of February in Shetland, with high hopes of the future. A few lingered and spoke of the continuing unresolved problems of shipping amid the North Isles in particular. They readily reminisced about the mail situation typical since a semblance of a system evolved.

It had been with characteristic initiative that the people of Unst, that most northerly isle in Britain, had ensured that there was a post of a kind as early as 1820. This had been maintained by the overland and ferry route from and to Lerwick, with a sixern deployed to give the "post runner" transport over the short seaways. The method was still in use, serviceable up to a point, but far from efficient. At least the inhabitants in the isolated croft-houses and hamlets, and on the route of the "runner", benefited to some extent by the service.

It was mentioned that there was a solitary postman for Unst and Yell. Davie Johnson of Haroldswick would leave from Baltasound, collecting the outgoing letters on the way. From Uyeasound he crossed the south end of Unst over the Scord, to Snarravoe, where he was rowed across Bluemull Sound to Cullivoe. There he would lift the mail from Gloup and Cullivoe before heading south to Gutcher, Sellafirth and Mid Yell. He carried on his back, eventually to Ulsta on the far side of Yell, all the outgoing letters from Unst and Yell. Next morning, with the incoming mail in a bag on his back, he would retrace his steps over the moorland track, delivering letters to the same places. And he had no one to help him, unless, as he grew older, his daughter would come the 12 mile return journey from Haroldswick to Snarravoe to meet him on his homeward trek.

The Shetland of the
Earl of Zetland

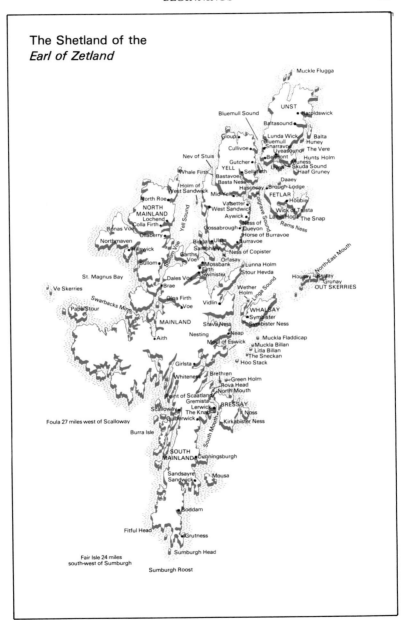

Muckle Flugga

UNST
Bluemull Sound • Haroldswick
Baltasound •
Gloup • Lunda Wick Balta
Bluemull Huney
Cullivoe • Snarravoe The Vere
Uyeasound
Nev of Stuis Belmont Hunts Holm
Gutcher • Muness
YELL Uyea Skuda Sound
Whale Firth Sellafirth Haaf Gruney
Bastavoe Daaey
Basta Ness Brough Lodge
Holm of Hascosay FETLAR
West Sandwick Mid Yell Hobbie
North Roe • Vatsetter • Wick of Tresta
NORTH West Sandwick Lamb Hoga The Snap
MAINLAND Aywick • Rams Ness
Lochend • Ness of
Ronas Voe Colla Firth • Gossabrough • Queyon
Ollaberry Horse of Burravoe
Northmaven Birga Ulsta Burravoe
Hillswick Samphrey Ness of Copister
Garths Orfasay
Sullom • Voe Mossbank Lunna Holm
Mossbank Stour Hevda
St. Magnus Bay Swinister
Dales Voe Housay Bruray
Ve Skerries Brae Wether Grunay
Holm OUT SKERRIES
Olna Firth North-East Mouth
Swarbacks Minn Voe Vidlin
Papa Stour WHALSAY
MAINLAND Symbister
Stava Ness Symbister Ness
Aith Nesting Neap
Moul of Eswick Muckla Fladdicap
Muckla Billan
Litla Billan
The Sneckan
Girlsta Hoo Stack
Whiteness Brethren
Green Holm
Point of Scaatland Rova Head
Gremista North Mouth
Scalloway Lerwick BRESSAY
The Knab
Gulberwick Noss
Kirkabister Ness
Foula 27 miles west of Scalloway
Burra Isle
SOUTH
MAINLAND Cunningsburgh
Sandsayre
Sandwick Mousa
Boddam
Fitful Head Grutness
Fair Isle 24 miles Sumburgh Head
south-west of Sumburgh
Sumburgh Roost

Yell Sound
Colgrave Sound
Linga Sound
South Mouth

Of course Shetland itself was far from well served by postal services. In 1810 there were ten mails a year "wind and weather permitting". That the climatic clause played an important part could be gauged by a complaint by one Neill, during his tour of the Shetland Isles in 1806, that "the letters of two and three months arrive together". He urged that a fortnightly service was essential. If people amongst the islands could write to each other after a fashion, any contact beyond Sumburgh Head was erratic in the extreme.

Some of the members of the newly fledged company recalled Sir Walter Scott's writing in his journal of 1814. That year the celebrated author had been invited to join a party of commissioners for the Northern Lighthouse Service in a voyage round the north coast of Scotland and through the various groups of islands to the west and to the north. That time on passage had to be accepted philosophically could be assessed from Scott's remarks: "We left the port of Leith on the 26th July, 1814, ran along the east coast of Scotland, viewing its different curiosities then stood over to Zetland and Orkney . . ." He went on, "2nd August — At sea in the mouth of the Moray Firth. This day is almost a blank, — light, baffling airs which do us little good; most of the landsmen sick, more or less . . . p.m. a breeze, and we begin to think we have passed the Fair Isle, lying between Shetland and Orkney, at which it was our intention to have touched. In short, like one of Sinbad's adventures, we have run on till neither captain nor pilot know exactly where we are. The breeze increases — weather may be called rough; worse and worse after we are in our berths, nothing but booming, trampling and whizzing of waves about our ears, and ever and anon, as we fall asleep, our ribs come in contact with those of the vessel . . ."

"3rd August — At sea as before; no appearance of land; proposed that the Sheriff of Zetland do issue a *meditatione fugae* warrant against his territories, which seem to fly from us. Pass two whalers; speak the nearest, who had come out of Lerwick, which is about twenty miles distant; stand on with a fine breeze. About nine at night, with moonlight and strong twilight, we weather the point of Bardhead, and enter a channel about three quarters of a mile broad, which forms the southern entrance to the harbour of Lerwick . . . We were some time detained by the wonders of a country which displayed so much that was new to us; and having seen what was curious in the Ultima Thule of the ancients, where the sun hardly thought it worth while to go to bed, since his rising was at this season so early, we doubled the extreme northern termination of Scotland, and took a rapid survey of the Hebrides where we found many kind friends."

Thus a voyage progressed under sail with further calls at Staffa, Oban, the northern coast of Ireland, including the Giant's Causeway, and . . . "At length about the middle of September we ended our voyage in the Clyde, at the port of Greenock."

Subjected to the variety of wind, the yacht, owned by the lighthouse commissioners, could but take advantage of how little or how much was offered. They might well have been assisted on their passage to Shetland had they possessed the powers of the legendary King of Sweden, "in his time held second to none in the magical art; and he was so familiar with the evil spirits whom he worshipped that what way soever he turned his cap, the wind would presently blow that way. For this he was called 'Windy-cap'." There was also the legendary Bessie Millie who could have offered wind to Shetland-bound sailing vessels from Orkney. She lived on the Orkney mainland at the beginning of the 19th century and helped her existence by selling favourable winds to mariners. He was a bold master who left the roadstead of Stromness without paying his amount to the aged Bessie. Her fee was extremely moderate, being exactly sixpence; for which, as she explained herself, she boiled her kettle and gave the vessel the advantage of her prayers; because, unlike the King of Sweden, she was not influenced by the ways of the devil. The wind thus petitioned for was, she said, sure to arrive — although frequently the ships and their crews had to wait some time for it! Conversely the motivating force could come too quickly and in too great a volume! Bessie Millie was, reputedly, the notion for Norna of Fitful Head, the ancient sybil of Scott's novel "The Pirate". Bessie was nearly 100 years old when Scott talked to her in her hovel on the side of Brinkie's Brae in Stromness.

It also was recalled by the group of Shetlanders that great seas generated by a mighty wind out of the north-west had crippled a sailing vessel off the top extremity of Unst, a story that had been often recalled. She was being carried rudderless, broadside, rolling drunkenly into the north end of Bluemull Sound. The crew tried to launch their boat, but it was smashed alongside and they could only await a dreadful end on the black, wave and spume-drenched skerries off the Westing in Unst. By the grace of God she came safely through the narrow gap between the rocky islets, scarcely visible in the half light and the maelstrom of whitened sea, then drove ashore, mercifully on the sands of Lundawick behind the massive cliff, the Blue Mull. To that day there was still the outcrop of rock on the sands, round which the men of Unst had contrived to get a hawser before the crewmen of the vessel were dragged ashore. Willing hosts took them to the warmth of the peat fires in the croft-houses.

Then it was discovered that she was the ship *Fivla,* from Iceland with a baled cargo. The sweeping, thundering seas coming straight

The smack *Columbine* in smooth weather.

into Lundawick out of the northern ocean made short work of the *Fivla* and she pounded herself to pieces. Out floated the bales to be swept ashore. Local men waded up to the armpits to retrieve what they could, everyone for himself. Each bale was heaved up the face of the sands above the high water mark, each man creating his own private pile. Remains of the ship went up the beach too.

When little else was coming in, the islanders set to and began to open the bales. Soft as the contents appeared to be, what emerged was hardly what might have been expected. As they tore aside the sacking a drift of white, like blown snow, flurried over the round stones and grass above the sands. Feathers, tiny white feathers! For a while it was thought that the soft down was the outer packing for something valuable, yet, delve as they might, the men came to nothing but feathers. And that was all there was to be had.

Oddly enough, not only the contents, but the casing found a way into the croft-houses of the Westing on Unst, although there was a whiteness about the immediate landscape for a time to come. The sackcloth, in considerable quantity, proved a fine material for covering the walls of but or ben. It was a strange end to a cargo of swansdown! The members of the inaugural meeting of the newly created shipping firm parted in jovial frame of mind. Swansdown indeed! No cargoes like that were likely to be carried in the new North Isles steamer!

Positive action followed. By 25th April, 1876, marine draughtsmen in Aberdeen had produced drawings of a steamer "considered suitable for the inter-island trade". It was a quick result within two months of the decision to go ahead. Mr Mylne, the North of Scotland and Orkney and Shetland Steam Navigation Company's secretary in Aberdeen, had agreed to work in liaison and had acted quickly with initiative. The dimensions of the proposed ship would be 120 feet in length, 20 feet in breadth and 9 feet in depth. Mylne recommended that she should be built under Lloyd's requirements for the 100A class. His suggestions were acceptable to the board. The next move was to have specifications made.

Time was of vital significance. The passenger certificate of the *Chieftain's Bride* was due to expire on 18th May, 1876, and there would be a stop-gap period after this, since a meeting of shareholders in the Masons' Hall, Lerwick at the end of February had accepted the views of the directors. It was a big meeting. The "Crab" had brought a dozen shareholders from Unst alone. And with good reason, because no island of the group would suffer more from the withdrawal of the steamer, previously intimated by circular. It was a Lerwick man, Mr John Robertson Snr., who had moved that the

Shetland Steam Shipping Company be wound up with a view to the establishment of a new company.

Although Unst opinion was concerned about short term inconvenience, all conceded that the financial questions and need for foresight in seeking a practical ship specially designed for their situation, were of paramount importance. Yet, memories were only too readily kindled about not only the shortcomings of the "Crab", but difficulties experienced over 30 years back, in 1839, when the small 10 ton sloop the *Janet* provided an erratic service, then, more recently of course, the *Imogen* and *Matilda*.

In fact trading to and from the North Isles had tended to by-pass Lerwick. Each little port in Shetland communicated directly with the continent in the 16th and 17th centuries. The lairds and clergy found it convenient to get supplies from areas like North Germany and Holland. Bremen merchants purchased fish cured in Shetland, offering in return goods unavailable in the individual islands. Later, when the fish trade was taken up by the lairds native to Shetland, the network of continental contact was maintained because the demand for fish remained. Therefore, the little sailers continued to voyage to the east rather than to the Scottish mainland. Inevitably they traversed great expanses of the empty North Sea which could help or hinder, coming and going in conditions which could be fraught with danger. They sailed from Norway, from Denmark, from Germany and from Holland. And there was no "Windy-cap", King of Sweden, to convey help with an encouraging wind! Not even a Bessie Millie!

But then the Shetland fishermen faced the immensity of the ocean and took their calculated risks in craft infinitely more vulnerable than any smack. Sixerns played their part in the ferry system, across such as Bluemull Sound from Unst to Yell or Whalsay Sound from Whalsay to the Mainland, as evinced by Sir Walter Scott in his journal. "One can hire a six-oared boat, whaler-built with a taper point at each end, so that the rudder can be hooked on either with pleasure. These vessels look very frail, but are admirably suited to the stormy seas, where they live when a ship's boat stiffly and compactly built must necessarily perish . . ." Essentially, however, they were used as fishing craft in their hundreds and eventually their vulnerability had been cruelly exposed in the gale of 1832 when 105 men lost their lives.

The facts stressed the uncertainty of the movement of people and goods; some kind of stability was essential for the long term. Little wonder then that the board of the Shetland Islands Steam Navigation Company and their shareholders were anxious to forge ahead. It was not merely a question of the security of their money, rather a basic desire to see justice done in coping with a human problem.

Charles Merrylees corresponded with Mylne in Aberdeen to take the planning of their new steamer a stage further. During the period of waiting and with the *Chieftain's Bride* due to leave Shetland in May, Merrylees organised sailing vessels for the interim. Towards the end of the month the smack *Absara,* owned by Messrs Hay and Company, Lerwick, was chartered for £4 per week. Joining her on the North Isles passage was the *Petrel,* owned by a Peter Garriock, at £4:10/-. The company had to find crew and their wages. Thereafter both smacks worked steadily in pleasant summer weather.

By early June, 1876, the company had been registered and certificated, the fee for this being drawn from the account opened with the Union Bank of Scotland in Lerwick. At the company board meeting on the 3rd of the month, George Hay announced the plans and specifications for the projected steamer, forwarded by Mr Mylne. The directors had these laid before them for discussion. Heads grouped together as the men bent over the table, and for a time there was silence as each of them appraised the layout. Conversation developed, accompanied by nods of approval at what they saw. The only dissent was about the manually operated anchor. They knew that amongst the islands a vessel had to anchor on eight to ten occasions each working day, and unanimously they agreed that a steam powered anchor was vital.

As the directors sat down once more it was realised that the replacement steamer would not be available for months to come. There was a feeling of frustration at the thought of too long a spell with the inconvenience of sail, having sampled the potential of steam power, albeit under far from ideal conditions. The vagaries and inconsistencies of the old "Crab" still rankled. A resolution was passed that efforts must be made to procure another steamer.

Subsequent correspondence and negotiations in Aberdeen and Glasgow produced an encouraging telegram which stated concisely, "Steamer, *Lady Ambrosine* available Glasgow. On passage early August." This was read at the late July gathering of the directors and greeted with acclaim. Merrylees was instructed to advertise sailings to the North Isles in "The Shetland Times" and by hand bills.

There was further news, pleasurable in one sense, disconcerting in another. Plans and specifications for the proposed steamship had been put out to tender the previous month and several offers were now lodged, ranging from £6,890 to £9,100. But even the lower

figure was in excess of the capital of £6,000 decided upon in
February. Each director had before him a list of firms and prices.
They were wide ranging:

Black and Noble, Montrose	£6,890
James Howden & Co., Glasgow	£6,900
C. Mitchell & Co., Newcastle	£7,150
A. & J. Inglis, Glasgow	£7,500
Palmer & Co., Newcastle	£7,650
Stephen & Sons, Govan	£8,000
J. Wingate & Co., Whiteinch	£8,750
John Elder & Co., Glasgow	£8,750
Railtone Dickson, Middlesbrough	£9,000
D. H. Henderson, Partick	£9,100

A prolonged discussion ensued, which taxed George Hay's
chairmanship. It was well into the evening of 25th July before the
board submitted to inconclusive findings. Financial questions had to
remain unanswered. Every one of the ten firms responding to the
advertisement for tenders had posed the same problem — too dear a
submission. Even the least expensive was in excess by £890, but D.
H. Henderson's figure of £3,100 more than the capital of the
Shetland Islands Steam Navigation Company Limited caused many
an eyebrow to be raised.

No decision was taken. Merrylees wrote in the minute book the
next day: "All these offers being so much in excess of the company's
capital, the meeting resolved to adjourn the consideration of the
building of a steamer until the general meeting of members to be held
on 10th August, and until the subject has been fully discussed with
the directors of the North of Scotland and Orkney and Shetland
Steam Navigation Company who hold such a large interest in this
company. Meantime they instructed Mr Merrylees to intimate to the
several builders who have lodged tenders, that their offers cannot be
entertained on account of their being so much higher than the
company anticipated or can afford to meet." This was inevitably a
disappointing outcome, although at the very least it was progress of a
kind.

On Saturday, 15th July, "The Shetland Times" showed relief
with the statement: "We are glad to learn that the directors of the
company anticipate being able to place a steamer on the North Isles
passage about the first of August".

No doubt "the first of August" implied, in the Shetland idiom,
early in the month rather than an accurate date. In fact the *Lady
Ambrosine* appeared in the south mouth of Lerwick harbour on the
night of Monday, 7th August, 1876, having come up from Glasgow

during the weekend. Under the command of Captain William
Nicolson, who was destined to have considerable influence in the
construction and layout of the postponed new steamer, the *Lady
Ambrosine* immediately sailed out of the north mouth of the harbour
for Yell Sound ports on the Tuesday morning, returning the next
day. On the Wednesday she made a trip with directors of both the
shipping companies, then set out on her second run to the north, this
time to Unst and the intermediate ports at her moderate speed of
eight knots.

The *Lady Ambrosine* proved to have about the same capacity as
the *Chieftain's Bride* although her internal layout was more functional.
She had been launched in December, 1873, from the yard of J. and
R. Swan of Dumbarton. Originally owned by the Western Isles
Steam Packet Company, the steamer operated in the Inner Hebrides.
In 1875 she was auctioned and bought by John McCallum and had
the distinction of serving the remote St. Kilda community. In 1885
the *Lady Ambrosine* was lengthened by 20 feet and when on charter to
Shetland she was still owned by the Glasgow firm, McCallum and
Company, who charged £80 per month. Strangely enough despite the
fact that her successor was of similar size to the old "Crab", the new
steamer was much more acceptable in the eyes of the islanders. This
was high-lighted by a letter from Alexander Sandison to "The
Shetland Times" at the end of October, 1876:

"As I have just accidentally heard that the little steamship *Lady
Ambrosine* is about to be withdrawn from the service in which she was
engaged at the beginning of August, I think it right to bring before
the shareholders of the company and the public generally the services
she has rendered since her arrival here. I think I am not overpraising
anyone when I say the captain, crew and vessel have given
satisfaction, and that the trade of the islands has been carried out in
an efficient manner. My experience has been that both the agent and
directors have studied the interests of the shippers of stock and done
what they could to accommodate all parties. From this port
(Baltasound) alone 277 cattle, 1474 sheep and 11 ponies have been
shipped. It would be as well to ascertain what she has done at all the
other ports, and then consider whether it is better now to renew the
charter of the *Lady Ambrosine* on the best possible terms rather than
return to the sailing craft for the winter months. The directors and
shareholders of the North Company must be aware that the sailing
craft will entail a loss, and without any satisfaction or security of
regular communication. There may be even a greater loss with the
charter of the *Lady Ambrosine,* but there will be the satisfaction of
carrying on the trade in a proper manner; yet I hold that it is a matter

for the serious consideration of the directors and shareholders of the company whether it is not their duty to maintain steam communications and assure the public that even at the risk of a loss they are determined to carry on the trade in an efficient and proper manner. As a small shareholder I would say by all means produce the steamers whose loss cannot be ignored in the interests of the general public, not to be overlooked or trifled with.''

Merrylees had been in correspondence with McCallum and Company, the Glasgow firm, but they wanted £90 per month during the winter, with the Shetland firm paying all running expenses. The directors were unhappy about the finance and despite Sandison's letter they resolved to discontinue the charter of the *Lady Ambrosine.*

Meanwhile, under Captain Nicolson, the ''peerie'' steamer (peerie: Shetland dialect, ''small'') had continued to voyage north through the treacherous channels. The North Isles population were better served and pleased than hitherto. About the middle of October the schooner *Venus* ran ashore on the island of Bigga and but for the intervention of the *Lady Ambrosine* would have gone the way of many a sailing vessel before her. The master of the *Venus,* Captain Goudie, had agreed verbally with Captain Nicolson at the time of the stranding that £50 would be a fair sum for saving the schooner, for undoubtedly she would have been knocked to pieces had the sea got up at Bigga, but her owner considered otherwise. He proposed £20. Leask, the owner, attended the meeting of the directors to state his case. When he left it was considered reasonable to compromise, and £35 was offered.

The risk of the premature departure of the *Lady Ambrosine* was avoided when a telegram appeared from her owners reducing the charter fee to the previously arranged £80. Also they wished to withdraw the mate put on board by them, and gave the company the option of terminating the charter by a month's notice, a reservation they claimed for themselves.

Thus the steamer maintained her work. Her earnings for October and November amounted to £452:6:3 with expenses of £382:12/-. The surplus of £69:14:3 was thought reasonable, since a loss had been anticipated.

At the end of 1876 Captain Nicolson was delegated to travel south to check on the construction of the new ship. Robert Sinclair of the local schooner *Aeriel* was given command of the *Lady Ambrosine* at the rate of £2 per week with provisions when on board. It was no fault of his that the profit and loss account for December showed a deficit of £47, but it was enough to sway opinion to decide to end her charter on 4th February, 1877. Her demise was accelerated after she ran foul of rocks at Burravoe and carried away her forefoot on 4th January. Thus the second pioneer of steam in the North Isles of Shetland made her exit at the end of the month. The smacks *Absara, Spell* and *Spy* replaced her. The steamer's departure stressed the gap between the quality of service of steam against sail, and the advertising showed the anomaly of the situation, with sailing vessels operating under the heading "Shetland Islands Steam Navigation Company Limited"!

2

The Birth of a Steamer

Alexander Sandison's misgivings about the ill-fated *Chieftain's Bride* and concern regarding the premature withdrawal of the *Lady Ambrosine* had had considerable justification in the light of events. The year 1876 had been fraught with teething troubles of the transition from sail to steam. In the interim, here was sail having the last word as the smacks worked the North Isles passage, but, despite the temporary setback, the wind of change was continuing to blow.

Back in July, 1876, the directors had reluctantly agreed to postpone the order for the ship, although a study of the tenders had

The shape of things to come.

revealed that James Howden and Company of Glasgow, with their price of £6,900, which was the second lowest, had made an extremely objective assessment. Indeed, the Shetland Company approached them again so that at the board meeting of 10th August the directors had on the table the original plans and specifications plus amended versions by Howden. George Hay had a full meeting to govern since a deputation of Aberdeen directors appeared for the important occasion. Every conceivable factor was thoroughly scrutinised. They studied the vessel's plans from stem to stern. They considered and re-considered her from keel to masthead. Eventually Hay stated from the chair, and asked to have minuted, that the original plans and specifications could not be departed from except that she was to have a straight stem and no figurehead; the poop and fo'c'sle would be carried up straight and not rounded in, and that the Lloyd's classification would be 90A instead of 100A.

By the end of August Howden had confirmed that they could construct the steamer for £6,650, the vessel to be ready for trial by

15th March, 1877, but it was said that the directors in Aberdeen had negotiated a reduction of £50 on this sum, thus the cost would be £6,600. Some alterations had been made to the steering gear aft. Also there was no stipulation in the printed specification about steam power for anchor operations, a factor which had been considered earlier by the directors. They aimed at a speed of ten knots for their ship on a consumption of not more than four cwts. of coal per hour.

After deliberating at length the board agreed to increase the capital. The £6,000 designated would fall short of the all-in costs. Probably another £1,000 would give them a better chance of coping with the renegotiated pricing. It was resolved to bring the shareholders to Lerwick to discuss a special resolution: "That to meet the cost of the new steamer about to be built for the company, the capital of the company be increased to £7,000 by the issue of 200 shares of £5 each . . ."

On 7th September Merrylees read a letter to a meeting. Howden had not agreed to concede the £50 mentioned earlier, and the price as far as they were concerned remained at £6,650. From Aberdeen Mylne corroborated this, having retreated from the stand made previously. The meeting in Lerwick acquiesced. A speed of ten knots on the engine design was considered by the prospective contractors as being optimistic, although they were attempting to ensure something very close to it.

Mr Mylne had consented to act in liaison with Messrs Howden and Company to ensure "symmetry in the vessel's rig". In addition, and as had been stipulated earlier, Captain William Nicolson would travel south in mid-December, 1876, to supervise and check the layout to make certain that detailing would be in keeping with the tasks of the steamer in the demanding work in Shetland.

The idea of travelling to Glasgow, and Paisley, where the keel had been laid, appealed to William Nicolson. It was unusual for a master to control the fittings by the builders and he was aware of being given a privilege and no little amount of responsibility. He was not unduly concerned since he accepted and administered authority, and he knew he could cope more than adequately with his designated role of superintending the layout. And, as a Shetlander, he would do so unassumingly.

Then, en route south, he stood on the bridge of the *St. Nicholas* beside her skipper as the "sooth" boat raised anchor and got under way past the Knab to starboard and, presently, the point of Kirkabister Ness on Bressay to port. The deep bass note of the steamer's whistle echoed over the Lerwick roof tops, a momentary interruption to his thoughts about forthcoming weeks. He wondered what Paisley would be like. In a way he was surprised. Glasgow was certainly a centre of building. The Clyde and shipbuilding were synonymous, but Paisley was more off the beaten track, and despite his widely-travelled seafaring career, in his experience it was unknown in that respect. A day later, after the *St. Nicholas* had berthed at Aberdeen and the captain had taken the journey by rail to Glasgow and Paisley, he looked for a representative from Howden or Fullerton to greet him. And it was John Fullerton himself who offered an outstretched hand in greeting as the passengers descended from the suburban train at Paisley. It was the beginning of a close association between the two men as they worked in conjunction at the shipyard.

During the ensuing weeks the Shetlander learned a great deal about Clyde and Paisley industry. With the long tradition, superlative quality and exacting standards of Clyde shipbuilding, renowned throughout the world, there was considerable incentive for a supporting role from the communities on the fringe of the mainstream of marine construction. While the major yards were producing great steamers, it had to be remembered that those had been pioneered by such men as James Watt and Henry Bell. The *Comet* had been the first steam vessel to ply for profit in open tidal waters some 64 years previously.

Nicolson was amused. Like the old *Crab,* the *Comet* had had her detractors. The first appearance on the Clyde aroused a medley of emotions in the populace. There were those who laughed at her owners' pretensions and as many others who were much diverted by the absurdly long smoke-stack which also served as a mast for a square sail. There were the pious who regarded the contraption with dismay, and who maintained that ships should proceed by kind permission of "the Almighty's ain wind and no' wi' the devil's sun-fire and brimstane". Also, as happened with the *Chieftain's Bride,* the *Comet* was never a success according to the ledgers. Her hull was not practicable for the work she had to do, and Henry Bell had her beached at Helensburgh to be lengthened by 20 feet. Coincidentally, although Nicolson was not to know it then, the ship he was supervising was destined to be lengthened by a surprisingly similar amount only seven years after her launching. Unlike the *Comet,* however, in the long term she was to prove her mettle in the realm of finance and other areas.

Basic and primitive though Bell's steamship had been, she created a precedent which had to be acknowledged by the protagonists of sail, and steadily, as the years passed, firms became established and flourished. Gradually a great and romantic industry was phased into a 22 mile stretch of the Clyde and tributaries. Before he had died, less than two years previously in 1875, Alexander Stephen had made a great business at Linthouse. He built good ships, graceful ships and fast ships. And firms like Denny's of Dumbarton, Lobnitz of Renfrew, Fairfields, and Brown's of Clydebank, were all specialising in their own spheres. While these yards were producing ships like the huge prestige-evoking passenger liners, there were other firms concentrating on smaller vessels. Paisley, on the River Cart, supported three such shipbuilders all with good order books and in healthy rivalry. After the middle of the century there was a period of innovation and inventiveness. Naval architecture developed spectacularly and the Paisley yards, through vigorous planning and imaginative salesmanship, kept to the forefront. Local competition amongst existing firms ensured quality in design and construction. Conventional vessels were produced, but so too were increasing numbers of specialist craft like dredgers, colonial river-boats and, then, revolutionary torpedo-boats. It said much for the local yards that they competed successfully with the established masters in these fields.

John Fullerton and Company was one of those lively firms. Founded in 1867 the company expanded under the leadership and drive of John Fullerton, concentrating on building, with the ships being engined by firms like James Howden and Company of Glasgow, Aitchison Blair of Clydebank or McKie and Baxter of Paisley. Fullerton was a strong personality, taking a daily personal interest in all that was going on at the yard, from drawing office to launching slipway. Since he did not employ a large workforce he knew the great majority of the men by name — a personal touch which was not lost on his staff as individuals. If Fullerton's was the smallest of several firms based in the Inchinnan Road at Paisley, sandwiched as it was between Bow, McLachlan and Company and Fleming and Ferguson, it lost nothing in quality and energetic production. Many a small boy stood at the great double doors of Fullerton's to watch with bated breath the skills of the men wielding their adzes. It was a proud yard, and it was said: "If you served your time at Fullerton's you could go anywhere else in the world". Clearly, with such leadership over the decades, the Merksworth Yard of John Fullerton and Company was capable of creating fine craft, and it was appropriate that the firm had been commissioned by James Howden and Company, the co-ordinating contractors, to construct the hull and fittings of the Shetland ship.

By the time Captain Nicolson reached Paisley the as yet un-named steamer was swiftly rising plate by plate on one of the five berths at Merksworth. The place was a cacophony of sound, an ear-splitting din of clattering cranes and chattering riveters. Every berth was occupied. The captain picked up a copy of the "Paisley Daily Express" of 1st January, 1877. In it was a report of excellent progress.

"Messrs J. Fullerton and Company have during the year been well employed, the vessels launched being: s.s. *Devon,* 205 tons, s.s. *Souza Franco,* 81 tons, s.s. *Larne,* 252 tons. *Surf Boat No. 31,* 50 tons.

"The vessels now building are a screw steamer for the Shetland Isles Steam Navigation Company Limited, and a screw steamer for the coasting trade in Australia."

Three hundred miles to the north, the Shetland directors kept in close touch with Aberdeen and Paisley. A letter arrived from Captain Nicolson and in it he intimated satisfaction with the workmanship and progress made on the ship. A second instalment of over £1,000 on the price was forwarded to the contractors at the New Year.

On 24th January, 1877, prompted by a telegram from Mylne in Aberdeen, the directors discussed the name which would be most appropriate. Hay, chairing the meeting, had his own ideas but they finally settled on a short list of three names, *Countess of Zetland, Princess of Thule* or *St. Olaf.* The last name seemed to have decided possibilities because it was so much in keeping with the names of steamers in the employ of the North of Scotland and Orkney and Shetland Steam Navigation Company, who had a firm stake in the subsidiary firm. These were the *St. Nicholas,* the *St. Clair* and the *St. Magnus.*

Merrylees, as secretary, was authorised to wire Aberdeen, where Mylne, Lord Provost Jamieson, Simpson Shepherd and Alexander Webster could select whichever name they considered best. For reasons polite or diplomatic the recommendation came back for *Earl of Zetland* or *Countess of Zetland.* Whatever the Shetland directors may have thought, a letter was despatched to Lord Zetland putting forward the proposals and leaving it to him to decide whether the steamer would be "Earl" or "Countess". Lord Zetland was prompt. He replied by letter on 2nd February, 1877, intimating his willingness to allow either name to be used.

By 16th February the decision had been made and it was a name which was to endure for nearly enough a century, carried by only two vessels on the same route. The anonymous hull on the stocks at the Merksworth Yard at Paisley would be named the *Earl of Zetland.*

Throughout the islands there were repercussions. Many people were not happy with the name and were not slow to comment or to criticise. Letters appeared in "The Shetland Times".

"As most of the shareholders of the Shetland Islands Steam Navigation Company must now be aware that their new steamer has been "gracefully" named *Earl of Zetland,* it is to be hoped that they will embrace the first opportunity of awarding a vote of thanks to the directors for the great amount of taste and discernment they have shown in choosing a name that must sound like music in the ears of every native of the islands, and it is hoped that his Lordship will feel a due sense of the honour that has been conferred on him by his humble worshippers.

"Shetland, although a poor place in some respects is certainly not so in either historical or traditional names . . . Is not a living Lord better than a dead Lion? And is it not better to toady to a live Lord than to pay any amount of compliment to the memory of a defunct Norse hero? But why should the Earl of Zetland have been selected as the man whom the directors delight to honour? Has he done anything with his enormous wealth to further steam navigation to, or amongst, our islands? Has he shared any of the heavy losses that we have had to bear in opening up the trade with the old *Crab?* I am afraid not. Or has he ever even visited the islands? Certainly not as the Earl of Zetland . . . As the s.s. *Earl of Zetland* is too long a name to write on an address card, or even to say, when a shorter one can do, the chances are that the public will write "per steamer" and that the vessel will be known as the *New Crab* or *Peerie Steamer,* same as formerly. Or if the public would like it better they might call her *The Lowrie,* which would also be a compliment to her first mate, who is certainly far more deserving of it. It is to be hoped that in return for the honour conferred upon him, his Lordship may purchase any shares as may yet be unsold, and do it in a true spirit of charity, hoping for no reward in the shape of dividends." The letter was signed "A Shareholder".

It was a curiously prophetic letter in parts. Locally the ship, from her first appearance off Sumburgh Head, was christened *Da Earl* and then in the fullness of time *Da Auld Earl,* although these terms were not in any sense derogatory, but given affectionately as the steamer showed her dignity from her early days in the islands.

Another irate shareholder referred to the previous letter: "As another disappointed aspirant to the directorship permit me to say that I was glad to see in your issue of the 24th (March) that your correspondent had the courage of his opinions and gave expression to the feeling of dissatisfaction with which Shetlanders generally regard the name assigned to the new North Isles steamer. Really it seems so much of toadyism and snobbery that all Shetlanders ought to know that they are indebted to the Scottish section of the board of directors for the high sounding name *Earl of Zetland* . . . Just one word to say that there has aye been several aliases suggested for the same peerie steamer. One more can't hurt. Suppose now she takes the name of that fine bit beastie *The Toad of Aberdeen*. Well, that she may be successful under whatever name she sails, is the prayer of your petitioner.''

Again there was an element of anticipation, for the *Earl of Zetland* established success from the outset. Maybe there were even occasions during her career when the Good Lord intervened for her salvation!

In Paisley, Captain Nicolson observed the day to day progress throughout January and February. He attended the yard punctually, watching riveters and fitters, engineers and joiners, caulkers and journeymen, painters and plumbers, men and apprentices alike, all working towards keeping progress right up to schedule. He came to know management and men intimately because Merksworth was a friendly place.

The straight, vertical stem of the steamer towered above him, her red lead anti-fouling paint gleaming dully below her waterline, the entire hull raised up on the blocks of the slipway, the ship poised to enter her natural element. He noted the fresh white numbers at the bow, indicating her draught, and his gaze swept upwards, appraising the clean curve of the sheer of the top of her plating swinging in perspective down to the drop of the for'ard well deck. The white rails were etched clearly against the leaden late February sky, both contrasting with the solid blackness of the plating. An atmosphere of near completion prevailed, and an enormous amount of work had been done by the shipyard team. Fullerton pushed his men hard, yet was not unstinting in his praise of a job well executed. And she was obviously a sound, strong steamer.

William Nicolson had found his task fascinating, through discussions with management and foremen, workers and apprentices, and gradually his satisfaction increased. Steadily there came to be less noise on board, less space cluttered up with a variety of tools and shipyard equipment, less untidiness, less dirt. The workmen ascended the gangway in decreasing numbers, and sundry parts swung into place by the yard cranes took on a unity, so that the un-named hull began to develop the appearance and feeling of a ship. It was an exciting prospect.

The directors felt confident about the potential of their ship as ''being a much faster and more commodious steamer than any hitherto on the passage''. Charles Merrylees was requested to try for a contract with the Post Office for the carriage of the North Isles mails, and they felt ambitious enough to talk about a fortnightly trip to Bergen in Norway, 180 miles distant, during the tourist season. Further, they decided ''the necessity for there being a qualified

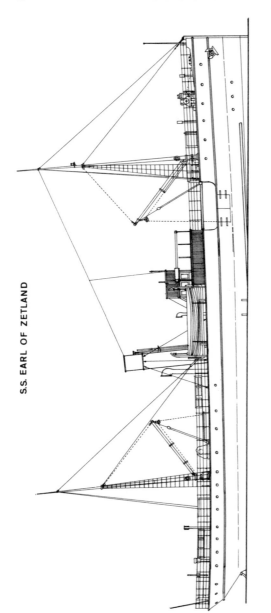

S.S. EARL OF ZETLAND

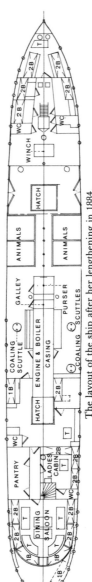

The layout of the ship after her lengthening in 1884.

steward on board the new steamer to keep the cabins in proper order and to manage the victualling on account of the company''.

James Howden and Company Limited, Marine Engineers and Shipbuilders, the original contractors, were in no way surprised at the efficient approach of John Fullerton and Company. There was a mutual appreciation and respect between the two firms, based on high standards and uncompromising efficiency. It was common practice in the 1860s and subsequent two decades for ship owners to place their contracts with the designers and builders of the propelling machinery. At the time when boiler and steam engine designs were developing and improving rapidly, the engineer was the obvious person to receive the main contract for a vessel because the success or failure of a ship depended largely on effective machinery. On the other hand, builders like Fullerton were masters of their own art and had been so for many years, but many of them had no engineering facilities. With so much natural inclination towards the newfangled machinery it was appropriate for the owners to seek the specialist advice of the marine engineers in the first instance. Therefore the Shetland Islands Steam Navigation Company Limited found themselves in the hands of a forward looking group of marine engineers.

William Nicolson discovered that Howden's had pioneered a significant range of improvements in steam propulsion. In the late fifties, and earlier, steamships were driven by simple single cylinder engines working at steam pressures as little as 20 to 25 lb. The compound engine was in its infancy and, although its importance was recognised by engineers as progress, pressures continued to be low and seldom were above 50 to 60 lbs. per square inch.

By the time he was 27, James Howden had done impressive research into the problem of steam vessels which needed a ludicrous quantity of coal for long voyages. Along with Alexander Morton, Howden took out a patent for "Improvements in Motive Power" and the two pioneers quickly established a reputation for original thinking. The Anchor Line of steamers had their *Ailsa Craig* (225 tons) engined by Howden, and a water-tube boiler and compound engine using steam at 100 lbs. per square inch were indicative of that enterprise and courage characteristic of all his work.

His continual striving for improved proficiency resulted in note being taken of his imaginative concepts. The "Glasgow Herald" of 21st July, 1869, gave him fair credit: "The screw steamer *Xanthe* of Leith, 100 tons burden, which had just had her former engines taken out by Messrs James Howden and Company of this city and replaced with that firm's Patent High and Low Pressure Compound Engines of 110 nominal power, had her new machinery tested on Monday last, 19th instant, between the Cloch and the Cumbraes. The mean of four trials taken, with and against the tide, gave the rate of 10.31 knots per hour, and the consumption of Scotch coal, weighed accurately under inspection of the owners, during the trial — the engines going continuously at full speed — was exactly five cwt. per hour: a result in the point of economy probably the highest yet obtained in marine engineering. The advantages arising from the use of these improved engines may be more strikingly shown by the fact that the engines which they replaced, though of equal nominal horsepower, and of comparatively recent manufacture by an English firm of note, gave a speed of only six to six and a half knots per hour on a consumption of nearly 14 cwts. per hour. We understand that Messrs Howden and Company have already fitted a number of steamers with their patent compound engines, all of which have shown remarkably high economical results, which have in every case been fully sustained during lengthened voyages.''

In endeavouring to improve the machinery he was building in his Scotland Street, Glasgow, works, Howden investigated many technical problems. Among these was the poor performance of the natural draught boilers of the day. His first attempt at improvement in this direction had taken place in 1863. He had applied mechanical draught below the fire grate, using an axial flow fan driven by a ''steam wheel'' on the fan shaft. The force draught fan was therefore a very simple type of steam turbine driven axial flow fan. While these trials resulted in an increased output from the boiler, the quality of performance he sought was not forthcoming and he turned his attention to the engines. He had experimented with favourable results on different designs of engine valve gear and the compounding of cylinders. He had also won success by the introduction of exhaust steam for feed water heating. At the same time, of course, work continued with the design and production of marine boilers and engines and the undertaking of contracts for complete ships.

Nicolson had an impression of craftsmanship and integrity after his visits to Scotland Street and, coupled with the neat but strong hull he had watched grow at Merksworth, he knew that his owners were going to have delivered a sturdy and reliable little ship. She was the fiftieth vessel to be contracted for by Howden, he discovered, the first being back in 1863 when the *Teen Chang* was built. Now, 14 years later, a new hull awaited launching and the installation of another set of well formed compound engines.

The Fullerton work team gradually lessened the untidy variety of materials in and around the ship. Piles of shipyard rubbish were attacked and disposed of. Within and outwith the hull, clutter vanished until, at the end of February, they were all set for the event.

Speculation and anticipation were the reactions of Shetlanders to the news that the launching was imminent. All that the vessel implied had caught the imagination of the bulk of the population. For too long frustration had been prevalent, and now opportunity knocked as never before in the history of North Isles conveyance of people and their belongings in all their diversity. If the practical issues were dominant — because the sea was the highway and the ship the life-line of communication — there was also a romantic appeal to people with the sea in their blood. They speculated on the appearance and convenience of the *Earl of Zetland,* the name itself grudgingly mentioned in town, on the mainland and amongst the islands alike; they speculated on how much of an improvement she would be on the old *Crab;* they speculated on the date of arrival in "da Sooth Mooth". Judgment would need to be deferred until then, but they expected a steamer that would be a vast improvement on the performance of the smacks when an entire week could pass on a return voyage Unst to Lerwick! They could hardly foresee that Shetland was about to receive a ship which could reasonably be upheld as the epitome of the spirit of the inter-island steamer in the world-wide sense, a ship with few equals in indomitable service to an island people. Any worthwhile vessel would make her mark, yet some more firmly than others. The *Earl* was to acquire an outstandingly individual personality that was to last throughout her seagoing life in Shetland and beyond. It was an indefinable atmosphere, that could not be identified with design or engineering, but it created an aura of romance which influenced those who sailed in her to care about her welfare and her career. Perhaps any well-found steamer — the *Lady Ambrosine* had shown some promise — would have acquired such singular distinction, having served with consistency year in and year out, performing feats of endurance and showing powers of survival, yet the *Earl* did this with a peculiar aplomb. In terms of indefatigable service to humanity she was due to give incalculable value to a way of life. Hers became no ordinary task, particularly during the first four decades of a career that was to last for 73 years. She was not simply a means of transport; she was the sole means of regular communication. As a result she was to become an integral part of the community, and long before more sophisticated modes of transport evolved, *Da Auld Earl* was to earn her laurels in the eyes of Shetlanders, particularly those of the North Mainland, and the North Isles of Whalsay, Out Skerries, Yell, Fetlar and Unst. Her presence and function in the islands were due to provide a microcosm of Shetland life, revealed and revealing.

But no-one had the crystal ball of foresight as the silent, impersonal hull became lost in the darkness of the night prior to her meeting with the waters of the River Cart the next day. Friday, 2nd March, 1877, the scheduled day for the launching of the s.s. *Earl of Zetland,* emerged grey and still. Below the attractively ginger-breaded counter stern of the steamer, poised to surge into the river, the tide moved barely perceptibly, on the flow.

By mid-morning Captain Nicolson was at the yard. A small number of workmen still clustered around and on board his ship, but the thunderous shipyard sounds came from the other berths at Merksworth. Two tugs were being built and two other hulls, one to be the s.s. *Wakefield* and the other the s.s. *Marie.* William Nicolson had noted that one of the tugs, the *Tweed,* was to be propelled by two screws, one at the stern and one at the bow. He was interested to learn that it was James Howden who had pioneered this principle of propulsion, and that the *Tweed* would be only the fourth ship of its kind in the world. However, his thoughts reverted to his own steamer. The two and a half months in Paisley had been all that he had hoped for. Fullerton and Howden had done a splendid job, he reckoned. Already he felt a keen sense of pride in his peerie steamer — not that she seemed small standing out of the water on the slipway, now receiving final touches for the happening to which he had looked forward so enthusiastically. To his sympathetic eye the vessel was immaculate.

A ragged cheer heralded the movement of the hull towards its native element that afternoon. As the drag chains uncoiled in a grind of metal the ship gathered momentum and swept downwards, stern first. She took the water cleanly and splendidly, setting up a surge which dashed itself to pieces on the far bank of the Cart, well lined with spectators. The Merksworth work force had stopped for the launching and, as the *Earl of Zetland* came to rest, a throaty spontaneous appreciation rose from a hundred men. Captain Nicolson and John Fullerton shook hands, their fundamental task well done.

The "Paisley Daily Express" of Friday, 2nd March, 1877, gave the event coverage under a headline "Launch of a Steamer at Crossflat Today". A slightly inaccurate description of the Shetland situation was followed by a glowing account of the new steamer.

"During the past few years various new routes have been opened up to places where the tourist may enjoy views of the picturesque or recruit his energies which have been exhausted by the fatigues of a city life. One of the most pleasant of these is the group of islands lying to the north-east of Scotland of which Shetland is the

William Nicolson
W. Sinclair

John Scott
E. J. F. Clausen

Peter Johnson
Shetland Library and Museum

William Spence
Mrs D. Mann

Tom Gifford
Mrs A. Gifford

Adam Tait
E. J. F. Clausen

Skippers who were key figures in the career of the *Earl of Zetland*.

principal, and for a few years past it has grown so much in favour with the public that the facilities for travelling through the islands have become inadequate. The Shetland Islands Steam Navigation Company (Limited), finding that they could not overtake the whole of the traffic with the small steamer at their disposal, *The Chieftain's Bride,* contracted with Messrs J. Howden and Company, Glasgow, in September last year, for a screw steamer of the undernoted dimensions, and these have now been carried out at Messrs Fullerton and Co.'s shipbuilding yard on the Cart. *The Chieftain's Bride* has been plying between Lerwick and the Islands of Whalsay, Fetlar, Yell and Unst — the furthest north spot in Her Majesty's home territory — and other places; but the influx of tourists has been so great, and the intercourse between the islands is increasing so rapidly, that the want of proper conveyance by water has been much felt. The pleasant climate enjoyed by the islands, during June and July especially, and the many opportunities for shooting and fishing, have led to so many tourists selecting to spend a few weeks amongst the islands which Sir Walter Scott has so vividly described in 'The Pirate'. It may be mentioned also that there are inns on the principal islands.

''The building of the new steamer has just been completed, and this afternoon the launch into the River Cart took place at Merksworth Shipbuilding Yard, in the presence of a large company of ladies and gentlemen, invited to be present by Messrs Fullerton & Co. As the ship left the ways, Mrs John Henderson, sister of Mr Charles Merrylees (secretary to the company at Lerwick) gracefully named it *Earl of Zetland.* Immediately afterwards it reached the water and floated successfully. As it lies in Cart, the vessel presents a very handsome appearance and shows remarkably fine lines. The dimensions are 120 feet betwixt the perpendiculars; 20 feet beam; and 9 feet depth of hold. She has been built under Lloyd's survey, and is classed in their books 90 A1. It is to be fitted up with engines of 50 horse power, inverted and direct acting, on the compound principle, by Messrs James Howden & Co., Engineers, Glasgow, the original contractors. As the ship is intended, and is specially adapted for, a large passenger trade, as well as carrying general goods, the internal fitting up has received careful attention. The engines, engine room and hatches are all placed in the centre, so as to allow ample room fore and aft, and also increase the steadiness of the boat. There is a large saloon and ladies cabin in the poop, furnished in a handsome style with sofas, tables, etc. The steward's pantry and other accessories are adjacent. The saloon is lighted by windows on both sides, and cupola on top of the poop, and the cabin is also well lighted. Forward there is a steerage saloon on the main deck for steerage female passengers, and on the deck below a large apartment for male passengers. These are also fitted up with sofas and cushioned backs to correspond. Above the saloon is the poop deck, which will form an excellent promenade for passengers in fine weather. The vessel is to be schooner rigged, and it is expected from her fine build that a high rate of speed will be maintained. She has fore and aft holds for cargo, and a steam winch which is to be placed at each hatch. The anchors are also to be worked by steam, and in every way the ship has been constructed so as to give the least possible delay on the voyage at the different ports of call in discharging or shipping cargo. There is no doubt that this commodious vessel will be a great boon to the inhabitants of those distant islands, as well as a source of enjoyment to the tourists who frequent the country.

"Captain Nicolson who has been in the Shetland Co.'s service for several years in the same trade that the ship is designed for, and who is to take command of the *Earl of Zetland* when ready for sea, has superintended the internal fittings for about two months back, and he expects to take the ship north about the end of the month, after the engines have been put aboard by Messrs Howden and Co.

"After the launch, Mr Fullerton entertained a select company in Merksworth House, to cake and wine, when prosperity was drunk to the *Earl of Zetland* and her builder."

Any toast will be given in a spirit of optimism and good will, but that offered to the already proud hull was, in effect, a toast to a legend within a lifetime.

"The Shetland Times" of Saturday, 3rd March, described the launching, although it tended to emphasise when the *Earl of Zetland* would arrive in Shetland waters to begin her life's work.

3

The Way Ahead

Payments on the ship had been forwarded to the contractors at regular intervals and on 30th March another was made. The fourth instalment on the price of the *Earl of Zetland* had been £1,662:10/-, additional belting came to £40, and the estimated expense of furnishings not otherwise stated, and of bringing the vessel to Shetland, was £200.

Charles Merrylees could scarcely contain his enthusiasm when he reported to a meeting in Lerwick that the ship would be ready for trial very early in April. This was greeted with an approving

Off Sumburgh Head, 14th April 1877.

atmosphere of comment. The directors knew just how successfully the launching of their creation had been accomplished. "The Shetland Times" of 7th April reported: "Bailie Robertson and Mr Arthur Laurenson went south by last boat as members of the piers committee, along with Mr Charles Merrylees, for the trial of the *Earl of Zetland* on the Clyde. We trust everything will prove satisfactory and that we will soon have her here. However much our correspondents may quarrel about her name (Ships' names do confuse the grammar sometimes) I think we may venture to say she will be welcomed by everybody. Owing to the unsettled state of the weather the isles' carrying trade is in a most unsatisfactory state."

Meanwhile domestic matters relating to the crewing were resolved. The skipper would have a pay of £3 per week, the mate £1:5/-, the fireman £1, all with food allowed for. Without provisions were the engineer at £3, sailors at 1 guinea, and the clerk at 15/-. Naturally Captain William Nicolson was already in command of the *Earl of Zetland* and Charles Merrylees was requested to engage one

D

John Smith as mate to assist in bringing the ship north after her trials.

The company and the Shetland population were primed and ready, and on the Clyde, birthplace of a multitude of vessels made by Scottish craftsmen, the *Earl of Zetland* settled to her correct displacement as the engines and diverse sundry fittings were placed. Finally by Friday, 6th April, she was bunkered and had steam up that evening. Prior to the arrival of the Shetland contingent, William Nicolson had found himself fully involved in innumerable tasks in preparing his charge for the sea. It was now the eve of the fruition of weeks of complicated planning and discussion involving patience and tact. Now he was about to embark on a challenging venture with a determination to prove himself and his ship. The Shetland situation and its ever-present difficulties he knew well enough, but he could only trust that the capabilities of the *Earl of Zetland* would meet with the approval of the professionally critical eye of the Shetlander himself. The past had not been reassuring. Now what of the future? But the steamer herself looked the part. Certainly, as the "Paisley Daily Express" had expounded, she "presented a very handsome appearance". It occurred to Nicolson that "looks are only skin deep". The morrow would bring its events for better or for worse. The captain felt rather philosophical.

At first light on the Saturday the *Earl of Zetland,* a plume of grey at her smoke stack, awaited her first assignment. She was on trial. Representatives from Fullerton's and Howden's joined the Shetlanders on board, and by mid-morning the ship was off Dumbarton, proudly thrusting downstream with first Greenock and then Gourock to port, and Dunoon to starboard, as she came round into the more open areas of the Firth of Clyde. There they opened up full throttle. The little steamer, streaming black smoke astern, giving her a purposeful look which was to become so characteristic, turned aside the water in hissing whiteness and moved into the measured mile at Skelmorlie, a ship alive. This was the keenly anticipated moment. Howden's thoughts concerned his engines. Fullerton appraised the hull shape and the clean-cut wake arrowed further astern as the *Earl* increased speed. Nicolson on his maindeck, sensitive to the throb of life about his ship, savoured the moment in its fullness. Merrylees, Robertson and Laurenson thought of many things, including the consumption of fuel! Below, a fireman shovelled coal, an engineer eyed his gauges and the *Earl of Zetland* raised 10½ knots. Howden had noted previously that 10 knots on the engine design was optimistic, yet here he had his power unit producing that and more! He was well pleased.

William Nicolson looked north beyond the island of Bute and

Toward Point as his ship, trials over and successful, returned to the upper reaches of the river. He greatly relished the voyage to home waters, looking forward to trying out the *Earl of Zetland's* sea-going qualities as well as anticipating a triumphal entry of the ''sooth mooth''. He did not have long to wait. With all the celebrations of launching and success of the first venture into semi-open waters over, the steamer was ready to depart from her birthplace by the following week, and on Thursday, 12th April, 1877, she sailed at first light. Arran, with its magnificent backdrop of mountains above Brodick, was abeam by mid-morning. The weather was overcast, though quiet. Her screw biting strongly at the water, the ship rounded the Mull of Kintyre, south of Sanda Island, then headed north between the Scottish Mainland and Islay. By late afternoon visibility had worsened. In the Sound of Jura, the island of Jura itself to port and the mainland to starboard, became ill-defined and lost their form, merging into the encroaching mist and approaching night. There was no credit in taking risks. Nicolson ordered slow ahead, then stop, and activity at the bow followed by a splash signified that the anchor was down in the shelter of Crinan Bay. And there they remained until the dawn.

With steam up, and away early on the Friday, course was set between Scarba and Luing, through the Firth of Lorne, thence into the Sound of Mull. Sixty-three years previously Sir Walter Scott had traversed these same waters to Oban, though sailing in the opposite direction, during his protracted tour with the lighthouse commissioners. Nicolson had heard of the events of that trip. Out past Ardnamurchan Point the straight stem of the *Earl of Zetland* dipped into the hint of an Atlantic swell as she came onto a more northerly course to take her up past Rum and Canna, with the spectacular backdrop of the Skye peaks etched cleanly against the cloud cover in greatly improved conditions. By midnight on the Friday the Butt of Lewis lay far to port unseen by the *Earl's* crew, but at 3 o'clock on the Saturday morning they could discern the land mass at Cape Wrath. Now the open sea expanded before them.

If the captain wished his ship tested against the elements he was not to be disappointed. Once clear of the Scottish mainland, and with Orkney to the east, the wind built up out of the south-east bringing breaking seas with it. John Smith, the mate, had admired the *Earl's* counter stern; now its functional value became apparent as it lifted buoyantly in the quartering waves, the fresh black paint gleaming with the wetness. By noon on the Saturday they had seen Westray in Orkney, and later could just observe the crofts at the south end of Fair Isle as the *Earl of Zetland* steamed north in the moderating seas.

The surf on the perimeter of the lonely island was obviously still rising high in the air, a measure of the now dying gale.

On a clear day Sumburgh and Fitful Heads at the south tip of Shetland stand above the horizon as seen from Fair Isle, 24 miles away. Conversely the lightkeepers at Sumburgh have a clear view over the Roost to the south and Fair Isle. With a low and hurrying cloud cover and smear of drizzle they saw sea and sky blend obscurely that day, although they scanned the greyness for a first glimpse of the new steamer.

It was fact that she was a tiny coastal vessel of a mere 186 tons, comparable to a trawler, and to the uninitiated apparently of little consequence; yet to the vast majority of 29,000 islanders her arrival in Shetland was looked upon as a solution to past problems and a realisation of the present and future. Somehow, much was expected. Whatever the consequences of opinion, for William Nicolson it was an experience to relish as Sumburgh Head came abeam, its massive shoulders descending into the ocean, the lighthouse, diminutive by contrast, perched precariously on the crest. Observers saw the steamer and the telegraph flashed news to Lerwick that she had passed Boddam, just north of Sumburgh, at 6 o'clock. Now the *Earl of Zetland* was breaking waters which were to be so much part of her existence. She surged along at her steady 10 knots. As the island of Mousa, with its broch belonging to a long departed civilisation, came up to the west, the crew and passengers could then see the outline of Ward Hill on Bressay, the island providing security for Lerwick Harbour.

To the ever-gathering group of curious and much enthused spectators on the Knab, the headland flanking the "sooth mooth", a tiny dark impingement on the face of the otherwise empty sea slowly but inexorably revealed shape and form. Although she looked anything but big, the ship appeared impressive with a "bone in her teeth" and white breaking water along her hull on the gradually darkening sea. It was 8 p.m. as the way came off her on that spring evening, 14th April, 1877.

On board, a rumble of the shaft and a boil of foam at the stern brought the newcomer to rest off Craigie's Stane. In the mid-18th century most of the property along the main street in Lerwick was owned by the Craigie family who had had a popular landing place named after them. It was the scene of hectic activity as the flitboats from the steamers were unloaded at the lodberry at Craigie's Stane. A lodberry was a store-house — often with the gable end projecting into the sea — the name itself derived from the old Norse language "Lladberg", meaning a loading rock. A gateway on the side of the

Craigie's Stane lodberry was used for manhandling goods into the store, and the flitboat men suffered many a "soosin" and the boats many a resounding thump in choppy waters alongside. It was primitive and far from practical, but Lerwick simply possessed no berth at which steamers could tie up securely and regularly. So the *Earl's* anchor sought the Shetland sea bed for the first of innumerable occasions, and an astonishingly big crowd thronged the foreshore to cheer and wave a greeting to ship and crew. A throng of small boats clustered round the *Earl,* a token of events to come in the virtually pierless islands. The entire crew already felt a consuming pride and confidence which were amplified by the warmth of the welcome. For Nicolson in particular the safe delivery and reception, the prospect of things to come, the whole concept, were a heady combination.

Approval was formally recorded in "The Shetland Times" the next Saturday: "The s.s. *Earl of Zetland* is advertised to leave on Tuesday first for the north of Shetland, and will sail regularly thereafter on the mornings of Tuesday and Thursday until further notice. Next week, however, owing to the Sacramental Fast day she will make only one trip, taking goods for both voyages on Tuesday first . . . On Tuesday morning the *Earl* was brought alongside the quay at the docks and was visited by crowds of people all day. We have already given a description of the vessel when recording the launch and it is only to be added that she is fitted up in a very substantial and handsome manner which reflects great credit upon the directors and Captain Nicolson, who has superintended the arrangements and taken every care to ensure the comfort and convenience of his passengers."

In the North Isles, which would benefit so much directly and indirectly by this new presence, people looked south for a first visit of thousands destined to be made to a number of little ports. Leading citizens made sure that flitboat crews were briefed to welcome *da Earl* in places like Symbister (Whalsay), Houbie (Fetlar), Burravoe (Yell), and Baltasound (Unst). The significance of her coming was clearly shown at Haroldswick, north of Baltasound, when the children were allowed out of school to see the first arrival of a steamer in their bay. Thus throughout the remainder of April and into May the ship began her Shetland career in varied but not unpleasant weather. The North Isles people liked what they saw, but there were those who were reticent, even sceptical. The experience of other steamers had not been convincing. It would need a winter to prove her mettle. It was easy enough to maintain a timetable in the soft days of summer, although they were prepared to make allowance for delays when the islands merged into a shroud of fog, the biggest hazard of all. Still, this ship had something about her it was said. Somehow she looked the part. It was also said that she had cost over £7,000, which was correct — £7,060:13:11½ to be exact.

::   ::   ::   ::   ::   ::

At the end of July, 1877, the directors presented a first report in which it was minuted that "the *Earl* has been well appreciated by the travelling and trading community of the islands and has secured a very fair return for the ten weeks she has plied." Of course the bald statement scarcely did justice to human contacts being created and moulded. There was the trip to the head of Sullom Voe, an empty yet strangely beautiful place on a day of subtle lighting and atmosphere peculiar to Shetland (and due to feature spectacularly in world news a century later as a major oil and gas terminal); the visit to Foula; the voyage to Out Skerries. The islands were opening up to the islanders.

There was the first of many cases of salvage, the rescue of the derelict schooner *Milberg und Engstrom* of Drammen. She had become uncontrollable south-east of Bressay and taking water through a damaged hull into a tightly packed cargo of barrel staves which, in their sodden and swollen state, were exerting pressure on the frame of the ship. A distress message eventually reached Lerwick through one James White, a fisherman who had sighted and boarded the stricken schooner. The *Earl* was made ready and sailed the 25 miles to the derelict which was heaving sluggishly in the swell. With a hawser on board the *Milberg und Engstrom,* the two vessels crept back to port where the schooner, lying low in the water, was anchored off the docks. A supervisor was put on board to take charge on behalf of the company. Meanwhile the Receiver of Wrecks was approached by Merrylees to put the vessel alongside the quay to be discharged.

The legal aspect of the salvage then emerged. By mid-July the underwriters of the cargo had paid £150 to the company, but the salvage of the hull had been brought before the Sheriff since the agent for the underwriters declined to pay without permission of the court. Mr Sievwright, acting for the salvors in his capacity as a solicitor, had been unable to find anyone to value the derelict as she lay and adjournment of the case was sought until the hull could be properly inspected. The Sheriff adjourned the case accordingly.

On 27th July, 1877, the hull of the schooner having been assessed, the directors accepted the decision of the court and Sheriff that the value was £40, whilst the amount of salvage would be £16 with expenses to the pursuers. His Lordship apportioned the amounts, including the £150 for the cargo. James White, the

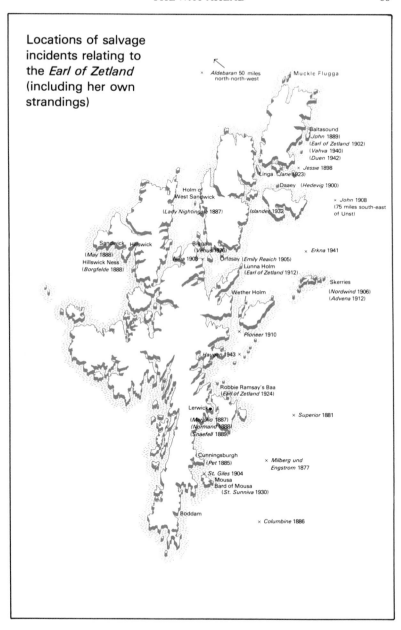

Locations of salvage
incidents relating to
the *Earl of Zetland*
(including her own
strandings)

× *Aldebaran* 50 miles
north-north-west

Muckle Flugga

Baltasound
(*John* 1889)
(*Earl of Zetland* 1902)
(*Vahva* 1940)
(*Duen* 1942)

× *Jessie* 1898

Linga (*Jane* 1923)

Daaey (*Hedevig* 1900)

× *John* 1908
(75 miles south-east
of Unst)

Holm of
West Sandwick

(*Lady Nightingale* 1887)

Islander 1932

Sandwick Hillswick

(*May* 1888)
Hillswick Ness
(*Borgfelde* 1888)

Bigga
(*Venus* 1876)

Nina 1908 Orfasay (*Emily Reaich* 1905)

Lunna Holm
(*Earl of Zetland* 1912)

× *Erkna* 1941

Skerries
(*Nordwind* 1906)
(*Advena* 1912)

Wether Holm

× *Pioneer* 1910

Haugen 1943 ×

Robbie Ramsay's Baa
(*Earl of Zetland* 1924)

Lerwick

(*Matutia* 1887)
(*Normand* 1888)
(*Snaefell* 1889)

× *Superior* 1881

Cunningsburgh
(*Pet* 1885)

× *Milberg und*
Engstrom 1877

× *St. Giles* 1904
Mousa
Bard of Mousa
(*St. Sunniva* 1930)

Boddam

× *Columbine* 1886

fisherman, received one eighth, as did Captain Nicolson; the crew were awarded one quarter, and a half went to the shipping company. Eventually the sum earned by the *Earl of Zetland* for salvage was £74:1:3 plus £2 for coals and running expenses and £4:10/- for a damaged warp. The directors also resolved to have a special arrangement with the crew of the steamer about future cases of salvage.

The draft form of agreement about salvage did not suit the captain and crew and a verbal suggestion by Merrylees was rejected by Nicolson. A directors' meeting instructed the secretary to write formally to the captain, stating that in future no salvage work should be done without instructions from the board. At the same time it was agreed that in any salvage affair where the crew were endangered or involved in saving life, then a higher proportion of salvage could be offered. But in an ordinary case like the *Milberg und Engstrom* the amounts proffered were fair, taking into account the interests of the shareholders. A slight undercurrent of dissatisfaction prevailed amongst the crew, revealed when Merrylees told his directors that Captain Nicolson had stated verbally that he had read to the crew the formal letter of salvage terms. The directors insisted on written verification that he had done so. This request was complied with reluctantly.

Back in the month of February, 1877, the secretary had written to Mylne in Aberdeen to seek a contract with the Post Office to carry the North Isles mails, from time immemorial subjected to the uncertain and vulnerable method of post-runner and boat. An acknowledgement was sent to the effect that the matter would receive the consideration of the postal authorities, but by July there was no other information. The wheels of bureaucracy ground slowly. Eventually a Post Office surveyor, Warren by name, arrived in Lerwick, talked to the directors and despatched his clerk to the North Isles on a fact-finding mission. By November a draft scheme prepared by Gibb, the surveyor's clerk, following a discussion with islanders on Unst, was submitted, accompanied by a letter from David Edmonston of Unst. The company then required a detailed statement about their obligations in conveying mail by the *Earl of Zetland*. Mr Warren replied on 15th November to the effect that he was not in a position to give a definite answer on the points raised, thus several more weeks elapsed. At the end of January, 1878, the company was offered 4/- per week by the Lerwick postmaster to take the mails from Lerwick to Whalsay on the regular voyages, and this was approved conditionally. Yet the accepted route was a fragment of the company's proposals, and the original overtures to the Post Office had apparently been ignored. By the end of May, 1878, the directors had abandoned hope of achieving anything with a strangely reluctant Post Office. This was unfortunate for the populace when the steamer was making a fundamental contribution already. As an instance of this, a letter from James Inkster of Brae asked for the traffic of the port to be taken by the *Earl* instead of the sailer *Saucey Jack*. The directors agreed on condition that all competition was withdrawn for a year and flitboat facilities were considered good enough.

Business expanded in parallel with a series of pleasure voyages which contributed much to the improved image of sea travel by steamer. It was written of Foula: ''Quite a sensation was caused by the first visit of the *Earl* and the sudden appearance of the ship steaming up from the north side towards Ham, having on board some south-country and Lerwick gentry on pleasure trips. The Foula people were both surprised and delighted, the *Earl* being the first steamer that had ever anchored in the bay. Captain Nicolson, who in his early days along with his father came into the small voe of Ham for shelter, seemed to have great pleasure in gratifying the curiosity of all who had a desire to visit his handsome little vessel, and it is hoped that he will make many more trips with her yet to this romantic and isolated island, and also that those gentlemen who expressed their opinion that a mail and lighthouse might be got for Foula as well as Fair Isle will, in the interests of humanity, give it their support now that it is being brought into public notice. The poor people of Foula have felt the want of some kind of regular communication with the mainland, especially in serious cases of illness when medical aid might have been of service and yet entirely out of reach.''

This type of visit to hitherto inaccessible areas had a powerful appeal, as evinced by the writing of another correspondent who unwittingly referred to the Holy Land, on the shores of which the *Earl of Zetland* would end her days over three score years and ten later. ''Having found the former trips very enjoyable I no sooner found the notice of another voyage when I resolved that I would improve my geography by having a look around the coast of Northmaven. By the by, speaking of geography it is wonderful with all our educational advantages nowadays how little most people know of the lie of the land, distances and general information of their own local districts. At the examination of one of our schools not long ago a class was examined for an hour and a half or so on the geography of Palestine. Now the geography and history of that country must always continue to be of great interest, but one cannot help feeling that a little more attention might be given to the geography round our own doors . . .''

The outing organised to Skerries early in August, 1877, was typical of the success of imagination and initiative by the shipping company. Few Lerwick people had ever had a chance to go ashore on islands which, on a good day, were shadowed narrowly on the horizon beyond Whalsay, as seen from the slopes above the town. As a result the response to the advert was good. The ship was billed to sail at 9 a.m., and a shuttle service of flit-craft transferred passengers to the *Earl*. A showery, mainly overcast morning failed to dampen the sense of adventure abounding, and Captain Nicolson, despite having come off the Yell Sound run only four hours before, proved to be in appropriately jovial mood. The last bells having echoed through Lerwick and with the anchor apeak, the ship swung east round the south end of Bressay to make passage close by the Ord, the Bard, and the island of Noss, towering and magnificent rock ramparts alive with gulls, fulmars and gannets.

With little swell on the sea and few goods in the hold, a hatch cover was removed and those passengers who had the urge, descended to dance to the strains of "Jeems" Williamson's fiddle, the sound of which complemented the steady throb of the compound engines and beat of shaft and propeller. There was the added interest of the unexpected heave of the ship which gave rise to unorthodox movement amid the dancers! The indefatigible Jeems kept them going tirelessly until the lure of the expanding panorama of Out Skerries drew them on deck. Now the islands commanded attention, just as the ever-nearing steamer was the subject of interest for those ashore.

Skerries, with Grunay (green isle), Housay (house or inhabited isle) and Bruray (brother isle) adjoined by the Bound rock on which the lighthouse had recently been built, formed a remarkably sheltered anchorage which astonished the *Earl's* passengers. They sailed through the north-east entrance with the strikingly tall white lighthouse to port, then the ship settled at anchor in the compact harbour, a secure base for the fishing industry. The group of islands was held in feu from the estate of Symbister to the estate of Busta, with T. M. Adie and Sons of Voe acting as factors and carrying on an extensive fishing. John Robertson Snr., who had been involved in the formation of the Shetland Islands Steam Navigation Company, also had fishing connections in Skerries which provided summer bothy accommodation for the men from Lunna on the mainland, almost due west of Skerries. Being near the grounds, the tiny islands made a fine base and a haven of shelter.

Shouted greetings from the flitboats gave a warm welcome. The *Earl's* for'ard well-deck doors were opened, and there were handshakes all round before the hundred plus passengers were put ashore at Robertson's fishing station. The storekeeper there, known as "Sockie", passed round his ram's horn cup liberally filled. They toasted his health and wished success to the fishing season. From the steamer in the harbour centre the crew could see the tiny dark figures gradually extending further afield in exploration.

To the islanders this was indeed an occasion in their near isolation. Up to the coming of the *Earl* to Shetland they had depended on the recently acquired sailing vessel for lighthouse work and, prior to that, could be remote for weeks on end. It was, in fact, a general holiday. William Peterson, known as the "Bishop of Skerries", was

The open doors of the well-deck.

teacher, preacher, lawyer, general adviser and friend to the whole community, and well established over a long number of years. His dwelling, like every abode in Skerries, was "open house" that day and the little ship, the means of it all, lay awaiting the pleasure of the people.

Humphray, the storekeeper for Adie, was away, but his wife extended open handed hospitality to allcomers and it was on a green by the shop that Jeem's fiddle stirred the feet to rhythm so that islanders and visitors swung into Shetland Reels, Boston Two-steps,

Quadrilles and Lancers. Some friendships had been renewed, many formed, and it was not easy to bid au revoir to the friendly islands, but the *Earl*, the already familiar billowing dark smoke at her funnel, eventually carried her complement south towards Whalsay, after many a hand and handkerchief on land and on ship were raised in farewell. They put in to Symbister Bay at Whalsay where the catering of R. & C. Robertson, the Lerwick grocers who had been appointed as suppliers, added to the satisfaction of the passengers. A two hour stop for tea over, the steamer was back at anchor in Lerwick by mid evening. It was a memorable addition to the growing list of visits made to previously little-frequented places and communities.

The administrative background since the appearance of the company had been ably handled by Charles Merrylees. His prowess was recognised when he became manager of the North of Scotland and Orkney and Shetland Steam Navigation Company at Aberdeen, the appointment to begin in January, 1878. In accepting the resignation, the directors of the Shetland Company voiced their confidence. He had done a splendid job in the formation and management. Correspondence, books and accounts had been well maintained. They spoke of his ability and faithful diligence in business over 20 years, and it was said that he would be generally appreciated and esteemed in his new home, as he had been in Shetland. Mr William Shand was made Merrylees' successor at a salary of £50 a year.

It was no reflection on either gentlemen when the *Earl* was found to have an alarming amount of water in her holds and engine room one day at the end of January. It was discovered when some of the crew went on board in the early morning. The captain and engineer were hurriedly summoned, and surveyed their lamp-lit images in the water below the open hatches. Packages floated disconsolately. The ship's pumps, aided by the crew with buckets attacked the encroaching sea water and the steamer had been emptied by early afternoon.

William Shand instructed the captain, engineer, fireman and two seamen to appear before the board. It appeared that a cock used for clearing accumulations of bilge water had been left open the previous day, giving a steady, if restricted, flow into the *Earl*. Undoubtedly given some hours longer she would have gone down. Strangely enough there was conflicting evidence, because whilst the board unanimously decided that the cock must have carelessly been left open overnight, the engineer and the fireman testified that the cock was found to be shut immediately after the water was seen. Yet there could have been access in no other way. It was found also that the sluices used for clearing out bilge water from the holds had remained open, which accounted for the water there as well as in the engine room. Although the engineer had to accept responsibility for the accident the element of mystery stayed. Being in charge overall, Captain Nicolson was formally requested to make regulations to prevent a recurrence of the incident.

Then there was evidence of further slackness. The ship returned from her first Board of Trade survey in Aberdeen with a complaint from the surveyor that the engines were in a dirty condition. This led to another letter to the engineer stating: "The engines and everything connected with your department should be kept in the utmost state of cleanliness and efficiency possible." The account of £170:12:3 for the overhaul might well have been less!

However, despite such minor items the ship was paying her way. Company revenue for 12 months ending June, 1878, was £2,643:6:7, while for the same period ending June, 1877, it was £519:15:5 less. The directors looked for a gradual and permanent development of traffic taking advantage of "the regular first class accommodation afforded by the company's new ship the *Earl*." There had been thoughts about introducing a service for the Westside of Shetland, but no support was given from the North Company. "I don't think the directors can be expected to move in the scheme of a steamer for the Westside. It is a matter for the local directors of the Shetland Company to promote. If they see their way to give the thing a trial, this company's directors, as shareholders, will offer no objections to the thing being tried . . . The s.s. *Express* lies at Kirkwall doing nothing. She could, I believe, be chartered cheaply for the summer and is, I understand, a very economical vessel to work. I think you had better have a meeting with your directors and find if they are prepared to negotiate with Robertson in regard to the *Express,* which Captain Nicolson might take a run south to see, if he could get any dependable man to take his place on the *Earl* for a week." The *Express* had been built at South Shields in 1869 for George Robertson's Pentland Firth run, and sailed between Kirkwall and Scottish ports. But, whatever her merits, the Shetland directors decided that she was unsuitable for the trade contemplated and no further action was taken in the scheme to have a companion ship for the *Earl*.

Much later, in 1883, the *Lady Ambrosine* returned to Shetland waters to ease the pressure on the *Earl* during the herring fishing season in the summer, when special runs were made to Fraserburgh, Peterhead and Aberdeen. The *Earl* might have on board up to 150 herring gutters. She could cope admirably in the spring season, but trade built up into the month of June towards the height of the industry. The extent and enormous scale of the bonanza is illustrated by the astonishing numbers of barrels of herring cured. In 1877 there were 5,451, but by 1881 the number had multiplied to an impressive 59,586. The army of fishermen and boys, fish curers, coopers and others expanded from 3,921 to 4,654. Larger boats of 18 to 30 feet of keel grew in numbers from 357 to 397, while those of 30 feet of keel and upwards increased spectacularly from only 11 to 117. With such an explosion of the herring industry in the 80s the pressure on shipping space was severe, and inevitably a vessel of the size of the *Earl* was badly compromised. In 1883 the *Lady Ambrosine* was re-introduced from the beginning of April at £105 per month, skippered by John Scott, mate of the *Earl.* She was collected at Fraserburgh and given a "floating" brief without definite timetable or regular routes, to be run in conjunction with the south steamers and as traffic demanded. The spring fishing was not a success, although the extra ship was run without any appreciable loss. In fact her five month charter proved to be timely since, during the previous year, doubts had arisen about the cargo and passenger capacity of the *Earl* due to increased trade. These uncertainties led to an exchange of ideas about having her lengthened. Co-incidentally the boiler had been surveyed by Thomas Lamb, superintendent engineer of the North Company. He remarked to the Lerwick directors that extensive repairs would be needed to maintain the present pressure, and in deciding to recommend a new boiler they felt that it would be opportune at the same time to have estimates for lengthening. Opinion in Aberdeen confirmed that both proposals would be acceptable.

Charles Merrylees, now resident in Aberdeen, arranged for a new boiler priced at £600 from Hall, Russell and Company, but the section to be slotted into the steamer raised questions of seaworthiness, speed and aesthetic qualities. Lloyd's requirements were class 90A. The two Aberdeen construction firms, Duthie and Sons and Alexander Hall and Company, tendered £1,950 and £1,830 respectively to add 23 feet in accordance with Lloyd's. Later, Hall increased the amount, due to additional strengthening needed.

There followed an exchange of telegrams. Neither group of directors seemed anxious to assume responsibility. Lerwick to Aberdeen: "Subject to full approval of Aberdeen directors, unanimously approve accepting Duthie's offer to lengthen *Earl* 23 feet. Maintenance present speed great importance." Aberdeen to Lerwick: "New offers lengthening *Earl* with all strengthening required by Lloyd's — Duthie's £1,980, Hall's £2,000. Directors here wish sanction Shetland directors before accepting lowest offer. Wire.". Lerwick to Aberdeen: "The directors here sanction

Aberdeen directors accepting either of the offers which will complete work in shortest time.'' Duthie's price of £1,980 was taken, and the firm undertook to have the *Earl* ready for sea by the beginning of March, 1884.

In the original state the funnel was equidistant between foremast and mainmast. The for'ard well-deck was longer than the after one and the ship's boats were set abreast of the funnel. Her crew had found that the after well-deck served no real practical purpose, thus when she was dry-docked at Aberdeen a decision was taken to cover the after space as well as lengthen the hull. She was cut behind the for'ard hatch and the 23 feet long insertion gave scope for a deck house and open bridge, and enabled the boats to be moved forward by 10 feet. Finally the foredeck was also lengthened, which gave cover for the derrick winch in the well-deck. Duthie's produced an excellent standard of workmanship which gave master and crew satisfaction, though they noted that the resultant extra buoyancy for'ard raised her bows fractionally when afloat.

Undoubtedly the lengthening was functional. It gave her hull a subtle sheer, provided a spaciousness on deck, and altered her proportions, producing a certain grace of line. If these qualities were not the "raison d'être" they certainly added to the practical features, and the steamer was the object of further interest and enthusiasm in the eyes of the Shetlanders when she came north to home waters. The carrying capacity was doubled, speed fully maintained and working expenses were not expected to be greater. She was described as "a much more serviceable steamer, in all respects as good as new".

Prior to the lengthening, the many facets of the existence of a small cargo and passenger vessel on an island run had continued to develop. Occasionally sail tried to re-assert itself. In the spring of 1878, despite a prior arrangement not to do so, James Inkster of Brae re-introduced his sailer *Saucey Jack* to carry goods from Lerwick to the north of Shetland. The directors saw this as an unjustifiable violation of the agreement to withdraw all competition to the company for 12 months. They therefore wrote to the owner that the *Earl* would cease to call if the *Saucey Jack* was not immediately withdrawn, and a similar communication went to Anderson Smith, Merchant, Lerwick, who managed the smack. Undeniably the *Earl* was already becoming an integral part of life, and her presence essential, for without resort to the ultimatum the *Saucey Jack* was taken off the run.

Financial matters were inevitably foremost in the minds of the directors. A circular latter to shareholders reminded them that the company did not insure against sea risk, it being left to the individual to protect his own interest. At a later date a resolution was passed to

insure the *Earl of Zetland* for £5,000 for 12 months, the premium being
£270.

The ship's regular contribution to livestock shipment was
emphasised when Tom Hamilton of Symbister made application for a
season ticket over the company's routes. A sum of seven guineas
would grant him the use of the steamer, but the directors
reconsidered this in view of Hamilton's considerable trade and they
reduced the sum to five guineas for one year, payable in advance.
Hamilton, however, was not mindful of the concession when a claim
appeared for £19:3/-, being the alleged loss suffered when a horse was
injured in transit. He intimated that unless the claim was met within
six days, proceedings would be instituted to recover the debt. No one
in the company was prepared to accept responsibility. A summons
was issued, the damages now restricted to £12. Eventually a
compromise sum of £5 was settled.

There was another informal approach by the Lerwick
postmaster, nothing having come of the company's overtures to the
Post Office in Scotland when Warren came up to Shetland. The
request was for what sum per trip or per annum the company would
charge for carrying mail to and from Fetlar on the Unst voyage. The
proposal was made to do this for 6/- per week, subject to trading
which would have priority, the mail to be transferred at Wick of
Tresta or Brough Lodge, depending on weather. Lady Nicolson of
Brough Lodge thought otherwise. She arranged for a letter from her
solicitors to the effect that the shipping of weekly mail at The Lodge
would prove injurious to her interests and steps would be taken to
prevent it. The directors were at a loss to understand the attitude and
replied that the Post Office would be responsible for landing and
shipping at Brough Lodge, but the calls of the ship there were more
for the convenience of the public than any direct benefit to the
company. In fact, if any measures were taken to prevent the travellers
sharing in the facility, then it would be necessary to withdraw the
steamer's calls to that station. Apparently Lady Nicolson appreciated
the situation. Nothing further was recorded.

A variety of special trips highlighted the steamer's place in the
many-sided structure of island life. The 1880 election was contested
in Orkney and Shetland by Samuel Laing and he chartered the *Earl*
for use "within the limits of the Orkney and Shetland Islands." The
charter was for £35, the charterer paying for "coals, engine stores,
provision and all other expenses whatever." Then another booking
was made by Mr Muir, inspector of schools. Special trips took place
on Saturdays from Lerwick to Foula (£20 for charter), Fair Isle (£15)
and Out Skerries (£10).

Salvage incidents were to become regular features in the activities of the *Earl*. Already she had salved the *Milberg und Engstrom* and now, on 13th November, 1881, she picked up the disabled brig *Superior* of Aberdeen, another matter not without its controversy. She was reported adrift to the east of Noss where Captain Nicolson had a tow rope put on board, then they took the brig into Bressay Sound where she was moored, her cargo of oil and skins intact. Obviously she was ripe for a claim, and the company proposed an amount for salvage at a third of the ascertained value of ship and cargo. The secretary handed a letter to the brig's captain intimating the claim for salvage and asking for details of ship and cargo. The solicitor to the company, Mr Galloway, recommended that proceedings be taken at once before the Sheriff to recover salvage, reserving claim on the cargo for later. This would give time to question the crews of both vessels. At first, figures of £250 or £200 were mooted, but these were modified later to £200 or £150 for the services rendered. Then it was decided to accept not less than £150 in settlement of salvage of ship and cargo. The agent at Peterhead for the owners of the brig declined to accept this amount and immediately the company's solicitors instituted proceedings to bring the case before the Sheriff in Lerwick. By the beginning of March, 1882, the matter had been settled, although hardly to the liking of the salvors, whose preliminary figure of £250 was whittled down to £100. The ruling of the Sheriff was final. Eventually £50 went to the owners of the steamer, £20 was given to Captain Nicolson and £30 was distributed amongst the crew, each according to his wages. It was July before the £100 was forthcoming, plus £1:13/- interest — small compensation when so much more was envisaged originally.

E

4

The Work Horse

Sail had had its protracted limitations; the first ventures into steam had hardly been notable for success, but at least the new steamer had made a strong bid for consistency and popularity. By 1890, during the first 13 years of her long sojourn in Shetland waters, she had carried a multitude of passengers and become a regular and familiar caller at ports over routes which covered well over 200 miles each week. Harry Pearson Taylor was one of those passengers. He was a Yorkshireman who had studied medicine in Aberdeen and, after graduating in 1890, he returned to his home in Northumberland. It

Inward bound off Rova Head.

was there that he received a request from one of his former lecturers asking him to relieve in Shetland. Harry Taylor agreed and visited Aberdeen en route where, coincidentally, he encountered a former colleague who had done locum on the island of Yell and the newly fledged doctor found himself regaled by accounts of the rugged beauty of Shetland, tempered by descriptions of roadless landscape and miles to walk on professional visits, crossing moorland in wild weather. Yet it was with a sense of optimistic anticipation that Dr Taylor travelled from Aberdeen to Lerwick on one of the steamers of the North of Scotland and Orkney and Shetland Steam Navigation Company.

Like hundreds of people before him Taylor transferred to the *Earl* for the voyage amid the islands. In describing his initiation into a unique experience in sea travel he wrote: "Passage was taken on the small local steamer the *Earl of Zetland*. The journey from Lerwick to Mid Yell took about four hours, including calls at two ports to deliver H.M. mails, passengers and goods. The first call was at Whalsay

(Symbister) about fifteen miles north from Lerwick and two miles east from the mainland of Shetland. This island looked very beautiful on this calm bright day. Little wonder that it goes under the name of "The Bonny Isle". It was here that I got a glimpse in the distance of the island of Yell which was to be my future home and the seat of my joys and sorrows for the rest of my life."

In fact Harry Pearson Taylor spent forty-five years of his medical career, from June, 1890, until November, 1935, based in Mid Yell as doctor for Yell and Fetlar. And he lived the ten years of his retirement in Mid Yell in his home, the Haa of Reafirth, evidence of a man captivated by a place, a people and a way of life.

His reactions to further passages on the *Earl* continued, "With the exception of Baltasound, the chief township and port of Unst, the most northerly of the North Isles group, there are no piers at which steamers can berth, so mails, passengers and goods have to be transported to the shore in large boats called flitboats. These boats, generally used by fishermen in the past and replaced by much larger sailing vessels later on, were called 'sixerns' because they were propelled by six men each using one oar, when not under sail.

"When the steamer dropped anchor a flitboat and other smaller craft came alongside, the owners of the smaller boats taking off their friends, relations and goods for themselves, while other passengers, mails, animals and general cargo for the local shops were deposited in the flitboat. During this transfer of men, women, animals and material from steamer to boats, those of us who had further north to go amused and interested ourselves in watching the proceedings of the steamer and 'skipper' of the flitboat. The badinage which took place between these worthies, although at times unprintable, was efficient in the highest degree and would certainly have made a Thames bargee envious and astonished a Billingsgate porter. The skippers of the flitboats were usually the victors in the wordy, but always friendly and humorous conflicts. This could be accounted for because the officers — generally the mate — superintending the transfer of goods were required to exercise restraint in their language while the skippers of the flitboats could let rip."

Unlike Dr Taylor the vast majority of hundreds of voyagers did not commit their experiences to the pen, although the character and industry of crew and ship would be apparent to all. The *Earl's* timetable, despite being inevitably slow-moving, was demanding. She was seldom still. About the time of Harry Taylor's arrival in Yell the steamer's sequence of service was firmly established. On Tuesday she left Lerwick at 9 a.m. on what was known as the Unst Passage, for Symbister, Gossabrough, Mid Yell, Uyeasound, Cullivoe,

Gutcher, Haroldswick and Baltasound with fortnightly calls at Tresta
(Fetlar) and Bastavoe. There was an overnight stay at Baltasound,
then the steamer returned to Lerwick at 8 a.m. on Wednesday, via
Uyeasound, Cullivoe, Mid Yell and Symbister.

The Yell Sound passage occupied the end of the week and she
worked her way north again, sailing from Lerwick on Friday at
9 a.m. for Symbister, Vidlin, Burravoe, Mossbank, Ollaberry,

. . . large boats called flitboats.

Lochend and North Roe, with fortnightly calls at Sullom and Garth. Also included in the timetable was a monthly call at Swinister and Ronas Voe on inducement. The visits to ports such as Ronas Voe on the west side illustrated the poverty of overland communication even on the Mainland. On the Yell Sound run, a second overnight stay was made at North Roe, after which the steamer returned south on the Saturday at 8 a.m., calling at Ollaberry, West Sandwick, Ulsta, Mossbank, Burravoe and Symbister to end her week in the early evening of Saturday. No five-day week for a dedicated complement of officers and crew on a vessel dropping and raising her anchor thirty times a week!

Changes in her timetable had been made at irregular intervals. In September, 1888, the Unst trip on a Tuesday took in Symbister, Mid Yell, Uyeasound and Baltasound. The *Earl* also called at Aith (Fetlar) and Tresta on the 2nd, 16th and 30th of the month, and Gossabrough, Bastavoe and Gutcher on the 9th and 23rd. Then from the Baltasound terminal on a Wednesday, anchoring at Uyeasound, Cullivoe, Mid Yell and Symbister en route to Lerwick. On a Friday the voyage included Symbister, Vidlin, Burravoe, Mossbank, Ollaberry, also Sullom, Brae and Garth on 5th, 12th and 26th of the month; and Swinister on the 5th and 19th. Ollaberry was an alternative terminal to North Roe and the *Earl* departed at 7 a.m. on a Saturday touching at Lochend, North Roe, West Sandwick, Ulsta, Mossbank, Burravoe and Symbister; also Mid Yell and Uyeasound when considered necessary. Symbister in Whalsay was the only port common to the Unst and Yell Sound passages, and was privileged to be visited both outward and inward.

Whatever was scheduled could never be accepted literally due to manifold uncertainties in operating the route. Flexibility and patience were key factors and the unexpected was a feature of existence. This was dramatically highlighted by a unique affair of the sea which put the name *Earl of Zetland* into the columns of the great national newspapers like the London ''Standard'' and Edinburgh ''Scotsman'' and caught the imagination of the reading public at home and abroad.

The annual survey of the steamer was a matter of careful routine and undoubtedly her eventual longevity could be attributed partly to the regular maintenance. Her machinery was in good shape. Such a survey had been done at Aberdeen over the second fortnight in January, 1886. William Nicolson brought her back, having left port at noon on Saturday, 30th January. With the bitter wind from south-south-east the *Earl* wallowed northwards; late on the Saturday night she was well north, and into the Sunday morning the ship anchored at

Lerwick. Captain and crew were relieved that the return trip had been no worse. January could be treacherous. But anticipation of some well earned rest became consternation and deep concern. Lerwick people were in a state of alarm and despondency which was immediately shared by the ship's complement. Tragedy had struck the islands and there was obviously prospect of even greater tragedy. There had already been one drowning; there was apparently every chance of another. A turmoil of near despair and intense speculation permeated the population and a grim sequence of events unfolded as the returning men listened to the subdued but strangely avid talk. Maybe there were some conflicting versions of a bizarre incident, but the facts gradually emerged through it all. James Jamieson, skipper of the smack *Columbine*, was dead. A respected seaman and known to every man on the *Earl*, he worked a weekly service between the south mainland and Lerwick, with fortnightly runs to Fair Isle. They found his death difficult enough to accept, yet could scarcely credit the outcome.

They knew the *Columbine* sailed on a Saturday for Lerwick from Grutness in the south-east point of Shetland and it was said she had left the bay there on the Saturday, also about mid-day, encountering the same south-south-east wind. Half an hour later she was off Boddam, rolling northwards in the following gale with double-reefed mainsail, staysail and jib, apparently well controlled.

Today, in the great diversity and variety of transport, the movement of shipping causes little comment, but in the 19th century the departure and arrival of the packet or steamer were features in the lives of the people in the sequestered Shetland hamlets, thus the *Columbine* was closely observed as was the custom. The experienced eyes of the old seafarers were suddenly aware that there had been a mishap, and could assess from the smack's erratic behaviour that it was not a triviality. But none could guess what had come about. The vessel had been seen to turn sharply to seaward, to the east, and then a snow squall had hidden her. When it lifted she was still headed away from the coast, clearly helmless. The seas were large enough to hide her hull from view below the wave tops and the watchers were further puzzled and alarmed when a dark object appeared on a crest, seen momentarily, then hidden in the trough. They knew it was the *Columbine's* dinghy. Two shapes indicated two people. The mystery deepened. Undoubtedly the fragile craft was directed shorewards, while the fleeing smack was becoming a shadowy form amid the gathering stormwrack. The flood tide was on, and offshore the sea was a white mass of breaking water. Knowledgeable men drew bated breath and gnawed at nervous lips as the silhouette of the dinghy dragged through the last few hundred yards, each yard fought for by the two oarsmen. But they made it, shocked and exhausted as they were. Grasped desperately by many hands the dinghy grated on the shifting shingle and was manhandled up to the grass — the two occupants still on board. They proved to be two unrelated Smiths, Jeremiah the mate and Oliver, deckhand of the *Columbine*.

In the nearest house, blanket-clad and with hot restoratives thrust into their quivering hands, the two survivors stammered through a tragic story to an incredulous and bewildered audience. Their tale fluctuated between concern for a passenger on the *Columbine*, now out of sight in the January twilight in an ever-increasing wind, the drowning of James Jamieson, and their own conscience-stricken uncertainty at decisions taken. Jeremiah Smith, the mate, described violent pitching and gyrating in the tideway, gusting wind, cracking sails, and the sharp report of the main sheet giving way. He and the skipper went for the wildly whipping rope ends, were caught off balance and lost footing to plunge into the white boil of wake amidships. Jamieson had failed to grasp a trailing rope and was yards astern in seconds. Smith miraculously hauled himself back onto the deck. Oliver Smith said he had hauled the staysail bowline to windward to keep the way off the *Columbine*, although he could not be sure if he had secured the rope in a frantic urge to reach the skipper by launching the dinghy. They had seen the outstretched arm of the skipper, raised in desperation, showing that he was fighting the all-embracing clutches of the sea. Too far for rope or lifebelt; too long to wear ship; the dinghy was the only way to go after him. Frantically the two men had swung the boat overboard and rowed hard in the direction of that final gesture by James Jamieson. But he had lost his battle. He had gone. Jeremiah despairingly recalled his glance back to his ship, after it was obvious that his fellow seaman had submerged, to see the mainsail against the port backstay, the jib drawing and the staysail sheet flat amidships, all trimmed by the perversity of fate to make her self-steering.

Jeremiah Smith indicated that the smack had temporarily come up into the wind as they hesitated. Hope revived and they pulled frantically, but a breaker almost swamped the dinghy and made them think about their own perilous position. They were a few miles off; they could never reach the smack under sail; they might not even make the land. Numb from despair and cold they struggled back. The two survivors established basic facts to the listeners which were duly embroidered and coloured. News had travelled fast over the south mainland and to Lerwick. Thus the *Earl's* men returned to a drama; a death by drowning, not unknown in the islands, was bad enough in itself, but a sailing vessel out of control in worsening weather with a helpless female passenger on board, was unprecedented.

The mail steamer *St. Clair* had also come to Lerwick from Orkney arriving on the Saturday night/Sunday morning. Her skipper had seen nothing of the missing smack.

John Bruce of Sumburgh, owner of the *Columbine,* was greatly concerned about the situation. Never before in living memory had there been such a dearth of decked vessels in the voes. Nothing was available on the east mainland to risk the conditions developing that night, but he discovered that a steamer, the *Gipsy,* was lying in Mid Yell and he promptly chartered her for a search. She left there at 6.30 p.m. on the Saturday night. By daylight the sea had moderated and the wind had veered westerly with improved visibility. The *Gipsy* steamed 75 miles to the south and east of the mainland, then came back on a north-easterly course, covering almost 200 miles in a fruitless and frustrating search over 25 hours. Bruce was not content to abandon the efforts. Early on the Sunday afternoon Captain Nicolson learned that he had been in contact with the company through George Hay, the chairman, and the directors generously agreed to provide the *Earl* free of charge for further search. Her crew were more than pleased to be involved. It was something positive. At 4 a.m. on the Monday the *Earl* put to sea. On board was Jeremiah Smith, the luckless mate of the *Columbine.* The wind was still near gale strength and snow was falling as the steamer passed Kirkabister Lighthouse. Nicolson ordered a course east-north-east and by daybreak they were 30 miles out. As far as it was possible to see, the ocean was empty. Men's eyes strained from maindeck and open bridge as course was shaped east for ten miles and south-east for ten miles. Nothing. Thick snow flurries, gusting in the near gale force winds, seas breaking over the fo'c'sle and stinging spray spurting across the ship made life extremely uncomfortable for men on watch, and oilskins were poor protection against their exposure to the fierce cold. Nicolson wondered just what could be achieved in these conditions even if they chanced to come across a shadowy shape in the murk. Short of standing by the smack, little could be done. No boat could be launched. There was no way of putting a tow rope on her. All ten men on the steamer said little, but wondered if Betty Mouat, the passenger, might have succumbed to the sea like the ill-fated James Jamieson. Doubts arose about the practicability of continuing. Eventually Nicolson gave a course change and the *Earl* swung onto her new track, homeward bound, still battering at the monotonous regularity of steeply pitched seas.

It was the first day of February. Rumour was rife over much of the Shetland mainland. A telegram reached Lerwick that the *Earl* had been seen off the south mainland with the *Columbine* in tow. The news spread rapidly. The people gathered. Women and children left their homes; shopkeepers their shops. Men stopped work early and stood in expectant groups at the quay to await the two vessels. The February twilight had almost gone as the *Earl of Zetland* came in — alone. The telegram had been the result of gossip and misguided optimism. One man on shore had seen two vessels close together, he had confided in a neighbour, and presently the tale had acquired conviction — one vessel towing the other. They could only be . . .

But it was not so, and the dejected throng at Lerwick foreshore gradually dispersed as the grim weather at sea was described. Captain Nicolson was reported in "The Shetland News" later in the week: "I don't think the vessel could have got as far as Norway. If she is down there is no doubt she met her fate at 12 o'clock on Saturday night. We were at sea then and the wind blew very strong from the south-west, the sea being terrific. I believe she would be crippled at that time. The forehatch was off and the companion was open, so that any waves that might break over her would very soon fill her. I am confident that I have covered all the ground that the vessel was likely to go over, or to be on and I don't think there is the slightest use of continuing the search. We would certainly have gone further than 60 miles out if the weather had been favourable, but it was a regular storm and we judged it to be of no use to go further even if we could have gone with safety. The day was one of the worst I have ever been to sea in. The sea was frequently breaking over our head. In at the land no one could form any idea how stormy it was."

The episode was an awesome example of the uncaring sea, but despite the declared futility of further efforts many reckoned that the rate of drift of the *Columbine* had been underestimated. Even her surviving crew, the two unrelated Smiths, thought she would be not far short of 50 miles out by midnight on the Sunday, yet the *Earl* had ventured only 10 miles further than that, and hours later. Some reckoned that Nicolson should have gone up to 120 miles out, yet to have done so would have been to risk ship and crew. The apparent lack of initiative by the North Company was also noted and widely discussed. Since the information about the disaster had reached Lerwick during the Saturday afternoon fully an hour before the *St. Clair* left Kirkwall in Orkney, there had been time available to telegraph and divert her course north for a sweep eastwards off the south mainland of Shetland. The omissions of the authorities and individuals heightened the poignancy of the situation, although criticism was tempered by thoughts of the fate of the passenger, Betty Mouat.

Such was the magnitude of the event that it was the talking point for the ensuing week. There could be no certainty that the *Columbine* had foundered and the optimistic Shetlanders speculated on the seemingly remote possibility that the smack had reached Norway. Opinion on board the *Earl* varied. Captain Nicolson seriously doubted if the vessel could have survived into the Monday. Inevitably the steamer was a carrier of widely divergent theories. At every port of call on her North Isles and Yell Sound trips that week comment was bandied between the steamer's well-deck and flitboat. It was all inconclusive and futile, yet had to be said because people must give vent to feelings in such circumstances. The pessimists predicted that the mystery would prevail, that the derelict smack would have been swamped, and that Betty Mouat and the *Columbine* would be added to the long list of unresolved losses at sea. Yet many people were hopeful. They respected the sturdy qualities of a well-built hull, the deep draught, even the protective embrace of the Almighty for a woman in dire peril.

Dramatically and finally the anguished rumour and gossip were ended by a blunt message telegraphed to Lerwick. ''Stavanger, Norway. Smack *Columbine* with woman safely brought into Lepsoe, near Alesund. Johnsen, British Consul.'' It was 8th February. There was a vast reaction of relief in Shetland. The widespread speculation was ended. Betty Mouat was safe, which was the essential factor, although the discussion featured how in God's name the *Columbine* had miraculously reached some shore to enable Betty to be rescued. For a further week the guesswork continued amid crew and passengers during the *Earl's* runs to the north, whilst the very unusual circumstances and dramatic ending had caught the attention of the world's press. Interest was intense. Not only the Shetland press carried extensive detail. Reporting went on stage by stage through such newspapers as the ''New York Herald'', ''The Scotsman'', and the ''Times'' and ''Standard'' in London.

That the 50 foot smack survived the menace of the reefs off Lepsoe was remarkable enough in itself, but that she had done so and saved a life was cause for rejoicing. And the passenger? Betty Mouat, a partial cripple, came from the community of Levenwick on the south mainland of Shetland and was travelling to Lerwick for medical advice and, at the same time, carrying knitwear for sale from the womenfolk. Her journey should have been one of under four hours, with a following wind. It took 180 hours of dreadful uncertainty, her morale sustained by a simple Christian faith and her body by a few biscuits and milk. There could have been a thousand calamitous landfalls, yet providentially the *Columbine* sought out one of the four possibilities in an awesome barrier of a thousand miles of hostile coast.

A "Shetland Times" report of 6th March carried a headline which illustrated the public reaction to an amazing survival. "The Heroine of the Columbine." A short article perhaps implied a touch of conscience by the directors of the North of Scotland and Orkney and Shetland Steam Company when mention was made of a "free passage to Miss Mouat from Leith to Lerwick when the lady feels herself able to undertake the voyage." The comparatively brief remarks hid a poignant sequence of assistance and kindness by the two fishermen of Lepsoe in the first instance, who braved the surf at the only acceptable stretch of shingle on the island, to bring ashore a 60 year old woman who had endured privation at sea, day after day, night after night, for most of the time without food or water. Hospitality was liberal in Lepsoe and Alesund. A mixture of curiosity and kindly interest brought many Norwegians to Bergen and Stavanger, ports of call for the steamer *Domino,* en route to Hull.

On 24th February, Betty Mouat reached Edinburgh by train to be greeted by a huge crowd, full of awe and adulation. She endured the attentions stoically, weak as she was, and found a measure of security and a degree of peace with Shetland friends in the city, although men, women and children flocked to see this remarkable woman who had cheated death.

After three weeks the survivor had recovered well enough to travel north on the *St. Clair,* which might well have been the vessel to find the *Columbine* had initial rescue attempts been correctly anticipated. As the *St. Clair* anchored astern of the *Earl of Zetland* off the Lerwick foreshore a great cheer welled up from an immense mass of well-wishers, and when the small boat came ashore from the steamer the crowds surged enthusiastically forward in scenes unprecedented in the northern capital.

Sympathy was universal. With the chief magistrate of Lerwick, Bailie Robertson, also of the Shetland Islands Steam Navigation Company, Elizabeth Mouat was driven in a carriage round the town. The people were celebrating a miraculous return and acknowledging respect for someone who had preserved a modest dignity during the entire affair. A practical outlet for public feeling through a subscription list brought further acclaim. Queen Victoria contributed £20, as did Mr and Mrs John Bruce. Leask, the clerk of the *Earl of Zetland,* collected £11:7:6 from crew and passengers and this sum played its small but important part in a total of £400. Yet Elizabeth

Mouat remained unmoved by it all and was content to return to her quiet, retiring way of life for another 32 years, whilst the *Columbine* survived to complete a life of 72 years. In due course she was to be emulated in longevity by the *Earl of Zetland.*

Throughout the 1880s the work of the steamer brought colour to the pattern of existence. If the Betty Mouat drama was a highlight, the years of the decade repeatedly featured salvage and social activities which added to the vast amount of trade in passengers, animals, goods and fish in which the ship was involved. A work horse indeed! Despite the occasional unaccountable setback through lack of fish the transport business was potentially lucrative now, although previously it had been on a tiny scale commercially.

Traditionally the Shetland fishing industry had been based on the use of the small open sixern of keel length 18-22 feet, six feet beam and double ended with a sheer at bow and stern reminiscent of the Norwegian "attring", a descendant of the Viking boat. She was really better fitted in size for inshore fishing rather than the demands made by the methods and scope of the offshore industry which developed fast in the 19th century. The haaf fishing (from old Norse hav or sea) made punishing demands on a crew. A boat would make two trips a week, Monday to Wednesday and Thursday to Saturday. Sleep was at a premium and cooking facilities in exposed conditions difficult in the extreme. The lines were laboriously baited, paid out and hauled by hand. Thus life was hard and the risks had already been cruelly exposed in the 1832 disaster. But a second, more recent, calamity was fresh in the minds of Shetland seamen. In July, 1881, seas tormented by a terrific wind from the north caught the sixern fleet over 30 miles at sea. The price was the loss of ten boats and another 58 men. From the haaf station at Nederton, Gloup in Yell, alone, 36 men had lost their lives. The *Earl's* men knew that the haaf fishing had recovered from the first disastrous summer gale, but it was common opinion that the second appalling loss spelt the death knell of the faithful sixern as a fishing craft, and effected its practical retirement into ferry or flitboat as described by Dr Taylor or, more sadly, to serve upturned as a store at the gable end of many a croft-house.

Larger vessels had appeared as early as the 1830s although there was a reluctance to abandon the sixern, partly for economic reasons. She was reasonably cheap to build, a remarkable sea boat for her size and no other craft could have made the trade viable for men who received such a meagre return for their fish. However, bigger sailing boats gained comparatively large catches which opened up the market year by year. In 1872 fishermen from Buckie on the Scottish mainland had shown initiative by coming to Shetland with a fully decked sailing vessel, working long lines and taking far more fish than any sixern could hope to achieve. This type of vessel paid her way and about the time of the arrival of the *Earl* in Shetland the men from Burra Isle on the west side of Shetland could repay the cost of a boat within a season with long-line fishing at the haaf, hand-line for cod or drift-net for herring. Thus the sixern was being gradually ousted, although the island fishermen generally were concerned about abandoning a type of craft in which they believed, despite the risks. Shetland was centred on an area rich in herring, a situation much exploited by the Dutch, not unnoticed by Scottish interests. In the late 1870s there was fresh impetus which brought large decked herring smacks north and the output of the fishing industry grew enormously. The boom showed itself in many ways. Curing stations sprang up all over the islands, an army of gutters and packers enlisted in Scotland arrived for the season, shipping increased with direct trips to the continent, and trading within the local communities was greatly enhanced.

With the directors seeking ways of improving remuneration, the *Earl* was added to the list of steamers active in the fishing industry. She logged hundreds of miles. On 14th February, 1887, she brought a large consignment of fish from Mid Yell, then two days later transported 40 tons from Scalloway round Sumburgh Head to Lerwick for shipment south by the North Company steamer *St. Clair*. On 13th July, in company with the steamer *Corsican*, she left Lerwick for Fraserburgh and Aberdeen laden with 150 herring gutters. The use of the steamer increased further. Her week's work was extended to continue with a run direct to Aberdeen each Saturday evening if there was enough fish to transport. The ship left the island capital at 5 p.m. on Saturday, 12th November, for a first run south, called at Scalloway for additional cargo, and sailed for Aberdeen at midnight. She carried 180 boxes of fresh and smoked fish from Lerwick and the North Isles, and 38 tons fresh and 15 tons dried fish from Scalloway. The time of year brought its weather problems. While the passage from Scalloway to Aberdeen took 21 hours, the return voyage featured heavy seas which caused slow time, and Captain Nicolson and his crew did not reach their home port until 7 a.m. on the Tuesday.

Subject to such uncertainty the service could hardly be consistent. But the new sailings were noted in the south. Messrs. James McLennahan and Company of Peterhead approached the directors with the proposal that cargoes could be taken to Peterhead. They added that the Great North of Scotland Railway might give a subsidy of £100 as inducement. The idea was rejected since the meeting reckoned that Shetland curers had no direct interest in the district and would object to the cost of carriage between Peterhead and Aberdeen. Further, at Peterhead the *Earl* could not arrive and depart on the same tide, whereas Aberdeen offered enough depth of water at any stage. The £100 was not enough to cover possible loss from cancelled sailings due to bad weather. Thus the previous decision taken in October was confirmed, to sail direct to Aberdeen, provided each trip raised a minimum freight of £30. The fears of cancellation were illustrated early in the New Year of 1888 when the "Scalloway Notes" in "The Shetland News" had a critical flavour: "On Friday negotiations were made with the Lerwick agent as to getting the *Earl* to make a direct trip to Aberdeen on a Saturday, which mode of conveyance would have been a considerable advantage to the curers, as carting across to Lerwick over 30 tons of fish incurred much expense. We understand the service of the *Earl* was sanctioned and curers advised accordingly. The curers having satisfied themselves as to the genuineness of this arrangement made no other preparation for forthcoming emergencies. However, on Saturday afternoon the scene was changed, as evidently the decision arrived at the day before was too good and accommodating for the Scalloway curers, and information was despatched, probably from 'Lerwick and District Maritime Government', that it was too rough for the worthy *Earl* to show her face westward of Sumburgh Head and that if curers wished to send their fish by the *Queen,* which was sailing on Sunday morning, they would have to cart them across to the metropolis.

"A rather unusual incident took place here on Saturday night. Just as the hurly burly of men and women working hard and the clatter of carts and the treading of horses, combined with the strains of music whistled aloud by the carters, it was observed that part of our bay was frozen. Who knows but what nature had a fore-knowledge of the fact that the good ship *Earl* would not that night molest our bay with its fearful propeller, which at the command of its master's muscular arm might have strewn our shores with an impassable mass of ice. Fortunately this was not the case and next morning by the rays of the warm sun the tiny ice field disappeared.

"We are glad to state that the curers, notwithstanding their difficulties, got the bulk of their fish south by the *Queen,* and little praise to those who had the power of helping friends in need, especially with a perishable subject and did not do it, nor even considered it necessary to give timely notice. It seems we are wholly under Lerwick's government as regards steamer movements, and

that disappointing the Scalloway curers is nothing but a jest, but we
hope that a sweeping revolution will yet be made when we shall have
our wants better attended to. The day may yet come when the
Ancient Capital shall again resume its title and have a Government of
its own inspired by the thought that, 'Scalloway wis Scalloway when
Lerwick wis nane. An Scalloway 'ill be Scalloway when Lerwick is
ga'en.' ''

Whatever Scalloway's claims to be the premier town in Shetland
the relevant difficulties of keeping viable a small firm and a small
ship were only too apparent to directors who had no wish to readily
cancel the trips of their steamer, yet who were uncomfortably aware
of that expanse of winter sea south and west of Sumburgh Head.

If the fish trade proved erratic, apart from the North Isles and
Yell Sound routine runs, other uses for the ship were sources of
income, although hard wear and tear on steamer and seamen. There
were various milestones in the unfolding saga of Shetland's
strengthening links with the south. These grew in the closing years of
the Shetland Islands Steam Navigation Company.

Lerwick harbour works had been gradually improving, with the
herring industry a particular incentive to organise better facilities,
especially for berthing. Bailie John Robertson was largely responsible
for a small pier at which the *Chieftain's Bride* could moor, but at the
time of the advent of the *Earl of Zetland* no regular berth was available
and she lay off-shore. In May, 1876, a conference in Lerwick had
established the principle of a pier capable of taking vessels like the
Earl and North Company steamers. Legislation and questions of
finance created delays, but at the end of 1877 Lerwick Harbour Trust
was formed and a policy of progress became viable. The great
upsurge in the herring industry with its resultant concentration of
boats on Lerwick led to the spread of the town itself, and the trustees
felt obliged to plan a harbour in keeping with the new trend.
Although another five years elapsed before there was physical
evidence of building, the planning had been thorough and a fine new
pier named after Queen Victoria was envisaged. The foundation
stone was laid by Sheriff Principal Thoms in 1883. Then began a
process of transformation of the appearance of the Lerwick foreshore
with its conglomeration of beach, rock, piers and lodberries. A great
many people looked forward to the time when it would be possible to
disembark from ship to pier. Already Shetland-bound passengers
from the south were accustomed to improved accommodation and
timings on the North Company's steamers, yet were faced with the
risks of transfer in open boats at Lerwick, at best uncomfortable in
summer, often extremely dangerous in winter. Also for the *Earl of*

Zetland, carrying such a diverse cargo, the continual shifting of goods on several occasions each week in the flitboats at Lerwick was very inconvenient, but the new facilities could not be produced overnight and another three years elapsed before the jetty materialised.

Wednesday, 23rd June, 1886, was a better day than promised. There had been frequent heavy showers the night before, but good weather welcomed the Lerwick populace on what was a public holiday. The people appeared in force to witness and enjoy a public and historically significant occasion. In the late morning William Nicolson had the *Earl* lying at the Albert Wharf immediately to the north of the new structure, ready to be the first vessel to moor at the Victoria Pier, now at an advanced stage of completion, with the big steam driven crane on the landward end and another on a barge alongside, both symbolising the advance of technology. At 1 p.m. Sheriff Thoms boarded the *Earl* accompanied by Vice Admiral Thoms, Sheriff Mackenzie, Bailie Mitchell, Councillors Halcrow, Robertson jnr. and Tulloch, Mr Sandison (Town Clerk) and Mr Bryden. Mr Charles Robertson and Mr Shand of the Shetland Islands Company were also present. The little steamer, having come direct from Baltasound, was in immaculate condition for her important and prestigious event. She flew colourful bunting, seen at its best in the sunlight, from foremast and mainmast. The brilliant colours were echoed by an array of flags on the Victoria Pier itself, and a naval vessel, *H.M.S. Eagle,* was dressed overall. Several Grimsby smacks and Dutch herring boats flew flags and pennants. It was another memorable moment for Nicolson as his steamer drew away for an hour's cruise during which lunch was served at the horse-shoe table in the saloon.

In Lerwick at Fort Charlotte, begun under the instructions of Oliver Cromwell suspicious of the activities of Dutch fishermen in the 17th century, a representative procession gathered and, headed by the town's brass band, marched to the pier to greet the *Earl of Zetland* as she moored at the north side, her regular berth for 60 years to come. Sheriff Thoms was invited ashore to perform the opening. His remarks were followed by acclaim from a great concourse of Shetlanders on the pier itself, and lining the new Esplanade. The procession reformed with the band again to the fore. Martial music, cheers and applause accompanied the formal march to the Town Hall in its commanding situation above the harbour and the trustees entertained the party to cake and wine. No doubt the *Earl* was an obvious choice for the occasion, being the local steamer and readily available, yet she seemed to be cast in an appropriate mould with ship

F

and crew capable of conveying the festive spirit, something which was experienced in a wide variety of forms.

Some weeks after the opening of the Victoria Pier there was an excursion to Fair Isle for the inauguration of the Wesleyan Church there. Passengers joined the ship at Sand Lodge and Grutness, John Bruce the proprietor of Fair Isle being amongst them. The steamer headed south in suitably brilliant sunshine and quiet seas, the flat southern horizon empty apart from the clearly defined blue impingement which was the island. In little over two hours from Sumburgh the east rock bastions of Fair Isle provided striking sculptured masses at Bu Ness and Sheep Craig before the *Earl* swung into the south harbour to be met by half a dozen small boats. Friends and supporters of the Wesleyan faith from ship and island filled the new building to hear the Rev. William Moister, a veteran missionary from the south, preach on the theme: "The glory of this latter house shall be greater than that of the former." After the public service there were two wedding ceremonies, which added a final touch to a day of fulfilment for Fair Isle. Progress in spiritual and material things. Another church added to the isles of the northern seas; two couples wed; and at Lerwick a new pier at which the *Earl* could berth on her return late that August night.

Every summer brought its balmy days of peaceful seas and serene skies. Two of the most important occasions in island life in 1886 had been blessed with such weather, but the decade saw a series of ship incidents and disasters which involved the *Earl of Zetland* in a sequence of assisting crippled vessels. The majority of these salvage affairs happened in winter. She had already salved the brig *Superior* in 1881. Prior to the saga of the *Columbine*, the schooner *Pet* of Wick had been driven ashore at Cunningsburgh, badly mauled by an easterly gale. After inspection it was found that the damage was not so serious; she would float and could be repaired. Therefore the *Earl* was commissioned to tow her to Lerwick for docking. A calm day was chosen and the two vessels reached the south mouth on Monday, 21st December, 1885.

The weather in the first weeks of 1887 was boisterous and unsettled. Within a few days of the beginning of the year a smack, the *Lady Nightingale,* missed stays in the swift tide of Yell Sound, came down on a lee shore, struck a rock off the Holm of West Sandwick and filled quickly. Her crew of three barely had time to put the dinghy over the side before their ship was engulfed, then they contrived to land on the barren Holm. Sympathetic and concerned islanders on Yell had seen their plight, launched a boat and took the three survivors to West Sandwick. The *Lady Nightingale,* her mast still forlornly visible in the January greyness, gradually broke up, spewing her cargo of 20 tons of dried fish into the heaving waters of the sound. Later the same week the *Earl* called on her routine run and took the men to Lerwick.

Steamers were also at risk. A month after the Westsandwick incident there was the case of the *Merjulio* of Leith of 981 tons register, bound for Burntisland from Bergen in ballast, and in Lerwick for coaling. She had anchored in the middle of the harbour prior to going alongside the coal hulk off Garthspool. A strong south-west air stream prevailed at the time and when her anchors came up the vessel's head swung round to the south, the wind caught her large exposed hull, and with her screw partly out of the water she was unable to steer. Her master and crew could only await the grind of going ashore and the *Merjulio* struck a rock known as the Skate off the pier of Maryfield on Bressay. And there she stayed with the short, steep waves within the harbour exploding vertically against her rust-streaked sides. Strenuous efforts were made to release the ship with kedge anchors, but all attempts proved futile and the master of the *Merjulio*, Bailie, asked for help from the *Earl* which was in harbour and available with steam up. Payment was arranged at £60 if unsuccessful and £200 if successful. With hawsers linked, salvage began. The *Merjulio* at first showed no signs of being willing to move, which caused concern because the tide was almost at its height. Work went on for almost two hours until the ship suddenly eased off the shoal and slid into deeper water. Captain Nicolson decided to lie hove-to until he saw the steamer alongside the coal hulk, then he returned the *Earl* to her berth at the Victoria Pier, two hundred welcome pounds to the good. Apparently the *Merjulio* had suffered no serious damage, although after coaling she left for Leith to be surveyed.

The mid-1880s brought changes in the officers. William Nicolson had played a significant part in the first decade and his prowess as commander was recognised when he was appointed to the North Company's *St Clair* on the Leith and Kirkwall passage. Another alteration was the position of mate now to be taken by Tom Moffat, destined to hold the post for 35 years as a committed and dedicated seaman. Nicolson's replacement was Captain John Scott, who proved to be a capable skipper. He had to be, because of the demanding, unequivocal routine of keeping the ship available for the expected and unexpected. At the end of August, 1888, he sailed round the north mainland to Hillswick whilst on the normal Yell Sound run and loaded material from the wreck of the steamer *Borgfelde*. She had gone ashore, laden with 3,000 barrels of herring, at Hillswick Ness. A month later the barque *May*, of Mandal, a timber-laden derelict after being wrecked at Sandwick, Northmaven, was towed to Lerwick by the *Earl*.

Despite the grim conditions so characteristic of winter and the inevitable dangerous trips in flitboats at the ports, no life had been lost associated with the *Earl's* voyages until a distressing fatal accident at Lerwick after Christmas, 1888. She was due to sail for the North Isles, including Fetlar, at 7 a.m. in the gloom of a December morning. As often happened there was a delay. It was a bleak day, a thick drizzle of rain intensifying the darkness, relieved only by a solitary gas lamp at the inshore end of the Victoria Pier. There were several passengers for Fetlar including old Margaret Robertson who was already on board, but who remarked to a friend that she would go back to her lodgings. It was the last decision she ever made. The steamer sailed before 8 a.m. and Mrs Robertson was not missed, but within half an hour John Kirkpatrick, the Bressay ferryman, had found her floating, devoid of life, below the south side of the pier. A formal verdict of accidental death was returned, although there were strong words about the inadequate lighting at the embarkation point for the North Isles.

About the same time in December yet another sailing vessel fought the North Atlantic and came second best with a smashed wheel, and poop rail and stanchions swept overboard. For three days the crew of the Norwegian brig *Normand* were constantly at the pumps fighting the ever encroaching sea. It was estimated she was making water at about three inches an hour. The sleepless men maintained their struggle until the *Normand,* laden with her cargo of coal from Burntisland and her unwanted burden of water, limped into Lerwick where, still under pressure from the gale, she dragged her anchor and finished up ashore between Lochaber Baa and the Holm of Cruister. On Christmas Day she was taken by the *Earl* to the Lerwick side of the harbour where her cargo was discharged, rather distant from its intended destination of Christiania (the former name of Oslo).

Shortly after the New Year of 1889 Captain Scott was involved in efforts to move the schooner *Snaefell,* an additional victim of dragging, this time in the vicinity of Gardie House on Bressay. Earlier attempts to move the schooner had been frustrated by persistent gales and yet again the vessel refused to budge. Like the *Normand* she had had appalling seas to contend with. In October, 1888, the schooner had left Gothenburg, Sweden, with timber for Ramsey, Isle of Man, and voyaged to within 20 miles of Noss Head, Caithness, when she was assailed by a hurricane of wind. Unable to make the Pentland Firth she was driven 60 miles north-east of Shetland, by sound seamanship won back the lost ground, and came to the land at Whalsay Skerries before reaching the north entrance to Lerwick in November. Once anchored it was thought she was secure, but like the *Normand* before her, the schooner had failed to hold, which led to the grounding below Gardie House, damaging her keel in doing so. Despite the further misfortune the ship remained dry. The cargo was unloaded, but the broken keel section seemed to have gripped the bottom and even with six inch hawsers around the *Earl's* bits the *Snaefell* obstinately refused to come off. Such delay was frustrating to Captain Corlett of the *Snaefell* and indirectly led to his death. He had been ashore in Lerwick and was returning to his ship with a local man Alex Henry, when their small boat was suddenly swamped in the wind-torn harbour waters. Nothing could be done for them and it was a tragic coincidence that the same tide which unexpectedly released the captive schooner also cast up the pathetic remains of her skipper. It was a fortnight before the body of Alex Henry appeared.

Surprisingly the *Snaefell* suffered only minor damage and by the end of March she sailed from Lerwick for Ramsey with her original cargo under command of a relief skipper. Also in January, within hours of her abortive attempt to free the *Snaefell*, the *Earl* hauled the barque *John* of Stockholm through the narrows leading from the North Isles. The barque was a powerless hulk having had her decks denuded of her cargo of pit props, her main and mizzen masts shattered and nothing but a stump of the foremast left standing. Great seas, charging before a south-east gale had swept her with green water from stem to stern when off the east side of Shetland and she had been limping towards Haroldswick when sighted by the Unst men. They put off and piloted the *John,* under Captain Barmauso, into Baltasound where she lay until the steamer came north.

Such ferocity from wind and sea played havoc with sailings on occasion. Immediately after her efforts with the *Snaefell* and *John* she departed from Lerwick on Tuesday, 8th January, for the North Isles. Impossible weather held her in Baltasound for another two days after which she worked down the east and south of Unst to Cullivoe, which proved to be too exposed. She then ran round to Uyeasound where she sheltered all day on the Friday. Her annual survey was due and the steamer should have left for Aberdeen on Saturday, 12th January. Yet again gales kept her back with another week's delay. As if that had not been enough, when at last she made for the south it was a slow trip and Captain Scott had to face a 36 hour labouring return voyage from Aberdeen, during which progress was reduced to 20 miles in nine hours! The series of gales had lasted intermittently for a full month.

Competition had not been a problem at any time apart from the abortive excursion into the *Earl's* province by the sailer *Saucey Jack.* However, at the time of the lengthening in 1884 the directors of the Shetland Islands Steam Navigation Company Limited were forced to consider the question of a replacement ship during January and February. William Shand contacted Charles Merrylees in Aberdeen and it was agreed that the North Company steamer *Queen* should take in the Unst passage once a fortnight (rather than charter an alternative steamer) while the smack *Cynthia* would be chartered for the Yell Sound run. The arrangement seemed entirely satisfactory except that a mid-January gale put the *Cynthia* out of action from her anchorage. She dragged and was driven ashore on Bressay and damaged.

Divergence of opinion between the Shetland Company and the North Company had emerged in February, 1884. It appeared that the North Company directors recommended the purchase of a derelict lying at Stornoway for £250 to be moored at Baltasound as a floating pier to be used in the first instance during the forthcoming fishing season, when the *Queen* would be on the fish trade. The local directors reacted adversely in that they felt that the North Company had more to gain than they, and could not agree to the joint purchase of the hulk. A compromise was reached when the smack *Petrel* was hired as a floating store for both companies on "the most favourable terms". Financial factors were always in evidence. The enlargement of the *Earl,* including her new boiler and fittings, had accounted for over £3,500. This forced the directors to negotiate a loan for £1,500 from the North of Scotland Bank. The loan brought the first elements of doubt into the viability of the Shetland Islands Steam Navigation Company Limited and embarrassment was accentuated in April, 1884, when the North Company put the *Queen* on the Leith, Fraserburgh, Lerwick and North Isles traffic.

Another historically meaningful meeting considered the altered circumstances. The *Earl* had, of course, been lengthened but Charles Merrylees, present at the gathering of directors on 10th May, 1884, explained how the directors of his company, holding about half the stock of the Shetland Islands Company, had no desire or interest in entering into opposition, but had been compelled to run the *Queen* to the North Isles to cope with the fish trade in particular and prevent encroachment by outside parties. It was in the nature of a classic dilemma for the Shetlanders. Amalgamation seemed the right remedy and they agreed to recommend to their shareholders: "That the North Company take over the *Earl* with any other property belonging to the Shetland Islands Company together with all debts due to and by the company . . .'' The factors were explained at the A.G.M. of shareholders in Lerwick on 31st July, 1884. Interestingly, ordinary freights had fallen about £160, yet passage fares had increased by £100, evidence that the travelling public were utilising the steamer. No further progress was made regarding amalgamation although in July, 1886, the minutes of the Shetland Company recorded that: "The ordinary revenue however, both from freights and fares during the half year just expired, has not manifested the same buoyancy characteristic of the corresponding period in previous years having receded to the extent of £280, but this curtailment has been partially compensated by increased receipts derived from special employment of the steamer.''

In 1887 the deterioration continued. "During the past year the revenue has been injuriously affected by the continuing exceptionally adverse fortune attending the prosecution of the fisheries combined with the consequent general depression in all branches of Shetland business.'' The employment of the *Queen* still rankled. A letter to the North Company mentioned the unsatisfactory state of the Shetland accounts being partly attributable to their steamer's presence in the North Isles. It added that something should be done either to counteract the effects of the opposition by arrangement of through rates, or proposals of amalgamation acceptable to shareholders.

The precarious state of the finances gave even more concern at the end of December, 1887. It was hardly a Christmas present for the ailing company! When entering Sullom Voe the *Earl's* fireman and engineer were aware of a serious fault in the furnaces and reported to Captain Nicolson. They discovered that two of the furnace tops had collapsed. Blowing off steam the ship limped into Garth's Voe and dropped anchor. Nicolson walked to Mossbank, about three miles distant, and telegraphed Lerwick. The all too familiar *Queen* sailed up from Lerwick, went alongside the crippled *Earl,* took on her cargo and did the round of ports, returning to Garth ready to tow her south. In fact the tow was made to Aberdeen, where the *Earl* was repaired. Local opinion was sympathetic towards the ship's misfortune. People knew well enough the considerable pressures on her. Once more the *Queen* substituted on the North Isles passage, whilst the smack *Farmer* coped with the Yell Sound visits. The *Earl* returned to her familiar surroundings on 8th January, 1888, taking 22½ hours from Aberdeen to Lerwick.

In mid-1888 the minutes of the Shetland Company noted that: "The very exceptional depression in all branches of Shetland business referred to in the last annual report as having detrimentally affected the company's revenue has continued and been even more acutely felt throughout the financial year just closed.'' Although the *Queen* had been discontinued in the North Isles in July, 1887, leaving all the trade to the *Earl* — apart from the period of repair — receipts from ordinary freights and passenger fares had only advanced by £65 while earnings from special services receded by £300. The boiler repairs had also been a hard setback. The disconcerting sequence of financial deterioration was halted in 1889 with a sense of relief: ''It is satisfactory to note that the ordinary traffic of the company has mainly contributed to the substantial improvement in the revenue accounts.'' Thus the *Earl* on her everyday round had succeeded in temporarily relieving the situation, and of course she had been thoroughly overhauled at the time of the boiler repair to meet the 90A Lloyd's standard. Therefore, maintenance was expected to be mimimal in the future.

It was the thirteenth year of the Shetland Islands Steam Navigation Company and their steamer *Earl of Zetland,* unlucky in the sense that an identity was about to be lost, but lucky in that ship and service were to be put on a secure basis. The tentative proposal of amalgamation of six years previously was again put forward, this time formally. The shareholders, having been aware of the rather fragile condition of their company, obviously felt that the islands would have nothing to lose and probably much to gain, and voted locally with clear majority in favour of the Shetland Islands Steam Navigation Company Limited being wound up voluntarily and ''The North of Scotland and Orkney and Shetland Steam Navigation Company to take over the s.s. *Earl of Zetland* with all other assets and become responsible for the whole liabilities of the Shetland Islands Steam Navigation Company Limited.''

At an extraordinary meeting on Tuesday, 10th June, 1890, a statement was made referring to a circular letter of August, 1889. The secretary, on the instructions of the directors, indicated that 475 shareholders had voted approval, to which had to be added 618 shares held by the North Company. Of remaining holders 41 gave conditional approval, 80 did not vote and 166 disapproved of the amalgamation.

The clear majority vote of about 75% had given the directors a mandate for the meeting and the arrangements were outlined to the assembled shareholders. The chairman, Bailie Robertson, described it as the most important meeting to be held for the shareholders. Certainly it generated considerable feeling. A view was expressed that local directors had proved themselves utterly incapable. This was countered with the idea that they deserved a vote of thanks and that all the blame should be put on the Aberdeen men!

The opinion of "The Shetland Times" was that the time for fighting was now past. There had been a chance when amalgamation was first mooted in 1884 for Shetland shareholders to buy out the North Company to acquire the *Earl* for their own control, but the opportunity had not been taken. It was pointed out that the primary object was the extension of trade in the islands. This had been a success. Trade had been greatly developed and steam communication was now a necessity. The newspaper mentioned that the work would probably not have been accomplished without the support of the North Company.

A second extraordinary meeting confirmed the resolutions passed in June, and in November the company, now in liquidation, showed a net profit of £373 from which a dividend of 5% was paid to the shareholders. Boats, equipment and stores of the *Earl* were valued at £4,925. This amount gave £3:10:4½ to each dissentient shareholder.

Appropriately the final meeting was held on 14th June, 1890, in the dignified surroundings of the Town Hall, Lerwick. John Fullerton, whose firm had built the *Earl* at Paisley, was to act as valuator of the ship, and Mr Alexander Duthie, Aberdeen, responsible for her lengthening, was appointed valuator on behalf of the North Company. The valuators would settle for a referee in the event of a difference. As a reflection of the work rate of the steamer, an application from the crew for a wage increase was before the meeting. But in view of the winding up of the company only a grant could be made. An allowance of nine pounds was distributed amongst the master, mate, engineer, four seamen and two firemen! Mr Shand, the liquidator, did rather better. He received seven guineas! Symbolically a letter was sent to the Registrar of Shipping, Port of Lerwick:

"Lerwick, 1 December, 1890.

Sir,

I request as authorised by the Shetland Islands Steam Navigation Company Limited, Lerwick, that the registry of the steamer *Earl of Zetland* of Lerwick, 68187, be transferred to the Port of Aberdeen.

Yours faithfully,
'W. M. Shand' Secretary."

5

The North Company: Early Days

The verbal and written skirmishing centred around the rather controversial amalgamation reverberated through the islands, but the deed had been done and, accordingly, newspaper notice of sailings of the *Earl of Zetland* for July, 1890, appeared without the familiar heading of "Shetland Islands Steam Navigation Co. Ltd.". Neither did it appear under the North of Scotland and Orkney and Shetland Steam Navigation Co. notice; instead under a separate heading of "Sailings to the North Isles".

The *Earl's* berth.

At the June decision Bailie Robertson remarked: "When the *Earl* was put on passage in the North Isles people thought it a great advance, but ideas grow rapidly in these days and now a strong demand has been made for a direct communication with the south. Had the islands company had the means to meet the demand, it is hard to say to what dimensions it might have grown, but unfortunately the pinch came there and the Aberdeen company, with a natural eye to their own well-being, must provide for that eventuality. It gives the company a virtual monopoly of the trade in the islands and for many reasons that is to be deprecated, but it may be presumed that the interests of the islands are so bound up with the interests of the company as to ensure the highest consideration and fair dealing."

In the eyes of some, the ideals were not put into practice. If the local papers carried the legend: "Goods are carried at the lowest rate", there was many a person who complained about the outstretched hand for another 3d for the run from steamer to shore in

the flitboat, or the "excessive" charge of 5d freight for a parcel to the
North Isles from Lerwick.

But the peerie steamer, indifferent to human foibles, responded
to the needs of her new owners, the trade and the travellers, just as
she had done previously. In 1890 her overhaul was made in October
instead of the following January as had been the custom, and the *St.
Clair* of the North Company replaced her for the island run. The *Earl*
carried mail to and from Aberdeen, meeting a gale on her return
voyage which reduced her to seven hours of hard steaming to cover
the twenty miles from Fair Isle to Sumburgh Head. Under old and
new management, timetabling was complex and sometimes
seemingly inconsistent, and intending shippers and passengers were
well advised to check the notices. In 1890 the ship was available for
special trips on Mondays "when sufficient inducement offers". She
loaded 15 tons of fish at Lerwick and 35 tons round at Scalloway on a
January Saturday night, sailing from the west side at 10 a.m. on the
Sunday, and was 30 hours on the passage to Aberdeen! Five weeks
later the steamer was relieving the *St. Ola* from Stromness to
Scrabster while the *Queen* operated the *Earl's* routes. In April, 1890,
the Yell Sound passage was Tuesday and the North Isles passage a
Friday. Again, in May, 1891, the long-suffering and patient crew
took her away to the Pentland Firth as a replacement vessel on the
mail run. The *St. Nicholas* served the North Isles in the interim.

In October, 1891, the *Earl* left Lerwick at the early, but not
unfamiliar, hour of 4 a.m. on a Monday for Uyeasound direct,
returning by Cullivoe, Mid Yell, Burravoe and Symbister the same
day. She next sailed for Ollaberry and Yell Sound ports at 9 a.m. on
the Tuesday. Later that month she undertook a second weekly voyage
on a Friday to various North Isles ports. Such variation was
inevitable with relatively limited shipping space, and the North
Company kept the situation under review.

A "Shetland Times" editorial comment in May, 1891, revealed
some of the uncertainties: "It is intended to run the former mail
service commencing on 1st June under a new contract with the Post
Office. It will be perused with much interest and, we fear, will not
meet with satisfaction in some of the details. As has already been
noted, the Post Office only agreed for four months for four mails a
week, but the Company indicated that they were willing to run five.
It is a pity this could not have been attempted after it had been so
publicly stated . . . One weak point seems to be that the direct
steamer is expected to do too much by running twice a week all the
way to Leith. In consequence during the whole month only three
sailings are timed from Aberdeen in the mornings, while two are late

at night, some 15 hours after the arrival of the London mail. Also, livestock shipped at Lerwick on Saturdays are not guaranteed to be landed at Aberdeen until Tuesday and may be carried to Leith and back . . . Again with regard to the return mails, the arrangements practically limit them to three. Also objection will be taken to the sailings of the *Earl*. The letters from the North Isles leaving on Thursday and those leaving on Saturday will both be despatched south from Aberdeen on Sunday . . . but the timetable will require careful consideration before the issue of another sailing bill.''

With these problems ever before them the North Company tried to make amends by chartering a 282 ton steamer named *Nigel* in November, 1891. She had an unfortunate introduction to Shetland. The *Earl* was south for her Board of Trade survey early in 1892 so the *Nigel* was in the North Isles on replacement. She had a defective windlass which delayed her with the result that she did not come into Lerwick from Whalsay until midnight on a Saturday. Three hours later the *Nigel* sailed for Aberdeen in blustery conditions which blew up into gale velocity, produced seas which knocked a man down and injured him, and forced the steamer into a passage of 39 hours.

An emphasis on priority for HM Mails led to criticism of the North Company by the Free Church Presbytery of Shetland. For some time the advertising for the sailings carried the following announcement: ''North Isles Passage. From Lerwick every Saturday night or following morning for Uyeasound and Baltasound . . . '' The studied avoidance of the word ''Sunday'' was no doubt an attempt to allay offence but, in fact, it was generally the Sabbath when the steamer left Lerwick. Angered at this desecration of the Lord's Day, numerous Shetland ministers were intensely critical, the more so because it was alleged that drinking took place at some of the ports. Clerk to the Presbytery, the Rev. William Rogerson of the Free Church Manse, Lerwick, was delegated to contact other denominations and enlist support. In April, 1893, the Shetland Synod met. It was suggested that a petition had been sent from the people of the North Isles, but John Bicket and John Watson, Ministers of North Yell and South Yell respectively, could not substantiate this. Feeling was unanimous that there should be a strong request to stop the Sunday sailings. An inter-church committee was formed composed of Rev. David Johnstone, Quarff, Rev. John Love, Mid Yell, and John Tait, Elder, of Lerwick, with Rev. William Rogerson as secretary. However, by September a petition was drawn up by the committee, with the Wesleyan Church also participating, but the reply from William Shand of the North Company, while fair, was unequivocal. He outlined a tight schedule for the ships. Every Friday after 5 p.m. a steamer left Aberdeen with mail and arrived in Lerwick through Saturday. Outgoing mail was sent south on the Monday evening. He argued that the *Earl* would be impossibly restricted if part of the Sunday was not used, having six ports at which to call on the week-end trip to the North Isles before connecting with the south-bound steamer on Monday. Also, he pointed out that the arrangement was solely for the benefit of the people of the North Isles, although a reasonable proposal for change would be considered. Although the Synod had serious reservations, it was agreed that the practicalities were vital, and so the issue was abandoned.

It was no fault of an overworked vessel that so many adverse comments were aimed at the service. Complaints were received from country districts through a joint committee of county and town (Lerwick) councils. Also a letter from the Mid Yell manse described how the *Earl* would pass within a few miles of Mid Yell en route to Uyeasound, yet incoming mail was delivered only on her return journey, with disconcerting delay because of cargo working. Shippers of fresh fish from Yell Sound added their criticism. The joint committee received a reply from William Shand, the North Company secretary. He regretted that the mail needs of the North Isles could not allow the *Earl* to make special runs with fresh fish from Yell Sound ports, although he mentioned that several times that winter the steamer had been deflected from the Unst passage on a Saturday for trifling quantities of fish, the freight of which was not even enough to pay the extra coals needed by the *Earl*. If the traffic had not been such a failure that winter the company might have arranged for the steamer to call in Yell Sound on the way south from the North Isles, yet it was doubtful if small quantities of fish could justify hardship to passengers on a bad day, and delay to the mail.

In such testing situations, the shore and sailing staff, the crew in particular, had much with which to cope, dealing with the complex nature of the trading programme. Inevitably there were demands on the leadership and integrity of the skippers, but then men like Nicolson and Scott had a depth of character partly derived from the discipline of training in sail and shaping up the hard way. John Scott was born in 1842, at South Shields, of parents from the west side of Shetland, his father being a seaman. It was on a long voyage that the father was a victim of smallpox which proved fatal, and the mother naturally turned to her ain folk with John, aged three, and a younger brother. John left school at 13 to learn the ways of the men of the sea, at first locally for two years, then, like William Nicolson, in the testing school of the Faroe smacks. There he learned to cope with the tough grind of weeks at sea where payment was by results, with the monotony of incessant work, of dousing the mussel bait with salt water, of repairing his line, of lifting the heavy fish on board, of gutting and beheading, of stacking the catch into the hold between protective layers of salt.

But his ambition encouraged him to search for other scope and he industriously worked at the mysteries of arithmetic and mathematics. The call of the sea took young Scott away to the East Indies, on which voyage he was befriended by a seaman who had originally trained for the Church, had developed a love of alcohol, and had taken off for the sea to seek some kind of remedy. This man was scholarly and gave his friend the incentive to go for promotion. On his return to Britain John Scott passed as second mate and after another spell at sea, including a trip to Quebec, won his mate's certificate. Thereafter he was given the mate's berth on the *Earl* and within two years was awarded the master's rating for home trade. By 1888 he had added the foreign trade qualification — now a mature, intelligent man of energy and drive.

His versatility was emphasised in March, 1894, when "The Shetland Times" announced that "Captain Scott of the ss *Earl of Zetland* will lecture in the Wesleyan Schoolroom on Phrenology next Wednesday. During the evening Messrs J. and M. Scott (his twin sons) will give violin and cornet solos, and at the close of the lecture Captain Scott will give illustrations of reading character from persons in the audience. The chair will be taken by Captain Nicolson at 7.30 pm." At the lecture the chairman observed that he did not know much about what was inside people's heads from seeing the outside of them. Evidently Mr Scott professed to be able to do something of that kind. All he could say was that often he and Mr Scott had had to lay their heads together in times of difficulty and always with good results. He referred of course to their teamwork as captain and mate on the *Earl*. John Scott's talk on the unlikely subject of the science by which character can be assessed by examining the skull was received so well by the Lerwick populace that he was asked to do a repeat the next month.

At the second lecture the audience again sang the 100th Psalm and the evening once more took on a slightly devotional flavour. It was a reflection of the simple faith of so many of the era whose lives were respectfully centred on the great sea. One member of the audience from the first lecture, a Mr Hargreaves, who had given the vote of thanks, sent his apologies. He had acquired a bad cold through travelling on the *Earl* a few days previously! Captain Scott convincingly discussed the bone structure, the circulation of the blood, the nervous system, and their relationship to the brain. It was a remarkable effort by a man of limited education and the Rev. W. Bruce evinced wonder at the quality before pronouncing the Benediction.

Sadly there was another benediction at the death of James (Jeems) Williamson in June, 1894. He had been a centre of attraction for years through his dexterity with the fiddle and he had responded enthusiastically times without number to many a Shetland reel on the *Earl,* and the cries of "Faster Jeems, faster!". If there was mourning for Jeems, at least folk appreciated that he had long outlived the three score years and ten allotted life span, and done so with vigour and vitality. He would be missed when in July the North Company encouraged excursionists to join in the more routine type of voyage to make a week-end jaunt to Unst.

The newspaper correspondent wrote: "For real enjoyment let those who have a few hours to spare from business, shake the dust of the city off their feet, get on board the good ship *Earl* and go to Unst, leaving Lerwick on Sunday and returning on Monday. 'All ready aft, Sir', is the usual sound which greets the ears of passengers as a brazen throated Son of Neptune prepares to throw off the warps on leaving the quay, but no such sound was heard aboard the *Earl* on the occasion when we sailed in her. It was Sunday evening and the still of the sabbatic rest seemed to prevail everywhere. There was no shouting, no commotion perceptible. The mails having been got on board, the command was given 'Cast off the warps', in a tone which might have been used at a drawing room tea. The engine-room bell signalled and with a few strokes of the propeller we were clear of the pier and fairly started. The harbour was pretty and the presence of the stately ships of the training squadron added much to its attractions. Scarcely a breath of wind ruffled the surface of the water which sparkled and gleamed in the bright sunshine, while the sound of the church bells inviting worshippers to the evening service came stealing over the waters in tones sweet and mellow. After passing through the north entry and shaping the course the congenial commander, Mr Scott, left his perch aloft and came down to the deck. A little over an hour later we reached the bonny isle of Whalsay, and it is evident Sunday is observed here in the orthodox Shetland fashion. The big herring boats were all at anchor while men lounged about the doors of their houses, smoking their pipes and enjoying their well earned Sunday rest . . ." Such a departure by the steamer and the relaxation of the Whalsay men were a tacit reference to the revered Sabbath, not as a repressive measure but as a respectful admission of the value of the restful Lord's day.

The ship then went on to Mid Yell before calling at Uyeasound. It would seem, therefore, that the plea from Mid Yell manse of a few years previously had been heeded, and mail was now unloaded at Yell on the Sunday run north. Doubtless the deviation to the west of Hascosay, into Mid Yell voe, was of great benefit to the Yell population and that is what mattered, although as a result the *Earl* was late into Baltasound. ". . . although it was midnight when we reached the shores of Baltasound there were a few people astir and lights gleamed from several windows, while on the pier were gathered such of the islanders as were expecting to meet their friends." In this pleasant manner the *Earl* catered for leisure and social pursuits even during her more routine runs. The impressive range of attractive places to visit encouraged the North Company to offer the public evening and holiday cruises just as their predecessors had done so convincingly and successfully. From 1890 right through the early years of the 20th century the ship played her part notably in the face of competition.

Towards the turn of the century many islanders had felt that the one company monopoly was too expensive and shipping space too restricted, and the concept of another company seemed worthy of consideration. Circulars were issued in 1902, with such encouraging results that a steering committee decided to float the Shetland Isles Steam Trading Company Limited. The registered capital was to be £12,000 made up of £1 shares. By May, 1903, the steamer *Mona* had been chartered. Owned by the Ayr Shipping Company she ran cargo, passengers and livestock between Ayr, Campbeltown and Belfast. She had 20 berths plus steerage space. Posted to leave Leith on 22nd June, 1903, the *Mona* was due to call at Aberdeen, Dunrossness and Sandwick before visiting Lerwick and going on to the North Isles ports. Skippering the *Mona* was James Leask, latterly chief officer of the *St. Rognvald,* which had been wrecked in Orkney in 1900. Announcements were made about special lower fares for passengers, which would inevitably ask questions of the North Company's fares on the *Earl.*

When the new ship arrived at Lerwick on her first voyage common opinion was that she looked a smart vessel, perhaps better fitted to cargo work, although passengers who had come north on her were well enough pleased. At the end of July her north-bound cargo was 139 tons general and 1,200 empty barrels, and her south-bound 140 barrels of herrings, 10 tons of wool and three ponies. About the same time the *Earl* was away to Stromness to run the Orkney mail as replacement for the *St. Ola,* after which both ships were on special consignments of lambs direct from Lerwick to the south.

G

Captain Peter Johnson and passengers in 1905. The bridge seems very exposed!

The Manson Collection, Shetland Library & Museum

Between West Sandwick and Ulsta in 1930. Note the large funnel and the bridge rails encased in canvas. Colin Henry at the wheel.

G. Donaldson

A youthful and unknown passenger looks non-committedly at the camera and a helping hand is not far away.

Shetland Library & Museum

The portly figure of Jimmy Garriock, Chief Steward, contrasts the style of an elegantly-clad lady on the stern of the *Earl*, a photograph taken at the turn of the century.

Shetland Library & Museum

In the autumn of 1903 the directors of the Steam Trading Company chartered the s.s. *Trojan* to replace the *Mona* during the winter months. She was a steamer of 260 tons with no passenger accommodation and she made her first trip from Lerwick on Wednesday, 7th October. Within a fortnight she was the subject of a lively discussion in the committee of Lerwick Harbour Trust. Normally the *Earl* had her long established berth on the north side of the pier, but in her absence the *Trojan* had been laid alongside there one day at the dinner hour when Captain Allison, the harbourmaster, was not available, the *Trojan* having arrived earlier than expected. Mr John W. Robertson, secretary of the Steam Trading Company, stated in a letter that if the harbourmaster had so instructed they would have put the *Trojan* anywhere he wished if only notification had been given. Robertson's case, however, had a weakness for he wrote that the harbourmaster came down and "expressed regret" that the ship was in the *Earl's* berth, then returned in half an hour "just when we had got under way with the discharging and ordered us to shift the vessel". Arguably the "expressed regret" by the harbourmaster before discharging should have been enough reason for the *Trojan* to be removed, but the captain and crew did not see the situation that way and when the *Earl* arrived she was forced to go to the south side of the pier.

The committee opinions varied. Mr Johnston said that apparently partiality was being shown by Captain Allison to the North of Scotland Company. Mr Ganson countered that it was merely an incident between the two companies. The Trust was not giving preference to one more than another and a thing like this would not happen again. Mr Tulloch remarked that there were times when the *Earl* lay ahead of another vessel at the north side and this could have been done, but Mr Ganson commented that they might think two could lie there while the harbourmaster, with his knowledge of the weather and conditions at the pier, knew better. It was said that Captain Allison did show partiality and "it looked very like it sometimes if they could believe the stories told", but the moderate Mr Ganson tempered their feelings and ultimately the harbourmaster was instructed "to endeavour to make such arrangements with steamers using the pier as would prevent any inconvenience or loss of time in future".

The weekly calls made by the Steam Company ship to ports south of Lerwick on the east mainland and the North Isles were short lived, for by December, 1903 these were fortnightly, although any suggestion of recession was countered by the announcement that the steamer *Minihinde* of Belfast would be purchased to replace the *Trojan*.

She had been built in 1891 of 409 tons gross with a 75 hp engine. Rather smaller than the North Company's *Queen* she carried 30 cabin and about 60 steerage passengers. Her name would be altered to *Norseman*. By the middle of March, 1904, the new steamer was ready to take on the route with a very competitive fare structure. Leith to Lerwick would cost 20/- cabin and 8/6 steerage; Aberdeen to Lerwick 15/- cabin and 7/- steerage; Leith to the North Isles — a long voyage — 24/- cabin and 11/- steerage, and Aberdeen to the North Isles 19/-cabin and 9/6 steerage. (All fares return.) Such reductions in charges were warmly welcomed by Shetland merchants and travellers, because the North Company freights and fares had for long been criticised. Now here was competition to put on the pressure and it came as no surprise when the North Company's annual report stated: "The directors have under consideration at present the modification of their service to Shetland, consequent on the falling off of goods and livestock through opposition."

On 16th April, 1904, the *Norseman* entered a domain hitherto the prerogative of the *Earl,* when she was billed to make an excursion trip to Whalsay, Yell and Unst, followed by another to Baltasound on Victoria Day of that year. Simultaneously the North Company advertised a trip to Collafirth and Ronas Voe, weather permitting. Thus the two steamers were in direct competition on the same day. If anything the *Earl* had a tactical advantage with the prospect of her passengers visiting whaling stations then in full production. They had created a stir in Shetland because their presence was the result of the banning of whaling on the Norwegian coast and the British Government's permission for Norse firms to set up in Ronas Voe, Collafirth and Olnafirth. The response from the public was very good, with 150 joining the *Earl* at Victoria Pier — north side! At the Norrona's Whaling Company's station at Collafirth, the manager described whale catching and processing, perfectly illustrated by the coincidental arrival of the whaler *Fritjof* in the voe, with two 60 feet carcases in tow. The whales were drawn up onto flenching boards by steam capstan prior to attack by the workers with knives to cut the blubber into strips, reduced further by a cutting machine, then taken by an endless chain of buckets to eight hours of boiling in large vats. The resultant oil was put into barrels, shipped to Glasgow and used in soap-making. In earlier days the remains of the carcase had simply been set adrift, but plant had been introduced to reduce the enormous portions to workable size for processing and manufacture in Norway into foodstuffs for cattle, and manure.

The Lerwick visitors were highly entertained, although the powerful odour of whale flesh had seemed to permeate everything, and Captain Johnson (whose advent to the *Earl* has yet to be discussed), despite being anxious to escape from the clinging smell, delayed the *Earl's* departure by half an hour to allow his passengers ample time to return on board. It had been a resoundingly successful outing.

Meanwhile the *Norseman,* billed for Unst, did not have the same success. She had had the misfortune to run aground temporarily at Fraserburgh on her run to Shetland, which compelled her to reach Lerwick at 1.30 p.m. on that Wednesday. She left for Baltasound an hour later with about a dozen people. Obviously the *Earl* had scored over her competitor.

By June, 1907, about four years after its origin, the rival company had debts of £6,000. It came as no surprise when in May, 1908, their coal hulk and other plant were put up for auction. The plant fetched a reasonable amount, but the hulk failed to reach the reserve price and, in fact, was sold privately. It was a sad end to a venture with a worthy motive.

Each phase of the *Earl's* career was punctuated by a selection of incidents of assistance to other vessels. The late seventies, eighties and now the nineties and into the new century brought accidents, albeit in diminishing numbers, since sail was being steadily ousted by steam. Shipping was less vulnerable, although winter weather remained utterly and universally treacherous. In early December, 1895, a Williamson man set off for Girlstavoe to dredge mussels. He and his four crew had a good day's fishing, but had the weather forecasts of the late 20th century been available, he might not have gone. By mid afternoon in gathering gloom the wind raised the sea from south-west and as they came out between the Brethern and the Green Holm, it was hard going. Off Rova Head the rising gale split the sail from top to bottom, so that they were left trying to keep the boat clear of water from steep breaking seas, and were being driven away from the land north of Bressay. Their salvation was the *Earl,* under Captain Nicolson at that time, coming towards Lerwick from the North Isles. She was immediately manoeuvred to give a lee and the five fishermen thankfully boarded the steamer, leaving their boat under tow until they came in through the narrows to shelter.

Three years later, in April, 1898, some south fishermen were not so fortunate. A Peterhead boat was lost with all hands off Bressay lighthouse in a hell of a storm from the south-east. Several boats were unaccounted for, but the *Earl* on reaching Lerwick reported two Scottish craft, the *Lily of the Valley* and the *Reeds,* secure in Cullivoe, and the rescue of the Mid Yell owned *Jessie* which had been given a hawser off Uyeasound, having lost her sails and an anchor. That the aid given was appreciated was evidenced by Charles Mann and crew of the *Jessie* in a letter to "The Shetland Times". " . . . We were in great extremity when the vessel came to us and we think we would be neglecting our duty if we did not in this manner tender our best thanks to all who assisted us . . ." On that occasion Captain Williamson was in charge of the *Earl*.

No respecter of men or property, the weather once again played havoc with a sailing vessel on the appalling afternoon of 17th February, 1900. The Norwegian barque *Hedevig*, 472 tons register, owned by Carl Dahl of Frederickstadt and built in 1852 at Moss, Norway, was homeward bound from London with 200 tons of loam. After ten days heading north, she met with a terrific pounding from seas which punished her to the extent that deck gear and rigging were destroyed, her hull badly strained and her crew forced to work the pumps incessantly for four days. Somewhere off the south end of Unst she became unmanageable and was thrust mercilessly south-west towards the hidden north coast of Fetlar. Denied sight of any shore her crew could eventually discern the roar of breakers somewhere ahead. Both anchors could not halt the *Hedevig's* headlong dash and she crashed into the tiny island of Daaey a mile off Fetlar. As the doomed barque twisted and ground in her death throes, the crew fought through the vortex of tortured water to reach land devoid of any semblance of shelter. Only the mate failed to gain a footing and disappeared. Realising that their only salvation was to be active, the men contrived to keep on the move throughout a long, perishing winter night, but another life was lost through exposure.

Wind and sea had eased in the grey dawn, revealing the battered remains of the *Hedevig*, an unusual dark shape in the white surf observed by a shepherd in the employ of Sir Arthur Nicolson. His attention riveted on Daaey, the shepherd saw movement and ran to arrange a boat. The local men won through and the survivors of the barque were landed at Brough Lodge and the warm hospitality of Sir Arthur. The following day the mate was retrieved from the sea to be buried in the Fetlar churchyard at Tresta alongside his colleague. Later the hospitality of the *Earl* was given to the survivors when they were taken to Lerwick and it was there that the remains of the barque, cargo and fittings fetched a lowly £9 in auction. The storm had made a lasting impression in the North Isles and the wrecking an indelible memory to the extent that folk, when recollection was kindled, spoke of the "Hedevig Gale".

In December, 1900, 19 years after the '81 fishing disaster, tragedy again devastated a Shetland district. This time it was North Delting. The sea took four boats and 22 men, depriving 15 wives and no fewer than 51 children of their breadwinners. Again, on a Friday, the weather had changed dramatically and swiftly into a demon gale with flying sleet and spindrift which covered such large rock-faces as the Horse of Burravoe, denying visibility to anxious watchers on the shores from Mossbank to Swinister. The suspense was eased with a report that the other five boats might have won their way into shelter at Fetlar or Skerries. As the *Earl* was due at Fetlar the people reckoned she might bring information, yet no steamer appeared, leaving the families with the burden of doubt. Saturday into Sunday was a long night for a group of desperately worried wives, and their concern was not eased when they learned that the steamer was not available to check at Skerries. The fishery office at Lerwick also reported that their cruiser had gone south. Telegrams were exchanged between Lerwick and the Edinburgh Fishery Board, who promised an effort to get a cruiser to Shetland, obviously a futile exercise, by the Monday.

But strong indignation prevailed in Delting at the failure of the *Earl* to search, and locally it was said that if the agent had heard the cries of Mrs Nicholson at Firth, who eventually mourned the loss of a husband, four sons and a son-in-law, something might have been attempted. In fact the *Earl* had been confined to Lerwick until 9 o'clock on the Saturday morning, 24 hours behind her posted time, and when the telegram arrived from Mossbank the extent of the disaster was not appreciated. By that time Captain Scott had taken the ship right north and she could not have come to Skerries before dark on the Saturday night when the narrow north-east entrance would have been impossible. Although it was further explained that if any good could have come of it the steamer could have sailed towards Skerries, opinion was intensely critical at the failure to attempt anything at all in such a dire situation.

Apart from small incidents, the *Earl of Zetland* had remained remarkably trouble free during her 25 years of ranging all over the northern seas from north-east Scotland to the multitude of islands, skerries and baas of Orkney and Shetland, from the reefs and outcrops of rocks of the Pentland Firth to the pinnacles of Muckle Flugga. She had successfully competed with all the extremities of the climate, albeit taking shelter if need be, yet digging into and throwing off seas of alarming proportions during her exhaustive year-round work. It was, therefore, hard luck for Captain Peter Johnson that she sank in harbour in calm water on Saturday, 7th June, 1902. Captain Scott had taken command of the *St. Sunniva* the previous month with Johnson moving into his place.

The herring fishing, then in its halcyon days, was in full

production and the steamer had gone to Wick to bring back fishworkers. They came in their hordes, the fisher lasses full of optimism and high spirits, the men, coopers, a hard industrious breed, bound for Scalloway, Burra Isle, Hamnavoe, Ronas Voe, Cullivoe and Baltasound. By the time the *Earl* entered Baltasound, the number of passengers was down to 16. Captain Johnson was faced by the forest of masts and spars of a multitude of herring boats, the whole fairway and harbour being fully occupied. Accordingly he took the only available path along the north side of the voe, moving cautiously not far off-shore in the early morning daylight. Abruptly all on board felt their stomachs tighten at the harsh grating of stones on the underside of the *Earl* as she unexpectedly ground to a halt and lifted fractionally against the bottom on an ebbing tide. There was no great concern for they thought she had run against a heap of ballast stones discarded from some fishing boat. Engines full ahead and astern had no effect for the moment, but surely she would come off on the tide. So they waited. What happened was not expected. Two and a half hours later the sea gushed into the hull with incredible and frightening speed, flooding the engine room and hold, then accommodation, so fast that the crew had little time to rescue their belongings. Within 20 minutes she had filled. At least the passengers and their luggage had already been taken off by flitboat. The water encroached until it covered bunks and winch in the fo'c'sle, washed across the top of the bulwarks on the well-deck, submerged the animal stalls, purser's desk, galley stove and everything right aft to the ladies' cabin and the carefully polished stove and tables and plush seats in the dining saloon; it reached up as far as the portholes and was near enough the upper deck. The *Earl* was, to all intents and purposes, sunk.

Five days later, when the tug *Empress of India* arrived from Aberdeen, the steamer presented an odd sight lying on an even keel, but submerged right up to her main deck. Steam pumps were unloaded from the tug, fitted on the *Earl* and at low water they began to pump her out. Divers then came on a large gash near the keel under the engine room. A sharp stone upstanding had pierced a plate and, with no protective bottom, the hull was vulnerable in such a grounding.

By the following Tuesday morning the hole was watertight and Captain Johnson and the men, having worked hard at ridding their ship of the effects of sea water, got her under way for Lerwick and, despite a rough tideway off Muness, she handled well. Once at the Victoria Pier a diver pronounced that the ship was fit to go to Aberdeen. Accompanied by another tug, *Clyde,* of Leith, the *Earl* set off south for repairs. The saloon, pantry and all other rooms had fittings destroyed or damaged by sea water. Bare boards in place of the normally richly upholstered saloon seats were severely utilitarian, contrasting with the normal tidy presentation. Fortunately the engines remained unscathed. Repairs to the upholstery took the longest time.

The Shetland newspapers expressed Peter Johnson's thanks. "Captain Johnson is anxious to return his sincere thanks publicly to all the people of Baltasound for having shown such kindness to the crew of the *Earl* while she was submerged there. Especially he would like to thank Messrs. Anderson, Edmonston and Sandison for giving accommodation to the crew." Public comment was made about lack of markers for the ballast heaps in Baltasound and much sympathy was shown for Captain Johnson.

That the *Earl* had confidently survived her mishap was shown by her work-rate three weeks later. She took fishworkers south on the Sunday from the North Isles, came back to Lerwick on the Tuesday, travelled to West Sandwick on the Wednesday, and Baltasound on the Thursday for the same purpose.

The sequence of misfortune to shipping continued. In April, 1903, there was the predicament of the 684-ton *Nina* of Porsgrund, timber laden, swept into Yell Sound with only the stump of one mast left standing. Pushed by the north-west gale, the *Nina,* awash and abandoned, came close enough to Ulsta to encourage a group of men to board her. Off the west side of Samphray they succeeded in getting a footing on the wave-swept decks, becoming immediately aware of the risk of destruction if they allowed the derelict to drift towards the reef between Fish Holm and Linga. Being so low in the water, green seas surged over the decks with the men up their armpits in water and gradually losing their stamina. It was a vast feeling of relief when they became aware of the *Earl* bearing down on them. Once within hailing distance the voices, carrying thinly on the wind, suggested a tow and this was agreed. The voe at Swinister was the best shelter nearby and ropes were passed, but the dead weight of the waterlogged hull was too much, despite hard steaming by the *Earl.* Although she eased the *Nina* out of the worst of the seas the tow had to be abandoned and, to the chagrin of the would-be salvors, the cargo of timber was spilled along the shore as the abandoned vessel drove onto the rocks — now a write-off.

Although the majority of mishaps came about through gales, fog was always a potential hazard. It was an irritating inconvenience at the very least and sometimes frightening in its very emptiness, the sea and land merged into grey nothingness, silent, swirling and menacing. Men could be so affected as to misjudge situations because of the blanket which stifled sight and mind. In Shetland the profusion of geos, promontories, holms, baas, skerries and shoals, lost in the all-pervading greyness, put even detailed local knowledge at question.

North Company ships had been at risk. The *St. Rognvald* was lost at Burgh Head, Stronsay on Orkney in April, 1900, followed by the *St. Giles* near Rattray Head on the Scottish mainland in September, 1902, and it was a curious twist of fate that her successor of the same name ran ashore in a pea-souper at the north-east end of Mousa early one morning in October, 1904. Providentially little sea was running and Captain John Scott ordered a boat away to Sandwick to telegraph for aid.

Meanwhile the rising tide had the firemen in the engineroom up to their ankles in water, and the *St. Giles* was badly hazarded. John Scott put her full astern with the aid of a kedge anchor and, as the steamer slid off after an hour, he took the only course of action open to him and made full speed round the north end of the island, headed for Sandwick. The folk there heard her siren blowing frantically before she reached the shore and was grounded at Sandsayre, a little west of the pier, within a stone's throw of the post office from which the boat's crew had telegraphed Lerwick. Such information was near sensational. William Shand had the *Earl of Zetland* available since she had not left for her Friday run to the North Isles, and with steam up she was away within minutes of the order to help the *St. Giles*. Passengers, mails, livestock, luggage and cargo were transferred to the smaller ship as she lay alongside in smooth water at Sandsayre before the *Earl* returned the 11 miles to Lerwick in improving visibility.

The *St. Giles* seemed to have escaped serious damage, since her holds remained clear of water as she rested in an upright position on a bottom of large, loose shingle, and her pumps easily took care of the water elsewhere. And there the steamer remained for a week until temporary repairs stopped the leaks and the *Earl,* in her familiar role of assistance, helped to ease the stranded ship back into deep water.

Within a year the North Isles steamer was again similarly involved, this time with the Peterhead steam drifter *Emily Reaich* which had stranded on a baa off the tiny island of Orfasay, near the Ness of Copister at the south tip of Yell. During the afternoon on a Wednesday in late April, 1905, the drifter was at full speed headed north through Yell Sound making for the fishing grounds when she lurched onto the shoal at high tide and remained fast. Again it fell to Captain Peter Johnson, as with the *St. Giles,* to attempt salvage. He had his vessel standing by the *Emily Reaich* in the early hours of the next day. By four in the morning his crew had two warps attached to the stricken drifter. Despite high water she refused to budge. Peter Johnson persevered for an hour, but had to abandon the attempt when both ropes parted. William Reaich, the drifter's skipper, and Johnson then decided to remove some boat-loads of ballast and pump water into the drifter's fore-peak to lift her stern, which was gripped by the rocks. In the late afternoon they made another effort, this time from the north-west. After another hour's hard steaming, abruptly the grounded vessel rolled off and immediately began to settle.

Damage was obviously serious and her rudder had apparently been sheered off. A tow to Lerwick was impossible, steering was out of the question and the *Emily Reaich* could sink within a short time. Although the sea was quiet the only safe place for beaching was at Burravoe, two miles away. So the drifter was lashed alongside the *Earl* and the steamer, rather like her predecessor the *Chieftain's Bride,* moved crab-wise across the tideway and into the narrow inlet at Burravoe where the *Emily Reaich* was run ashore. Little did Peter Johnson know that within a few years his own ship would be similarly badly compromised with unlucky and unhappy results.

As the 20th century developed, fewer and fewer sailing vessels were seen in Shetland, although several more were wrecked before the end of the first decade. But even the *Earl* needed moments of assistance. Although a foresail was carried on the steamer to facilitate turning in narrow anchorages its minute scale was hardly large enough to utilise the motive power of the wind. This was unfortunate when near Whalsay on 12th May, 1906, the intermediate shaft broke and the *Earl* was rendered helpless, a very unusual happening. Captain Johnson elected to despatch a boat in the smooth conditions to row the 12 miles to Lerwick for help, a hard 3-4 hour pull and an illustration of the versatility of the crew. They were thankful enough to have the relaxation as the *St. Giles* brought them and their boat north before the bigger ship towed the *Earl* back to the Victoria Pier. Less then two years previously the *Earl* had towed the *St. Giles*!

When disasters occurred to sailing ships in the North Isles or North Mainland, the *Earl* invariably had had some part to play in the drama. Over the six years from 1906 till 1912, there were four major incidents. The first was at the end of December, 1906, when the steel barque *Nordwind* of Hamburg, on a voyage from Gothenburg to Melbourne with a cargo of dressed timber and cement, fell on her beam ends off Out Skerries. Despite the jettisoning of sails and cordage the ship failed to right herself in a full south-east gale and was thrust onto the crags flanking the south mouth of the harbour, where she was held fast with a mass of breaking seas seething over her angled deck. Captain Casper Gerwohl was drowned by an all embracing wall of water as he reached solid rock from the *Nordwind's* jib-boom, and carpenter Willie Solze and deck boy Felix Groysmann also lost their lives and failed to have the luck of 17 survivors, who were so deeply grateful to the Skerries people as well as to Peter Johnson and the crew of the *Earl* who took them to Lerwick. The *Nordwind* was scythed in two an hour after her grim fate and went to the bottom in deep water.

Seventeen months later Captain Johnson had 12 men from the wooden Norwegian whaler *John* of Sandefiord aboard on the *Earl's* trip from Baltasound to Lerwick. An exploding lamp in the accommodation set fire to the *John* some 75 miles south-east of Unst. Desperate efforts by the crew failed to contain the outbreak, and the skipper, Johannesen, ordered the boats away only a moment before the entire ship became a mass of roaring flames, gradually extinguished by the eager sea. The whaler was in her death throes before the eyes of her crew in the two boats when the Norwegian fishing steamer, *Ludolfreade,* appeared and carried the 12 to Baltasound and characteristic warm hospitality from the islanders.

The third affair featured an act of bravery and skill on the part of Whalsay men, with salvage as the incentive, and the *Earl* had the pleasurable brief of carrying £418 salvage money to be divided among 17 salvors. Events leading up to the saving of a battered hull could rank among the sagas of the seas. A Norwegian barque, the *Pioneer,* had left Liverpool for Skien near Porsgrund on 21st November, 1910, battled against tempestuous weather, caught sight of the Norwegian coast, been assailed by an onslaught of wind and sea unknown to her master and crew, and carried westwards in catastrophic conditions. Survival was crucial. The coal-laden barque was being battered day after day by cataracts of water, rolling maliciously, heeling on occasion so that her crew thought she would turn turtle. Her rigging was tensed far beyond what it had been designed for and when cordage tore apart it was the skipper who lost his life in efforts to cut away the wreckage. A toppling mass of sea took him overboard. For another eight days the mate used all his seamanship to no purpose in an incredible prolonged fight with the sea. What control he had went with the destruction of the steering gear and when the menacing roar of breakers on a shore could be heard above howl and shriek of wind, he ordered the men into the boats, leaving the barque to whatever fate Nature decreed.

Shetland had also suffered long from this gale of gales. The Whalsay men were confined to their homesteads, although often enough at the gable ends of the croft-houses looking to the east and

the semi-obscured sea and leaden sky. One day it would lift!
Presently the sting had gone out of the wind; there were thoughts of
getting back to the fishing, and discussion centred on the big seas still
running beyond Whalsay Sound and over towards the Nesting shore.
But in the haze of a watery morning there was amazement at the
appearance of a vessel with sails awry, certainly out of control. Three
boats went out of Symbister and bore down on the derelict, now in
the grip of the flood tide. Even from standing off, the 17 men could
see no sign of life and she seemed ripe for salvage if they could board
her. The 900 ton barque presented a streaming wall of hull on the one
roll and gunwale under on another, making boarding a chancy
business, yet they tried and succeeded. Knowledge of set of tide, skill,
and gradually easing weather, all combined, enabled them to
manoeuvre the *Pioneer* up into Linga Sound, where she was anchored,
a feat which would have been unlikely had her crew remained with
her. As it was they survived a four hour tussle to win ashore at Eswick
in Nesting. They were relieved enough to have their lives; the
Whalsay fishermen were glad enough to have £24:10/- each, for it
was well nigh Christmas 1910!

The south-east has, from time immemorial, been a source of
worry about gales in Shetland. Such a storm played havoc with
shipping in mid-January, 1912. "The Shetland Times" carried the
headline: "Great Storm in Shetland. Mail Service Unhinged." The
Earl left Lerwick on the Friday morning and reached Baltasound that
night. On the Saturday she made for Mid Yell in worsening seas and
was forced to lie there until the Monday morning, something she had
managed to avoid for 20 years. During a brief lull the steamer came
back to Lerwick where people were talking about the spray being
carried over the lighthouse on the heights of Sumburgh Head. In
such awe-inspiring conditions it would have been surprising if some
ship had not come to grief, and almost inevitably it was a sailing
vessel which was wrecked.

A 424 ton Swedish barque, the *Advena,* was bound for Kalmar,
her home port, from Sunderland with a cargo of coke. Like the *Pioneer*
of two years back the *Advena* had been within sight of the Norwegian
coast when the devil-gale made its diabolical presence felt directly out
of the south-east. It came fast and fearsome, taking sails apart and
lifting the sea into unprecedented fury, urging the barque relentlessly
to the north-west over the North Sea. Shetland lay across her path
and she came to the land at Out Skerries where the folk watched the
life or death struggle of a tiny symbol of mankind against the might of
Nature. About 4.30 on a Friday afternoon she was coming into the
south mouth of the harbour when a gigantic comber took her bodily,

slewed her round, and in a smother of whiteness crashed her on wave-battered rocks. One moment there were seven minute dark figures clustered on her stern, the next they and the barque were smothered in a welter of foam.

Five Skerries men, William Anderson, John Henderson, David Anderson, Andrew Johnson and Peter Anderson, regardless of risk, took the lighthouse boat and went off. The *Advena* had gone within five minutes and the chances of the seven seemed utterly remote, yet two, Ragmar Larsson and Karl Yonsson, came through the ordeal. Later, as the *Earl* sailed from Skerries with them, the broken and splintered keel and lower planks of the hull lay at the high water mark, the stern had disappeared, and the deck with remaining timbers floated near the shore. Larsson and Yonsson had been fortunate, thanks to the Skerries men. Two from the lighthouse were given inscribed binoculars plus £3 each and the three others, fishermen, an aneroid barometer and a similar sum of money; just reward for venturing into such forbidding conditions, yet reacting in a way entirely appropriate to the great traditions of the sea.

From time immemorial loyalty and integrity have been associated with the behaviour of men in all the great seafaring nations of the world and clearly the crew of the now indispensable North Isles steamer had become personalities of note. Her first skippers had shown seamanship and friendship and they were backed up by a team of worthy shipmates. There was Tom Moffat the mate. At the time of the *Advena* wreck he had already served near enough a quarter of a century on the *Earl,* aware of every conceivable situation and a vastly experienced seaman. And being mate on this ship made demands unlikely to arise in any other vessel. Awareness and experience were vital. That he took his work seriously was without question, although tensions and stress might bring quiet, though telling, reaction. The mate had to be a blend of everything from stevedore to acting skipper and Tom was responsible for the remark: "I cannot work and navigate at the same time!". No doubt it happened in acute circumstances!

Tom Moffat had to be quick off his mark from his home in Market Street, Lerwick on a winter's morning to begin working cargo. If it was to be a six o'clock start then he would be there, prepared to play his part in lifting and loading. There were no dockers then, no lines of demarcation, no strikes. A man did his day's work and more if need be. Colin Henry, seaman, was of this stamp, but he chanced to be late on a dark winter's morning. The mate, already at work, saw Colin arriving and observed, "Colin, it's three minutes past six, three minutes past six, three minutes past

Exhaust steam from the derrick winch flurries round the bows as a small boat is rowed ashore. The big flitboat prepares to go alongside.   *National Maritime Museum*

The well-deck, centre of activity. Tim Petrie, the cook during the early 1900s, has a word with two young travellers.   *Shetland Museum*

Heavily laden at Whalsay, but two oars preferred.

Four oars in evidence at Ulsta as the flit-boat comes off in 1905. The small pier is a vivid contrast to the ferry terminal of some 70 years later.   *Shetland Library & Museum*

six . . .''. He made no reply, began his work and was never late again. Or so it is said.

Maybe the criticism was not surprising because the mate sailed close to the wind, as it were, between order and chaos. The steamer carried an incredible variety of goods. She would take everything from cotton reels to barrels, coarse soda to Portland cement, matches to roof beams, pliers to ploughs, porridge oats to tar chips. There would be bags of flour, casks of brandy, bottles of beer, chests of tea, boxes of tinned soup, packets of soap . . . And the mate contrived to create a pattern which ensured that there were barrels for Baltasound, chests of tea for Cullivoe, matches for Mossbank . . . his sheaf of cargo-handling papers waved in direction, frustration or anger from the cement-lined floor of the *Earl's* forward hold or 'tween decks. He was directly answerable to the captain at Lerwick for clearing the pier or putting the warps ashore when berthing, responsible for lowering and raising anchor at each port, navigation when the skipper was unavailable or indisposed, had to bear the idiosyncracies of the flit-boat men through the North Isles and North Mainland, and many a scathing remark in the traditional banter had to be countered in a manner inoffensive to the company and the passengers. Thus Tom Moffat had a demanding existence on which he appeared to thrive.

Although the hours were arduous the *Earl* had about her a leisurely atmosphere, due mainly to men like Moffat. Time was always relative. As was customary the mate rang the warning bells prior to departure from Lerwick, and the sharp sound would reverberate and echo through Commercial Street and the stepped lanes to the Town Hall and beyond on a still, frosty morning. Each of the three bells would be delivered in staccato fashion with the characteristic one, two, and then three, prior to casting off. But even after the final bells, if mate or skipper knew of a latecomer or if some forgetful passenger had left a package or case behind, then there was time to wait. It was this kind of generous concession, albeit delivered in a gruff but not unfriendly way, that made people affectionately disposed to the steamer and her men.

Jimmy Garriock had become steward back in 1894 and was there until 1904, when he was appointed to the *St. Rognvald*. He was an enormous round man of great good humour and his jests added colour to life about him. Jimmy Young, known as "Swifty", of the Fetlar flitboat, was not noted for his alacrity, immaculate appearance or turnout, while haircuts seemed unknown to him. His hair was long and unkempt and he shaved as little as possible, without actually producing a beard. Banter between the two men of the same Christian name was customary and one day as the gap between flitboat and ship's side narrowed, after the *Earl* had anchored at Houbie, Jimmy Garriock greeted his namesake: "Aye, aye Jimmy hair's thick". Young was quick with his parry: "Aye, aye Jimmy, so's beef!", with a meaningful glance at Garriock's portly shape!

Of course Moffat saw several skippers come and go and most of them acknowledged his experience in the avoidance of the masses of underwater and tidal rocks on the routes, and he would act as navigational adviser to any newcomer. Nevertheless he was a man of few words, as a boatman at Brough Lodge on Fetlar discovered. Sir Arthur Nicolson was expecting a visit from nobility and sent off a small boat to meet the *Earl*. It was Tom Moffat who greeted the boatman from the well-deck. The man had forgotten the name of the titled gentleman and Moffat was unaware of any stranger, so to the question "Is the Lord aboard?" he replied, "If he is I've no seen him!".

Seasonal changes of captain were standard practice and Tom Moffat accepted these as routine. In May, 1904, Peter Johnson left the *Earl* and was replaced by William Johnson who had been sailing as chief mate in the *St. Ninian,* then Peter returned for the winter season. In 1905 and 1906 this system was again used. Thus, if skippers would come and go through company policy, there were the men who, like Moffat, were loyal servants of Shetland on the *Earl of Zetland.*

Colin Henry would be one of the longest serving seamen. He came from the little community of Gutcher in Yell and had worked on the steamer for a decade before he decided to move wife and family to Lerwick, from which base he did over 25 more years to emulate Tom Moffat's 35, although he continued several months after the mate before retiring to Lerwick. Colin had a kindly nature, friendly and helpful to many a fretting passenger in the throes of seasickness, while he was a familiar figure at the old wooden wheel on the open deck below the bridge, hands protected from the bitter cold by knitted mittens, often renewed by the efforts of grateful fisher lasses who appreciated his agreeable disposition.

Then there was John Fraser, who hailed from Cullivoe in Yell, a survivor of the 1881 fishing disaster. He lived in Lerwick, and such was the extent of his commitment to his beloved ship that he would go to her berth at the Victoria Pier and check the moorings during a menacing night of wind. It was an act typical of seamen motivated by a total loyalty to the *Earl of Zetland.*

6

Milestones and through World War One

The remarkable fragmented range of involvement in community work never lessened. Politics, postal services, livestock cargoes, the Up-Helly-A' annual festival and pleasure trips, all contributed to the variety. In January, 1906, Mr Cathcart Wason, Liberal candidate, chartered the ship to take Skerries voters to Whalsay and those from Fetlar to Mid Yell, although Mr Dunlop, the Unionist candidate, did not wish to be involved in the expense. Early in February 10 electors

A flitboat alongside in fog.

from Skerries and 27 from Fetlar travelled to vote, then the steamer's crew went back to Lerwick to record their votes. The result of the poll in the Parliamentary Election was Wason, Liberal, 3,837; Dunlop, Conservative, 1,021; Liberal majority 2,816. Perhaps poetic justice had been done!

Criticism of the postal service in open boats was made in March, 1906. It was pointed out that the *Earl* dealt with much of the mail, but there was the anomaly of quantities of mail being taken by horse and gig over rough roads on Sunday evening from Lerwick to Mossbank where it was carried by open boat across Yell Sound to Ulsta, then again by gig over Yell itself to Bluemull Sound and once more by boat to Unst. Frequently mail failed to reach Unst until the Friday. This was regarded as incredible at the beginning of the 20th century and a likely source of disaster with open boats in such frequent use. Further complaints were made about the poor postal arrangements for Out Skerries.

In the sphere of livestock shipments ''The Shetland Times''

noted that the *Earl* made a special run to Aberdeen early in September, 1909, carrying 1,097 lambs.

Annually, on the Wednesday prior to the first Friday in September, the steamer would cross from Lerwick to Bressay about 6 a.m. to tie up at More's herring curing station at Leiraness or Buchan's station at Cruister to begin loading of lambs from the farms of Maryfield, Hoversta and Setter. Hard work had gone on to gather the animals from the Bressay hills and green fields, carefully herded down into the makeshift, but effective, enclosure on the shore and stage, formed from full herring barrels and wooden hurdles. (The fishing stations still had barrels to ship away in the early autumn.) The *Earl* could lie comfortably alongside either of the piers. More's had deeper water, though Buchan's possessed a fine sandy bottom.

The concentration of hundreds of disturbed sheep, barking dogs and shouting men produced a babble of noise clearly heard in Lerwick, as the lambs were funnelled into the narrow gangway and into every available space on board; deck, 'tween decks and cargo space all were utilised. The din of bleating animals crammed into the hold and acrid odours were in sharp contrast to the fiddle airs, shouts of revellers and smells of roasting Shetland lamb in the galley on the pleasure trips. A voyage south could take the *Earl* over 30 hours, with occasional loss of animals from exhaustion as a result of heavy slamming into large seas. In later years the Board of Trade's regulations denied such trips, which were so much a feature of the *Earl's* activities from the turn of the century and for more than a decade thereafter.

Up-Helly-A' had been a well established Viking fire-festival celebrated in Lerwick at the end of January each year and was tremendously popular throughout the islands. The 1910 celebration was no exception and, "notwithstanding the cloud-laden and grey sky a large number of young people undertook the journey to the capital and arrived at Lerwick on Monday evening. The s.s. *Earl of Zetland* brought down visitors from the North Isles on Monday afternoon and later in the evening these were added to by that steamer's arrival from Sandwick." For many years it was the custom that the firing of the signal gun and the lighting of a flaming torch on the *Earl* heralded the start of festivities and from 1889 the feature of a locally constructed Viking galley, the focal point of a procession through the streets, made an exciting impact, and the climax of hundreds of flaming torches tossed into the galley charged the January night with a spectacular column of fire. This tradition, continuing through the 20th century, has emphasised the Norse flavour and kinship with Scandinavian lands. The culmination, of the galley consumed in a mighty pillar of fire to represent the funeral of a Viking chieftain, had been the inspiration of the blind Shetland poet J. J. Haldane Burgess. A brilliant academic career had been cut short by the loss of his eyesight and he became deeply interested in the Norse heritage. With a natural flair for poetry he created verse in the Shetland dialect and in 1897, his imagination caught by the old Norse literature, he wrote the Up-Helly-A' song about the spirit and independence for all. The song was to become immortal.

Just as the old steamer attracted attention each year at Up-Helly-A', so she remained a focus of interest on other special occasions. In May, 1911, she carried 200 passengers on an outing down to Grutness in the extreme south of the mainland, landing a number at Sandwick en route. The lighthouse on the crest of Sumburgh Head and the magnificent cliffs were popular with the visitors.

In December, 1911, there was a significant change in the crew. Andrew Jamieson had come from the Scalloway office of the North Company in 1907 to be purser. He had served the travelling public particularly well for the four years but, like so many of his generation, he had elected to emigrate to New Zealand. David Gray from the Lerwick office took over the position and was destined to be a character long associated with the *Earl of Zetland,* amazingly until after the second war.

The year 1912 might so easily have been one of normal routine sailings. Certainly the *Advena* incident, with which the *Earl* had been indirectly involved in January, had caused a stir in Shetland, but in the spring of 1912 a disaster of unprecedented dimension shocked the entire world, and the sea-sensitive island people were appalled at the magnitude of the loss of the *Titanic* as 1,500 individuals (rather less then a quarter of the Lerwick population) perished in icy seas. The pre-maiden voyage publicity had declared the *Titanic* absolutely secure from risk — "God himself could not sink this ship" — yet an unobserved knife-edge blade of ice had ripped through compartment after compartment in the bowels of the great liner, leaving her mortally wounded and exposed to the inrushing sea. Her 46,328 ton bulk sank in less than three hours. Her boats were adequate for only a fraction of her human complement. But then they had thought she was unsinkable. Court of Inquiry reaction was strongly critical of the complacency and assumptions of the designers and owners of the liner whose safety regulations were based on an outdated and absurd formula determining boat requirements. The net outcome was an ultra-sensitive Board of Trade in months and years to come, a sequel which almost inevitably brought about an unfortunate milestone in the career of Captain Peter Johnson of the s.s. *Earl of Zetland.*

The morning of Friday, 26th July, 1912, was no different from average. About 90 passengers and 50 tons of mails and general cargo had been taken on at Lerwick for the North Isles and Tom Moffat ordered "Warps away" on Peter Johnson's instructions. It was 9.30 a.m. An hour and 20 minutes later the ship unloaded into the Whalsay flitboat, the men working in a gathering haze which steadily restricted visibility. As the steamer got under way for the ten mile run to Burravoe the clammy tendrils of fog blotted out Linga to port and the Whalsay houses to starboard, although passengers on deck saw the shadowy form of Wether Holm to port as it was passed. Captain Johnson rang down for reduced speed from nine to six knots, posted the mate and John Fraser in the bow and conned his ship carefully for the five mile stretch of ebb tide water up to Lunna Holm, the six knots ensuring steerage way in the conditions. He had no doubts about his actions. From the bridge he gave careful course changes to Magnus John Scollay, A.B., at the wheel below, who in over six years had steered the course some hundreds of times. The figures on the fo'c'sle beyond the dark hole of the well-deck were wraith-like. Beyond was an impenetrable blank mass of grey. Below, shipboard work and travel were normal. Tom Sutherland, the chief engineer, had reduced speed when the order came as he had done many times before in thick weather and he was not unduly perturbed. Crewmen like David Gray and Colin Henry regarded the fog as a nuisance causing a late arrival at Yell, and passengers such as Gracie Robertson of Burravoe knew that her folk would take her when she arrived. The *Earl's* timetable was never that punctual.

Those at the bow were acutely aware of the unusually repressive vapour and the sullen, low swell and surge of the bow wave below them. Even the beat of the engines seemed remote. Looking aft, the foremast, bridge, and funnel with its wreath of smoke, lost definition as the ship slid on through the tideway and a waft of wind from the east. Moffat and Fraser saw the dark shape simultaneously. The mate yelled "Holm ahead" in the direction of the bridge, and Peter Johnson reached for the engineroom telegraph. Tom Sutherland reacted to "Stop" and "Full speed astern" and waited. It was 12.15 p.m. He found the following two minutes the longest in his life. The grind of iron on rock when it came sent a chill through 85 stomachs and suddenly the *Earl of Zetland* was firmly aground on Lunna Holm and taking water. Just ten years previously she had been sunk in Baltasound, but here was extreme exposure with her underside vulnerable to whatever rocks might pierce her plates since the tide had another two hours to fall before low water, and to port and astern water deep enough to swallow the ship for all time. Full power astern brought no results, although a kedge from the starboard quarter prevented her from swinging broadside to the land with the force of the tide. Peter Johnson himself checked the hull and sea from a lowered boat and found no rocks all round apart from a ledge on the starboard side on which his steamer seemed to rest.

A report of an increased flow through the breached plates and the horrific thought of that deep water and the possible end of the *Earl* forced a decision about the passengers. Since the green grass on the holm was a mere 20 yards away it was a simple matter to lower the second boat for the transfer of people, luggage and provisions, anticipating some enforced time ashore. So close was the ship's side to the rocks that the boats could be used pontoon fashion and as the red-bearded Tom Moffat supervised the transfer it was a male passenger who remarked of the *Earl's* encounter with the grassy islet:"'Boy is du tinkin tae gie her a corn o' green girse i' da morning?''. (''Are you thinking to give her a drop of green grass in the morning?''.) Moffat's reply was never recorded! The operation moved smoothly in a steady drizzle of rain through the fog. Tarpaulins were rigged, offering a barely adequate respite for a three week old baby, most of the women and a quantity of luggage including a recently purchased mattress in Lerwick, from which the owner steadfastly refused to be separated. Hot tea and sandwiches from the steadily filling *Earl* helped to ease the discomfort on Lunna Holm.

About 1.30 in the afternoon a local boat appeared. Her occupants had heard the siren booming its deep throated alarm and had anxiously put to sea. They returned to telegraph Lerwick, while the crew continued to try to free the ship. Repeated use of the engines failed; the propeller shaft tunnel began to flood; water seeped into the engineroom. The donkey pump repelled this well enough, being used in addition for emptying the after hold, and the afternoon dragged on in attempts to keep the sea at bay. At 4 o'clock they lifted the kedge to the port side in the hope that it would help the now flowing tide, and full power astern, to release the *Earl* from the grip of the ledge. A dozen male passengers had elected to remain aboard, although there was little they could do but wait, while the 60 passengers on Lunna Holm surveyed the stricken steamer and speculated on her fate. The pumps had ensured enough buoyancy for the *Earl* to rise with the tide and about 5.30 p.m. Peter Johnson again rang for power. Fifteen minutes later she eased off into the low swell. Water pressure immediately built up through whatever iron plates were burst open and the 25 men on board wondered if they might yet be forced to take to the boats, now back on board, if the *Earl* sank under them in the south mouth of Yell Sound. Tom Sutherland had every available pump in action. Despite their efforts the ship was clearly losing the battle to survive. He worried about the fires being extinguished because that would mean the end.

As the *Earl,* significantly down by the stern, was swallowed up in the miserable drizzle and mist, the desolation of the moment gripped the landed passengers on the tiny island. Those who needed shelter most crouched under the scanty cover provided by the tarpaulins. At least darkness was a long way off, yet little imagination was needed to visualise the possible fate of the steamer. By the early evening visibility had improved. They could see the north tip of Lunna Ness and about half way across the gently undulating waters of the sound, although the shores of Yell were still obscured. An hour passed, two hours, until three boats, led by the Burravoe flitboat, emerged from the murk over the providentially calm sea — so flat that the oarsmen kept way on, close into the rocks. Anxious questions were shouted and brought confirmation that the steamer had been beached. As had been the case with the drifter *Emily Reaich* in 1905, Burravoe was their salvation. Half way over the three-mile stretch of sound there was three feet of water swilling threateningly around the engineroom and passenger space aft was awash. When she wallowed into the narrow inlet at Burravoe the depth had reached five feet, but they had won a race for survival as the ship was carefully run ashore on sand and shingle. Most men on board figured that she had only ten minutes to spare. It was a close call!

The news of the labouring steamer had brought the population out, a wave of sympathy permeating the crowd as they saw how low in the water she was, and information about the stranded passengers had engendered much preparation in the houses in Burravoe when the boats had set out. By mid-evening, heavily laden, they had returned from Lunna Holm and were alongside the pier below the shop at Burravoe. About 60 bedraggled people, mainly women and children, climbed ashore to disperse to the houses under the guidance of the Rev. John Watson who, himself, took a group to the Burravoe manse.

It had been a nerve-wracking situation for Peter Johnson, although he could console himself that there had been no panic and no loss of life. Also the folk talked about their sympathy for his predicament. There was plenty of goodwill. Many hands cleared mails and luggage from the now stationary and forlorn *Earl of Zetland,* preparatory to the arrival of the *St. Sunniva* in response to the telegraph signal to Lerwick. She reached Burravoe after 2 a.m. on the Saturday morning, loaded mails, passengers and luggage and visited the ports, all agog with the news of the mishap.

No opportunity had been missed: the *Sunniva* carried a team of workmen. They laid steam pumps in the *Earl* early on the Saturday, when it was found that plates were ruptured abaft the engineroom bulkhead on the starboard side near the keel. A temporary repair soon reduced the penetration of the sea. The effects of salt water were gradually and laboriously removed for the second time — memories were readily kindled of the inundation in Baltasound ten years previously — and by the Tuesday morning, with the arrival of the salvage steamer *Ocean Bride,* the crew had their charge looking in reasonable shape, so much so that she entered Lerwick under her own steam, to be greeted by a large crowd of curious citizens. On the Wednesday, 31st July, she sailed south to Aberdeen with the *Ocean Bride* in attendance and such was the speed of the repair that she was back in Lerwick on the Sunday afternoon and away to the North Isles the same evening under command of Captain Mackenzie, formerly chief officer of the *St. Nicholas.*

The Board of Trade had had no formal inquiries when several North steamers met with accidents. In March, 1891, the first *St. Rognvald* stranded near Kirkwall and finally met her demise in 1900 when she was wrecked off Burgh Head, Stronsay. Her successor, the second *St. Rognvald,* struck rocks at Fair Isle a year later, though not seriously, but the unlucky stranding so similar to that of Peter Johnson's *Earl* was when John Scott's *St. Giles* had fallen foul of the island of Mousa in 1904. Johnson would recall that accurately since his steamer was there to render aid and it was a bitter pill to swallow when he found himself chief witness at an official Board of Trade inquiry at Aberdeen in late August following an almost identical situation with his own ship. John Scott had had no such ordeal. Sheriff Young presided, with Captains Bett and Davis as nautical assessors. William Merrylees, the North Company manager, sat throughout the trial. Mr N. M. Duncan and Mr G. Duncan, advocates, Aberdeen, represented the B.O.T. and owners respectively.

Peter Johnson was called. He said he held a master's certificate in Foreign Trade. He described his ship and confirmed that he thought his compasses were in good order, although no action had been taken recently despite a request to the marine superintendent to have them checked. There were two boats which could take 43 passengers; two life-rafts each catering for five people. Eight lifebuoys and 232 lifebelts completed the safety equipment.

The captain was followed by Tom Moffat, Tom Sutherland,

Magnus John Scollay and John Fraser, each describing the events of the day. Scollay confirmed that there was no shipping in the area. He had concentrated on the ordered course at Wether Holm. The master was on the bridge. Part of Lunna Ness had been seen and a course change was given. Evasive action was taken when the holm was suddenly sighted but the ship had only partially answered the wheel which was then made fast, and he went round the ship after she grounded. Fraser stated that he had been 15 years on the ship. The assessors wanted to know how often the boats were launched. "Once a year?". He replied, "More often than that, about once a month." In his opinion they were in good order that day.

Mr Thomas Lamb, who had been superintendent engineer for the owners, was asked by Captain Bett how many passengers B.O.T. regulations allowed. "232, including the crew." "You carry 232 but you had boat accommodation for 53. Do you think that is fair to the public?". Lamb replied "That's the proportion the Board of Trade allow." Bett pressed for an opinion " . . . leaving 180 to sink or swim? As a man do you think that is a fair thing? I am not asking you for your opinion of the Board of Trade." Lamb stated that he would prefer a place for every passenger. Captain Davis queried further "Do you remember the captain asking you some time ago to adjust the compasses?" Witness could not say. He thought they were adjusted a year ago by the B.O.T. surveyor.

Peter Johnson, when recalled, stated to Captain Bett that he corrected his compasses by transit and sun observations, but had no record. However, the compasses had been ashore to be examined two years before.

Mr G. Duncan wanted to know how many passengers would be on the ship at any given time. It was mentioned that she would carry near her full complement during the herring fishing season, but probably an average yearly number would be under 50. Sheriff Young commented, "I suppose many of them will not be passengers for the whole distance?" Johnson responded, "Some will come on at Whalsay and go off at Burravoe." The sheriff replied "I think I have seen that. It is more like a river steamer with passengers as on the Clyde." The remark was greeted with one or two wry grimaces. A comparison with the waters of the Clyde brought recollections of the inadequacies of the *Chieftain's Bride* of over 40 years before.

In the summing up, the severe formality and bureaucracy of a government department showed. Mr N. M. Duncan presented the questions for the Board of Trade. What was the number of compasses for the vessel? Were they in good order and sufficient for the safe navigation of the vessel? When and by whom were they last adjusted?

Did the master ascertain the deviation of his compasses from time to time? Were the errors correctly ascertained and proper corrections for the courses applied? Was the vessel supplied with proper and sufficient charts and sailing directions? Were the right measures taken to check the position of the vessel when off Wether Holm at 11.50 a.m. on 26th July last? Was a safe and proper course set and thereafter steered? Was due and suitable allowance made for tides and currents? Having regard to the state of the weather was the vessel navigated at too great a speed? Was the lead used? If not, should it have been used? Was an appropriate look-out kept? What was the cause of the stranding of the vessel and was she seriously damaged thereby? Was the vessel navigated with proper and seamanlike care? Was the damage to the *Earl of Zetland* caused by wrongful act or default of the master?

They were questions which might have been asked of any stranding, but in the unfeeling and analytical atmosphere of the inquiry, they took on a daunting significance which was not in keeping with attitudes in the islands, where many a man looked at Peter Johnson's ill-luck rather than his lack of judgment. At least the court took into account an unblemished record and difficulties in these waters, and in cautioning the captain to be more careful in future, the findings were that safe alteration was not made to the course when Lunna Ness was sighted at Stour Hevda and the vessel was steaming too fast.

As Peter Johnson took a pride in his seamanship and had an affection for his charge, he felt that the caution put him in an invidious position and his reactions prompted him to resign from the *Earl* and to withdraw from the North Company. Throughout the islands the reaction was of concern, and appreciation for his work, to the extent that a subscription list was opened with a return which revealed the esteem in which he was held. In September, 1912, he was invited to the Masonic Hall in Lerwick to receive a purse of gold sovereigns, presented by Mr J. C. Grierson, county convener, who said they were there to extend sympathy and brotherly feeling as they should do to a countryman who had been in difficult circumstances recently which, he thought, had not been owing to his fault, but he, like many other men, had had to pay the penalty for bigger men. If the *Titanic* had not been lost there would have been no inquiry into the accident to the *Earl*. He then recalled the several wrecks of ships belonging to the North Company, and felt that Peter Johnson had been made a scapegoat. It was a matter of sincere regret that the captain had felt it necessary to resign because all who travelled knew him to be an excellent seaman and thoroughly capable in every way.

In a moment of emotion, Peter Johnson said that he could not make a speech at any time, more especially since he was overcome in this manner, for the handsome present he had got was not only unexpected, but he could not see how he had deserved it. He found it difficult to appreciate Mr Grierson's complimentary terms because he had just tried to do his duty.

Thus Captain Peter Johnson's association with the *Earl of Zetland* came to a premature end, an end as unfortunate as it was untimely, and an apparently strange consequence of the sinking of a giant White Star liner.

Alterations in personnel continued. In the inevitable change of skipper, Captain Mackenzie, of the *St. Nicholas* took over the captaincy early in August, 1912, although he was then succeeded in the early spring of 1913 by David Burgess, who had sailed as mate of the *St. Rognvald.* Tom Sutherland had already been given the chief engineer's post on the second *St. Giles,* then almost at the end of her careeer with the North Company, and he left the *Earl* in August, 1912, to be replaced by John Robertson, who had been second engineer on the *St. Giles.*

The 1912 Lunna Holm drama had avoided loss of life, but Tom Moffat found himself in the witness box again within a year of the stranding, this time in connection with the death of three Whalsay men lost in a boating capsize. On Tuesday, 15th April, 1913, James Anderson, Tom Arthur and John Irvine had left Symbister for Neap in Nesting to collect the mail which would have come overland by gig. All were experienced men — Irvine skipper of the fishing boat *Silver Spray* and Anderson and Arthur hands on the boats *George* and *Topaz.* Whalsay folk at the south end saw the boat returning with sail on her well into the intervening expanse of sea, which was being lifted by an increasing southerly wind. They saw the sail taken down and in a moment the boat, men and sail had disappeared. Four days later the buckled remains of mast and sail were discovered by searchers, along with keel and bottom board of the hull, all washed ashore at the Groot of Stava Ness. Tragically the men were never found. Of course the North Company had the contract for H.M. Mails, normally carried by the *Earl of Zetland,* but the steamer was south for her Board of Trade survey. In her absence no formal alternative was made and it was standard practice to take an open boat, a method long criticised as dangerous and mentioned publicly in 1906 and earlier. Moffat confirmed that boats running the post bags across Bluemull Sound and from Brough Lodge in Fetlar to Mid Yell were 12-12½ feet of keel. He commented that these stretches of water could be just as

formidable and dangerous as Whalsay Sound on a bad day. Perhaps
the inevitable had come about.

Despite the hundreds of crossings of such seaways, the sad loss to
Whalsay was the only serious misfortune with mails within living

Heavy slamming into large seas . . .

memory, and it brought about a question in Parliament from Mr
Cathcart Wason, who wanted to know of the Postmaster General if he
would enquire of the contractors if they had compensated the families
of the men lost. No claim was received by the North Company and,
in fact, the Post Office offered no assistance, presumably on the
grounds that their obligation did not go beyond ensuring that suitable
men took the mail over to the islands as required. A formal verdict
was returned with the recommendation that men so involved should
have expenses to cover an overnight stay on the mainland in the event
of rough weather. The lack of human understanding evident in the
cold facts led to an exchange of views between the Postmaster
General, the Zetland County Council and Nesting Parish Council.
Despite the delay of several days if the steamer was off passage the
Post Office refused permission to the North Company to transfer the
post bags in open boats . . .

*   *   *   *   *   *

Meanwhile the domestic scene was gradually being
overshadowed by events in Europe. As far back as 1904 some units of
the German Fleet had anchored off Lerwick, lying between Breiwick
and Bressay — a Prussian show of strength which was closely
observed from the heights of the Knab and which caused some
misgivings in Shetland when relations between Britain and Germany
were not improving. Increasingly in the following years British Naval
presence showed around Shetland.

In June, 1913, warships of the Third Destroyer Flotilla were
deployed in exercises around the islands and the crew and passengers
of the *Earl* saw the spectacle of the high-speed destroyers in Yell
Sound and east-side waters. The cruiser *Blake* supported by 20
destroyers utilised the peaceful expanse of Sullom Voe as an
anchorage, the normally tranquil atmosphere being transformed by
the activity of fleet launches and resounding bugle calls on still, calm
mornings. The naval men were given a traditional welcome
whenever ashore and on a Sunday the tiny Congregational Church at
Sullom Voe reverberated to the throaty depth of male voices in such
praise as "The Lord's my Shepherd" and "Onward Christian
Soldiers". And many a sailor there was in the last stages of young
life, for the war which came in August 1914 was an awesome carnage.
Because a prosperous, strong and self-willed Prussia, with ideas of
territorial gain and eventual world domination, had elected to invade
Russia and attack France, Britain, as their ally, had no choice but to
challenge Germany. Shetlanders contributed almost immediately.

Hordes of Naval Reservists left; thousands were already at sea in what proved to be a highly vulnerable area of the war — the merchant marine — and within weeks the newspapers were referring to "the Great War", as the extent of hostilities became apparent.

It was true that the *Earl* was for the most part in waters contained by units of the British Fleet, because Swarbacks Minn, off St. Magnus Bay on the west side, became an anchorage for the 10th Cruiser Squadron, but she still sailed south on occasion, often commanded by David Burgess, to relieve on the Pentland Firth or for her annual overhaul. She would thread through a motley collection of shipping, lying where the German warships had anchored off Lerwick ten short years previously, and ranging from Faroe smacks to square riggers and large steamers, all reputedly neutral and brought in for examination by British warships. Massive boom defences were rigged across the south and north entrances of Lerwick harbour, one from Ham on Bressay to the Knab, and the other from Heogan on Bressay to the Point of Scattland. During these uncertain war years the North Company kept the inter-island timetable on familiar lines. In 1915 the steamer left Lerwick early on the Monday for Uyeasound, and called at Cullivoe, Brough Lodge, Mid Yell and Whalsay on her return the same day. She then did the Yell Sound ports on the Tuesday, returning on the Wednesday from Ollaberry at 7 a.m. At the weekend she sailed up to Baltasound on the Friday and was back in Lerwick on the Saturday. There were few delays to her timetable on account of the war, but her crew were uncomfortably aware of its proximity.

Warfare between surface vessels, though exacting in its toll of men and materials, was fundamentally a fair conflict in which manoeuvre was visual, tactics based on skill and trained sea-craft, and when forces were equal the outcome often in doubt. When war came on 4th August, 1914, the sea-scene was set in distant waters as German cruisers sought out and destroyed British shipping, but later in the month of August, the enemy was on the receiving end during a skirmish of light cruisers in the North Sea, followed by a wider engagement between battlecruisers in January the next year. The encounters of these enormous fighting machines were spectacular visually and aurally, culminating in the war milestone of Jutland at the end of May, 1916, when the Prussian war-lords realised that their sea-power was gradually, steadily, being eroded by British naval might and tactics.

The German answer was premeditated and carefully planned. Their research and preparation were typically methodical to ensure a repeating blow against the island which was proving to be a tough

I

obstacle to their hopes and aspirations. Through the unseen underwater threat of the submarine they planned a campaign, the severity of which would cripple the sea communications of Britain and leave her in a state of seige, born of starvation of supplies. It was a grand plan put into execution through an enormous fleet of submarines which played havoc with unsuspecting merchant shipping. It was designed to shatter the economy from Shetland's Muckle Flugga to Cornwall's Land's End. It might well have succeeded.

The British Navy had no immediate answer to this new threat with the result that the submarines sank ship after ship, confidently appearing within sight of land to strike at the very heart of a community. Shetlanders realised with dread that the war had been brought to their doorsteps by the U-boat when during a bright June morning in 1915, within a few miles of the *Earl's* frequent route via Out Skerries, the herring fleet was faced by the daylight surfacing of a raider which systematically sank by gunfire 15 fishing craft. It might well have been a horrendous slaughter of the innocent, but a U-boat commander with a degree of chivalry spared two boats and allowed all the crews to take their frightening tale to Lerwick. Stealth and deception under the covering sea allowed the submarines to come close inshore undetected and made places like Burra Isle and Whalfirth useful hide-outs. Indeed, it is said that after the war a Shetlander, a sailor, made the acquaintance of a works manager in Hamburg who showed immediate interest in his nationality. "Do you know Yell?" asked the manager. When the sailor confirmed that he certainly did, the next query was "Do you know Whalfirth?". "It is near my home, but do you know it?". The reply astonished the Shetlander. "Many a night I have been there. I was in command of a U-boat and when your ships at Busta got too nosey, we would shelter under the cliffs." The German described the Nev of Stuis and the geo at the foot of the Lumbister Burn at Whalfirth entrance, the barren slopes tenanted only by sheep, and the lack of human habitation. It was easy, therefore, to slip ashore at night and kill off a sheep. This they had done on numerous occasions. It usually made a marvellous delicacy in a rigid and featureless diet, but he remembered the last killing. It was a ram and too tough to eat. And the sailor recalled a Shetland man who had lost a ram just at that time! This was the epitome of carrying the war to the enemy camp!

The British Government viewed with concern the mounting losses of ships and men — 12,000,000 tons of shipping and 44,500 either killed or seriously injured in the merchant service alone by 1918. The staggering total in cold figures belies the anguish of thousands who died in agony. From Scapa Flow, in Orkney, and Swarbacks Minn, armed liners, cruisers and destroyers tried to meet the menace of the U-boat, but shipping was severely restricted. The southern waters of the North Sea were virtually closed to the enemy, thus the northabout route between Orkney and Shetland was essential for the Atlantic, while the Norwegian coast, abounding in shelter, was said to be widely used by the submarines. It was not surprising that those who crewed the *Earl,* or who travelled on her, felt vulnerable during the almost daily visits up the east side of the islands — local talk was often about sightings of German U-boats. She remained unmolested, however, with more delay caused by winter weather than by enemy action, the steamer with the distinction of using the Lerwick harbour boom defences more than any other! In one January gale in 1916 the *Earl* was forced to abandon her Friday morning North Isles voyage until the Monday at 5 a.m. Deep snow brought all landbound transport to a halt and the winds persisted throughout most of the month, so strong that at Weisdale a sixern was lifted off the beach, killing two sheep when it fell.

Often enough the *Earl* carried conversation about shattering events. In February, 1916, northern Unst folk were badly shaken by reports of the battle within sight of Muckle Flugga when the 16,000 ton armed liner *Alcantara* took on the strength of the German cruiser *Greif* at the expense of both ships. It was one of a diminishing list of individual battles, because the British began to realise that there was strength in numbers and heavily protected groups of ships would stand a better chance of survival than those sailing independently. It was the beginning of a convoy system which was to prove valuable, though not invulnerable, in two World Wars. That problems would occur was illustrated in October, 1917, only six months after the establishment of the system, when two speedy and heavily armed German warships attacked a convoy midway between Shetland and Norway. Two British anti-submarine destroyers *Mary Rose* and *Strongbow* fought until sunk in an unequal engagement which had the sad outcome of leaving a defenceless group of vessels, and the Germans, careless of property and lives, and without examination or warning of any kind, pounded the unarmed steamers by gunfire. Five Norwegian, one Danish and three Swedish vessels were lost, while the raiders retreated with no thought of survivors. The anger generated by this kind of atrocity led to Admiralty strengthening of convoy escorts, and the efficient blockading of the North West Approaches, greatly helped by American intervention in the war, gradually pressurised the U-boats into submission. By early 1918 the problem had eased tremendously, yet not before further heavy loss of life, including that of many a Shetlander. In fact when the Great War ended, Shetland mourned six hundred dead, including those who had emigrated.

Although the islands had no threat of invasion, strict wartime routine was established and in August, 1917, the folk read in the Shetland press: "We would remind our readers that the Lighting Clauses of the Defence of the Realm Regulations are still in force. This reminder seems necessary for with the long spell of fine weather and the benefit of The Summer Time Act, little or no artificial light has been required in Shetland for some time back, but, with the sudden change on Thursday evening there was a need for artificial light in most households. A walk round the town late in the evening revealed a sad lapse from the obscuration of lights so rigidly practised in winter. It would be wise for householders to see that their lights are properly obscured."

The trend of the war was by that time moving in favour of the allies, and the German menace through the submarine was gradually subdued. Despite the movements of North Company shipping in the gateway to the Atlantic and North Sea there had been no loss of ships or life during the hundreds of voyages made by the *Earl* and, more dangerously, by the mail steamers running to Aberdeen and beyond. Maybe incidents were inevitable, but it was not until January, 1918, within months of the end of the conflict, that the *St. Clair* was faced by a U-boat while on passage to Lerwick from Stromness. The surfaced enemy opened fire, which was returned by the *St. Clair's* gunner. Although the attack was repelled he, along with the ship's cook, died from a shell burst. A month later the *St. Magnus* featured in the only sinking of a North Boat on passage to or from Shetland. Off Peterhead she was mortally struck by a U-boat's torpedo and foundered with the loss of three lives, mails and cargo. Crew and passengers were landed at Peterhead. Nevertheless by November, 1918, when the Armistice came, the steamers had made 412 voyages to Lerwick in safety. Another North Company ship, the *St. Margaret,* was torpedoed on a voyage to Iceland. She was on charter to G. and J. Burns Ltd. of Glasgow. Attacked without warning some thirty miles east of the Faroes, the ship was struck in her bunkers and foundered within minutes. Amazingly eighteen members of the crew survived. Four were drowned. It was felt that the loss of two ships was bad enough, yet the company had escaped lightly considering the number of voyages made and the colossal tonnage lost through enemy action in northern waters and elsewhere.

When it came, the end of the Great War was acknowledged with tremendous relief and great rejoicing, tempered by the sobering thought that no community in Shetland had escaped the dreadful carnage, whether at sea or in the appalling conditions of the trench warfare in France. A host of young Shetlanders had paid the ultimate price. Amid the festivities of 11th November, 1918, they were remembered as those who had died fighting for the freedom so thankfully won, but at the supreme sacrifice. In the seafaring community the ships made a significant contribution to the celebrations with a colourful display of flags, while the sounds of their sirens echoed round the shores of Lerwick harbour, mingling with the ringing of bells in the Town Hall and churches. At Victoria Pier the *Earl* lent colour and sound, her crew gathered on the fo'c'sle to watch the Lerwick Brass Band playing at the Market Cross before an enormous gathering of townsfolk. As the daylight faded, shipping again introduced a cacophony of sound and signal rockets shot skywards in the gathering gloom of a Sunday evening, while the little *Earl* voyaged to the north on her never-ending routine, her bunting still streaming in the wind. And as if to sympathise with the human situation, the heavens released a fantastic display of the aurora borealis from a deep base in the north-east, superb streamers of multi-coloured light shimmering skywards, all in a scintillating demonstration of the grandeur of nature.

The North Company returned to peace-time work, the only remaining war hazard being wayward mines. Once more the emphasis was on the domestic affairs of the sailing programme, but it was not until June, 1919, that advertising reappeared and ship movements were noted in the Shetland press. Fares from Lerwick to Uyeasound and Baltasound were 10/- first and 7/- second cabin, to Mainland, Yell and Fetlar ports 8/- and 5/6, to Vidlin, Mossbank, Burravoe and Skerries 7/- and 4/6, and to Whalsay 5/- and 3/6. The *Earl* took mails north on a Monday at 5 a.m., they went overland on a Wednesday, and again by steamer on a Friday at 3 p.m. This illustrated the growing interest in road transport throughout Shetland and the very gradual but insistent erosion of the sea routes to the North Isles.

Accidents to the crew of the *Earl* were confined to isolated incidents over the years and not always on board, as John Fraser discovered when he was struck down by a bolting horse and trap, in the street but Jamie Jamieson of Breiwick Cottages in Lerwick (originally from Papa Stour) was a victim of a knock which might have had more serious results. It was standard practice to lay wide planks from the quayside to the edge of the hatch coaming at the forehold, so that some packages could be slid down. As Jamie stood by the hatch at Victoria Pier one day in March, 1919, he chanced to turn his back on the planks to look into the hold, was thumped firmly on the behind by a sliding box, lost his balance and pitched head first the nine feet into the hold. Almost immediate examination by a doctor showed that he had escaped with a scalp wound and was badly shaken.

Alterations in crew brought significant changes again. John Robertson, engineer for seven years, was promoted to the *St. Clair* and his place was taken by Sammy Harrison, a young townsman of Lerwick who was another Shetlander to serve long and well. The old ship seemed to attract and retain a considerable number of seamen who had a great deal to offer in every respect. If work was not necessarily a labour of love, what was done was accomplished ungrudgingly and without regard for time, with the result that they confirmed an atmosphere to which the public had for long responded. Long serving skippers, characters like Nicolson, Scott and Peter Johnson, had each established his individuality with one common factor of good communication with the crew, company officials, flitboat men, steamers' agents at the ports and all who travelled. They created an informality on board which had become something of a tradition over the 40 years of the steamer's existence. Captains William Gifford and David Burgess had ensured a continuity during the war years and they were succeeded by Captain William Spence in 1919.

If other captains had been held in considerable esteem, Willie Spence, often known affectionately as 'Spencey', was the doyen of them all. He had a compelling and magnetic personality coupled with a powerful physique, and to those of his own and a younger generation, Willie Spence and "da auld *Earl*" were synonymous. He was part of her. If experience — and experiences — are to be a measure of qualification, then Willie Spence was well fitted for seafaring. His career was a sequence of adventure. One of five sons, he was born in Cullivoe, North Yell, destined for the sea from the outset. Like too many Shetlanders, economic hardship near the poverty line curtailed his early ambitions. Providentially the arrival of a school of whales and his part in driving them ashore gave him enough money to travel south to ship on the brig *Ocean Belle* of Blyth. After sailing in numerous coasting vessels he joined the *Jane Porter* of Belfast. She left, coal laden, for Valparaiso, Chile where a revolution was in progress — her cargo was sold to the rebels! A chequered voyage for the best part of a year ended in Falmouth. He then enlisted on the *King James*, a Glasgow registered four-masted iron barque, in June, 1892. She took on coal at Newcastle, New South Wales — a load which never reached San Francisco, its destination.

Far into the Pacific Ocean spontaneous combustion set the cargo alight, and the crew fought the deep-seated smouldering conflagration in daylight and darkness until forced to abandon the barque. For two long days the 42 crew watched her burn until the sea swallowed up her remains, leaving two boats in worsening weather to seek salvation to the east and America. They lost contact with each other. Exposure claimed 18 men in one night, and after several days the survivors caught sight of land which was inaccessible for a boat through big seas driving ashore. Willie Spence alone, struggled through the surf to discover that he had landed on Santa Rosa island off Los Angeles. Local people cared for him until he was taken off by the San Franciscan tug *Fearless,* and learned that from his boat only the skipper, the sailmaker and an apprentice survived, having been lifted on board a coaster after he had taken to the sea; and the second lifeboat had found access further along the coast of Santa Rosa. There were 24 survivors from the *King James's* complement of 42.

A spell of four years in San Francisco followed. Willie crewed on tugs, worked cranes, did stevedoring — in fact anything available. In 1896 he came back to Shetland to visit his folk, but joined two last sailing ships, the *Wasdale* of Liverpool and *Carrick* of Glasgow. A variety of steamers came next; the *Lord Elise, General Gordon, Raphael, St. Hillier* and *Saxon.* As if determined to prove that "variety is the spice of life" he again looked to Shetland, this time to join in the herring bonanza, and made his first acquaintance with the *Earl of Zetland* in 1900 when he crewed in her for a fortnight. Since he had married it suited him to work locally, so for a number of years prior to the war he served on numerous North Company steamers, including the *Queen, St. Giles* and *St. Sunniva.* Perhaps anticipating the conflict, he was in the Royal Naval Reserve and in 1914 was despatched to China to join the armed liner *Empress of Asia* engaged in a search for the German raider *Emden.* Some months later, as quartermaster, he was transferred to another armed merchantman, the *Suva,* which was employed in patrol work in the Red Sea. The exceptional variety continued when in May, 1915, he became skipper in a trawler section in the Dardanelles. Two years later he reappeared in Shetland, having been a victim of recurring bouts of malaria which damaged his health, yet he bounced back for the last months of the war, firstly as a coaling officer at Ardrossan and secondly as a pilot under the convoy scheme, working out of Lerwick for three months and Methil for nine.

So Spencey came to the *Earl* right at the end of the war as a seaman of experience and distinction. As skipper he immediately made an impact on the North Isles. People reacted well to his forthright and jovial personality. However, he became mate on the *St. Sunniva,* commanded the 350 ton *Fetlar* owned by the North Company for some months, then, when she was sold in 1920, he returned to the *St. Sunniva,* again as a deputy. The North Company policy of frequent change among their captains returned Spencey to the *Earl* for some months in 1920-21, and gave him charge of the *St. Clair* from June till November 1921 when he went back to the North Isles passages. Curiously enough, when on the *St. Clair* in September, 1921, he took her north to Unst for a consignment of ponies and cattle bound for the south.

For 17 years the *Earl of Zetland* was an outlet for Willie Spence's outstanding seamanship and he was familiar with success born of an adventurous and confident demeanour. Thus when he was let down one Saturday in January, 1922, it must have been an anti-climax to his expectations. Yet she had done what she could with her 50 h.p. engines.

The incident involved the Norwegian full-rigged ship *Maella* which had anchored off Maryfield, Bressay. She was riding high, a big hull surface exposed to the south-easterly winds which so often prevail in Shetland around the turn of the year; it had been easy enough to come into the harbour from the south end. After a short visit to Lerwick the *Maella's* captain, Nyhus, looked for a favourable wind, ideally northerly, but when the wind offered no change he approached the North Company for a tow out of the confines of Lerwick harbour. The request to the crew of the *Earl* met with some misgivings because William Nicolson, her first skipper, had died at the fine age of 83 and his funeral was taking place in Lerwick that afternoon. It was unfortunate that they could not be there to pay last respects.

Around noon, Willie Spence took the *Earl* across the bows of the *Maella* and a heaving line was put over, followed by the heavy towing hawser. Once made fast they took up the strain and the two ships gradually got under way, flanking the Bressay shore as closely as possible to give sea room. It was intended that the tow should be over the ten mile stretch to the Bard of Mousa, ordinarily a straight-forward task, but the first difficulty was off Bressay light when a snapped hawser cast the *Maella* adrift in a strong south-easterly breeze and within easy stranding distance of the Ness of Sound or the Knab. After two hours of manoeuvring another hawser was put over in a still freshening wind. The *Earl* was given full throttle, the rope fully taut, but then the second problem emerged when Spencey discovered that the power of the wind plus the strong-setting tide were too much for his engines, and he suffered the ignominy of being towed by the

Maella! Left with no alternative Spence signalled to Nyhus that they would put back into Lerwick, so the two ships returned to the anchorage rather faster than they had done on the outward leg. Their reappearance about 9.30 p.m. created some amused comment, although no doubt Willie Spence would have the measure of that!

Overnight the wind veered westerly and on the Wednesday afternoon local men from Gulberwick assisted the *Maella's* crew in the tricky operation of moving her, unaided, out of the narrows between the Knab and the Taing of Ham, this time keeping as close as possible in the lee of Lerwick. The full rigged ship made a magnificent spectacle as she moved slowly under maximum sail, edging out, skirting Kirkabister Ness and the Bressay light, forming a course for Tonsberg in Norway. Apart from the restricted sea room, there were no difficulties and the big vessel reached her port on the Sunday while the *Earl* pursued her familiar routine, the subject of a certain amount of good humoured raillery.

Eighteen months later she was associated with a different kind of incident when she brought from Yell 14 crew members of the steamer *Jane* of Gothenberg which had foundered after running on the rocks of Linga, off Gutcher. The ship, of 500 tons, had come to Lerwick from Boston with a load of coal, discharged, voyaged north to Baltasound for a cargo of 475 barrels of herring, then sailed for Lerwick at 11 p.m. on a clear, smooth night. Caught by the south-going tide race she had rammed the island, filled, and was sunk in deep water. There was no loss of life. And there were those on the *Earl* who thought back to her own stranding at Lunna Holm with 30 fathoms of water below her keel!

7

Between the Wars — The Twenties

By the beginning of the third decade of the 20th century the big events of the Great War were put into the background of the thoughts and activities in the lives of the people; only the poignant memory remained of those who fell. Domestic matters relating to the *Earl* became more evident as civilisation recovered, and the relative trivialities like recreation and entertainment returned.

There had been regular maintenance of the ship, although in keeping with the war effort new fittings were minimised, and she was certainly due improvements in the immediate post-war years. In

Hard-worked flitboats at the *Earl's* well-deck.

September, 1922, "The Shetland Times" featured: "That old friend of the travelling public, the *Earl,* has just been fitted with electric light throughout. The contract for the work was in the hands of James Thomson, electrical engineers, Aberdeen, whose representatives have been in Shetland doing all the wiring of the vessel. The current is generated by a General Electric Company dynamo driven by a Ruby engine. Mr Davidson, superintendent engineer of the North Company, together with a representative of the engineering firm, inspected the installation on Tuesday and found it very satisfactory. There are about 60 lights throughout the vessel, including navigation lights and passengers' accommodation and crew's quarters. There is also a deck cluster for loading and discharging cargo, giving much superior facilities, especially at the country ports. There can be no doubt as to the improvement in the lighting, and this last advance in equipment puts all the company's vessels on a level, the s.s. *St. Ola* having been fitted with electric light by the same firm last week".

The alterations met with full approval. Suddenly the onerous

routine task of filling, lighting, and maintaining old-fashioned oil lamps was reduced to the flick of a switch, and the new-found brilliance of the lighting was a near revelation, hitherto shadowy corners now being illuminated. Considering that for near enough six months of the year much of the ship's work was accomplished in semi-darkness or darkness, the men appreciated beyond measure what had been done. Many said it was not before time!

In 1920 a traditional feature which reappeared in Lerwick was Up-Helly-A', while excursion trips by the North Company had obviously lost nothing of their popularity of the pre-war years. Only the weather did not relent. January, 1922, produced shocking conditions. On the 22nd, a Saturday, the *Earl* reached Symbister and discharged mails and cargo. On her way north she came up against seas of such ferocity that her crew were compelled to sling oil bags over the side, and the steamer made for Mid Yell and shelter. On the Sunday morning she managed to reach Uyeasound where there was danger in unloading as the flitboat rose and fell alongside the open doors of the well-deck. The more open water to the east of Unst and up to Baltasound was too rough to negotiate, and the *Earl* put back to Mid Yell. Once more she lay overnight and at daybreak traversed the same stretch towards Uyeasound, this time south of Uyea Isle, then tackled the difficult area north to Balta Isle. All on board were relieved to enter Baltasound late on the Monday afternoon. A temporary lapse in the wind strength allowed the return to Lerwick on the Tuesday, yet back came the gale to ensure that the warps stayed on at the Victoria Pier until the next Saturday. The storm had persisted for a full week.

Considering the frequency of such exposure to gale force winds, it was surprising that disaster was closest in near windless conditions, and in 1924 two contrasting incidents happened within four months of each other to remind the populace that there were omnipresent hazards in working the ship and in operating the flitboats. The first of these was at the end of the summer of 1924.

Captain Spence was employed in his summer capacity on the south boats, and Captain Donald McMillan, who hailed from Tiree in the Western Isles, was in charge on Thursday, 28th August, as she approached Lerwick from the North Isles late in the evening. She had taken a considerable number of people north to Fetlar for the popular agricultural show held annually there, not being expected back in Lerwick until well into the night. Accordingly the ship was on schedule as she came into the narrows at the north end of Bressay Sound, and all on board were in high spirits after a good visit to hospitable Fetlar. The run south had been very agreeable in smooth conditions, which enhanced the congenial atmosphere, and near-disaster could not have been further from the minds of crew or passengers.

When it came, the crash was a shocking reminder of the treacherous sea. The *Earl* had more way on her than she had at the time of the Lunna Holm incident 12 years before, and there was a horrific grating and grinding of metal on rock, accentuated by the calm, dark night, as she drove onto the infamous Robbie Ramsay's Baa, a reef which lurks a few feet below the surface at the northern approach to Lerwick. The rock had proved a threat on more than one occasion and, in fact, was so named in 1874 when the whaler *Nova Zembla* came to an abrupt and unexpected halt. She was returning from the Greenland whaling and was approaching Lerwick by the North Mouth to land the Shetland contingent of her crew. Robbie Ramsay, a Yell man, and reputedly a harpooner on the whaler, was at the wheel. According to popular belief the captain remarked: "Isn't there a rock somewhere about here, Ramsay?". He had hardly uttered the words when the *Nova Zembla* ground her underside on what was known as Skibba Baa. Robbie answered: "Day ir dat an you're upon im!". From that time onwards it was Robbie Ramsay's Baa. The whaler was eventually towed off for repair at Hay's yard in Lerwick, but not without the kind of underwater damage the *Earl* had sustained. Sammy Harrison reported water in the engineroom and there was a distinct list to port, but the passengers showed no real signs of panic, most noise coming from agitated livestock. Distress rockets from the ship alerted the coastguard on duty at Fort Charlotte, followed by two more from the fort itself in acknowledgement, and to call out the crew of the life-saving apparatus. Lieutenant Faint in charge of the coastguard unit ran to the Alexandra Wharf, aroused the crew of the fishing boat *Mizpah* with the news of distress signals from the north entrance, and asked the skipper to go out. Within minutes the motor-driven vessel was off the Point of Scattland where her men realised that it was the *Earl* seen silhouetted in a blaze of flares to the north. And a long night followed for master, crew, passengers and would-be salvors.

The *Mizpah* was greeted with relief by Donald McMillan. Although his ship was firmly held on the ledge he was deeply concerned about the 50-60 passengers and, in a mixture of feelings, glad that the sea was smooth enough for the fishing boat to nose up to the *Earl's* side in deep water. By 1.30 a.m. all the passengers had transferred, leaving the stricken steamer to an uncertain immediate future. About 3 a.m. the coastguard on duty noticed that the lights of the *Earl* had apparently disappeared, assumed that she had submerged and hurriedly contacted Lieutenant Faint who consulted Alexander Stephen, the local North Company agent. The *Mizpah* was again despatched, her crew wondering what would materialise if the steamer had toppled off the reef and was sunk. Meanwhile Stephen and Faint travelled out by motor car towards Gremista as far as they could and to their vast relief saw the lights still burning, though barely discernible. They decided that the dynamo had probably failed. As they stood and watched and speculated they saw the first signs of the dawn, a barely perceptible paling of the darkness. And soon the vague bulk of the two vessels showed, the fishing boat at an angle to the canted deck of the *Earl*. Presently the two men could see movement of figures as livestock and cargo were man-handled over. Full daylight revealed that about half the starboard side rested on the rock with the bows and stern overhanging. She still listed to port to the extent that at high tide water found access through the main hatch and portholes aft to the cabins and saloon, where it rose and fell according to the state of the tide. The ship herself never moved in the first long hours after the stranding, aided by weather which was a model of consistency with a gentle offshore breeze from the west. For a third time Lady Luck appeared to be with the *Earl of Zetland*.

The *Mizpah* eventually took off the tired and haggard Captain and crew about 10 a.m. on the Friday, leaving the old steamer abandoned, albeit temporarily. A watch was kept during the night, into the Saturday morning. Another tide rose and fell; still the sea remained docile, still the wind stayed light. At 1 p.m. the salvage steamer *Henry Lancaster,* a frequent war-time visitor to Lerwick, appeared from south and anchored near the baa. Well equipped by the Aberdeen Mutual Insurance Salvage Association, the salvage vessel produced four eight-inch and two six-inch motor pumps which were installed aboard the *Earl*. On the Saturday a diver probed for the damage, which tended to be obscured by waving fronds of kelp on the baa, but he discovered a hole on the starboard side of the engineroom and no other very obvious fault. He utilised two wooden boards to stem the flow into the hull before the pumps were tried after the ebb tide, and when the salvage crew started up the six pumps they watched as the water level in the hull was gradually reduced while outside it rose. With this assurance it was decided to begin operations at eight o'clock on the Monday morning.

So that the stern would lift, some 20 tons of ballast had already been removed by the salvage crew under Mr Alexander Stirrat, Aberdeen Salvage Officer, and North Company dockers, with an arrangement to retain some water in the forehold to ensure the buoyancy aft. And with the six pumps spewing at full pressure the unwanted water had been removed in two and a half hours, which enabled the steamer to lift gently off the reef to be brought alongside the *Henry Lancaster*. Steam was raised and the *Earl of Zetland* limped through the North Harbour to her berth at Lerwick where so much speculation and rumour brought very large groups of the curious to the Victoria Pier to look and to discuss, as she lay with the salvage steamer moored outside her. On the Tuesday two divers checked the damage again. Apart from the gash and some indented plates the hull was intact to the extent that a decision was made to sail the next day for Aberdeen and dry docking.

The aftermath for the old *Earl* was the renewal of numerous plates and the fitting of a larger rudder during a month's stay in Aberdeen. For the North Isles and North Mainland folk it meant a variety of shipping. The *St. Sunniva, St. Magnus* and *St. Fergus* were all seen on the passage. For the Lerwick Harbour Trust it meant a question about the sectors of the Rova Head lighthouse in relation to Robbie Ramsay's Baa. Mr W. Sinclair said that he was always under the impression, until the recent accident to the *Earl,* that the baa was covered by a sector of the light, but now knew that there was no indication for vessels coming from the north. It was not the first occasion on which a ship had gone on it and it was lying in a very vulnerable place. Mr Sinclair moved that they approach the Northern Lighthouse commissioners to have the rock marked by a light, an idea which was unanimously approved, and heartily confirmed by Donald McMillan when he resumed command of his ship on Sunday, 27th September.

"The Shetland Times" of 21st February, 1925, stated that the lighthouses commissioners had agreed to change the coloured arcs of the Rova Head light to ensure a warning sector for the infamous baa. When the light remained unaltered the Harbour Trust prompted the commissioners in the November, but received a reply which stated that it had not yet been possible to effect the alterations. Not until the spring of 1926 was anything done.

Considering the constant movement of the *Earl* in her year-round commitment amid such a mass of unmarked outcrops of rock, which could be known only through an intimate knowledge of the local geography, it is not surprising that problems arose, and even although the established crew could sense instinctively that there was danger, a skipper was still alone in his decision-making. The men who commanded the "sooth boats" had no easy task in the rigours of winter, yet if it blew up they had vast tracts of open sea in which to heave-to or run, and no North Company ship ever sank in that great area of water wracked by winter storms between Sumburgh Head in

The well-deck, a focal point of island life. Lowrie Gifford and Robbie Gray take time to pose for a photograph.

L. Gifford

Left: Davie Gray the Purser who "could take the *Earl* to Uyeasound or anywhere else he liked on a Tuesday". Right: the long-serving Engineer Sammy Harrison in a lighter moment.

E. J. F. Clausen

Shetland Library & Museum

Erty Moar, half brother to Willie Spence dressed for a wet day in summer. Willie adopts a typical stance. *Mrs D. Mann*

Tom Gifford, Mate, and Willie Spence, Skipper, pose for the camera. Magnie Fraser, brother-in-law of Tom Gifford at the wheel. *Mrs A. Gifford*

William Spence and Sammy Harrison (extreme right) with a group of male travellers. Note the variety of headgear.

Shetland Museum

A busy morning at Victoria Pier as passengers come ashore from the ill-fated first *St. Sunniva*. The *Earl* lies in her familiar berth.

The *Earl* at her berth at Victoria Pier. She has the lovely second *St. Sunniva* for
company. The big *St. Magnus (III)* lies on the south side.   *R. Williamson*

Steam herring drifters dominate this sunlit scene. The *Earl* seems hemmed in. A
photograph taken in the Thirties.   *J. D. Ratter*

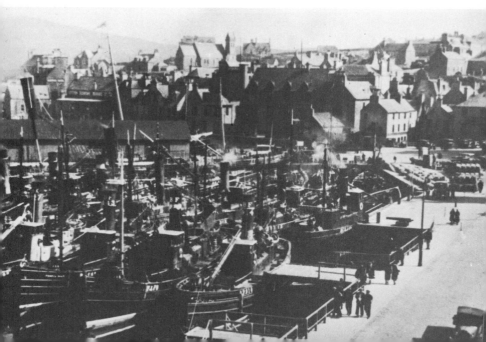

the north, the east side of Orkney, the triangle of the Moray Firth, and Kinnairds Head and Buchan Ness in the south. Thus in some respects their voyaging held fewer risks than did that of the inter-island steamer. Losses were due to collisions with the land, apart from wartime sinkings. The inter-island steamer's captain, however, had land, visible and invisible, as a constant companion, frequently friendly, occasionally downright unfriendly. It did not matter whether the sea was calm or rough, a gentle swell or high breakers, the proximity to the unyielding gneiss or blue-grey limestone of baa or skerry or rugged coastline was the risk factor. And so it was that Robbie Ramsay's Baa almost brought about the downfall of the *Earl,* while only weeks later a ship deprived of her steering, driving onto a lee shore in storm and darkness, illustrated the variety of events which could so easily go wrong.

Willie Spence was on the *St. Sunniva* and Donald McMillan was in command of the North Isles steamer on Monday, 29th December, 1924, when a call was made at Symbister en route south. In the early evening darkness of winter Captain McMillan used the steam whistle to inform the flitboat crew, as was customary even in daylight, and he dropped anchor some 500 yards offshore. When the boat appeared, a shadowy form amid the wave caps, lit by the *Earl's* recently installed electric lights, she had her crew of four, two men in charge of a cow, a few passengers and a small quantity of goods. The time was 6.50 p.m. In a quarter of an hour the flitboat had been unloaded but, in the interval, the tide had turned and was running against a sudden rising wind from south-south-west with accompanying steep breaking seas worsening by the minute. All six Whalsay men watched the old sixern plunging madly, lashed alongside the well-deck, and realised they would be lucky to get ashore again with a heavy craft propelled by unwieldy oars into the gale. Among themselves they decided that discretion was the better part of valour and elected to remain in the shelter of the steamer. Accordingly Captain McMillan attempted by ship's siren and morse lamp to inform those ashore that there was a problem, but apparently without success. He decided to remain anchored with 30 fathoms of chain out and await developments. The sixern was bumping heavily on the steamer's belting and beginning to ship water, so she was moored astern to ease the motion. Half an hour later it was realised that the steamer was beginning to drag. Another 15 fathoms of chain were paid out and Sammy Harrison ran his engines to hold the position. Further signals to the shore in the near pitch darkness brought no response, and as a full gale began to howl Donald McMillan saw the danger of swamping of the flitboat and brought her back from astern. It was 8.45 p.m.

No-one seemed to be directly responsible for what followed. It was said afterwards that Andrew Bruce and Henry Simpson, both flitboat men, suggested to the captain that he might move two or three ship-lengths further into the bay and they might be able to row ashore. But he did not hear or wish to hear. A short time later Andrew Bruce, who had gone to the engineroom for a yarn and warmth, heard that Donald McMillan had ordered the flitboat to be cut adrift. Bruce went for'ard with his knife to do so but found that she had already gone — swallowed up by the pitch black night and charging white-capped seas. It was 9.15 p.m. It was a dilemma with several possible solutions. The boat was too big to hoist aboard; even if they had moved closer inshore, which was dangerous in the darkness, the sea was immense and Symbister Bay exposed from the wind direction and the men might never have managed. It was unlikely that towing was practical; the tow rope might have fouled the *Earl's* propeller with disastrous consequences in the conditions. Whatever the outcome of the likely loss of the flitboat, Captain McMillan elected to look to the safety of his own vessel.

If the extreme state of the sea was a reason for his invidious decision, he was vindicated by subsequent events. The gale, now in unleashed fury, raised seas which were breaking on board, making raising anchor on the exposed fo'c'sle a dangerous business. McMillan knew that his ship did not have the power to drive towards Lerwick into the wind — in fact, even in less exacting circumstances, she had to be tacked in a bad gale — and the waters south of Whalsay were full of scattered hazards like Muckla Fladdicap, Muckla Billan, Litla Billan, Inner Voder, The Sneckan, and Hoo Stack; and further south the Green Holm, Brethern and Robbie Ramsay's Baa — the latter all too familiar! Only by running for Mid Yell could he hope to escape. He ordered a course of north-north-east knowing that he at least had open water before him over the 16 mile expanse of sea up to the Fetlar coast. Momentarily the *Earl* was in the trough; she sagged and answered her helm, the wheel kicking violently held by two crewmen, then the good buoyancy from her counter stern lifted her onto the next advancing wave and she got under way. So bad was the sea that even running before the wind there was the risk of being pooped, while the rudder was subject to hard buffeting which was transmitted to the wheel itself. For an hour they staggered to the north until tension on the wheel suddenly ceased, and the *Earl* lost direction, deprived of her steering.

John Henderson, the mate, hurriedly checked aft and found that the quadrant head of the rudder had snapped. Even the reserve wheel at the stern was useless. It was an alarming situation for Donald

McMillan since the hour's steaming with the wind had taken them well up towards the Fetlar coast somewhere ahead in the impenetrable darkness. With no steerage way they were pinned down to violent slamming in a welter of sheets of water and the awesome din of the storm. John Henderson had suggested a large piston spanner from the engineroom as temporary gear, an idea confirmed by Sammy Harrison. Even Jimmy Willie Spence, the chief steward, and the Whalsay men were among those trying to retain a footing on the gyrating deck, continually drenched by stinging, racing wetness as they strove to organise an emergency repair. In the engineroom the two firemen, Jack Anderson and Hugh Hughson, maintained power and the handful of passengers huddled below decks, some prostrate with sickness.

Captain McMillan, lonely in the responsibility of command, waited anxiously. His dead reckoning made the unseen banks (cliffs) on Fetlar uncomfortably close and he knew that no-one would stand a chance if the ship was driven ashore there on such as Rams Ness or The Snap. Also to the west was the Yell coast, the Ness of Queyon having already claimed a victim only months before, in April, 1924, when the skipper of the German barque *Bohus* of 1, 426 tons had mistaken Skerries for Fair Isle and had stood on in poor visibility into disaster. Curiously enough no-one on the *Earl* could see the White Hill lighthouse just south of the entrance to Mid Yell voe. It had been installed back in 1904. Meanwhile they were being badly knocked about and he was very concerned about the risk of someone being washed overboard with opportunity for rescue nil. Mr McMillan's relief was immense when Henderson appeared on the bridge to report that they had a jury rig organised. The large spanner, fully extended, had been keyed onto the rudder head stock and the steering was then controlled by tackle operated by winch-drum ends. Sammy Harrison had organised the work in near darkness, a bitter wind full of flying, icy spray, and a slippery deck constantly throwing the struggling men off balance. But they had made it. The time was near enough midnight.

McMillan and Henderson discussed their position, decided on a north-westerly course which should take them well into Colgrave Sound, and the *Earl,* once more under control, lurched and shrugged her way towards Mid Yell. Despite the proximity of the White Hill the first light they glimpsed — with great relief — was a lamp-lit window in the croft-house at Stoal to the south of the lighthouse. Local knowledge paid off as they briefly saw the gleam of surf at Vatsetter Ness, then careful observation of the loom of the land past Lusseter took them into the sheltered Mid Yell voe in the early hours of the Tuesday morning. And Mid Yell folk were astonished to see the familiar vessel lying near enough her customary position as a grey winter day dawned! If they were surprised, the reactions of the Whalsay families whose men went off to the steamer were rather different. The six men had been away from their homes for more than an hour when the steamer blew in the inky night, and it was known that she had come. Although the wind was rising the people in the houses had no real cause for concern; it had blown up before with the men off in the flitboat. No-one troubled to look in the direction of the *Earl* and the small craft. Lights were not seen and the offshore wind carried the sound of the steam whistle away to the north.

By 11 o'clock there were doubts; by midnight reason enough for one household to check with another. Long anxious minutes were spent peering into the black void. Nothing. They began to fear the worst. Had the flitboat reached the *Earl*? Why had the steamer gone? A sleepless night was inevitable and the hours dragged past until a reluctant day revealed great shaggy crests of waves driving under a low, hurrying heaven into a merging obscurity of murk — all devoid of life. The telegraph at Whalsay Post Office relieved the depression with news of the *Earl,* and the six missing men, at Mid Yell. Relief was replaced by a degree of anger when it became known that they had steamed off into the night after abandoning the flitboat and, it seemed, without any communication with the shore. Questions were asked in Whalsay and in the wider sphere of business.

Repercussions followed. The North Company was sued for £150, the alleged value of the lost flitboat, by Hay and Company of Lerwick, her owners. Sheriff Grant presided at the court while agent for the pursuers was Mr Thomas Johnston, and solicitor for the defenders was Mr David Shearer. Events of the night were carefully scrutinised. It was noted that the flitboat had seven oars, two painters, but no sailing gear, no anchor and no spare ropes on board. She could not reasonably have been towed in the conditions. Neither was it practicable for Captain McMillan to release spare anchor and ropes in such weather, with regard to the safety of his own vessel. The crew of the flitboat were not employed by the defenders or their agent in Whalsay, nor was the boat hired by pursuers to defenders. It was maintained that the crew acquiesced to the cutting adrift, and that the boat was not lost through the fault of the defenders' servants. Mr Shearer argued that the defenders' advertisements that they take no responsibility for boatage from their steamers to the shore were, or ought to have been, known to the pursuers. In the light of evidence Sheriff Grant gave decree in favour of the North Company, the defenders, with expenses. Hay and Company immediately questioned the decision. Subsequently Sheriff Principal Pitman gave further judgement and refused the appeal, finding the pursuers liable to costs.

Technically, therefore, Captain McMillan was exonorated, although the affair was a difficult matter of conscience, indicative of the problems posed for those who go down to the sea in ships. If the captain and crew had had some qualms about the affair of the flitboat, they no doubt felt vindicated to some extent when the insurance underwriters, impressed by the resource and seamanship displayed after the rudder quadrant came adrift, decided to give Donald McMillan and his crew an award of £50.

The Up-Helly-A' celebrations had always given scope to creative writing in the islands and it was customary to feature current or recent events in the "bill". Inevitably the Whalsay flitboat incident was a talking point throughout Shetland and at the January, 1925, festival jocular reference was made:

> *"Oh for the days when Scotts[1] was rife,*
> *A body could travel without fear o' life,*
> *Where loaf and saucermeat and aa sic so,*
> *Came oot o' da steamer wi freshness aglow.*
> *These were the days when aa da flit craft,*
> *Wisna left ta be washed up less oars and taft,*
> *Or towed wi da tide,*
> *And cast aff wi a grin,*
> *And a wave o da hand,*
> *And GUT-CHEER[2] ye win[3]. "*

1. Captains Scott of Lerwick and Orkney.
2. Gutcher in Yell.
3. Go.

In 1925 Donald McMillan transferred permanently to the south boats and Willie Spence maintained his celebrated command of the steamer, a man already a prominent figure in physique and reputation, quickly becoming a living legend. The routine work he took comfortably in his stride, but more than any other man he had the confidence to move his ship in weather which might well have confined her to shelter and, of course, the folk reacted well to this type of initiative. Hitherto the *Earl* might or might not appear round a point or headland into such ports as Vidlin, Ollaberry, Ulsta, Uyeasound or Baltasound, yet there seemed now to be more occasions when her black bows showed starkly against a light welter of sea and her whistle steam momentarily white on her funnel as

Spencey announced her arrival on a bad day. So it came about that people generally associated the captain with an adventurous spirit and the utmost co-operation (even although he sometimes sailed when the flitboats could not be worked).

Despite his willingness to go anywhere in the islands anytime, occasionally it would be foolhardy to venture out in winds of force nine or ten which would cause shipping all over the north to run for shelter. Sometimes then there was no steamer when she might have been expected. But Willie had the measure of any criticism and there came his famous remark, which showed his rapport with his ship, when to the question: "Weel Spencey, whit wis wrang dat doo didna come doon yesterday wi her?" he replied: "I wida come, but I coodna get her ta come!". On that occasion the *Earl* had sailed from the North Isles in the face of a south-easter and after several attempts to go beyond Symbister, the skipper had to give second best and lie overnight in the bay at Whalsay.

His unorthodox attitude led to unusual situations which called for quick decisions. There was the case of the fourern (four-oared boat) which came off for the mail at Cullivoe on a gusty day when the north-west wind was too strong for the big flitboat, yet reasonable for a four-oared boat and four men. Magnie Sinclair, the Cullivoe steamer's agent, in charge of the fourern, noticed that wind and sea were rising disconcertingly fast, though in the lee of the steamer there was a little shelter. He thought they might manage back ashore with a struggle against the ever-increasing sudden gale. Despite Willie Spence's plea to remain in security on board, Magnie thought they would go, but Willie had the last word when he gruffly ordered the fourern to be lifted by derrick onto the well-deck and there she, and the four men, remained in safety for a couple of hours until the wind eased and they were allowed to row up into the voe.

The *Earl* could roll in a beam sea, and the heavily built Captain Spence was always loath to accept adverse remarks about the stability or sea-keeping qualities of his ship, always maintaining that any rolling she did was only on account of his pacing from side to side on the bridge!

Like others before him Willie Spence gleaned the particular and personal lore of coastal navigation by word of mouth and gradual experience in working the ship in the infinite variety of flat calm to howling gale, brilliant sunlight to blank fog and black night throughout spring, summer, autumn and exacting winter. It required great sensitivity in bad visibility or darkness. Much was achieved by the "feel" of the ship, while the "scrap" log entered up at regular

intervals and showing timings and courses, was a ready reference. A
typical summer run to Lerwick was noted:

2.53 p.m.	Left Baltasound	Fresh westerly	Misty
3.09	Balta Light	Course SSW	
3.12	South point, Huney	SW x S¾S	
3.24½	Vere Rocks	SW x S¾S	
3.39	Hunts Holm	SW x ¾W	
3.48	Haaf Gruney	SW x W	
3.58	Wedder Holm	W x N	
4.08	Urie Lingey	SW x W½W	
4.15	Sound Gruney	W x S½S	
4.33	Point of Hascosay	SW x ½W	
4.45	Basta Ness	WSW	
4.47½	Kay Holm	W¾N	
4.53	Mid Yell. Stop.		
5.05	Left Mid Yell		
5.07	Geo of Hivdegarth	ESE	
5.11	Ness of Lussetter	SE x ½S	
5.16	Ness of Vatsetter	S x E	
5.22	White Hill	S x W	
5.51	Horse Stack	S x W¾W	
6.21	Swarta Skerry	SW x S¾S	
6.51	Wether Holm		
7.05	Whalsay. Stop.		
7.12	Left Whalsay	Strong north-westerly wind	
7.17	Symbister Ness	SW x ¾S	
7.35	Hoganeap		
7.48	Voder	SW x S¼S	
7.53	Moul of Eswick	SW x ¼S	
8.19	Brethern	SW x S½S	
8.25½	Rova Head		
8.55	Moored Lerwick		

The fluctuations of the climate in autumn did not always permit
such regularity when visibility closed in, even allowing for the precise
minute by minute checks and course changes of the scrap log, and the
rhythmical beat of vibration through the frame of the ship right up to
the tremor of the bridge rail. Such sensitive indications were useful
enough for timing into the narrow north entry at Lerwick from Rova
Head — they said there would be 99 beats from the throb of the screw
if the skipper put his back against the bridge, or a minute and a
quarter, before coming round onto a south-west course between the
Green Head and Bressay. This type of dead reckoning was used

frequently in the North Isles like the occasion when Willie Spence was taking the *Earl* from Unst to Fetlar via Yell for the agricultural show. On a relatively quiet day and with mist on the sea's face he navigated from point to point of land from Uyeasound to Mid Yell, then out past Ba Taing on Hascosay over Colgrave Sound to the south of the long finger of Lamb Hoga which shelters the Wick of Tresta. And with the aid of his watch he judged Rams Ness to a nicety before following the banks towards Houbie where he dropped anchor for the renowned Fetlar show and the concert which followed it, the rigours of the fog forgotten for a few hours.

That the elusive vapour had its risks was illustrated again in another situation when Andy Irvine of the Westing, Unst, then living at Snarravoe, set off for Uyeasound in his open boat on the first of the south tide to collect wood for a roofing repair. He came out from Snarravoe keeping a close watch on the shadowy rocks to port, remarking to Norman Tulloch who accompanied him: "Da *Earl* will be coming from Uyeasound to Cullivoe and I'm no wantin ta meet him in dis bruck; we'd best go in by him" (bruck: 'rubbish'. A reference to the state of the weather). Their boat swung past the tip of Hoga Ness, then Norman said: "Man he's in by wis". "Man", said Andy, "you must be mad!" "The *Earl* is in by wis I tell you; I hear her." "If she's in by wis then she's at risk". They waited anxiously, glaring into the unresponsive fog, thick about them, knowing that the steamer would be barely under way, yet wondering if she might bump them. Their uncertainty ended with the jangle of an engineroom telegraph. And there she was, a few boatlengths distant, her bows touching on the shingle between Hoga Ness and Belmont, a thrash of foam at her counter as she went full astern. Andy and Norman spoke with them briefly and the strength of the south tide keeping the steamer to the east was blamed for the near-stranding.

A skipper could never be sure whether to assess by dead reckoning or play safe, as illustrated by the "scrap" log noted in dense fog, which could bring visibility down to zero at sea level yet with a glimmer of light directly above.

4.30 p.m.	Hove up and proceeded
4.35	Full away. Dense fog.
Board of Trade Regulations in operation	
5.43	Eased down
6.00	Stopped and sounded
6.25	Sounded
6.35	Sounded
6.45	Anchored

Moderate south-westerly. Ebb tide.

Willie Spence may have been a man of independent spirit, bold and adventurous, but he was never foolhardy. If anchoring was the obvious and secure remedy then he would anchor. It was like that as the ship lay motionless in the stillness of a pea-souper, only the plop of water around bows, belting and stern, intermittent conversation on deck, the chink of crockery from below, the subdued hum of a dynamo and an occasional roar of blown-off steam interrupting the blanket of silence. The captain waited on the bridge, forearms and elbows over the canvas dodger, his patience contrasting with some increasingly restless travellers a few feet below him. "Captain," said a female passenger, "when can we go on?" He indicated the fog. "But there's blue sky above." Willie Spence glanced yet again at the opaque and oppressive wall, like cotton wool, looked back at the lady and intoned: "Aye, lady, but yon's no the way we're going!".

The ebullient Spence rejoiced in such jocular remarks, and stories abounded about his spontaneous comments, sometimes blunt rejoinders, to officers, crew, flitboat men and passengers alike. His outgoing personality knew no barriers of class or creed, and he could explode in colourful language should his ire be provoked. And he did not stand on ceremony as he clearly showed from his favourite corner of the bridge on a winter's day of snow and wind at the exposed Brough Lodge at Fetlar. A new Free Kirk minister was arriving at Fetlar, and he had already had a rough passage to Lerwick on the old clipper-bowed first *St. Clair,* which had done little for his confidence. His transference to the *Earl* hardly reassured him and by the time the steamer had anchored at Brough Lodge and he had seen the peerie boat rising and falling alongside the open doors of the well-deck in the near-darkness and snow, he was lingering by the cargo winch, naturally rather uncertain about risking the fragile-looking boat. "Is dat all now?" came from the flitboat. Willie, concerned about an open lee shore, shouted back: "Dat's all, come on git awa frae here!". "Na, but there wis a meenister coming ashore here. Whaurs he?". Spence roared at him: "Tae hell wi' da meenister!". And the gentleman concerned hurried, head down, into the heaving small craft, no doubt wondering into what sort of situation he had arrived, as the flitboat men cast off and Willie rang for full ahead.

Seemingly irreverent reactions by this remarkable character belied a great-hearted man of considerable faith. Yet any strangers around the horse-shoe table in the *Earl's* dining saloon might have suspected the faith. It was customary for the captain to say Grace before every meal in a saloon which had considerable style and atmosphere, with its deep scarlet cushions on the seats, the polished brass surrounds on the portholes and brown photographs of Shetland scenery, like Muness Castle in Unst and Hillswick on the mainland, set between the portholes. So they were seated and Willie raised gnarled fists with the four rings of command on the cuffs of his jacket and began: "For what we are about to receive may the Lord make us . . ." only to be rudely interrupted as something crashed to the deck above him. Without apparently pausing for breath he continued: "Hell and damnation what bloody noise is that!".

The strong reaction must have been repeated at a much later date when Robbie Robertson was mess boy and Jimmy Willie Spence, the steward (like his skipper from Cullivoe, but no relation), had mentioned to Robbie that the bogey funnel from the saloon needed a clean, so this came to mind and as he passed Robbie gave the funnel a swipe with his broom with unexpected and drastic results. The lum was indeed dirty for the caked soot within cascaded down into the well-tended fire below, creating a dense soot-filled acrid smoke which blasted out, permeating the entire saloon, and driving its occupants, including an irate and cursing Willie Spence, out, gasping into the fresh sea air.

Despite her lack of facilities and real comfort the *Earl of Zetland* proved to be a popular vessel with visitors to the islands in the period between the wars. The tourists came in ever-increasing numbers in the twenties and thirties and the crew from captain to mess boy were zealous in their efforts to entertain people from south who were so readily caught by the lore of Shetland. Of course the summer visitors were nothing new. Maybe Sir Walter Scott had been an exceptional tourist back in 1814 when he sailed north with the lighthouse commissioners, a man captivated and inspired by what he saw and experienced, to the extent that he wrote "The Pirate", and thus publicised a hitherto little known area in terms of holidays. However, until the steamers were running regularly and frequently the tourist market was intermittent. By 1883 the North Company were offering sea trips designed specifically for the summer holiday trade and were ambitious enough to list cruises to Norway. In 1886 a cruise to the Hardanger, Sogne and Romsdal Fjords was the first visit to Norwegian waters by any British shipping line. It was a splendid initiative by the North Company with such resounding results that they immediately ordered the ill-fated first *St. Sunniva* as a purely passenger vessel. She boasted three baths and a piano in her up-to-date inventory. Cruises to Scandinavian waters by the *St. Sunniva* and *St. Rognvald* continued until 1908, curiously enough receiving more attention from the company than cruising in the Shetland Islands themselves. In the last decade of the 19th century there were expeditions round Shetland on offer, and visits to Fair Isle and Foula

— nothing new after the pioneering efforts of the Shetland Islands
Steam Navigation Company in the late 1870s.

By 1898 there was an elaborate series of round trips organised.
The North Company brought the *Earl of Zetland* into their scheme.

Enjoying the sunshine during a special trip.

Tourists could switch from her at Ollaberry to make the overland trip, albeit over rough roads, to join the west-side steamer at Hillswick, or spend four successive days, Sunday to Wednesday, on the *Earl* during her North Isles and Yell Sound visits, a fascinating experience for any visitor, with an intimate glimpse of the Shetland way of life.

Much encouraged by the response of the public to the summer programme the shipping company invested in a specially built hotel at Hillswick, first advertised in 1902. It proved to be a signal success, opening up a new era of inclusive holidays. For the summer season of 1909 the *St. Nicholas* carried holidaymakers to the new St. Magnus Hotel where the price for a week was six guineas for the round trip and full board from Leith, and £6 from Aberdeen. The 3/- extra each way for the 100 mile sea trip between Leith and Aberdeen was good value at not much more than a farthing a mile! Alternatively the tourists could voyage from Leith on the *St. Sunniva* on a Wednesday, and Aberdeen on a Thursday to link with the *Earl of Zetland* for the North Isles run over a Friday and Saturday. Since the *Earl* made around a dozen calls the slow, leisured pace and involvement of the ship in each small community offered an excellent relaxation, yet stimulating experience, for those who ventured to the islands.

If this type of holiday inevitably ceased between 1914 and 1919, enough people had savoured its pleasures to ensure that it not only continued, but developed. Although the scale of tourist traffic never justified any frequent special cruises around Shetland by the North Company ships, the regular services in summer provided enough scope for the interested visitor. In fact the *Earl of Zetland* was the only steamer which made regular cruises even although these were of a limited nature. In the issue of 18th July, 1925, "The Shetland Times" announced a one day excursion for the July holiday the next week. The *Earl* would leave Lerwick at 9 a.m. for Whalsay, Burravoe, Mid Yell and Uyeasound. On that occasion over a hundred people went north for the day, well entertained musically by George Stark, the blind fiddler, and his band. They went ashore at Mid Yell to play to an enthusiastic audience. Fiddle music was generally a feature of the *Earl's* annual holiday voyages and by the 1920s had become a tradition. In August, 1927, it was reported: "Wednesday was observed as a general holiday in Lerwick, the particular occasion being the annual regatta and acquatic sports, but with the exceptionally fine weather prevailing, many parties left the town to spend the day in the country and large numbers crossed the harbour to Bressay. For the afternoon, when the sports were completed, the North Company had arranged an excursion trip round Bressay. The trip began at three o'clock and 200 people embarked. As the ship passed Noss the whistle was blown and the startled birds gave a fine display of their numerical strength on the cliffs there. On the return journey the vessel steamed up Dales Voe and arrived back at Victoria Pier just about six o'clock. As one participant remarked: 'The *Earl* left Lerwick at three o'clock on 3rd August on a three hours trip at a fare of three shillings.' And the combination of threes apparently proved a good omen, the trip having been most successful and thoroughly enjoyed by all who went. Captain Spence and his crew did all they could to make the voyage pleasant, while Mr George Stark, the blind fiddler, and his companion Mr Jordan, enlivened the outing with cheery music''. Such music provided an ideal atmosphere to set hearts beating faster, pulses racing and feet dancing or tapping, and the *Earl* became a renowned centre for Shetland fiddle playing. Not surprisingly Willie Spence utilised this in his inimitable manner. Bobby Gray was one of those musicians and Willie would say: "Man Bobby awa doon below tae da galley and we'll have one or two slow airs." And Bobby would play and Spencey would say to strangers to the islands on board, indicating the seals on Lunna Holm as the ship sailed past: "Listen now, listen. You'll hear da seals; see them dere. Now you'll hear them." Whether or not the tourists gave credence to such suggestions was never recorded, but they were sources of great amusement.

In keeping with the unusual, an issue of "The Shetland Times" for April, 1926, had a heading: "New Method of Killing Fish". A short paragraph described how twice during the past winter the *Earl*, commanded by Willie Spence, had dropped anchor and stunned fair size cod which were secured by the small boats which had come out to meet the steamer, and at Houbie, more recently, a third had floated to the surface, struck by the plunging anchor. It had recovered quickly and escaped.

Spencey liked to have strangers aboard his ship partly because he enjoyed leg-pulling. One Monday afternoon, as the vessel entered Skerries, a tourist, pointing to the shore-station for the lighthouse, asked: "What is that building?" and was solemnly informed: "Oh that — that's da hotel". And an hour or so later another query, as the ship neared Whalsay. Yellow weed on the rigs ashore waved in the breeze and the captain was asked: "What crop is that?" He replied: "It's mustard. They sell it to Colman's. That's just a sideline." On another occasion in conversation with a man who asked what kind of people lived in Skerries, Willie said: "Oh terrible people. You know we never lie here overnight." "Why not?" "They'd come aboard and scalp us!" And again one rather misty Sunday afternoon on the passage between Symbister and Burravoe, a tourist discerned the faint shape of land to starboard looking incredibly remote, and asked the captain: "What land is that?" There was a perceptible hesitation while Spencey may have toyed with the idea of saying it was the Norwegian coast before he answered truthfully: "Oh dat's Skerries". But Spence never suffered fools gladly. A youthful and over-confident visitor from "sooth" was travelling with a friend and was plotting the progress up through the islands with the aid of a map. "Yes," he said, "that's the entrance to Yell Sound on the left with Fetlar on the right." The remark was overheard by a Shetlander who pleasantly corrected the young man by saying that Bluemull Sound was to port and off the starboard bow was Uyea Isle. "I don't think so. I have my map here." The visitor was quite dogmatic. The captain was brought in to settle the difference of opinion and confirmed that they were further north than was thought. Still the man maintained: "But my map . . ." Willie Spence cut him short: "For as long as I've known, that has been Bluemull Sound and that has been Uyea Isle, but they might be hell and buggery for all I know!"

Such casual visitors to Shetland disappeared during the winter months although in January each year Up-Helly-A' attracted some from the south. Indeed the holiday season tended to be short and by September tourists diminished in numbers, leaving the ship to work her exacting sailing programme for eight months of the year with native Shetlanders, their goods and animals. Generally the even tenor of island life was uninterrupted, but occasionally the influence of an outside event percolated through. Withdrawal of labour by strike action was in principle anathema to the Shetlander, although in February, 1914, workmen engaged in the extension to the Victoria Pier at Lerwick asked for a pay rise of 1d an hour and settled for ½ d — which brought their lowly rate up to 5 ½ d! And again in 1920 there was a strike in Lerwick which hampered trade and was indicative of the post-war problems of unemployment and inadequate wages which had profound effects all over Britain. The difficulties of the 1920s brought about the great upsurge of industrial unrest culminating in the General Strike of 1926, which was felt in Shetland to be a "brutal and primitive" method of settling the issues. "History would be searched in vain for a parallel to the events which have transpired in Britain since Saturday, 1st May." The country ground to a halt and with the cessation of train services, mails and goods to the islands were abruptly terminated. The *Earl* lay alongside Victoria Pier for the unprecedented period of seven days, her hull still and silent in contrast to the perpetual motion of her normal work load. The massive nine day strike was ended unconditionally by the General

L

Council of the Trade Union Congress and "was received with great satisfaction" in Shetland.

As a contrast to the bitterness of the national scene the northern islands remained magnificently served within the comparative limits imposed by the sea. In October, 1927, the "Orkney Herald," the neighbouring Orkney newspaper, made a point of mentioning the ship which was relieving the *St. Ola* on the Pentland Firth connections: "During the past week the *Earl of Zetland* has been carrying the mails. Captain Spence is to be congratulated on keeping up to time all the week, especially on Saturday when the steamer was 20 minutes under schedule time both inward and outward."

The next month typical selfless service was recognised when John Fraser of Lerwick's St. Olaf Street was presented with an armchair by the crew after 30 years on the North Isles run. Such men as John Fraser were exempt from criticisms of the mail system which cropped up at regular intervals throughout the years and, indeed, received praise for good work within the limitations. Amid a welter of complaints in a letter to "The Shetland Times" in March, 1928, a writer rather grudgingly conceded: "We must admit that the mail service to the North Isles has been regular now for some time. Much praise is due to Captain Spence who has brought the *Earl* many times to Baltasound under unfavourable conditions, darkness and so on, and at the same time not disregarding the good service of the other masters." The letter emphasised the irregularities on Unst in that the *Earl*, having come into Baltasound on a Friday, did not discharge the mail for the Haroldswick Post Office until the Saturday morning, when the horse and gig came down to Baltasound pier with the outgoing mail. It was pointed out that as a result no letter could be answered by return.

Such anomalies were partly the result of slow transport on land — not that the ships epitomised the essence of speed — but by 1928 there was the transition already established from "Shank's pony" and pony and trap, to petrol-fuelled internal combustion engined vehicles. In many respects in mid-April, 1927, when R. W. Tait and Sons asked Peterson the coachbuilder of Market Street in Lerwick to build a bus on a Chevrolet chassis, it was the beginning of the end for the long established sea routes. Yet it was to take another protracted 47 years before the final demise of the consecutive service of the *Earl of Zetland* and her successor of the same name; and the symbolic and sympathetic letter to the North Isles public which appeared in "The Shetland Times" in December, 1974, summed up feelings: "With the termination of a splendid service to our island over the years by the familiar *Earl*, we, the members of the Houbie Flitboat

Committee, and on behalf of our fellow islanders, wish to state publicly that we have many regrets at the close of the service. We sincerely thank all those in the shipping company for a splendid co-operation.'' It was signed by Charles Brown, secretary of the Fetlar Flitboat Committee.

But much was to come in the saga of the ''old'' *Earl* and the 35 year colourful lifespan of the ''new'' *Earl,* a story in itself — the halcyon ''Thirties'', the horrendous early ''Forties'' and historic late ''Forties''.

8

Between the Wars — The Thirties

The decade opened disastrously for the North of Scotland and Orkney and Shetland Steam Navigation Company Ltd. With a coastline so indented and fragmented, Shetland inevitably had its extensive toll of wrecked shipping. Even the *Earl of Zetland* had been involved directly or indirectly on a variety of occasions in rescue or salvage services. Many vessels were foreign but, while local reactions were highly sympathetic, their loss did not strike the same chill at the stomachs of Shetlanders as did the involvement of those ships which sustained a life-line to the islands. The population had been appalled

The Bard of Mousa proved to be her downfall.

at the implications of the disappearance of the *Columbine* in 1886, shocked at the stranding of the second *St. Giles* on Mousa in 1904, and alarmed at the grounding of the *Earl* on Robbie Ramsay's Baa in 1924. Yet no North steamer had actually sunk irretrievably as a result of a collision with the shores of the islands.

When the news broke in Lerwick, with the firing of a maroon at 6 a.m. on the morning of Thursday, 10th April, 1930, that the lovely clipper-bowed *St. Sunniva* had run hard aground on Mousa in thick fog and that her survival was unlikely, the information was met with incredulity. Only a year before she had returned to the direct passage between Aberdeen and Lerwick, having been renovated from the lower decks up at considerable expense over a spell of three months. She had been a centre of interest at Victoria Pier, much admired as a modernised steamer after 21 years on the main route. But now her 864 ton hull was apparently in danger of being swamped by the eager sea.

The ship had left Aberdeen on the Wednesday at 1.25 p.m. on

her scheduled run. Visibility was extremely limited as she came up the east side of the south mainland after three o'clock in the morning in darkness, fog and drizzle. Nine miles beyond Sumburgh Head, and with its east side projecting three miles to seaward from the mainland, lay the island of Mousa, famous for its broch from a long bygone civilisation. Not ordinarily a menacing island with offshore skerries, Mousa was the only projecting land between Buchan Ness and Lerwick. A few degrees off course and a ship could be too far inshore for safety. So it was with the *St. Sunniva.*

The Bard of Mousa at the south-east corner proved to be her downfall. Not that she was moving particularly fast. Her skipper had asked for half speed when he noted the fog horn from Sumburgh Head lighthouse and the ship seemed to be on her normal course in the conditions. It was 3.40 a.m. when her underside was ripped by jagged underwater rocks in a gigantic gash which left the future of the *St. Sunniva* in no doubt. Temporarily she heeled over to port and more than 40 passengers, including women and children, scantily clad, straight from their bunks, came on deck to the roar of escaping steam and the deep mournful wail of the steamer's siren, noises accentuated by the report and swish of signal rockets. They were directed to boats already being swung out in readiness to put them ashore on Mousa.

When information reached Lerwick, the *Earl of Zetland,* accompanied by the fisheries cruiser *Vaila,* immediately sailed for the wreck. Over an hour later both vessels stood by the doomed *St. Sunniva,* now well down by the bows, her passengers forlorn spectators on the massive rock pile of the Bard of Mousa.

Her forward quarters were quickly submerged and inaccessible, but aft, salvage of all moveable objects went ahead with the use of her boats, which had already transferred passengers to the attendant ships. The crew removed her silver and cutlery, gathered linen, some bedding, cushions, rugs, discovered two caged canaries in the saloon, but were unable to salvage the well-used piano, a feature of the *St. Sunniva's* amenities. For several days parts of the stricken vessel were available to salvors, then the wind changed from a northerly direction to south-east, raised a big sea and the now completely abandoned hull began to disintegrate. The *Earl* and *Vaila* had done what they could. Now the water around the wreck became littered with cargo as the contents of the holds were ejected through shattered plates. Sides of beef, flour, oatmeal, barrels of petrol, boxes of butter, margarine and fruit all found their way ashore on Mousa itself, also around the bay at Cunningsburgh. Four sacks of mail drove ashore. One containing parcels had its contents destroyed, but the letter mail proved to be readable when dried out at Lerwick Post Office and was delivered on the Friday and Saturday. However, well over a hundred sacks in the lower fore-hold of the *St. Sunniva* were never recovered; any thoughts of further salvage were abandoned as the steamer finally disappeared from sight, battered into pieces by the relentless sea.

The *St. Sunniva's* tragic demise was a bitter blow to all who had a stake in, and affection for, her. A 43 year career had given yeoman service on the shipping routes, while she had earned the warm interest of a multitude of cruising enthusiasts. Such was her prestige that an immediate decision was taken to replace her by a vessel of the same name and style. Thus early in June, 1931, the *Earl of Zetland,* bedecked by bunting, was one of several vessels to welcome the *St. Sunniva (II)* to Lerwick. It was a triumph of sentiment and beauty over utility as the white yacht-like hull caught the afternoon sunshine in Bressay Sound. She had lingered momentarily and significantly off Mousa where little more than a year ago her namesake had met an unkindly fate, her crew and passengers with bared heads in appropriate gesture in the early summer sunshine.

The first years of the thirties unfolded with little undue drama on the east side of Shetland, although the *Earl* was in attendance at the seemingly inevitable incident, this time involving the motor boat *Islander.* Over the decades efforts had been made by a range of organisations and individuals to usurp the *Earl's* reign. The 52 foot *Islander* was the latest of these. Owned by John S. Ratter, the Cullivoe merchant, she was a large motor boat designed to offer faster passages and to carry passengers and goods between Lerwick and the North Isles, and had come into service in the late spring of 1931. She was scheduled to sail on a Sunday afternoon, on this occasion carrying passengers for Mid Yell, Cullivoe and Uyeasound. She faced a strong north-easterly wind as she came out of the north mouth, heading up between the Green Holm and the Brethern Reef, forcing into a short, steep sea. The *Earl* left Victoria Pier some time later and Willie Spence observed what appeared to be a stationary or drifting boat dangerously close to the notorious Brethern. As the gap narrowed he acknowledged hand signals from the boat, now identified as the *Islander,* clearly in a helpless condition and close enough to the heavy surf around the reef to be caught in the backwash. Spence eased the steamer gradually to within heaving line distance and they put a line over, not a moment too soon. The *Islander,* with a fault in the magneto, was towed back to Lerwick, where 13 passengers transferred to the *Earl* for the voyage to the North Isles.

A year later the *Islander,* like the *St. Sunniva,* came to an untimely end as a result of grounding on Whiting Baa, north of the Ness of

Queyon near Aywick, East Yell. She had called at Cullivoe, Gutcher, Brough Lodge, and both piers at Mid Yell on passage to Lerwick. When approaching Aywick she was met by a small boat with two passengers and their luggage, then moved off for Burravoe. Had there been wind, John Stewart of Mid Yell, the skipper, would have seen the breaking water on the underwater baa, but the smooth surface showed nothing. The big motor boat drove firmly and finally onto the reef at 10.15 a.m., now potentially a write-off as she began to make water. Two other small boats fishing for mackerel, and the Aywick boat, were alongside within minutes to take off passengers and luggage, leaving the skipper and engineer of the *Islander* standing by. Again coincidentally, the steamer going from Mid Yell to Burravoe appeared, hove-to, and embarked the people, including girl fish workers employed by J. Sutherland & Company, Fish Curers.

The *Islander,* a forlorn hulk, held by the rock, was abandoned eventually and an exceptionally low ebb proved to be her undoing. The transverse pressure on her keel broke her back. Within hours she became an unsalvable wreck and was destroyed by heavy seas. It was a sad termination to an optimistic and ambitious idea by John Ratter, although it was also a measure of his firm belief in Shetland, and the North Isles in particular, that he went on to purchase the motor boat *Madge* as a ferry for hire in the North Isles. She was 32½ feet in length, 8 feet in beam and 4 feet in draught, and a 35 h.p. Atlantic engine gave her a speed of ten knots.

Another scheme to compete had indifferent success. A vessel named *Innovator* was commanded by John Henderson, a former mate of the *Earl*. That she had her problems was illustrated by a newspaper report of January, 1933. In a prolonged gale the *Earl*, bound for Lerwick, had to take shelter at Mossbank and could not move until the next day. The same storm affected the *Innovator*. The report highlighted her problem: "The local passenger and cargo boat *Innovator,* skipper John Henderson, left Lerwick on Monday for Whalsay to take a consignment of fish to be sent south by the *St. Rognvald.* On the way north it was found necessary to cut adrift the small boat which was being towed by the *Innovator*. About 200 boxes of fish were taken on board at Symbister and the *Innovator* had a rough trip to Lerwick, a good deal of anxiety being felt for the safety of the boat which, however, weathered the gale well."

Such depressions in the weather were a reflection of the prevailing economic climate in the early 30s. The herring fishing had gone into recession as a result of the decline in the market in central and eastern Europe, and fishing as a Shetland industry became subordinate to agriculture, textiles and transport. Shetland could not expect to escape the general world economic depression. Also, there was a scarcity of herring, particularly in 1933, which reduced the number of outlying stations and personnel to staff these. The old steamer no longer carried the great complement of gutters, curers and coopers of another era, and her biggest passenger groups were confined to local holiday trips. But in many respects these were halcyon days for the ship because there was boisterous fun and wholesale enjoyment in which she seemed to revel. The tripping days of pre-World War II focused on the recreational interests of the islands in a variety of ways.

In May, 1932, for the Victoria Day excursion the *Earl* was billed to leave at 9 a.m. for Whalsay, Burravoe, Mid Yell, Fetlar and Uyeasound with the Lerwick Brass Band on board to play selections during the trip. The Lerwick competitors of the Thule Model Yacht Club, accompanied by their sailing craft, were to travel on the steamer to Burravoe where a regatta would be held by the Burravoe Model Yachting Club. The ideas were imaginative, but the weather vetoed that particular Victoria Day event! The Fetlar Agricultural Show coincided with Lerwick Regatta Day in August, 1933. Instead of the regular annual cruise round Bressay the steamer transported judges, officials and spectators north to Fetlar at the crack of dawn, leaving Lerwick at 3 a.m. A couple of years later, in July, 1935, Willie Spence took the *Earl* and about 180 passengers round Bressay, with a call at Noss, where the raucous seabirds drowned out the sound of the combined George Stark's and Radio Jollies bands. So successful was the trip that an identical outing was held a fortnight later, a feature being the large number of visitors to Shetland taking part. The aged vessel could certainly provide the atmosphere, particularly when she sailed in the full regalia of her dressed-overall bunting. Of course Spencey added his own individual brand of colour whether on festive occasion or routine voyage. C. A. Manson of Lerwick Post Office staff contributed an article to the Post Office magazine in 1936: "I left the Head Office at 10 a.m. on Friday and boarded the mail steamer *Earl of Zetland.* Captain Spence's good seamanship and geniality are well known as great assets to his passengers with a knowing twinkle to the unwary landlubber. 'Sailing in a fog would be dangerous here' remarks a timid tripper. 'Yes,' says the captain reassuringly, 'but we carry large shovels with which to clear a passageway when it becomes too thick.' Then someone spots the log-line. 'Oh that. It's for catching fish.' These and similar asides are punctuated by his business-like 'Nor'west by west half west' to the helmsman . . ."

Since its opening in June, 1886, the Victoria Pier had been a priceless asset in bringing shipping into the heart of the Shetland capital and the *Earl of Zetland* was a feature in her berth on the north side, a pulse of island life and trade. Lerwick folk found the pier splendidly central and it was fashionable to observe the steamer movements. Perhaps the frequency of use accounted for a certain notoriety due to people falling into the sea, and in the early part of the century the Lerwick Harbour Trustees, motivated by a letter from the Home Office, had guard chains fitted. The pier structure was slightly enlarged and changes were made to the north and south, particularly with the construction of the small boat harbour in the second decade of the twentieth century. Suggestions were made in 1923 about a tapered enlargement from base to point, but the Alexandra Wharf to the north of Victoria Pier was in poor state and funds were drained into repairs instead. The issue was raised again in 1930 and Captain Spence aired his views in public: ". . . I observed in the local press . . . a grant had been obtained for the purpose of widening the Victoria Pier, 80 feet at the base tapering to 20 feet at the point . . . I understand that the enlargement is to be done on the north side of the pier, and if so the direction of that side would be materially altered. I would respectfully suggest for your consideration that whatever widening is intended should be done parallel with the existing pier, which is at a well placed angle and convenient for going alongside in every kind of weather. During the 11 years that I have been Master of the *Earl of Zetland* I have never had any difficulty in getting alongside, and the pier at its present angle is most suitable for north-east and south-south-west gales which cause the heaviest seas at the pier. If the angle of the pier is altered as proposed the north side would be untenable with a north-east gale as a vessel would be lying broadside on to sea and wind . . .''

Undeniably extension was needed. The Victoria Pier was central to all Shetland, with the south side accepting incoming cargo and passengers, and the north side acting as clearing and transit area for the North Isles. The big shed in the centre of the pier directly opposite the berthing areas left little space between its corrugated iron walls and the side of the ship, and on steamer's day the milling throng would be tightly packed, the steam of humanity rounding such obstacles as the new-fangled cars, the *Earl's* bunker coal and enormous piles of stacked boxes, bales and barrels.

But the congestion continued and Willie Spence did not have to worry about north-east gales because nothing more was done due to lack of funds of the Harbour Trust, while the Scottish Home Department never seemed more than lukewarm. That the Victoria Pier was important historically and practically showed on 23rd June,

1936, when its 50th anniversary was celebrated. The second *St. Sunniva* and the *Earl of Zetland* were dressed overall, the *Earl* having had the privilege and distinction of being the first ship to berth at the Victoria Pier half a century before.

At length, by 1937, the Harbour Trust's finances allowed plans to be renewed for an enlargement, although by that time the days of the old *Earl* in Shetland waters were numbered. A new ship was on the drawing board. The pier project reached the tendering stage and a price of £36,632 was agreed. In fact the Lerwick Harbour Order was not confirmed until 29th September, 1939, by which time Britain was in the throes of war, and the work was out of the question. Thus the protracted query of the Victoria Pier dragged on. Captain Willie Spence never saw it resolved.

Timetabling of the domestic routes of the North Isles steamer changed little. In December, 1930: "The *Earl of Zetland* or other steamer will sail as under, weather, etc. permitting, liberty being reserved to alter the arrangements as the necessities of the trade or any emergency may require. North Isles passage from Lerwick every Monday morning early to Symbister, Whalsay, Mid Yell and Uyeasound, returning from Uyeasound same day at 8 a.m., calling at Cullivoe, Brough Lodge, Mid Yell and Symbister. From Lerwick every Thursday at 9 a.m. to Symbister, Skerries, Mid Yell, Brough Lodge, Uyeasound and Baltasound. From Baltasound every Friday at 6 a.m. calling at Uyeasound, Cullivoe, Gutcher, Mid Yell and Symbister. Yell Sound Passage from Lerwick on Tuesdays, 9th and 23rd inst. at 7 a.m. to Symbister, Houbie, Burravoe, Mossbank, also Sullom when required, Lochend and Ollaberry. From North Roe on Wednesdays 10th and 24th inst. at 7 a.m. to Lerwick calling at West Sandwick, Ulsta, Burravoe, Vidlin and Symbister.

Fares from Lerwick:	1st Cabin		2nd Cabin	
	Single	Return	Single	Return
To Uyeasound and Baltasound, Unst	12/-	20/-	7/6	13/6
To Yell Ports and Fetlar	10/-	17/-	6/6	11/6
To Mainland Ports, Burravoe and Skerries	8/-	14/6	6/6	10/-
To Whalsay	6/-	10/6	4/6	7/6
Between Intermediate Ports	5/-	8/6	4/-	6/6

The routine advert in March, 1934, showed the same sailings although the *Earl* was due to call at Bastavoe on the 8th and 22nd inst., a destination omitted from the December, 1930, advert. Astonishingly, fares had been reduced. First Cabin single from

Lerwick to Uyeasound or Baltasound cost 1/6 less, as did the return to Burravoe or Skerries. Other fares were correspondingly less. Amazingly the cheaper fares structure was maintained right through to the war years, although the timetable differed. In March, 1938: "North Isles Passage: from Lerwick every Sunday afternoon to Whalsay, Mid Yell and Uyeasound, returning from Uyeasound on Monday at 7 a.m., calling at Cullivoe, Brough Lodge, Mid Yell, Skerries and Whalsay. From Lerwick every Tuesday at 8 a.m. to Whalsay, Mid Yell and Uyeasound, returning from Uyeasound at 8 a.m. on Wednesday calling at Brough Lodge, Mid Yell and Whalsay, also Houbie on 9th and 23rd inst.

"From Lerwick every Thursday at 9 a.m. to Whalsay, Burravoe, Mid Yell, Brough Lodge, Uyeasound and Baltasound. From Baltasound every Friday at 6 a.m. calling at Uyeasound, Cullivoe, Gutcher, Mid Yell and Burravoe and Whalsay, also Bastavoe on 4th and 18th inst. Yell Sound Passage, from Lerwick on Saturdays 5th and 19th inst. to Ollaberry, returning same day and calling at West Sandwick and Ulsta, also Mossbank and Vidlin when required."

But a rival of real consequence was apparent in other advertising in the Shetland Press. "Overland Route to North Isles. Ganson's passenger service to and from the North Isles every Wednesday will continue to operate as follows: Leave Lerwick 6.45 a.m. Leave Mossbank 10.15 a.m. on arrival of motor boat from Yell. Travel by Ganson's — the Pioneer Overland Service."

The steamer had triumphantly overcome other serious, and more direct, rivalry but the "Overland" was a more insidious infiltration of her domain. In the long term there could be only one winner. History was to unfold in such a way that the old *Earl* escaped the ignominy of being completely phased out, and it took until 1974 before the sea road to the isles went into oblivion when her successor, the second *Earl,* vanished from the Shetland scene.

It was the growing challenge of the 'overland' which forced the hand of the North Company to institute the Tuesday-Wednesday sailing to connect with the direct boat to and from Lerwick. Reputedly this idea of enterprise came from the shrewd David Gray, the long-serving purser, who was so importunate that in the end he was told that he could take the steamer to Uyeasound or anywhere else on a Tuesday afternoon! The slightly built Davie was an energetic personality, his overalled figure a familiar sight to passengers and flitboat men as he cheerfully dispensed tickets at his office below the bridge or climbed down into the semi-darkness of the hold armed with his wad of invoices and orders to sort out cargo at each port. By the 1930s Tom Gifford of Bressay was mate, having succeeded John Henderson, and took over as Master when Willie Spence retired in 1937. It was nothing new for Shetlanders, brothers, to crew in the same ship, a feature which was a concern during two wars because of loss risk, and Tom Gifford served on the *Earl* together with his brother Laurence. This doubtless played its part in giving the steamer's complement that stability and continuity so characteristic of the extended years of her service in Shetland. Another long serving crewman was Robert Gray from Baltasound. He joined the ship at the age of 16 as a cabin boy, progressing to cook and finally chief steward during the Second World War. His daughter, Margaret, has described succinctly the essence of the meaning of working on the old vessel: " . . . the *Earl* always seemed part of my life and I have many happy memories of her. My father loved being on the *Earl,* although it was hard with long hours. He was always away more times than he was at home, even sleeping on board for an early start to the isles the following morning. We lived in Lerwick and my sisters and I made regular trips to Baltasound for our holidays. My father, then cook, was usually busy in the galley making huge roasts. We would go in there because it was lovely and warm. When the roasts were ready he carried them to the pantry which was some distance from the galley. It was also used as a post box. Before each trip to the islands people left letters and parcels there. The seas could be very rough and when I felt seasick my father would let me sleep in his bunk, which was situated at the back of the pantry. Also in bad weather when lady passengers were unable to get out of their bunks to make up their babies' feeds, he would fill the bottles at the galley and take them to the children. Of course the mothers were most grateful and many were the knitted socks and scarves he received each Christmas . . ."

The galley was a focal point with its warmth on a blustery winter's day, and was in some respects conveniently placed immediately behind the purser's office and the animal stalls, which were aft of the cargo hatch. It was the width of the engine and boiler room casing, a narrow space with the cooking range on the for'ard wall, with a door at each side originally. With the advent of the internal combustion engine in the islands, the deck space on the starboard side was utilised for the storage of petrol, oil and paraffin drums and, in the interests of fire-safety, the door was sealed off, leaving access from the port side only, aft of the animal stalls. Inevitably the handling of ponies, sheep and cattle, the bigger animals hoisted on board each with a canvas sling under its belly, brought moments of excitement. It was not unknown for an animal to

A fine view of the *Earl* surging along during a routine Yell Sound trip in the Thirties.

A special occasion. Dressed overall, she looks well in fine summer weather with a large crowd on board, all set for a trip round Bressay.

Mrs A. Gifford

An amused Colin Henry stands below the crowded bridge. Captain Spence takes care of a young passenger.   *Mrs D. Mann*

A jam-packed bridge. Tom and Agnes Gifford on the right. Willie Spence holds a rather disinterested young passenger.   *Mrs A. Gifford*

end up in the sea. However, there was one big stirk which chose the galley in its wild-eyed very physical panic. The galley was empty at the time, the door open and a possible release from the animal's confinement. Before it could be mastered, the stirk plunged through the doorway to find itself firmly wedged, held by its rib cage between range and after wall. A bruising battle ensued. Flailing rear legs and swishing tail, behind the high storm-step into the galley, made formidable weapons in the very confined space. Long minutes of scrambled activity with ropes subdued the creature, but not before many a bump and scrape to the crew.

With animals central to life and the economy of the islands, the steamer was in constant use as a conveyance and not surprisingly livestock featured in unusual ways. The more domesticated creatures like ponies and dogs travelled in some comfort, each important to the crofter for everyday existence. Shetland ponies have from time immemorial been distinguished internationally, so they were accorded that little extra care in transport, although it was customary to swim them ashore. A stallion used amid the islands for breeding purposes was quite familiar with the sea! Dogs were frequent travellers, generally tethered in the deck space in the fo'c'sle where they were out of the way and in safety. This was not always the case, however, because even in Willie Spence's time they had not forgotten about old Peter Clark's dog at the beginning of the century. The story was oft repeated. Peter was an Unst man who sold tea on that island and on Yell, so he was called "T.P." as a result, and was a character forby. Often he used the *Earl* from a port such as Uyeasound, to Cullivoe. About the turn of the century the ship was still rather primitive in fittings and the anchor chains emerged from the hawse holes on the foredeck and hung free and without any guard in the gloom of the fo'c'sle before entering the chain locker below. Peter had come aboard with his dog, happened to be in the fo'c'sle as the *Earl* got under way for the short run between ports, had looked for a convenient projection on which to tie up the animal, and had hitched it to a link in the chain. Peter Johnson, then skipper, had ordered an anchor down to await the flitboat, sadly the anchor chain to which the dog was attached. Instantaneously the unfortunate creature shot skywards to an untimely end. But the passing of old Peter's dog was the reason for the chains being boxed in — it's an ill wind that blows nobody good!

Yet it was an ill wind with no good to anyone on another occasion. A Yell woman had a vivid dream in which the ship in some miraculous way contrived to reach the porch on the croft-house in which she lived, far up from the shore. A black calf was unloaded and entered the ''but'' room. The next day the woman learned that her eldest sister had died in England at what must have been the same time as the black calf appeared in her sleep. If the calf achieved the impossible in the dream by ascending the hill slopes in the *Earl,* Charles Sandison of Baltasound recalled the reality of a whale with aspirations of becoming airborne in Yell Sound. Of course in the 1920s and 1930s one could hardly spend a whole day at sea without seeing a whale, and they were noted frequently from the steamer. Sandison was on deck as she headed south to Lerwick. Crossing the mouth of the sound the surface of the sea was broken in a great burst of white foam about a quarter of a mile away to starboard. A massive dark shape heaved upwards until almost clear of the welter of water, then, after a second hanging in the air, it collapsed in an explosion of spray, the noise of which brought passengers who were having lunch below, hurrying on deck. There remained only the disturbed surface of the sea to mark where an enormous rorqual whale had emerged. They lingered on deck hoping for a repeat performance, but the rorqual never re-appeared, perhaps tired after its prodigious leap. Since this species of whale is 60-90 feet in length the achievement required to lift it clear of the water left a sense of wonderment at the timing, power and thrust of body and tail in lifting it into virtually full view.

If the whale had successfully disturbed the placid waters of the sea, attempts made over the years to disturb the complacency shown in the postal arrangements had met with little success. Even in the late thirties proposals were being put forward to bring about some kind of improvement. While Whalsay and Fetlar District Councils accepted the existing service, a lengthy letter from Unst was concerned that the present steamer service to Shetland and the North Isles was no better than it had been 40 years earlier. A petition from Unst sought to increase the mail service by the overland route, but the Whalsay and Fetlar communities feared that this might prejudice the very existence of the *Earl.* The Unst council mentioned that mail left Aberdeen on Friday, reached Lerwick on Saturday and was not delivered in the island until Monday. Also mail leaving Lerwick Post Office on Friday before 9 a.m. reached Uyeasound too late for same-day delivery at the north end of the island. If the steamer left Victoria Pier at the posted time of 9 a.m. perhaps same-day delivery would be possible, yet invariably at departure time the *Earl's* derrick was still swinging to and fro from quay to forehold, taking on goods and mails from the steamer from Aberdeen. Departure from Lerwick could be any time from 9.30 till 10.30 a.m. or even later. The Unst council wondered why unloading of the vessel from south could not start

M

Willie Leask, a Lerwick docker known as "Whalsay Willie" strikes a pose with a fiddle on the foredeck. By his right elbow is Wilfie Goudie. Third from his left is Nana Moffat.

Mrs A. Gifford

A group of passengers seated beside the engine room skylight. Included top right are left, Professor Gordon Donaldson who wrote "Northwards by Sea" and right, Major H. W. L. Hunter of Unst who spoke highly of the *Earl*.

G. Donaldson

There were three flit-boats in Mid Yell. Sail was popular from Linkshouse. Note the small Austin car on the after hatch.

B. Spence

A bright morning at Out Skerries. Awaiting the flit-boat. Tom Gifford, then Mate, and Erty Moar see the anchor down.

Mrs A. Gifford

much earlier in the morning. There was no satisfactory answer to the North Isles in the autumn of 1936, and a couple of months later the weather succeeded in drastically disrupting communications, illustrating the vulnerability of sea mail. The sequence of gales was unprecedented. From 1st December until the 26th, 32 gales had been recorded at the Lerwick Observatory, a gale being a wind velocity of 39 m.p.h. and upwards. That month there were 17 days of gales, followed by 15 in January, with the storm of the 23rd of the month generating the heaviest seas for years. Even in March, gales, accompanied by sleet and snow, created havoc not only in Shetland, but south in Scotland, England and Ireland. It was an incredible winter, and the one preceding the retiral of Captain William Spence, who must have thought that the weather was making vast efforts to have the last word. Little wonder, perhaps, because on one occasion the valiant Spence had uttered another famous remark in which he described gale conditions as "a stiff breeze". With wind forces up 95 miles an hour, Mother Nature made every effort to call his bluff. There were varied situations over the long drawn-out months. The steamer left Victoria Pier one morning, reached the north harbour, was forced to anchor, then came back to berth in the afternoon. A Russian vessel, the *Ilman,* of 4,000 tons, was reported by Norwegian radio, through Wick to Lerwick, as slowly steaming towards Shetland with damaged steering gear. An S.O.S. indicated that she was about 120 miles east-south-east from the Bard of Bressay and she requested contact by the lifeboat. It was considered that the distance was too great for the small lifeboat based at Lerwick, thus Captain Spence was approached, the *Earl* being the only other vessel available immediately. He declined on the same grounds of distance and heavy seas. It happened that the *Ilman* survived the battering and sailed on independently. Even the berths in Lerwick were dangerous during these protracted gales. The *St. Catherine* had her upper belting on the starboard quarter badly damaged in the surge against the wall of Victoria Pier. On the same day, Saturday, 23rd January, 1937, the *Earl* had struggled from Lerwick to the North Isles. On the return she reached Whalsay at 1 a.m. on the Sunday, hove-to in the lee of the land, then in the grey daylight of Monday, Willie Spence took her into better shelter at Vidlin. At 10 a.m. on the Tuesday another effort was made to sail for Lerwick, only to be thwarted by the shipping of a series of enormous seas. On returning to Vidlin a boat was launched and some passengers, including a stretcher case, were landed to be taken for the rough run to Lerwick by car. Another abortive attempt to sail was made, denied by seas which threatened to swamp the old ship. Eventually some moderation in the wind force allowed her to move out and on to Lerwick. It had taken from Sunday until Wednesday noon. A stiff breeze indeed!

If the dauntless Spence had been posed insurmountable obstacles in wind-velocity and wave-size over that protracted period there remained occasions, times without number, when he had won through to an isolated community and earned the gratitude and goodwill of the folk. This was abundantly demonstrated during a sequence of events in the months of April and May, 1937. They marked the retirement of a man who had upheld and enhanced all that seamanship stands for, a man whose magnetic disposition gave a charisma to his exacting daily toil. North Isles people met together in crowds in the Mid Yell public hall on 19th May to pay tribute and to say farewell to a Shetlander of presence. Each of the North Isles was represented officially by a notable member of the community. Appropriately it was Dr Harry Taylor, who had given a lifetime's service as a general practitioner on the island of Yell, having come to Shetland in 1890, who gave the initial speech. He spoke of Willie Spence as a pilot of the dear old *Earl of Zetland* and how those who knew the physical conformation of the coast between Lerwick and Baltasound — studded as it was with skerries, baas and perhaps sunken rocks, which may never have been charted — the erratic tides, climatic conditions, cruel winter gales, darkness, flurries of snow, dense fogs — only they could realise the heavy responsibility and frequent mental strain which rested on the skippers. Robert Smith of Mid Yell, a native Shetlander, confirmed Spence's capabilities. The *Earl* had come round to Gossabrough in south-east Yell for a special call on her return Yell Sound trip to Lerwick. It happened that a severe south-south-east gale was blowing, but weather or no weather the steamer had come. The flitboat men were in two minds about putting off, yet, maybe influenced by Willie Spence's presence, they went, shipping water from time to time to Smith's discomfiture. He said: ''The worst was yet to come! Already under way two hours and 20 minutes, I noticed the Skerries o' Neapoback abeam to starboard and we appeared to make no headway. I mentioned it to Captain Spence and asked him if he thought we should ever reach Lerwick. 'Of course we will,' he replied. 'That's nothing. I'll keep her head to the wind a bit longer, and in a quarter of an hour there will be the south tide and I'll lay her head to the Skerries and get the tide under her bow.' We did arrive at Lerwick 8½ hours from leaving Gossabrough! I mention that as an example of the prowess and skill of Captain Spence. In fact he seemed to be in his glory when fighting the elements . . .'' Peter Sandison, the Cullivoe merchant, augmented this with the tale of Gibbie and

Ursula, who had had their supper. It was a fierce gale from the south, there was just the heel of a loaf left on the table and Gibbie held it out to the dog. "Boy," said Ursula, "dunna gie yon to da dug, for we hae little ida hoose, and du kens da *Earl'll* never come wi dis wadder." "Haud de tongue, due dusna keen Wullie Spence for as shore as daylight come da morn doo'll hear da whistle o' da *Earl* ida voe. Da Lord forbid he ever blaws a gale dat wid keep him frae comin nort. He kens we can get a corn plaster or an aspirin, or a mixture for wir stamics, fur we hae guid doctors, but he kens dat's poor feed for an empty stamic, and he will see that we get wir daily needs." And Gibbie and Ursula were not be disappointed, nor to be denied. The *Earl* came.

The Rev. William Carson from Fetlar confessed that his knowledge of seamanship was limited to two nautical maneouvres — that of splicing the mainbrace and that of yelling louder than usual for the steward for help in saving the saloon carpet from disaster when the *Earl* behaved skittishly, as she often did in spite of advanced years! But he bore witness to Captain Spence's skill in handling his vessel off the open beaches of Fetlar, offering maximum shelter to the flitboats, and consistency of service. William Carson proffered only one criticism — Willie Spence was not a Fetlar man. He had, however, been reminded that the captain had been born in the Parish of Fetlar and North Yell. There was a Scotsman who attributed every famous person to Scotland until an Englishman countered: "At any rate you cannot claim Shakespeare, the greatest of them all." "Maybe," said the Scot, "but he was good enough to be Scottish." And accordingly the minister felt that they could lay claim to William Spence. What he could do, and would do, was confer upon him the Freedom of Fetlar, "so that at any time you desire to boast, you can tell the world that you are a Fetlar man." A gift from Fetlar consisted of a wallet of Treasury notes, and Unst, Whalsay and Yell followed suit. Fittingly the Yell wallet bore the inscription: "Presented to Captain William Spence by the people of Yell in appreciation of his faithful and efficient service while Captain of the ss *Earl of Zetland,* 19th May, 1937."

Not surprisingly Captain William Spence was taken aback by the depth of feeling at the presentation and resounding rendering of "For He's a Jolly Good Fellow". "I have in my time weathered many a gale and braved many a tempest, but I must confess that speech-making fairly puts the wind up me. Words fail me to express my appreciation of your reception tonight, and while I am grateful to you all, and am deeply touched by the remarks of the various speakers, I must say I never expected such handsome presentations . . . I have always tried to do my best and while, as you all know, the *Earl* is no race horse, I managed to get her to crawl along somehow . . . I never lay on my oars whenever I could go and I think I can add that I never disgraced the Shetlander as a seaman. They have been bragging about me, but you don't need to believe them . . ." The Captain added his regard for the gifts from Whalsay and Unst folk given on their behalf by Dr Gilchrist and Mr John Stewart respectively, the former the incumbent Yell doctor, who mentioned that notorious strip of water between Whalsay and Lerwick and how Mr Carson's remark reminded him of the traveller who was informed by the steward that he could not be sick in the cabin, to which the victim replied, suddenly overcome, "Can't I?" John Stewart reminded the audience that Captain Spence took charge of the ship when Unst people were almost in despair. "Time and again we waited for the appearance of the well-known black funnel, but often we were not even favoured by the sight of the smoke. The *Earl* is now a very old ship and she seems to have had a charmed life . . . She still survives and as far we can judge she will still be going when we are all dead! In fact she has gone over the ground so often that one would imagine she could find the way herself!"

William Spence's brief response to near adulation was given with characteristic modesty and self-effacement, a man embarrassed by attention and affected by his own depth of emotion in realising his commitment to his calling and the prospect of giving up the rich and rewarding sea-life.

At other earlier presentations much credit was given. David Gray, the purser, proffered the gift from the crew. "Shipmates, I am honoured in making this presentation to Captain Spence and I feel that I should say a little in his praise. I have known him as long as I've known the company's steamer. As mate he was most energetic, always ready to help on all occasions. Then he gave up command of larger ships to take over the North Isles trade which was at that time very irregular. Since then he has made the best use of the material at his disposal . . . This inscribed ebony stick is a remembrance from the crew. I hope you will be able over a number of years to sport it and never require to lean on it. This is my honest wish and I am sure the wish of us all . . ." The Lerwick office staff added their appreciation when Alexander Stephen, the agent, handed over an engraved dressing case. A fourth gift was accepted from the Post Office in Shetland and given by the Postmaster in Lerwick, Mr F. C. Young.

Thus William Spence, of Cullivoe, departed formally from the island shipping scene, to be replaced by his mate, Thomas Gifford, whose captaincy of the old steamer was to be co-incidentally brief, lasting two years, although his service to the North Company was rewarded when in later stages of his career he was promoted to Commodore of the North Company fleet.

A week after his appointment, Tom Gifford took his ship to the southern approaches of Bressay Sound to bid welcome to the second *St. Clair,* a product of the Hall, Russell yard at Aberdeen and a coal-burning vessel of 1,637 tons. Dressed overall, the two steamers approached Lerwick in brilliant sunshine, watched by great numbers of the populace, the old *Earl* perhaps looking her years when set beside the handsome buff-funnelled *St. Clair.* Yet a moment of joy and cause for rejoicing in another improvement in communication.

Changes in personnel. Changes in ships. Time and progress brought these about, but routine had to go on. Throughout the summer of 1937 Captain Gifford coaxed the ageing *Earl of Zetland* round her oft-traversed route, and her existence continued to be punctuated by the unexpected occurrence or incident. At the end of May a Norwegian fishing boat, the *Alesund,* en route to Iceland, called at Lerwick for water. Her skipper misjudged distance and speed and despite the anticipated braking power of a hawser attached to a bollard on the Victoria Pier, he allowed his bow to strike the *Earl* a resounding thump on her stern. The hawser had snapped, and the *Alesund* had enough way on her to extensively damage the steamer's stern moulding.

In August, Tom Gifford supervised the immensely popular round Bressay trip for a hundred passengers who were rather more relaxed than the survivors of a Norwegian trawler who had come south on the *Earl* to Lerwick from Baltasound the previous week. They told an extraordinary story. The *Aldebaran,* a 55 ton steam trawler, was sailing in a position roughly 50 miles north-north-west of Muckle Flugga, the most northerly lighthouse in Britain. Laden with her cargo of barrels and salt, she was rising well to moderate seas and seemed stable enough. Not one of her 16 crew could have given a thought to what happened. A freak wave may have been responsible. Her skipper, Jakobson, confirmed later that in his opinion the cargo, including the bunker coal, was correctly stowed and could not have shifted. But one moment the *Aldebaran* was stable, the next she was laid down to port on her beam ends, 12 of her 16 crew being rudely shaken in their bunks. The ship slowly righted herself, staggered momentarily and immediately fell on her starboard side, struck by another sea. This time her rails went under and she began to fill. The men below had moved fast. Scantily clad as they were, before the trawler had come back onto an even keel following the first list, they were on the angling deck as she began to go the other way. As they struggled to loose the port boat, the other one already submerged, they saw the remarkable sight of the chief engineer emerging from the engine room skylight having literally risen with the inrush of water! The boat rested on the *Aldebaran's* side as all 16 crew, mostly dressed in only singlet and trousers, scrambled aboard, only in the nick of time as they launched the boat as if from a sloping beach. A couple of boatlengths away a roar and surge of sea indicated the end as the trawler was swallowed up. Three minutes had elapsed since the first warning, according to the story recorded, not even enough time to radio for assistance. The 16 contrived to keep the boat's head to the sea for another 18 hours before they were sighted by a Swedish motor vessel and landed at Baltasound. Undeniably the *Aldebaran's* crew had had a narrow escape from death by drowning, an ever-present risk for those who go to sea. Even so, 60 years of voyaging, year after year of close proximity to the might and treachery of the ocean, and no loss of life could be attributed to the old *Earl*. It was a proud, though unsung, record. If, then, the sea could not claim a victim directly, nor the ship be responsible, there was nonetheless a great sadness when William Carson, the Fetlar minister and a very frequent traveller, died on board in September, 1937. A man of wide interests and generous by nature, he had come to Lerwick for an education committee meeting and was returning to Fetlar from the Queen's Hotel where he had stayed.

One or two people thought that Mr Carson looked unwell as he came over the gangway onto the steamer. Moments later he staggered and was helped below to the saloon, where Robbie Gray attempted to make him comfortable with rugs, while the minister insisted that he would be all right in a few minutes. Captain Gifford went below when they were clear of the north entrance. He found William Carson in deteriorating condition and slipping from consciousness. An hour later at Symbister, Dr Orr, the Whalsay physician, was summoned by megaphone, but by the time he boarded the steamer from a small boat, the patient had gone to join his Maker, dead from a cerebral haemorrhage. Despite a lack of precedent, the *Earl* immediately retraced her course to Victoria Pier where the body was transferred to the mortuary at the Gilbert Bain Hospital. The following Sunday William Carson was taken to Fetlar on the old ship for burial in the soil of the island of his ministry, known as "the Garden of Shetland".

9

The Beginning of the End

From Christmas, 1937, the womenfolk who came to the shop at Burravoe frequently found that expected goods from the *Earl's* scheduled call were not there. This meant a return, perhaps over several weary foot-slogged miles, the next day. It happened too often, with the result that Bertha Lethbridge, for long a school teacher in Burravoe and public spirited, mentioned in a letter to the press the inconvenience if the steamer could not linger long enough to unload the essential items of food, clothes, household requisites, paraffin and livestock. Much of the cargo from Lerwick was perishable and if the

Two *Earls* at Victoria Pier.

ship happened to bypass Burravoe and landed goods at Mid Yell, 8 miles to the north, it was necessary for the merchant to wire the steamer's purser to ensure that vulnerable items were put ashore, then a lorry had to be hired to bring these to Burravoe. Additional expense for travellers was another factor.

It could be assumed that the non-appearance of the steamer on occasion was a reflection of the development of roads and vehicles — by 1937 an integral part of the Shetland scene. Eight short miles by lorry would not seem an undue inconvenience in the eyes of the *Earl's* men, when other priorities had to take precedence. Curiously enough the inconsistency of the visits to Burravoe was a corollary to the pressures induced by the Tuesday-Wednesday sailing to the isles on the instigation of David Gray, itself a result of the competition from the overland route.

Another comment came in the form of a letter to the editor of "The Shetland Times" in February, 1938. "From my first remembrance of the *Earl* we, the North Yell people, were

accommodated once a week, but now the arrangements are every
Sunday to Mid Yell only, and North and South Yell passengers have
to find their own conveyance as the small buses do not run until
Monday morning. I cannot understand why the manager of the
(North) Company should change a service which has hitherto been
satisfactory and been run to connect with their mail service through
the whole of Yell and Unst. If the manager would look at the advert
put out by the overland service he would observe that buses and ferry
boats connect with each other so that passengers have neither delay
nor expense. In the interests of both North and South Yell, I hope
the manager will see that the *Earl's* sailings are changed to Monday or
an arrangement made with the Post Office to send their mail buses to
connect with the steamer every Sunday.''

Timetabling for March, 1938, confirmed the reasons for the
criticism. The ship left Lerwick on the Sunday for Whalsay, Mid Yell
and Uyeasound where she lay overnight. Not until the Thursday was
the *Earl* scheduled to call at Burravoe as well as Whalsay, Mid Yell,
Brough Lodge and Uyeasound, with Baltasound as the terminal. The
Friday trip from Baltasound took in Uyeasound, Cullivoe, Gutcher,
Mid Yell, Burravoe and Whalsay, also Bastavoe, on the 4th and 18th.
Eventually authority acknowledged the representations from
Burravoe at least, since one of the 1939 Company advertisements
carried the details: *"Earl of Zetland* from Lerwick every Sunday at
2 p.m. to Whalsay, Burravoe, Mid Yell, Brough Lodge and
Uyeasound . . .''

The changes and spontaneous alterations were symptoms of the
prolonged transitional period of transference from sea-dependence to
land monopoly of transport, and with such fragmentation
dissatisfaction among customers was inevitable. Still the aged steamer
persisted as a focal point in what were noted to be her last months of
existence in Shetland, for a new vessel was planned. Indeed, a
discussion held by Zetland County Council in February, 1938, had
led to a request to the Clerk to write to the North of Scotland
Company with regard to the provision of a new vessel to replace the
Earl of Zetland. It was said that she would be a miniature of the new *St.
Clair* which had first been seen in the ''sooth mooth'' a year previously
and which was receiving plaudits from the public for style and
comfort. It would be another year — probably mid 1939 — before the
replacement arrived.

Meanwhile the old ship continued to traverse her perpetual
route. James L. Smith had recently become manager of the North
Company and was making a first managerial voyage on the *St. Clair*
in June, 1938. He had come up to Scalloway, then crossed by road to

Lerwick for a visit to the North Isles. No one could deny the quality of the hospitality on board the *Earl*, but her conspicious lack of passenger facilities was a talking point for the new manager, especially when contrasted with what was proposed for her successor, due to be built at Aberdeen. By September, 1938, the venerable steamer had carried vast numbers of holiday visitors who invariably responded to that peculiar and particular atmosphere, not easily defined, which was life on board, scene of personalities and a multitude of events supervised by successive skippers and ably continued by Tom Gifford. The habitual and popular range of special trips continued. That September the *Earl* transported a large group to Symbister for the annual regatta and a football match between Lerwick and Whalsay. It was a drawn game with a goal each. The weather was in agreeable mood with sunshine, shadow and a lively wind, in contrast to the severity of a December gale which pinned down the *Earl* during a North Isles Thursday run. She had been late in leaving Lerwick at almost 10 a.m., made fairly heavy weather of it up to Symbister, failed to call at Burravoe, often a difficult port in heavy seas at the mouth of Yell Sound, and finally ran for Mid Yell where Tom Gifford decided to lie until Saturday. He risked the exposed Unst east coast up to Baltasound that afternoon, but was storm-stayed again until the Monday morning. Finally a return was made to Lerwick at 3.30 p.m. the same day. The New Year was then imminent.

1939 was to be vitally significant in many spheres of life. It was a year of decison-making for numerous free nations of the world. It was a period of enforced change within countries as governments declared their opposition to the threat of oppression from Nazi Germany, oppression which had already taken its toll of human beings, the Jewish race in particular. As the little *Earl of Zetland* lived out her last official months no-one could visualise that she would ultimately have a role to play in the vast scenario of the Jewish people whose destiny lay in the land of Palestine. Neither could anyone envisage that the peerie steamer would have another six years of service to Shetland as the fates of war brought about emergency reorganisation.

Those factors were in the unknown future. Despite the shadow of war, life in Shetland continued, as everywhere else in Britain, with a veneer of normality. In April the North Company announced that the new motor-ship would carry the title *Earl of Zetland*. Application had been made to the Board of Trade to place the suffix "II" after the name of the existing ship. Tom Gifford wrote officially in the "Scrap" log: "17th May. Ship's name changed to *Earl of Zetland II.*" This was done at Aberdeen after she had left Lerwick on 13th May for overhaul. He added: "Thursday, 18th May. Went on a pontoon at Fish Market. 10.00 a.m. Left berth. 10.45 a.m. On pontoon. 19th May, 10.45 a.m. Came off pontoon. Coaling at Back Berth." Although the name had become an accepted part of the island scene, just as had happened in 1877, there was criticism about the proposal. "There are several names suitable for the North Isles boat," wrote one correspondent in the newspapers, "but whichever is chosen it should include *Yarl*, the Norse equivalent of *Earl*. Here are a few of the names suggested: *Yarl Olaf, Yarl Harold, Yarl Eric* and *Nordland Yarl* — the latter being considered by many as very suitable for an exclusively North Isles boat. Should any difficulty be experienced in selecting one or other of the above or similar names, then *The Yarl* itself would be quite suitable as the ship would be referred to by most people as *The Yarl*, just as today they refer to the present ship as *The Earl*." In fact the writer was not far wrong since, while the registered name was complete, the new vessel was due to be called *The Earl* for several decades to come.

Years of discussion in Whalsay concerning the need for a pier at Symbister led to a letter in "The Shetland Times" in May. "Fair Play" argued: "The Whalsay fishermen have lost three consignments of haddock this past winter through not getting them shipped in time to reach the market in fresh condition. I could name a dozen or more boats which have driven ashore for want of a breakwater or suitable anchorage. Some of them were got off again after a hard struggle and others become total wrecks. Then there is the steamer's service. On some occasions the *Earl* cannot get into the bay at all and has to anchor in the tidal sound. Not so long ago (1924) a flitboat was lost. The men saved their lives by scrambling on board the steamer, but the boat had gone. The *Earl* had to turn round and run for Mid Yell for shelter and the people of Whalsay did not know until the next day whether the men were dead or alive. On another occasion the flitboat coming back from the steamer drove ashore on the sands at Symbister. The men jumped onto the beach, but the goods were spoiled ..."

Also in May it was announced in the Aberdeen "Press and Journal" that: "The new motor driven vessel, *Earl of Zetland*, now under construction to replace her namesake on the North Isles of Shetland passage, was launched from the yard of Messrs. Hall, Russell and Company. She is 154 feet long by 29 feet beam and will weigh 548 tons." The announcement contrasted with a "For Sale" handbill distributed by the North Company with a photograph of the old *Earl* under the heading "Handy General Cargo and Passenger Steamer". A description mentioned 144 feet and 20 feet dimensions with estimated deadweight about 200 tons, including 100 tons of stone ballast. She had passed a No. 3 Special Survey in 1936 and was Class 90 A.1. at Lloyds. There was no mention of the 50 h.p. of her engines compared to the proposed diesel unit of the new ship of 850 h.p. Neither was there official reference to the remarkable fact that the same engines, which had been installed sixty two years ago, were driving the *Earl* along. The notes concluded: "This steamer was lengthened in 1884. From time to time she has had very large renewals and overhauls. She has always been well looked after and kept in excellent condition."

During the months of June and July the situation in Europe became more threatening, with Germany's obvious aggressive intent towards Poland, and Britain's alliance with that vulnerable country. The weeks slipped past and despite the radio news reaching Shetland and the resultant speculation, people still talked of matters of the moment. What would the new ship be like? The old *Earl* would be going. It was the talking point of the summer of 1939 in the North Isles, and inevitably the deep-seated attachment found formal expression in the public hall at Baltasound on Friday evening, 4th August. Tom Gifford had brought his well-loved steamer north on her routine call, moored at the familiar pier and had gone with his crew to join a crowded audience in the hall already decorated with the colourful bunting from the *Earl*.

Islanders from widely scattered communities came to Baltasound that night. It was a festive occasion with a variety of entertainment. Later in the evening Major H. W. L. Hunter described ship and achievements. On behalf of the people of Unst he wanted to extend a very hearty welcome to Captain Gifford, the officers and crew. This was greeted by enthusiastic and prolonged applause. Also he welcomed the visitors. Next he called the *Earl*. Mention was made of the difference her coming made to those who witnessed the transition from sail to steam. Major Hunter then introduced Mr. Fordyce Clark, an eminent Unst man.

"This is an occasion of more than passing interest. We are about to say farewell to an old friend, and contemplate the breaking of a tie which has existed for 62 years; and although we do not sorrow as those who have no hope — for we believe that a new and better era is about to dawn — yet we cannot witness the passing of such an old, familiar friend as the *Earl of Zetland* without a sigh of regret.

"The staunch old ship has been sailing these northern seas in all weathers since the oldest among us were boys, and long before the majority of us present saw the light of day. She has brought both

An historic occasion. The arrival of the handsome new motor vessel *Earl of Zetland*. Perhaps looking her years the old *Earl* lies alongside the Albert Wharf. The year is 1939.

Almost six years later a transformation is taking place as she is returned to peacetime garb at the end of the Second World War. The shrouded Colt Browning guns abaft the funnel, and the Oerlikon emplacement at the stern, are reminders of living dangerously in northern waters.

L. Gifford

gladness and sorrow to our homes. Year by year she has carried away from these shores the youth of the isles in quest of fortune, but she has brought few of them back except for a brief visit to those they have left behind. She has also frequently brought back the mortal remains of some for whom the struggle has proved too hard. She has helped to keep us all alive by bringing to our doors the necessities of life, together with such luxuries as we could afford, and she has carried away to the markets of the world our island produce, our sheep, our ponies and cattle. She has made herself indispensable to the life of the islands, and has proved herself to be a friend indeed.

"Yet when some of us have entrusted ourselves to her tender mercies she has at times treated us rather unkindly. Of course we should on these occasions have blamed the weather, but it relieved our lacerated feelings to have a grouse at the old *Earl*. In later years she has brought our mails, and that has made her arrival more of an event than ever. In short, she has become an integral part of the life of these islands; and despite her somewhat slow pace, and her admittedly indifferent passenger accommodation, she has a warm spot in all our hearts . . ."

Fordyce Clark mentioned that the *Earl* had come from Paisley under command of Captain William Nicolson, was lengthened, and remarkably she survived several mishaps. Captain Gifford, esteemed by them all, was about to take a new command and had their best wishes for his future success and well being. Davie Gray, the genial and popular purser, who had collected their fares for more years than Davie cared to remember, would continue to do so on the new vessel. Mr Clark appreciated the purser's consideration and tact. Then the capable engineer, Sammy Harrison, on whom so much had depended, and who had coaxed the old *Earl* along for so many years, was also to join the replacement ship.

The Rev. James Binnie, Parish Minister, followed with well-considered comments about his experiences of the ship. He said: "In this age of machinery and mass production, when romance and poetry are apt to be banished from life, this meeting is proof that romance is still part of our lives. It is not usual for us to lavish our affections on the merely material, but next to our wives and sweethearts, small boats and great ships, especially in these islands, claim our attentions . . . The Glasgow people and the Paisley buddies are apt to rag each other: 'Where were you born?' said a Glasgow man to his buddy. 'In Paisley, but as shair's death I couldnae help it!' How many people have realised that the *Earl* was born over 60 years ago in Paisley? Renfrewshire is my native county. The brass nameplate, her birth certificate, abaft the engine

N

skylight, was almost obliterated 12 years ago. It can just be deciphered today, I am told.

"The North of Scotland steamers are all Saints. The *Earl* is no Saint, but she is no Sinner. The New Testament word for sin means really to miss the mark! The *Earl* never missed the mark; she has always reached her goal, has never run ashore. What, never? Well, hardly ever! — in the words of Gilbert and Sullivan's Opera. A marvellous record over 60 years. I am credibly informed that no life has ever been lost from the *Earl*. She surely has earned her right to canonization and the title of Saint!

"Looking back across the years the old faces welcome again in memory the pilgrim to the North Isles — Captain Spence, Tom Moffat, Jamie Garriock, John Fraser, Colin Henry and Jamie Jamieson. The attention and courtesy of officers and crew of the North of Scotland Company is proverbial . . . Passing from the sublime to the commonplace, but necessary, creature comforts, one remembers the really good cup of tea on the *Earl* and the crisp yellow fried haddocks, tails in mouths, served between Whalsay, Skerries and Mid Yell. As I said already, this is an historic and romantic occasion.

"I believe there is one link between the old days and these. Mr David Gray is the only member of the crew I think who was on the *Earl* when I came to Unst for the first time. He carries the purse from the old vessel to the new. I hope to stay long enough to go down with the new *Earl*, not down to the bottom but down to Lerwick! We hope for the new vessel, her captain and crew, many years of useful and glorious service in linking this most ultimate corner of Ultima Thule with the regions of the South.''

Mr James John Hunter, boatman at Uyeasound, regretted the departure of the old *Earl*. In his remarks he made the point that she was easy to board in all weathers.

The Unst member on the Shetland County Council, Mr Andrew J. Irvine, found it difficult to express in words what he really felt; the good old ship had become so much part of life in Unst and had become a real and well known friend to each islander. He was proud that he realised the *Earl's* worth when she still had many years of service before her. Some 10 or 11 years ago the *Earl* went away for her annual overhaul and, as usual, a newer, faster vessel took her place; but within a week of her going everything was in a state of chaos. It was October weather and perhaps a bit stormy, but not the sort of weather that would have disturbed the ship from her steady run. Not so her substitute. Their Monday mail arrived on Tuesday, their Friday mail on Monday, and two or three lambs had to be taken back unshipped. One Monday morning at the end of the month Andy Irvine went outside to find a gale of south wind blowing and he thought that there would be no mail that day. A few minutes later he was greatly surprised to hear, sounding clear and loud above the howling wind, the cheerful note of the *Earl's* whistle. Then he saw the fine old vessel on her way to Cullivoe, shouldering aside the billows of a raging south tide in Bluemull Sound, with that air of calm imperturbability so peculiarly her own. He felt so glad, and such a sense of safety and security came over him at seeing the familiar ship back that he could not refrain from expressing his gratitude. He sent a poem to the press. This, he felt, expressed what the *Earl of Zetland* was to everyone far better than anything that could be said.

There was a contemplative and poignant silence in the Baltasound Hall as Andy Irvine spoke, with feeling born of sincere appreciation and understanding. His verse, created in a long moment of reminiscence, sentiment and thanks, eloquently interpreted the feeling of the islanders. Written originally on the back of a long envelope during the tenure of Captain Willie Spence, reputedly the indefatigable mariner had the newspaper version framed and honourably placed in his peerie cabin below the bridge. Furthermore the crew were impressed by this spontaneous tribute to their ship to the extent that Davie Gray said to Andy Irvine when he next was on the *Earl*: "No fare Andy". That intrepid commentator and satirist of the island scene remarked that it was the only poem that ever paid! It produced vigorous applause in 1939, then 33 years later, in 1972, it was to stir similar memories on the retiral of Captain Willie Sinclair from the *new Earl* when he particularly requested the famous poem during a retiral presentation in the self-same hall in Baltasound.

> Da simmer and da hairst is past
> An' winter comes in surly blast,
> Wi wind an' rain an' hail an' sleet,
> Da grund is just wan slush o' weet,
> Up here inta dis Northern Isles,
> Frae news and cities miles and miles,
> Dere's just wan thing at helps wis oot,
> We ken we'll hear da Earl's toot.
>
> Tro darkness, wind and rain an' hail,
> Shu comes twice weekly wi wir mail,
> Shu brings wis up wir Christmas drams,
> For Unst, like 'Lerwick Then and Now'
> Is weet and dry by turns, I trow.
> She carries doon my bit o' rhymes,
> She taks wis up da "Shetland Times"

Shu brings wis claes an' maet frae sooth,
At warms wir backs and fills wir mooths,
An' folk could never get aboot,
If it wisna for da Earl's toot.

Shu's been troo muckle strain and stress,
Shu's backit in frae Muness Ness,
Shu's had her rudder split in twa,
Shu's been on Robbie Ramsay's baa,
An' ae time apun her roond
She brook in twa at Baltasoond,
Dey raised da ends, shoved in a middle,
An dere she was as fit as fiddle,
Even sinkin' could na knock her oot,
Shu still could gie her cheery toot.

An whin da Earl gangs awa,
We miss her — yea, baith ane and a',
We daurna ship wir stock to sell,
We get wir mails ower land frae Yell,
We canna blame da onken men
Da "Road ta da Isles" dey dunna keen,
But when da Earl comes ageen
We greet her, yae, lak some auld freend
An' we a' houp, week in week oot,
Shu lang may gie her cheery toot.

Andy Irvine went on to conclude: The *Earl's* toot would soon be heard no more in the islands, but her memory would linger with the people for many a year. He could think of no more fitting phrase with which to close, than just to say of the *Earl* — "Well done thou Good and Faithful Servant."

The chairman asked one Rasmie o' Breetifield to "call on" the *Earl*. Rasmie said: "It wid be imposin on da tolerant spirit o' dis great assembly for me ta try ta add anything opportune to what's already been sed by mair accomplished speakers.

"Dis great community o' beings drawn tagither by common consent ta recognise socially da captain, officers and crew o' da auld *Earl* composes a far finer tribute to da noble vessel wi' a fine record o' service to da Isles, dan a da language at I cood summons, an da gesture I cood portray, or a da faces I cood set-up.

"As we experience dis transaction, we feel grateful that kent faces — though maybe no aye bonnie faces — frae da auld craft 'ill be to da fore ida new vessel, and so we'll no feel strangers.

"An noo, as we share dis farewell till a revered servant o' da Nort Isles, lit wis extend a hearty welcome to her successor, and express da hope at shu'll be privileged to maintain da same place in da affections o' da community."

Mr Hunter addressed Captain Gifford, thanking him for seamanship, courtesy and kindness to all who travelled on the ship. Amid deafening applause the captain rose to reply, "On behalf of the officers and crew and myself, I wish to thank you all for the kind thought that prompted you to arrange this gathering here tonight, and for the kind invitation extended to us through our good friend Mr William Hunter. I also thank you for the many kind things said tonight. It is very gratifying to know that the little bit we do is so well appreciated and I can only say that in the future, as in the past, we shall endeavour to give you our best. I feel confident that when the new ship comes you will have a worthy successor to the old one."

The inimitable purser, David Gray, was described by Mr Hunter as "one who has almost become part of the old *Earl*". It was not being suggested that he had been there for 60 years, but most of his life seemed to have been spent on the old ship. The only fault to be found with him was that he always appeared to be keen to "get hold of our money", and would even wake passengers from a sound sleep with "Tickets please!" Thanks to Davie Gray the *Earl* had made a regular additional Tuesday trip to Uyeasound and his persistence, on behalf of the community, had led the north manager to say that the captain could take the *Earl* to Uyeasound or anywhere else he liked on a Tuesday!

Davie Gray associated himself with his captain's remarks then went on: "The last time you entertained us was the farewell to Captain Spence from the *Earl of Zetland*, and tonight it is farewell to the old ship. I have been connected with the old *Earl* since I left school, and have seen many old friends pass from service. I am very pleased to tell you that the old ship is not going out of the North Isles service in disgrace. Why I say this is that on 29th July she did the journey from Symbister Bay to abreast of Lerwick Fish Market in one hour, which is a record, but tonight I would like to say something about the new *Earl of Zetland*; and the reason we are having this most up-to-date ship in the company.

"Mr Smith, our present Manager, has, I think, made only one trip to the North Isles, but his observations during that time eclipsed those of any other official of the company during my service. Our manager saw the necessity for better accommodation, also speed, for the people of the North Isles, who comprise over 25 per cent of the total population of Shetland, and all that is required now is your co-operation to give the new *Earl of Zetland* facilities at the ports of call which will add to the complete comforts of the voyage. I am not referring to Baltasound pier, as it is the one and only in the North Isles, and we all know the boon it is compared with conditions at other ports of call where passengers and livestock all have to be boated off, which causes loss of time and inconvenience to passengers. I hope that all of you here will make many trips in the new ship, and that she may be as fortunate as the old one.''

William Hunter summed up: ''And so we pass from the old to the new, but whatever ship may come to this northern isle of Unst, we shall always remember the old *Earl*.''

Wholeheartedly and fittingly the audience rose to sing:

> *''So goodbye old ship o' mine,*
> *And for the sake of auld lang syne,*
> *Your name will live on till the day is gone,*
> *Goodbye old ship o' mine.''*

The gathering dispersed in thoughtful and reflective mood into the August darkness, then at six o'clock on the Saturday morning, the birth of a new day, many came to the pier, some awoke and others stirred in their sleep as Captain Gifford tugged the whistle lanyard and the *Earl* sounded a farewell — and her thanks — when she turned south at Balta Isle for what they thought was almost her final visit to Baltasound.

Throughout the first half of August the routine run continued. The *Earl* had Uyeasound as terminal twice, Yell Sound — Ollaberry — once, and Baltasound on another five occasions. On the fourth of these on Saturday, 19th August, a familiar figure had been recalled. Just and righteous sentiment brought Willie Spence back. The *Earl* had called at Uyeasound, Cullivoe, Gutcher, Brough Lodge, Mid Yell, Burravoe and Whalsay, mooring at Lerwick at 1.25 p.m., then after a mere 20 minutes at the Victoria Pier she took part in a unique and intensely historical event in the annals of Shetland. It was a poignant yet joyous situation for four North Company skippers, all of whom had been associated in varying degrees with the old *Earl*. Willie Spence stood proudly on her bridge as she slipped her ropes from the north side of the pier, while the lovely white-hulled and buff-funnelled *St. Sunniva* moved out stern-first from the south side under command of William Gifford. It was 1.45 p.m. To the south, the spectators on the Knab (was it really almost 62½ years since a similar group had watched the little steamer come to Shetland?) observed two ships growing in size as they came on past Mousa having met off Orkney. They were the new *Earl of Zetland* from Aberdeen and the big *St. Magnus* from Kirkwall, captained by Thomas Gifford and Donald McMillan respectively. Thus for the first, and only, time four North Company vessels rendezvoused. If not perfect, the day was cloudy/bright with a gentle breeze. The spectacle stirred the

imagination, since it was symbolic of so much history and progress —
the past and the future. They came in line ahead up through the
middle of Bressay Sound, each ablaze with colour, dressed overall,
the old *Earl*, followed by her namesake, then the *St. Magnus* and the

"So goodbye old ship o' mine"

St. Sunniva. A great surge of people came round the shore from the Knab, anxious to witness the simultaneous arrival of four steamers, joining the milling crowd of hundreds already thronging the harbour front. Fittingly the entire scene was sun-lit, accentuating the white flurry of steam at the funnel of each of the steamships, visual evidence of the booming sirens which echoed round the shores from the north to the south mouth and the hills far beyond, the cheering welcome of a great concourse of townspeople, islanders and visitors temporarily drowned out by the noise. In came the old *Earl* to berth at the landing stages by the Albert Wharf. Her successor eased neatly alongside the "*Earl's* berth", the *Magnus* took the south side and the *Sunniva* came in astern of the new *Earl*. All eyes focused on the newcomer.

The motor-vessel *Earl of Zetland* looked magnificent. Many people felt it was unfair to her predecessor to make comparisons. She was just different, a new generation of ship. Yet the distinctive, practical well-deck with doors which, as James John Hunter had observed, had made the old *Earl* workable in all weathers, were a feature common to both. Superior power and passenger convenience were obvious enough and no one who looked at, or over, the new ship that day failed to be impressed.

An hour after the thrilling and soul-stirring arrival of the "fleet" the newcomer carried directors and guests of the company round Bressay and as far north as the Nesting coast for a cruise which lasted until 6 p.m. And the folk were still there at Victoria Pier in large numbers until late on the Saturday night, as if reluctant to lose anything of the spirit and atmosphere of the moment. Meanwhile the dining saloon on the *St. Magnus* was the setting for an excellent dinner. Local public figures and businessmen had been invited. The toast of "The New *Earl*" was proposed by Mr William (Billy) A. A. Tulloch, chairman of the Lerwick Harbour Trust. He congratulated the directors of the North Company, trusted that the ship would be loyally supported by the public, and would continue to run as long as her predecessor . . .

Mr Mitchell Williamson, chairman of Aberdeen Chamber of Commerce, toasted "The Old Rock". He commented: "Aberdeen hospitality is one thing, but Aberdeen hospitality dispensed in Shetland and in Shetland atmosphere is quite another! I wanted this toast to be 'The Old Rock' because it is a term of affection to all Shetlanders, more especially to exiles like me, because it arouses all manner of sentimental feelings. The old *Earl* is something of a chip off The Old Rock and the new *Earl* has much to live up to . . ."

Mr R. J. H. Ganson, vice-chairman of Zetland County Council, responded and said that books could be written about the incidents on board the old *Earl,* while the humour and hospitality of The Old Rock had always been features for visitors from the south. He paid tribute to a most excellent vessel and was very glad they had retained the honourable old name of the *Earl of Zetland* in spite of the controversy which raged in the local press. He was pleased that the name which belonged to the oldest ship in the company was to be allowed to go on.

In a toast to the "Town and Trade of Lerwick" Mr W. J. H. Dickson confirmed that the warmest tribute the North of Scotland Company could pay them was this new ship, and Bailie Magnus Shearer, who replied, spoke of their awareness of the links with the city of Aberdeen and the company which had presented them with such a magnificent ship.

"The Old *Earl*" was proposed by Mr J. W. Robertson. He spoke of a "utility" ship which could take part in any of the company's work. He had known her to load and discharge eight full cargoes in one week! Mr James L. Smith, Aberdeen manager, wondered what the old *Earl* might say if she could speak. "She might tell us that she has sailed in Shetland waters for a million miles. She might tell us that she has carried in safety half a million passengers. She might tell us that she has carried almost half a million packets of His Majesty's mails. She might tell us that she has carried about 200,000 ponies, cattle and lambs. That is not a bad record. She has carried Shetland people in health and she has carried them in sickness. She has served her owners and she has served her masters. She has known these masters. She has had their confidence. She has shared their anxieties. She has been officered by men who have cared for her, and she has been kept ship-shape by seamen. She has been well engineered and she has had firemen. She has had stewards, she has had pursers. All are typical of a type of man and a type of seaman second to none in this world. I will not attempt to say how much the company and the public owe to the loyalty of these seamen, and I will not try to say, when the day comes, as it shortly will, when she hands in her last log, whether or not she might expect 'Well done, thou good and faithful servant'. But I do know that the company wish to leave a memento of the *Earl's* departure. I have told you, and you know, that she has carried the Shetland people in sickness and in health, and I would like our friend, Sheriff Wallace, to accept a cheque for £100 payable to the Gilbert Bain Hospital. Further, I would be grateful if he would ask the three masters of the *Earl* to stand up and associate themselves with this gift. I would add that we, in the south, have watched with great admiration the way in which people in Shetland have made efforts on behalf of their hospital extension scheme."

Taken aback at the unexpected gift, Sheriff Wallace, who had made innumerable trips, found the moment very touching, but it was a splendid tribute to the old *Earl* and her association that the company should have thought fit to give this magnificent gift to perpetuate her memory in the Gilbert Bain Hospital.

In this evening of recollection, sentiment, and optimism for the future, Captain Halcrow toasted the builders. Mr C. S. Maclay responded on behalf of Hall, Russell of Aberdeen. He was very gratified at the interest created by the new ship. His firm had been greatly encouraged by the assistance of the directors of the North Company in the construction. The trial trip earlier in the week had been very satisfactory . . .

On the Sunday the celebration went on. Both North Isles ships sailed out of "da nort mooth", the "old" setting out on her final peacetime voyage to Baltasound, and the "new" bound for Yell Sound and Ollaberry, where she lay overnight, on a directors' cruise. Appropriately the old *Earl* visited each one of the North Isles on her return trip, and the islanders came out in numbers in Unst (Baltasound and Uyeasound), Yell (Cullivoe, Gutcher and Mid Yell), Fetlar (Brough Lodge), Skerries (north-east mouth) and Whalsay (Symbister). And she was back at Victoria Pier at 2.40 p.m. on the Monday, 21st August, her last berthing there before her demise to Aberdeen and possible oblivion.

The *Earl's* stay in Lerwick lasted not much over three hours, yet the precious minutes were utilised to the full in an extension of the astonishing evaluation and commendation. Lerwick Harbour Trust and their chairman William (Billy) A. A. Tulloch, a kenspeckle figure in Shetland, invited members of the shipping company and Captains John Scott, Spence and Gifford to the compact, heart-warming saloon. It was the final scene before the curtain rang down. Billy Tulloch wished to take farewell of a good old friend. Captain Halcrow, also of the Harbour Trust, rose and surveyed the seated people grouped round the ancient bogey-stove which had provided warmth and solace to generations. He addressed Willie Spence in particular: ". . . It is wonderful that she has responded to the service of men for this long period without a single fatal mishap, and unique in the way that she and successive commanders have woven themselves into the texture of public affection and public memory. Indeed, I do not know what will linger longest in island memories, the ship or her crews who sailed in her for decades and gave her the fine reputation she has. Some have joined the great majority, but mention of well-remembered names recalls the *Earl of Zetland* and vice versa . . ."

The people in that intimate atmosphere of the saloon were visibly affected, and James Smith, the Aberdeen manager, indicating the familiar, immaculately maintained stove said nostalgically: "As I have sat looking at the stove I have just been wondering how many stories have been told round here — some true and some not so true! It symbolises the history of the ship and her fine stature. I hope that in time the new ship will gather such a reputation and that she may be as much loved as the old ship has been. I give you a toast, 'Farewell to the *Earl of Zetland*'." The company rose and drank.

At 6 p.m. on Monday, 21st August, the Victoria Pier was packed with spectators in a final gesture of approbation from the folk she had served. Rockets soared heavenwards as the thrash of water at her stern pulled her away from the quayside for what was thought would be the last time. Her successor followed, black hull, white upperworks and buff funnel gleaming in the early evening light. A suggestion of variable wind ruffled the harbour waters as the *St. Magnus,* southward bound to Kirkwall and Aberdeen, fell in behind the new *Earl,* and the three vessels moved slowly out in line ahead. The low sunshine cast an ideal gleam on them. It was a moment of grandeur. Off Bressay Lighthouse Tom Gifford ordered the ensign to be dipped as his ship put about, a mere hint of diesel fumes a blur at the compact funnel, contrasting with the dark streaming smear emerging from the old *Earl's* tall smoke stack. The booming sirens again reverberated round the township, beaches, rock-faces and hills. A final parting. For a time the *St. Magnus* kept company until her superior speed took her away towards Mousa and the little old *Earl* was left on that great expanse of sea to the south, visible from the heights of the Knab. And there were many men, women and children who watched her out of sight.

The log recorded the voyage to Aberdeen:

Bressay Light	6.25 p.m. 21st S x W¼W	Log streamed	Light variable wind
Mousa	7.14 p.m. 21st SSW	7.4 miles	
Sumburgh Head	8.14 p.m. 21st SSW	16.8	
Fair Isle	10.25 p.m. 21st SSW	36.4	11 p.m. Fog. Later some lightning.
Kinnairds Head	10.05 a.m. 22nd S x E½E	143	3.30 a.m. Fog
Rattray Head	11.05 a.m. 22nd S x ½W	152	lifted.
Buchan Ness	12.20 p.m. 22nd SW½S	162½	5 a.m. Wind NW
Cruden Bay	1.03 p.m. 22nd SW½S	168½	light. Clear.
Black Doig	2.30 p.m. 22nd SW½S	180	
Pilot on Board	2.50 p.m. 22nd		
Aberdeen	3.15 p.m. 22nd		Moored in front of office

10

World War II and Milestones

The final days of peace in the last quarter of August, 1939, were shadowed by the deteriorating situation in Europe. A German-Soviet Pact to "desist from any act of violence, any aggressive action, and any attack on each other, either individually or jointly with other Powers", strengthened Britain's resolve to stand by Poland and precautionary measures were given priority. Amongst a multitude of preparations the Admiralty received authority to requisition 25 merchantmen for conversion to armed merchant cruisers; tension heightened. British shipping was alerted.

Wartime moments at Gutcher in Yell.

August dragged to a close. On the 31st the axe fell as Hitler issued his "Directive Number 1 for the conduct of the war . . . The date of attack on Poland, 1st September, 1939; time of attack 04.45''. Britain's response was an immediate mobilisation which reached into every sector of the community. Two days before the formal declaration of war the directors of the North Company met to consider the emergency and the requisitioning by the Admiralty of three steamers, the *St. Sunniva,* the *St. Magnus* and the *St. Ninian,* the latter being a veteran of the First World War.

Thoughts of selling the old *Earl of Zetland* were inevitably countered by ideas that she might yet be useful. Even in the early days of that fateful month of September she appeared to have a roving commission. On 30th August she was at Matthews Quay, in front of the North Company's office, ready to load, with Captain Logie in command. Then to Kirkwall with a heavy cargo, thence to Scrabster. She was there at 4.10 p.m. on Saturday, 2nd September, and even as Neville Chamberlain, Prime Minister, announced on the Sunday

morning to the nation that Britain was at war with Germany, the *Earl* departed for Scapa Flow. Off the Orkney shore there was a first hint of the wartime presence as an Examination Ship ordered her to heave-to for a check. Throughout the first month of the conflict the little steamer worked cargoes from Aberdeen to Scrabster, Stromness and Kirkwall, but on 3rd October she was berthed in Aberdeen and lay unused for the most part of two months.

Her old contemporary, the *St. Ola,* now 47 years of age, had continued the short, but exacting, run over the Pentland Firth from Scrabster to Stromness normally, an ever-increasing responsibility due to the build-up of the naval base at Scapa Flow. Such was the pressure that a decision was made to enlist the *Earl's* services again. On 26th November she sailed from Aberdeen bound for Scrabster. Off Buchan Ness she made heavy going in a westerly gale which forced her into Peterhead. The following day course was set north-north-west across the Moray Firth towards Clyth Ness, south of Wick, and in the 70 mile stretch the ship took some punishment in big seas which compelled her to anchor in Sinclair's Bay late that night. At 2 a.m. the wind had moderated enough to allow passage into the Pentland Firth and four hours later, on the 29th, the old steamer lay off Scrabster awaiting berthing permission. It was the beginning of an intensive month of activity within the area.

Elsewhere, the wartime pressures were building up. This was the period of the "Phoney War" or, in Neville Chamberlain's words, the "Twilight War". Britain and France remained impassive, action being confined to the dropping of leaflets on German cities. But at sea the action was instant and there were widely contrasting incidents. On the first day of the war in the Western Approaches the British liner *Athenia* took 112 lives with her when she was torpedoed and sunk. The North Company's *St. Clair* had a different experience. She was off Sumburgh Head on her run north to Lerwick from Aberdeen in that October. The day was still, with a flat sea, Sumburgh lying to port clad in an early morning mist. It was difficult to believe that seas and skies held any threat. Surprisingly, another sound filtered through the noises of a ship in motion. Heads on board the steamer turned, startled, and swivelled quickly as eyes took in the totally unexpected sight of an aircraft. The German, a JU 88, below mast height, came from astern and swept past to the north, a momentary crescendo of engines and blur of shape and insignia, and gloved hand of pilot raised in salute. The incredulous gaze of any crew on bridge and deck of the *Clair* followed the aircraft until it was lost to sight. Suddenly, then, the war seemed very near.

About the same time the major early disaster for Britain and triumph for Germany brought awesome punishment and toll of war into the heart of the Royal Navy's reputedly impregnable base at Scapa Flow, and into the hearts of men on steamers like the *Clair* and *Earl* the realisation that they were in the front line at sea. On 14th October, 1939, several torpedoes from the submarine U-47, commanded by Lieutenant Gunther Prien, tore into the vital parts of the anchored battleship *Royal Oak* in the Flow. Prien had skilfully taken his boat between two blockships, and through the strong tidal current of Kirk Sound between the Orkney mainland and Burray, the result of a pre-war visit to Orkney on a spying mission. Great columns of water rose skywards; the *Royal Oak*, deprived of her stability, rolled over within ten minutes and sank, taking 786 men to a watery tomb. Prien and his crew returned to a delirious welcome in Germany. The British counted the cost of a capital ship, and the price in death and in deprivation for a multitude of relatives.

Throughout the month of December it fell to William Banks, an Orcadian, to command the *Earl* in a series of voyages between Scrabster and Scapa. Navy cargoes and services personnel were carried as her contribution in the build-up of the base with extensive development in defences, accelerated by the sacrifice of the *Royal Oak*. The route taken across the Pentland Firth was the direct one from Scrabster, with Dunnet Head to starboard, then up through Hoxa Sound and across the Flow to Scapa at the north end. Poignantly and symbolically all that remained as an indication of the grave of a battleship was a solitary wreck-buoy, a constant reminder of the cruelty of war. Day by day it was forceful visual evidence as the old steamer passed close by.

Despite 30 crossings of the Pentland Firth during the third month of the war the voyages were uneventful. Apart from the sighting on Christmas Day of what appeared to be a mine, there was nothing to interfere directly with the steamer's routine. Yet her limitations were apparent. Her cargo capacity was restricted; her passenger facilities left much to be desired; she was anything but fast and, therefore, vulnerable. The answer was apparent, and the North Company had little choice in any event. Rumour had it that the new *Earl* would be requisitioned by the Admiralty, a suggestion which became fact early in January, 1940. She therefore complied with the wartime demands which were described in a booklet produced by the North Company after the war, in December, 1946. "Daily — hourly — requests and instructions from the Admiralty, the Ministry of War Transport, Army and other Service Departments were acted upon . . . Soon the Company's ships were drawn into the maelstrom of war — a bitter unceasing struggle between Merchant

Ships (at first ill-armed, almost defenceless) and a powerful enemy winging the skies and lurking below heaving waters . . . Widely varied was the cargo handled in the general trade to Orkney and Shetland, amounting to about half a million tons; from guns, explosives and ammunition to vegetables, ice, clothing, hardware, fruit, motor cars, vans and ambulances with as many as 2,000 individual consignments in a single cargo. Indeed a mixed bag from the means of dealing with death to the necessities of maintaining life . . . As for livestock, an important part of the Company's work, 176,000 sheep, 35,000 cattle, 4,500 pigs and 3,000 horses were transported over the war period as well as 1,300,000 packages of H.M. Mails. In the course of these sailings the Company's vessels completed 1,600 voyages, in addition to 1,800 trips across the Pentland Firth and 900 inter-island voyages in the North Isles of Shetland, steaming about 840,000 miles — a distance equal to more than 33 times around the world.'' But the fates were to bring infinite variety to the lives of millions before that retrospective booklet was to be published.

Of course, the hundreds of sailings by the *Earl* in the North Isles added another colourful chapter in the saga of the steadfast old ship as she returned to Shetland so unexpectedly. As the New Year arrived in 1940 she was still involved in her day by day three-hour run across the Pentland Firth, still skippered by William Banks. Frequently she was in Stromness, but generally the route was between Scrabster and Scapa. Twenty more times she crossed the Firth until Captain Banks took her alongside at Scrabster on Monday, 22nd January, berthing at 1.55 p.m. There she awaited her final phase in northern waters.

The requisitioning of the three steamers had placed a demanding burden on the *St. Clair* which had to maintain a tight, if irregular, schedule between Aberdeen and Lerwick, usually laden with troops. She was commanded by Captain William Leask, with Adam Tait, an Aith man with a skipper's ticket, as mate, now destined to play an important role in the last act of the *Earl of Zetland II* as a North Company steamer. The erratic sailings of the *Clair* gave little scope to crew members for leave, thus it was in the nature of a luxury when Adam Tait found himself relaxing at home in Edinburgh at the end of the third week in January. A Sunday morning was ideal for a respite, but his moments were rudely interrupted by a visit from the Leith agent of the shipping company. Apologetic though he was, the message was unequivocal, and to the effect that the *Earl* was lying at Scrabster in urgent need of a skipper to take charge of her for the North Isles of Shetland. Adam Tait had been put forward and they were anxious for him to take her north immediately.

Having caught the first available train from Edinburgh on the Monday morning, Captain Tait reflected on how quickly circumstances can change a life. The leave so suddenly ended had been more than welcome. His thoughts were many and varied. They were of home and family; the *Earl* and crew; the North Isles — unknown to him; Shetland in relation to the war; the islands and their strategic importance in the Northern Approaches; the question of Norway only 200 miles to the east of Lerwick and more than likely a German invasion there. An immense question mark was raised over the near future, and the look of the snow-bound countryside, grey and inhospitable, was anything but encouraging. The troop-laden train, further delayed by snowdrifts north of Inverness, eventually released its passengers at Thurso early on the Tuesday afternoon. Adam Tait was by then caught up in fast moving events. He was offered an overdue lunch, hurried across to Scrabster, given a naval order, taken down to the ship which lay alongside with steam up, introduced to Shetlanders like David Henry (a nephew of the fine seaman Colin Henry) from Gutcher in Yell, who was mate, David Gray still "part" of the steamer, and purser, and John Findlay, the engineer; and given orders to clear off as quickly as possible to the east or west of Orkney.

Thus he found himself on the bridge of the *Earl of Zetland II* at 5 p.m. on Tuesday, 23rd January, 1940, suitably clad to withstand the snow coming with a strong south-easterly wind. He chose to go up the west side. The landmarks came at irregular intervals. Dunnet Head abeam at 5.30 p.m., Rora Head 6.50 p.m., Marwick Head 8.27 p.m., Brough of Birsay 8.39 p.m. Off Mull Head on Papa Westray at 10.54 p.m. the wind began to ease and the snow turned into intermittent sleet, although the night remained very dark. Fair Isle and Sumburgh Head lighthouses, welcome beacons in happier days, were blacked out, but providentially, and possibly under Admiralty instructions, the Sumburgh light probed the murk to offer a bearing for a few minutes, enabling the new skipper to check his dead reckoning. Thus the little vessel retraced her familiar path north past the massive outcrop of Sumburgh and the island of Mousa, to berth quietly at Victoria Pier virtually unnoticed in the still, grey early morning of 24th January. During her five months' absence Lerwick had been transformed into a formidable wartime stronghold, with booms and shore gun emplacements at the south and north harbour entrances. But already the enemy had made his presence felt, though met with vigorous opposition from the anti-aircraft defences. Sixteen bombs failed to do significant damage on 13th November, 1939, but in a second go about a week later six Heinkels

O

went for a Sunderland flying-boat moored in the north harbour. Despite retaliatory fire from shore-based guns the Sunderland, blazing furiously, was destroyed. December brought further raids. A disconcerting type of warfare was introduced when defenceless fishing boats were shot up off the east side of Shetland. Then on 1st January, 1940, H.M.S. *Coventry*, lying in the now world-famous Sullom Voe, had a very near miss in a solitary bombing foray which rather interfered with the New Year catering arrangements, and was in stark contrast to the light hearted snowballing which had entertained the crew on the white-blanketed foredeck on Christmas day. A Dornier swept in from astern of *Coventry*, limiting her arc of fire, pressing home a determined attack. Two barrel-like objects left the aircraft and hurtled downwards on H.M.S. *Coventry*. As was fated to happen the next year to the men on the old *Earl*, the crew watched the bombs, spellbound. An eye witness commented later: "With relief I saw the falling objects splash into the voe a few yards from the ship's side. I was about to rejoice when *Coventry* was flung violently upwards. The deck seemed to rise and hit me in the face. Next there was a nauseating drop which tumbled me on deck. After this a deluge of salt water." The *Earl* was in a highly vulnerable situation, moving almost daily on the enemy side of Shetland, with even greater exposure to follow as Norway succumbed to German troops and armour. If vessels like the *Coventry* and the Lerwick Harbour environment were well protected, the defensive equipment of many merchant ships was noticeable by its absence. So it was with the *Earl*. But later, when fully armed with a bizarre array of weapons, she could have given a fair account of herself. Such armament, however, took time.

When Adam Tait sailed to Uyeasound on 25th January, 1940, on the first wartime voyage to the North Isles, the sole armament was his own Winchester ·5 repeater rifle! This ludicrous, totally inadequate state of affairs lasted until early July, when the *Earl* sailed alone — no convoys for her — to Aberdeen for some defensive equipment. A large kite to be flown at the end of a fine steel cable (in suitable wind conditions!), an ancient Lewis gun, and a gadget called a Holman Projector were fitted. The Holman was unique, temperamental and frequently more frightening to its users than to any enemy. The principle was simple. A Mills bomb was fired into the air to deter (or destroy) aircraft engaged in low-level attack. A length of steel piping formed a six-foot barrel which could be swung about freely. The firing power was either compressed air from a steel bottle, or a steam supply from the boilers. Utilised mainly by smaller vessels, the device was often only powerful enough to spit out the bomb uncomfortably close to the ship. All the weapons on the *Earl* were tried out, off Sumburgh Head, on the return voyage. They successfully projected one Mills bomb a respectable distance, fired off 20 rounds with the Lewis gun and flew the kite for 5 hours in a moderate easterly wind. The kite also had its limitations. To launch it the ship turned into the wind, the winchman slacked off the cable which was attached to a block on the foremast head, and the kite was "lifted off" with the aid of two crewmen on top of the compact wheelhouse (which had been fitted at Aberdeen earlier and which at last gave the helmsman some protection after 63 years). It was hardly ideal for a sudden attack, for sea-room was needed to fly it practically, as well as a reasonable breeze. Nevertheless the *Earl's* crew practised when the chance arose. It was on such an occasion that they found themselves an object of curiosity. The steamer was off east Unst, the wind was north-westerly and the kite up at its maximum of about 1,000 feet in clear weather, when a high-flying plane was seen. Focke-Wulf Condors were popular with the enemy for convoy spotting, often noted from the *Earl* flying at a great height. This time the steamer was no doubt noted too; and so was the big kite, a source of interest for this Condor's crew. The big aircraft swung in a wide arc, losing height until the men on deck sensed it uncomfortably close. Then, after a couple of circuits, its crew satisfied that this was no secret weapon, it regained altitude to the west and the Atlantic.

Variety had been a feature of the *Earl's* peacetime existence. Inevitably the diversity of war intensified the range of incidents affecting the ship and the people associated with her. There was the case of the stranded steamer. Winter darkness had reluctantly given way to grey daylight on 6th February, 1940. A west-bound depression ensured conditions which were uncomfortable on land and dangerous at sea. The scattered dwellings on Unst were obscured by driving, icy rain; the wind-torn waters in the voe at Baltasound, slate grey and punctuated by white crests, indicated the state of the sea outside. It seemed likely that the *Earl,* due that evening, would anchor somewhere for shelter. No other vessel was expected. There were raised eyebrows, therefore, when the shadowy form of a ship was noted steaming before the gale and apparently heading for the entrance to Baltasound at the south end of Balta Isle. In she came, gradually acquiring more definition, the hull distinctly etched against the whiteness of the seas breaking around her. Those onshore watched with curiosity as the strange steamer kept on coming, riding high in the water, probably in ballast. A three-island ship, she had a tall single funnel amidships and looked big, perhaps 5,000 tons. She was a unique sight so far into the long narrow inlet which is the voe of

Baltasound. Slowly the great slab-sided hull, black and rust-streaked, gleaming dully in the welter of flung spray and icy drizzle of rain, came up level with the pier. If she went any further she would be aground. The few watchers were aware of a flurry of white water at the counter stern as the vessel stopped and there came the fragmented sound in the gale of metal on metal, with a cloud of rust dust as at least one anchor chain roared from its locker. And there she lay, swinging bows-on to the wind. The unheralded arrival caused much suspicion and speculation: there was no indication as to her nationality. What a risk to take in coming so far in! Old ballast heaps were all over the place in profusion — even the peerie *Earl* had come to grief years ago. The weather at sea, although bad enough, was not impossible. From the pier the anonymous steamer loomed large against the low-lying land at the far side of the voe. She was secure enough from the sea, yet the large expanse of metal in the face of the wind was another matter. There was no communication and local men who had come out drifted away, back to the warmth of their homesteads, as the gathering gloom gradually swallowed up the big vessel.

Overnight the gale became squally with strong gusts. Imperceptibly the steamer began to drag in the darkness, but had drifted too far before the second anchor could brake her progress. By dawn on the 7th she had gone aground on shingle and sand at near enough the top of a spring tide, pressured by the gale, some 300 yards from the pier.

After daybreak Charles Sandison of Hamar, Baltasound, and the Coast Preventive Officer, boarded the stranded steamer by the proferred rope ladder. Lloyd's register listed the owners as Skjelbreds Rederi A/S Kristiansand, Norway. She had only recently changed hands, however, and in broken English her master, in semi-uniform winter clothing, stated that she was the *Vahva* from Tallinn in Estonia in ballast to a port in England. He had found her unwieldy to control sailing light so decided to seek anchorage in Shetland. Admitting that he had dropped only one anchor with a relatively short length of chain the day before, he could not explain why both anchors had not been used initially in such gusty weather. He was not prepared to accept the idea that with the aid of one of his boats and cable he could winch his ship off. In Estonia a tug would be provided and he would do nothing without one! Finally the Coast Preventive Officer temporarily disconnected the *Vahva's* wireless for security reasons and the two men went back ashore.

As anticipated Adam Tait had decided to lie overnight at Mid Yell on the 6th. On the 7th he logged: ''Strong SSE wind. Overcast.

Rain at times. Rough sea and heavy swell on passage to Baltasound. Boats having difficulty in coming off at ports of call." The new wing shelters on the bridge were proving a real asset. At least now there was a modicum of comfort in part of the ship which had been so exposed for so long. The *Earl's* counter stern had taken a knock at Lerwick just a few days previously when the steam trawler *War Lord* had rammed it, but yet again the full curve had risen well to the following seas up the east side of Unst and by 1.30 p.m. on the 7th the *Earl* was alongside the Baltasound pier.

Communications between Unst and Lloyd's resulted in a message to the North Company who, in turn, sent a brief to Captain Tait: "Attempt salvage of s.s. *Vahva* at own discretion." After mooring at the pier at Baltasound and cargo unloaded, Adam Tait met Charles Sandison, acting on behalf of Garriock, Lloyd's agent in Lerwick. Along with David Henry, mate, and John Findlay, engineer, he boarded the Estonian, where they found a worried captain. "It is blowing strong. I am in despair if the wind rises any more." He confirmed that there was no cargo, ballast tanks were full, and leaks as a result of the grounding not of consequence. The starboard anchor was out with 45 fathoms of chain, also an anchor run out from the stern. Soundings supervised by David Henry showed that the *Vahva* was firmly held. At the ebb the depth of water was eight feet except abreast the main mast on the starboard side where it was only five feet, exposing a vast area of discoloured underside. She needed over nine feet forward and 14 feet aft to float. The *Vahva's* chief engineer reckoned it was not possible to pump out the tanks between one tide and the next. Charles Sandison offered pumps which augmented those on the ship, and the machinery throbbed throughout the night. If they could get rid of the unwanted ballast before high water at 10.30 a.m. on the 8th, then the steamer would only need 12 feet aft. It was a race against time.

On the morning of the 8th, Adam Tait wrote: "7.30 a.m. Left pier. Strong SSE wind, overcast, raining." 75 fathoms of the *Vahva's* eight inch manilla rope were linked to a bridle of 2 - 45 fathom lengths of the *Earl's* five inch rope, the ends attached to bow and stern of the grounded vessel. The North Isles steamer was anchored to windward, which was the only possible position. Anchors had already been laboriously raised on the *Vahva*, so she would lie free once the water level was suitable. A signal by Aldis lamp informed the Estonian that towing was about to begin. It was 9 a.m. and ballast tanks had been emptied. Adam Tait rang for "slow ahead". The water churned white under her stern, ropes rose dripping from the water and the angle of entry to the sea of her anchor chains decreased as the strain came on. Vibration possessed the frame and structure of the old ship. Inch by inch the depth of water increased and crept steadily up the sides of the *Vahva,* but uncertainty remained as John Findlay manipulated the *Earl's* engines to maintain the right tension. For a long 45 minutes they persevered until, just before 10 a.m., a tremor ran through the stranded hull. Frantic waving from the *Vahva* was additional visual evidence that she was being freed from the sea bed and Captain Tait continued to exercise his delicate balance of power between anchors, engines and the weight of *Vahva's* hull at the end of the tow ropes. And slowly, very slowly, the *Earl* dragged the 3,655 ton bulk of the *Vahva* until by 10.30 a.m. she was 200 feet out, with enough water under her keel. A successful salvage, witnessed by the Unst people on the pier.

It should have been the conclusion of the episode, but another factor materialised, with unexpected results. The naval commandant at Kirkwall had had information about the stranding on the 6th and ordered HM Rescue Tug *St. Mellons* to Unst. She was hurriedly bunkered and left at 4 p.m. on the 7th. Her skipper recorded: ''Proceeded out of harbour through S.E. gale; high dangerous sea in Pentland Firth.'' At 11 a.m. on the 8th, by which time the *Vahva* was afloat, he logged: ''Arrived in Baltasound; contacted s.s. *Vahva*; vessel lying broadside on to rocky shore and aground fore and aft, strong S.E. wind and high ground swell. Vessel washing on shore. Island mail steamer trying to tow her off, but unable to do so.'' This was an astonishing interpretation of the situation, because Aldis communication between the *Earl* and *St. Mellons* confirmed that the two vessels would take the *Vahva* to a safer anchorage further out in the voe. And curiously enough there was no other mention of the *Earl* in the log of the *St. Mellons* apart from a note of her departure.

There was a touch of irony in subsequent events. The powerful *St. Mellons* transferred a rope to the stern of the *Vahva* while the *Earl* held her in the relatively safe position, ready for both ships to coax their charge out past the pier. Gusts of wind still swept round the hull and superstructure. The tug, water boiling at her stern, took the strain and the Estonian began to move again, but it was unfortunate that the tow rope was passed through a fairlead right aft on the *St. Mellons* which restricted her control. Had her hawser been on the tow hook amidships all might have been well. As it was she began to swing to leeward broadside to the wind and the shore just beyond the pier, with its group of interested local inhabitants. The choice was limited. Either she would run aground or she would drop the tow rope. Adam Tait could do nothing about it. From the *Earl's* bridge the little pier was totally obscured by the mass of the *Vahva's* hull, while from the other side the locals saw the stern of the steamer looming larger, much of the rudder and screw out of the water, and about to demolish their viewpoint. Assuming that discretion was the better part of valour, the skipper of the *St. Mellons* had cast off, which left the *Vahva*, a menacing powerless hulk, surging towards the pier. Had the water been deep enough she would have done a lot of damage, but the sea bed brought her to a grinding halt, yards short, all the valuable work achieved by the *Earl* undone.

Already Adam Tait had lost schedule time, but the day was too far spent and he anchored overnight. He left Baltasound early on the 9th February, leaving the *St. Mellons* to deal with refloating the steamer, not such a difficult task with only the after portion of her hull aground. By mid-morning on the 9th the Estonian was anchored securely. On the 10th the log of the *St. Mellons* recorded: "1400/10 *St. Mellons* and *Vahva* arrived safely in Lerwick. *Vahva* handed over to charge of N.O.I.C., Lerwick; safely anchored in harbour." A compromise situation resulted. Legally the *Earl's* efforts had merited a direct salvage claim. Yet the *St. Mellons* log implied failure. The Admiralty also had a demand to consider on the evidence of the log, but the *Vahva's* owners were reluctant to submit a suitable settlement and the issue went to arbitration. A sum of £3,000 resulted in August, 1940, £2,480 of which went to the Admiralty, leaving £520 to be disbursed to master and crew of the tug. Adam Tait had made the incident quite clear in a report to the North Company, who contacted the Salvage Association, and negotiations resulted in an award summarised by James L. Smith, the North Company manager, in a letter to the *Earl's* master. "Naturally we had to put up a fight to get a sufficient amount, but we considered the circumstances justified a reasonable payment, and that the good work undertaken by yourself and your crew deserved a generous part of the total paid."

The affair of the *Vahva* was a milestone for the *Earl's* crew; it had tested their teamwork, given considerable satisfaction and brought about a not unwelcome financial windfall. Routine followed. Week by week the steamer worked the North Isles including regular visits to Skerries, beyond which lay the threat of the wartime North Sea and ominous portents of German aims in taking Norway. Hitler had made the decision in mid-December, 1939, " . . . I am informed that the English intend to land there, and I want to be there before them." The German propaganda machine had already declared that: "To Norway will be restored the northern islands (Orkney and Shetland) as 'living space' when they have been liberated from the yoke of Britain." In April, 1940, a "cat and mouse" game developed. The British laid mines off Narvik. German warships were observed heading northwards. The enemy struck at a variety of Norwegian targets from the sea and by paratroop invasion. Seven divisions shattered resistance and within two days the Germans possessed all the main ports. With Scapa Flow as a main base Britain prepared for direct war at sea to the north and east of Shetland. The enemy was less than 200 miles from Lerwick. The sea itself was the main deterrent.

Short of an attack, nothing could have brought the news of Norway's downfall to Adam Tait and his crew more tellingly than the arrival of the seaplane. They were north-bound from Mid Yell to Uyeasound on a still evening when the drone of an aircraft penetrated the noises of a ship at sea. They looked and wondered as the plane banked and curved downwards — no sign of aggression. Then astonishment as it touched the sea's surface and settled in a great swathe of white water. Adam Tait rang down "Stop Engines", and the seaplane taxied over. Talk on the *Earl* had been about Norway. Information was not good. The war seemed frighteningly near. Suddenly it was all stomach-gripping fact as the Norwegian crew of the aircraft confirmed in English: "We just managed to get out. When we left the base the Germans were coming into Bergen. Only a few planes got away."

The Germans claimed a master-stroke in outwitting the British, who launched a major attack on a coastline for so long associated only with the colonising Vikings. An offensive in which the battleship *Warspite,* the aircraft carrier *Furious,* cruisers and destroyers, all fought, was ultimately futile despite exacting toll on the enemy. The main target, Narvik, remained in German hands. Norway had been pulverised into seeming submission. Another abortive attempt, this time to secure Trondheim by "Operation Hammer", was repulsed by the Germans. Although the fight for Norway became introverted, such had been the British commitment at sea that the German fleet was made impotent to the extent that it could be no factor in the invasion of Britain.

But these issues could not be known in Shetland. What was happening to the enemy was difficult to appreciate. What was seen was the succession of often badly damaged RN ships seeking shelter and repair, and an ever-growing fleet of an amazing selection of craft packed with Norwegians fleeing from the oppression, and seeking landfalls anywhere from Muckle Flugga to Sumburgh Head. In Shetland it all had the ominous threat of impending disaster; only a matter of time before the onslaught. On 17th April, 1940, the destroyer *Eclipse,* badly holed, limped into Lerwick, and a week later she was followed by the *Pelican,* minus 60 men and her stern. It was on 4th May that the first refugees came.

Since the *Earl* covered more than 45 miles of the exposed east side day by day, she was often a welcome sight to beleaguered escapers after the hazards of slipping away from German surveillance, and the rigours of the North Sea, in feats of bravery and endurance seen only in war. Adam Tait experienced the interception of small boats and large boats. The arrival of each in Shetland waters was the end product of months of subterfuge and patience in the face of a cruel enemy. A Norwegian naval officer, his wife and son, attained freedom and were on the *Earl* from Unst to Lerwick. He had been First Lieutenant on a warship which foundered at the abortive defence of Oslo, but escaped — every man for himself ultimately — and, travelling with his family, managed to reach an obscure, small community south of Narvik. There he found work in navigation instruction to young locals, carefully safeguarding his real identity. Obstensibly he found relaxation in fishing, but week-end by week-end secreted fuel and supplies on a suitably screened islet. For near enough a year he patiently fooled the unsuspecting Germans, until a settled spell of weather in February, 1942, encouraged him to go with the 43-foot craft he had used for his fishing trips. His family escape was screened by the jettisoning of all loose gear, including the dinghy, to suggest a drowning accident. Under cover of darkness they made the open sea without any hue and cry, promptly faced an unexpected gale which, although acutely uncomfortable, gave concealment, and four days later they made landfall at Baltasound. The Lieutenant was another of those who escaped via the *Earl* to fight for the liberation of his homeland. Like some other escapers' boats, the 43-footer was offered on the market for sale in Shetland and was bought by George Leslie of Sumburgh. She came on the Shetland fishing-boat register in May, 1942, and was listed as having been built in Norway in 1915. Named the *Duen,* she was used for fishing after the war, but subsequently was sold and appeared on the Buckie register in 1947.

The *Erkna* was a much bigger vessel. Originally she was employed in fish transport from ports in north Norway to Trondheim. At the outbreak of war a conversion was being made from steam to motor, and by the time this was completed the Germans were in occupation and she was commandeered by them for similar trade. In November, 1941, she lay at Stokmarknes in the Lofoten Islands, her engine temporarily out of commission. Her owner, Mathias H. Myklebust, learned through the "Jungel telegraffen" of the "Heimefronten" (Norwegian Resistance) in Alesund that the *Erkna* was urgently needed to transport a group to

Shetland, and that he should arrange for her to be "stolen". Mathias Myklebust had been given permission for engine repairs at the port of Gergen, then he took on a cargo of iced fish and herring for Molde, south of Kristiansund. An oil ration permit card enabled him to replenish the fuel tank after the voyage south, and he took his boat to Gurskoy, in the vicinity of Alesund, while he travelled on land to Trondheim for business with the German firm for which the *Erkna* had been requisitioned. He then abandoned the boat to be dealt with by the "Heimfronten", assuming that the enemy were ignorant of the scheme. Time would tell.

In the darkness of the night of 16th November two men, a skipper and an engineer, both members of the resistance, slipped the moorings for a stealthy, short run to nearby Ulsteinvik. No alarm was raised. They anchored the *Erkna* offshore and awaited the dawn. All the daylight hours of the 17th they half expected a German patrol boat. Nothing materialised. After nightfall boatloads of men climbed over *Erkna's* bulwarks to disappear into cabin, hold, wheelhouse and even engineroom. The final boat brought the total up to 60, including Martin Bjorlo and Peter Sperre, 17 years old and the youngest on board. That last boat was taken ashore by the resourceful resistance representatives, leaving the *Erkna* to get under way for Shetland and freedom. At 0130 on the 17th she abandoned her moorings ready for an exit to the open sea. Peter Sperre elected to remain on deck exposed to the chill of the North Sea in November rather than endure the confinement below, with more risk of seasickness in the long regular swell of the following day. During the 18th they swayed westwards in increasing wind and sea from the south-east, yet poorer weather meant better security, especially from the air. The 60 were vastly relieved as daylight faded and the now labouring *Erkna* was swallowed up in another black winter night. By 0500 they knew that Shetland, probably the east side of Unst, was very near, an unlit and unknown coast. The motor was run only to keep *Erkna's* bows butting into the steep seas and to await daylight. Until mid-morning poor visibility and restricted light denied them a sight of the white smear of surf which indicated what they assumed to be Unst. They then slowly motored south a few miles off the east side of Fetlar. By early afternoon the *Erkna* was north of Skerries, a gyrating and lurching hull in the near gale force conditions. Martin Bjorlo and Peter Sperre were in the shelter of the deckhouse with others when the ship was sighted. They saw a small grey-painted steamer on a south-south-east course hammering into the teeth of the gale. She looked like an inter-island ship, possibly bound for Lerwick — certainly she appeared friendly. It was providential they thought; contact seemed sensible.

Several hundred yards separated the vessels when two things happened. Simultaneously from each ship there was noted a dark shape swivelling, dipping into the troughs, lifting to the crests of the waves. Also, coincidentally, the *Erkna's* engine stuttered and then faded with compressor trouble and she swung broadside, rolling heavily within a few boat-lengths of the shape — now identified as a mine.

For the *Earl* — inevitably it was the *Earl* — the mine was a first priority. Mines had already proved a hazard by exploding on the Shetland coast, and gunfire from the steamer had already disposed of 13 in 1941. Crewman Magnie Fraser, from Papa Stour, had proved to be the crack shot with gun and armour-piercing bullets. Naval gunners, then additional personnel, considered Magnie, in a light-hearted way, to be something of a poacher. Mines shot at tended to fill and sink rather than blow up. So the crackle of gunfire was heard on both vessels as yet another menace was put to the sea bed.

Adam Tait and Davie Henry, his mate, had assumed that the drifting fishing boat of standard Norwegian design was a further escape effort. They figured that she would have been hazarded if the mine had not been destroyed. Such a small vessel could be blown to smithereens. And she seemed to be helpless as it was. A large number on board too, judging by the figures at her bulwarks. They wondered about her name. Time now to consider what to do about the strange vessel. The gap between them narrowed.

From the *Erkna* the unknown vessel had a purposeful air. Smoke swirled, fragmented, aft as she came up into the wind 200 yards away and her bows flung bursts of spray outwards. Oilskin-clad figures could be seen in the wing shelters of the open bridge. She looked an old steamer. She was a most welcome sight.

Captain Tait indicated a tow, acknowledged by a wave of an arm from the Norwegian. Momentarily the *Earl* rolled in the trough, came about, churned past the *Erkna's* bows so that a heaving line could arch over the grey-green swirl between the ships and the line fell across her foredeck first time. Chief engineer Findlay put his engines into reverse and they edged up stern into the wind until a hawser could be manhandled over.

Towing was not easy. The fishing boat yawed about in the beam swell like a reluctant puppy on a lead, swinging with such vigour that an abrupt sheer parted the rope after only three miles. And again they contrived the linking process. The second attempt was maintained. About four hours of slow progress took the two vessels into the lee of the land mass of the island of Whalsay. On the west side, at the bay of Symbister, Adam Tait dropped anchor and brought his charge close up astern in a swell which denied any attempt to bring her alongside.

Security was the next question. The enemy might try to infiltrate Shetland and beyond by landing agents through the refugee boats. It was Olsen's task to check. He was one of three Norwegian security officers whose activities extended throughout the islands and who operated a rota system on the inter-island steamer. In 1941 they were busy because not far short of 2,000 refugees found their way to Shetland. Since the *Earl* could have as many as 150 on board over a week she required a near permanent security presence. Olsen, known to Adam Tait as a graduate of Oslo and Cambridge Universities, moved informally, but systematically, amongst the refugees, a specialist in dialects whose knowledge of the Norwegian districts was matched by his understanding of the patois of Unst, Yell, Fetlar and Whalsay. It was said you would think that he had never been out of Whalsay all his life! Observation and scrutiny were his watchwords. His brief was to seek out spies or Quislings (named after Vidkun Quisling who was a Norwegian collaborator with the Germans).

The *Erkna's* masts traced uncertain arcs across the grey racing storm scud overhead as she rolled at the end of mooring ropes. All on board the North Company steamer curiously awaited events while the Security Officer, having boarded the refugee ship, conversed with his countrymen. An hour elapsed before Olsen came back with firm advice to leave the 60 where they were. He did not want the *Earl's* crew, and travellers, composed of services personnel and some civilians, to be outnumbered by transferring the refugees. No chances to be taken, he maintained.

Time pressed. The short winter day would be fading unless they got under way with the *Erkna;* and one of the most treacherous areas of water around Shetland lay before them. Still the wind kept the sea raised, starkly white over the notorious Voder and Brethern reefs as both ships, the Norwegian securely tethered, wallowed south to Lerwick. In the November twilight Adam Tait thankfully passed his "guests" to the care of the Naval patrol guarding the north mouth, and the *Earl* slipped quietly down the harbour to the Victoria Pier, her second wartime salvage completed. The incident was over for the ship. What remained was the bureaucratic salvage claim procedure. The captain's report elicited a prompt reply from Aberdeen. Manager J. L. Smith wrote: " . . . I congratulate you and your crew on this accomplishment . . ." Early in December he sought more details about when and where the *Erkna* was built, her value in sterling and whether or not she was likely to run ashore with no anchor and no power. At the time Adam Tait could not confirm where she was built. He estimated her to be not more than five years

old and the Norwegian Vice Consul in Lerwick assessed the value at
£5,000. " . . . she was certainly in danger of stranding. According
to the drift of the tide and direction of wind, she would have reached a
position in the dangerous area of Yell Sound within two hours . . .
when approached by the *Earl* she was lying stopped in the vicinity of a
German mine. This particular type being semi-magnetic may have
constituted an added danger to the *Erkna* as she was an iron vessel."

Although men on the Norwegian vessel had insisted that the
faulty piping in the engine could have been repaired, given time,
undeniably the vessel was endangered. They maintained that a tow
was acceptable to save time, not to save the ship. Yet tow there was,
with salvage resulting.

If the North Company and *Earl's* crew expected a speedy
financial return, they were to be disappointed. Not until 1st April,
1943, did Adam Tait have a letter from James L. Smith in Aberdeen.
For months no department or body was prepared to accept
responsibility or to make any offer for services rendered, until the
Royal Norwegian Government reluctantly remitted £250. The
shipping firm allocated only a small proportion to the salvors, which
put a few pounds into their pockets. Captain Tait was given £13,
Davie Henry, mate and John Findlay, engineer, £6.15/- each. Davie
Gray, as purser, Magnie Fraser, Robbie Robertson, Lowrie Gifford
and Jimmy Grains, as seamen, Bill Knights and Andrew Cormack,
as firemen, Robbie Gray, as steward and John Sutherland, as cook,
picked up £2.15/- each. Leask, the boy, had a single pound and 10
shillings! Wrote Mr Smith: "I trust that you and your members of
your crew will consider the result to be satisfactory in the
circumstances." Their reaction was never recorded. In terms of risks
amounting to danger, judgement in seamanship and responsibility
for a ship in distress, it added up to a paltry award.

Such relatively meagre returns were characteristic, given
reluctantly by the owners of the broken-down or stranded vessels in
each case. This occurred again after 17 eventful months of the *Earl's*
war. The location was the Unicorn Reef lying offshore in that
infamous expanse of water between Whalsay and Lerwick's north
entrance. The victim was the 80-ton Norwegian motor vessel *Haugen,*
more kindly treated by the jagged reef than the warship *Unicorn* of
1567 which was lured to a drastic end as she tore out her underside
under full sail. When the Earl of Bothwell, consort of Mary Queen of
Scots, had fled to Shetland, his vessel picked up a pilot in Lerwick,
sailed out the north mouth and cleverly enticed the pursuing *Unicorn*
to sail across the reef to her destruction. Her name was given to the
hidden rocks.

A moderate south-south-west wind had created a long ground swell, the sky growing overcast, as the *Earl* dipped her bows southwards into the undulating surface off Whalsay on 21st April, 1943. Adam Tait noted routinely in the log: "6.56 p.m. Passed Mull of Eswick Lighthouse." Fifteen minutes later Davie Henry observed a vessel: "That fellow's going to be in trouble if he's not careful." They watched as the other ship, unaware of the danger, lurched onto the Unicorn, was held, and ground against the unyielding gneiss. Within minutes she had lost her rudder, and other wood in the swell looked like portions of her keel. With the *Earl* lying as close as Adam Tait dared, the stranded vessel's small boat brought over a line to be linked up with a 6" manilla rope for towing. With deep water all round the reef, an effort was made to pull her off the way she had gone on. Ten minutes of power from John Findlay's engines brought no response, and they elected to try another tactic, although it seemed a forlorn hope. A wire-rope bridle was formed amidships on the starboard side to allow more scope to manoeuvre and Captain Tait again rang down for power. Fifteen minutes of regulating the engines brought success. The vessel twisted off the rocks and settled, swaying in the rhythmical swell. "8.10 p.m. M/V refloated. Engines in working order, but unable to manoeuvre owing to loss of rudder. Vessel leaking badly. Shortened tow rope and commenced towing towards harbour."

Twenty minutes later the *Earl* hove-to off Rova Head in shelter and her charge was brought alongside. Adam Tait met Bernhoft, the skipper, who confirmed his gratitude and stated his ship, the *Haugen,* belonged to the Royal Norwegian Navy and had been making for Lerwick prior to an assignment in occupied Norway. While the two masters talked there was frantic activity to keep the water level down. Her crew were helped by services personnel travelling on the *Earl,* all armed with a variety of buckets and containers. The engines were available to pump, but the inrushing sea was only just kept at bay by their herculean efforts. It was late evening and dark before the steamer released the water-laden *Haugen* to be berthed by another Norwegian ship.

There was more correspondence to the *Earl's* master from the North Company. " . . . War circumstances seem to have resulted in salvage opportunities coming your way and I trust that the effective services rendered by yourself, and your crew and ship, will be recognised in due course . . ." And later: " . . . We have found, by experience, difficulty in arranging matters with the Norwegian Authorities . . ." By mid-September the confirmation of payment reached Adam Tait. "Our (the North Company) usual procedure is to apportion the total award, after deduction of expenses, one-quarter to the crew and three-quarters to the owners.'' And finally by November, 1943, the Lords Commissioners had awarded £300 of which £225 was swallowed up by the company coffers. The Secretary to the Admiralty had advised that the nett salved value of the *Haugen* was £3,000. Adam Tait fared rather better than he had done with the *Erkna,* receiving £20. Davie Henry and John Findlay lifted £9.10/-. The rest of the crew shared £36.

It was the *Earl's* final major salvage adventure — the end of a formidable, impressive record, and a prolonged era of assistance to shipping in danger, given in the grand tradition of the sea, bringing the best out of a ship and her crew. It was, however, far from the end of her service in terms of wartime events prior to an unexpected, colourful sequence of shadowing by the British Navy, interception, and tow into oblivion, as a Jewish illegal immigrant vessel. Coincidentally she played her part in the vexed, poignant, yet romantic episodes in the creation of the Jewish Nation. No-one on board in the early forties could have, even in his wildest dreams, conceived of the ''Voyage of Vision'' to come. There were, however, newspaper and radio reports of the unbelievable systematic destruction, with extermination as the aim, of Jews in Nazi Germany. It had been a declared object in the German SS newspaper ''Das Schwarze Korps''. ''As early as 1933, the year in which we took power, we claimed that the Jewish question should be solved with the most brutal methods and completely. We were right then, but we were not able to implement our view because we lacked the military strength we possess today. It is essential; it is inevitable. We no longer hear the whining of the world. No power on earth can keep us from bringing the Jewish Question to its total solution.'' The prophecy was unfolding in all its grim reality.

11

The Enemy at Large

"Total solution" was the ultimate intention of an arrogant and confident enemy. Undeniably defeat for the British held the prospect of humiliation, slavery and the brutish disposal of those who failed to comply with the whims of a merciless dictator. If, in the immediate pre-war years, the Jews and the British — under their obligation to the 1921 mandate of the League of Nations — had not seen eye to eye on the question of free movement of immigrants to Palestine, they were of necessity united in the face of possible annihilation in these horrifyingly extreme circumstances during the 1940s.

The shape of things to come — shadowing by the Royal Navy.

On 3rd December, 1939, the Zionist Executive in Jerusalem had published a call to all young people to enroll in the Jewish units to fight Hitler. Over 130,000 men and women responded. The British appeared reluctant to accept Jewish volunteers unless a comparable number of Arabs came forward. Since the Arabs failed to react in numbers any formal acceptance by the British of Jewish volunteers was necessarily delayed. It was, however, the view of Winston Churchill that forces should be encouraged for the defence of Palestine by the Jews, thereby releasing eleven battalions of mainly British troops tethered there. Having been Colonial Secretary in the 1920s Churchill understood, and was sympathetic to, the Zionist cause, but the White Paper of May, 1939, which decreed a cut back on immigration and purchase of land by the Jewish community brought burning and embittered criticism which led Prime Minister Ben Gurion to declare: "We shall fight side by side with Britain in our war against Hitler as if there were no White Paper, and we shall fight the White Paper as if there were no war".

P

During the years preceding the terror the same Nazi Germans had embarrassed Britain by aiding and increasing systematic, if rather limited, movement of Jews from Germany into Palestine, even establishing Gestapo-sponsored training camps for the preparation of young Jews to run the British blockade (which was restrictive, not prohibitive). To add to the complexity, the savage campaign by the Germans against Jewish citizens gained in momentum. It was a paradoxical situation.

The outbreak of war rationalised the Nazi approach in an agonising and simplistic manner. No more immigration; only extermination. The chips were down. Early portents looked bleak. Auschwitz, Belsen, Buchenwald and Ravensbruck became horrific hells for multitudes of Jews reduced to grotesquely postured piles of bodies of men, women and children who died horribly and innocently in gas chambers — their only 'crime' their nationality. Birmingham, Coventry and London were three of a host of British urban areas blasted by the German air blitz. Four hundred people were killed in Coventry during one night. German radio proclaimed that other cities would be "Coventrated". Three nights later eight hundred lost their lives in Birmingham. For Jew and Briton alike the end was the same — death. Only the circumstances differed; the Jew could not fight back.

The "Twilight War" was a feature of the past. If surface sea supremacy had been denied to Hitler because of the battle at Narvik, he determined to break British morale through all-out air attack and U-boat activity. The capitulation in 1940 of Holland, Belgium and France led directly to the famous retreat of the allies and the miracle of the escape of British Forces at Dunkirk, and placed Britain with her back to the wall. From Land's End to Muckle Flugga, German invasion was expected. Only a narrow strip of sea denied a swift and final surge of German forces into London and beyond. Norway seemed a possible base for paratroop landings in the northern islands.

A "softening-up" blitz was directed by Goering, who had assumed command of the air battle. Kent, Sussex, the Tyne, Mersey, Clydeside, the provincial cities in England and, to a lesser extent, the Forth and Aberdeen all suffered the onslaught. Orkney and Shetland received frequent, but sporadic, attention.

In Aberdeen the North Company offices sustained structural damage which destroyed records, while Shetland experienced about 240 alerts over the war years. Bombs were dropped in 27 raids but without achieving major destruction. What stirred up anger was the German habit of indiscriminating attacks on defenceless people. School children in the country districts learned to dive for a ditch;

wives of two lighthouse keepers lost their lives in calculated machine gunning; a man had his arms smashed. With such callous disregard in targets, the crew of the *Earl of Zetland* realised that they would unavoidably encounter the enemy at some stage. For months, although German planes were sighted afar off almost daily, the little steamer was ignored. When the attack did come the *Earl* had the narrowest of shaves.

She had slipped her moorings at Baltasound in the early morning of Saturday, 4th October, 1941, a grey overcast day with moderate sea and reasonable visibility. An hour later she was off Muness, with Adam Tait preparing to alter course into Skuda Sound and anchorage at Uyeasound. The look-out called: "Aircraft off port bow, heading south-west". It was 7.40 a.m. The plane was far enough away — about 1½ miles — to make identification difficult. (The British Blenheim and German JU88 were remarkably similar.) It was then lost in the overcast. Fourteen minutes later the skipper scribbled in the scrap log: "7.54 a.m. Crew ordered to action stations. Unidentified plane bearing south at approximately 4,000 feet, distant ½ mile, heading westwards. Vessel rounding Ness of Ramnageo and heading NW x W."

Seconds later no-one on board was in any doubt. In a rising crescendo of engines the JU88 banked steeply and came at them from dead ahead. In the long moment of waiting, crew, services personnel and a sprinkling of civilians, were painfully aware of possible complete destruction. That the JU88's crew meant business became clear as five blobs detached themselves menacingly from the black underside and plummeted down towards the ship. Any one of the five missiles could have meant the end of the *Earl of Zetland* and her complement of crew and passengers.

The whistle of the falling bombs was lost in the chatter of the *Earl's* Lewis guns from fo'c'sle and bridge. The erratic Holman Projector immediately developed a leak in the air valve and was useless. Personnel on the bridge watched momentarily then flattened themselves on the deck behind the half-inch teak boarding where they doubtless prayed for salvation. Their escape could be regarded as a godsend. Captain Tait glanced up as the bombs came straight in line, but seconds later their flight was influenced by the beam wind which providentially altered their direction a degree or two off course, virtually at the last moment.

When the detonations came, Chief Findlay, below in the engineroom, felt the staggering shock of the missiles which had struck the sea about 90 feet from the starboard side. The old ship listed violently in the blast, and Grains and Cormack, the firemen, grabbed what they could to avoid being flung about. They wondered what to expect next. But the engines picked up the rhythm again and the steamer sailed on.

Adam Tait commented: ''That attack was a close call.'' Even then the result was sensational and petrifying. As the JU88 roared

. . . the JU88 banked . .

overhead, its guns spitting a shower of tracer, a vast wall of water arose, blotting out the coast of Unst and Ramnageo in cascades of white which slowly subsided. The deck canted alarmingly to port, then back to starboard, port again, starboard again, before the steamer settled onto an even keel. Pursued by return fire, the JU88 banked and was swallowed up by cloud to the south-east.

A quick scrutiny revealed that the sure hand of Fullerton, the Paisley builders, had made a strong ship. Not a rivet had sprung — only one or two coupling bolts at the tail end of the propeller shaft had broken. The funnel, which had a number of bullet holes in it, was the only evidence of damage. If the JU88 had escaped, so had its intended victim; although German radio reported otherwise. That same day as they headed towards Lerwick, Lord Haw-Haw, in one of his "Gairmany calling" broadcasts, announced satisfaction that a "large troop transport" had been sunk on the east side of the Shetland Islands. The captain and crew of the *Earl of Zetland* took the liberty of assuming that they were the subject of the broadcast!

Headquarters, Shetland Defences, responded to the report of the incident. "The defence commander has asked me to write to you and to convey his congratulations on your narrow escape in Skuda Sound on Saturday morning.

"He feels sure that the saving of the *Earl of Zetland* and her passengers must be accredited to your (Captain Tait's) able handling. The quick action of your crew in answering the enemy's fire is a pleasing sign and it is hoped that, if the occasion should ever arise again, a 'bull' will be registered.

"The commander further hopes that the *Earl of Zetland* and her captain will continue to run the service between the outer islands and the Mainland for many days to come, in spite of the Nazis' efforts. He wishes you and your crew the best of luck in future encounters with the enemy — may there be none!"

And there was none! But a contrasting and tragic episode created a great sadness amongst the crew just five months later. As the ship closed Out Skerries from Lerwick, again on a Saturday, 21st February, 1942, a twin engined plane caused "action stations". Through binoculars Adam Tait identified a slow-moving Blenheim fighter/bomber north-east of them. As the *Earl* swung round towards the north-east entrance at Skerries the aircraft banked about a mile off Bound Skerry on which the lighthouse stood, rose from about 50 feet to 300 feet, appeared to get out of control and, to their dismay, nose-down, accelerated into the south end of Grunay island. There was a grinding crunch, a flash and an immediate belch of fire-tinged purple smoke before their horrified gaze. Within ten minutes of the crash they had hove-to off the boat slip for the lighthouse stores and keepers' homes, and Davie Gray went ashore in charge of a boat's party. He reported: "Three of the crew and myself went ashore as soon as we arrived at the harbour at Skerries and ran to the plane in the hope that a rescue was possible, but regret that death must have been instantaneous on the impact. I assume that it was the rear gunner who was thrown clear. The other two were burning in the wreckage. At the time there was exploding ammunition and the heat was terrific, so we could not approach too near. But we made a careful check to make sure there were no more than three in the crew." A disconsolate purser and boat's crew rowed back to the now anchored steamer with the Skerries flitboat alongside, behind them an enormous mass of dark smoke towering heavenwards, a funeral pall for men who had run the gauntlet of German anti-aircraft fire in Norway.

Adam Tait described a range of situations: "Another incident happened when we were anchored at Skerries, and on a lovely summer afternoon. To get a quick turn-round I asked the gunners (services' personnel had been enlisted) to help the crew for the quickest possible discharge of the cargo. I kept watch and, as usual, would ring the alarm bells should the need arise. Amongst the passengers was a naval commander who was on the bridge for a yarn. Leaving him for a moment I went over to the wing of the bridge to check cargo-working. Without warning the 'J' Rockets were fired. Work immediately ceased and the crew scattered to action stations. The startled commander had the rough edge of my tongue. He had pulled over the safety lever and pushed the switch "to see if it would work"! I can never forget the sight of these two white parachutes with swinging wires attached, drifting slowly away over the Skerries lighthouse. These 'J' Rockets had replaced the inadequate Holman Projectors and only once did we have to use them aggressively. On passage in the North Isles at a later stage a plane came at us directly in the line of attack — it looked like a JU88 — and I fired, having held on until the last moment. The aircraft was forced to bank really steeply. It was only then the boys on the guns saw the RAF roundels and held their fire. A split second decision! Generally the signal was if the 'J' Rockets were fired the gunners could open up. British planes were instructed never to fly directly over friendly shipping — which meant we had an apology for the incident from the RAF.

"Towards the end of the war — as equipment became more plentiful — we were given Colt Brownings with shields, mounted to port and starboard on a platform abaft the funnel and over the engineroom skylight. The Colts could fire 2400 rounds per minute between them of tracer, armour-piercing, incendiary and ordinary ammunition loaded into belts in that order. They were fantastic! It was possible to swing right overhead, firing all the time, rather like working a hosepipe. Even an aircraft moving at 300 m.p.h could be holed like a sewing machine going through cloth. With the additional gun, an Oerliken in the emplacement at the stern, we were well equipped on the old *Earl*. Fortunately for us — and the enemy — we never had to use them. Unfortunate that we did not have that armament when the JU88 came for us.

"Another time it was a pity we could not have brought arms to bear, although an old fashioned ramming might have been possible had we known what there was before us. Once more we had left Baltasound in early morning before daylight dawned. Of course there was a working agreement with Naval Control about the *Earl's* movements at night with darkened ship. Timings had to be made clear if we were to avoid trouble with coastal batteries, and the North Isles Post Offices readily passed on a message: "The *Earl* has left Uyeasound", or "The steamer is on the way from Whalsay to Burravoe." So we had come out of Baltasound, not a pleasant departure with strong south-south-east wind blowing onshore. We were keeping well out, giving Vere reef and Baas of Muness rocks a wide berth, maybe a couple of miles off shore. The lookout reported a small light away to starboard and inshore. Davie Henry commented: 'That must be some fellow in difficulty.' We thought it might be a ship's boat, and I felt we had to investigate. With a lee shore and that sea someone could be at bad risk. I rang down to John Findlay for reduced speed as the *Earl* turned stern-on to the wind, and we progressed for a quarter of a mile or so, facing the mysterious light which moved vertically in the waves. We were just yards off when we made out the conning tower of a submarine looming up to one side. They must have been startled enough because there was a tremendous flurry of water, like an explosion, as they filled tanks and crash dived close by the *Earl's* stem. It was incredible.

"The affair was mentioned at Uyeasound and information passed on to Naval Control at Lerwick, who confirmed that there were no British submarines in the area. U-boats had certainly been observed in the early days of the war, even one in the narrow confines of Bluemull Sound on a moonlight night, running on the surface. Then on 9th January, 1940, the Greek steamer *Torris Chandris* ran onto the same nearly submerged Vere reef when fleeing from a U-boat. She sank eventually, taking her cargo of iron ore from

Norway with her, not directly by enemy action, but in the act of salvage. Possibly Lord Haw-Haw claimed her too!

"In those first months rumour was rife and invasion scares happened. About the time of Dunkirk, in June 1940, one quiet summer's night, an alarm did sound. This was of great concern because we had been told if invasion became a reality we would have the unenviable task of scuttling the *Earl* across the face of the Victoria Pier to prevent ready access. We felt the greatest relief when the alert was cancelled and Lerwick returned to the curfew's silence, a curfew which seemed unending. It existed each night for about two years of the war and was, of course, very restrictive. When we were berthed in Lerwick half the crew remained on board; the others had passes to negotiate a series of check-points amid all the barbed wire of the water-front on the way home, if they lived in Lerwick. The skipper's cabin was on deck; very vulnerable. There was a Bofors gun above Tammy Irvine's shop behind the usual berth, one at the Post Office and another at the Widows' Homes: and armed sentries, all trigger happy, posted at intervals right along the harbour. I felt it prudent to be below deck at night when we were lying in Lerwick!

"There was every justification for the curfew, although despite it there were attempts by persons unknown to molest shipping at Lerwick. Two of those affected us. The first concerned the compass in the wheelhouse. We were up in the north harbour bound for the North Isles, and Robbie Robertson from Burravoe, who was steering, was checking on the line of buoys when he glanced at the compass. 'Ah, but dis compass is all wrang,' he exclaimed. It was away SW when it should have been N 40° E or so. Since we were steering by the land it hardly mattered then, but fog would have been another issue. Once through the protective boom at the entrance, into clear water, we found the magnets had been altered, and we re-adjusted the compass by slowing down and 'swinging ship'. Half an hour and we were on our way. The second incident involved the engine discharge. John Findlay had gone below to give the engines a turn. Steam was up, but he almost immediately sensed that all was not well. Running topside he saw two ends of wooden planks projecting, cut and wedged into the square discharge hole just on the waterline. He shut off engines instantly since build up of pressure through the condensers could have burst the discharging pipe. A small boat was taken out to remove the offending wood. If they were practical jokes they were in poor taste. The security people informed us that there were saboteurs at work in Shetland over the war years, hence the concern in screening all the Norwegian refugees — a method of infiltration which would have suited the Germans particularly well. Olsen and his colleagues had a vital task indeed. But no-one ever knew who was responsible for the suspected sabotage on the old *Earl.*

"Risks in peace time in Shetland waters were bad enough, although it was at least safe in harbour! During the war the weather was often at fault, just the same, but other problems arose too. If we went south for refit we usually sailed alone. On one memorable occasion we got away from Shetland in winter darkness and found the lighted channel marker-buoy ten miles east of Noss Head, miraculously it seemed after having done the 100 miles or so from Lerwick in a fresh to strong south-east wind which gave the ship a lot of leeway. Davie Henry and I felt pleased with the calculations. Thereafter we had to get into the channel kept clear of mines six miles wide and three miles each side of a marker buoy every 30 miles and stretching right round Britain. We had been warned we would meet a north-bound convoy, so had to make sure we were in the south-bound channel which was to the right of the marker buoys. From the mouth of the Pentland Firth we kept closely to the south-west side of the three mile width across the Moray Firth, heading for Kinnairds Head. Everything was black as pitch with bad visibility as well as darkness, between two and three in the morning. I remember saying to Davie Henry: 'They must be due any time now.' Off Kinnaird we were to turn through 90°, but suddenly out of the murk there loomed the bows of a huge ship, sailing light. She was so big we seemed to be looking up at her! We were horrified. Immediately we switched on navigation lights at 'dim' and were forced to sail down through a convoy of perhaps 60, all on the wrong side of the channel! They were going slowly, probably delaying for daylight before passing through the Pentland Firth. A close call in another way! We were relieved to reach Aberdeen unscathed.

"The old ship certainly had unusual experiences. The Germans had developed the magnetic mine which looked like providing a knotty problem until the Naval scientists demagnetised ships by girdling them with electric cable, something which was called 'degaussing'. The North Company's *St. Magnus* had about 30 miles of degaussing wire in her, cable about two inches thick. Instead of this the smaller ships went through a demagnetising process called 'wiping'. The *Earl's* turn came and we went to Lyness in Scapa Flow. She was given the standard treatment, then put through a check. There is no record of how she treated the instruments, but the Naval people were taken aback when they discovered that she had been given too much and gone the other way! She was so old that she was unique in her iron construction, as distinct from the modern steel, with enormous heavy plating, built like a battleship. And the iron had upset the calculations to the extent that she had the unusual experience of being at Lyness for over a week instead of two days until she passed the test and we could sail with less concern on the routine North Isles run.

"All the *Earl's* skippers had bad moments with weather. I had heard about the narrow north-east entrance to Skerries and how it could be treacherous there in certain wind conditions. One day in winter it was a relief to escape from a heavy sea into Skerries, which was quite well land-locked, and we worked cargo and passengers in reasonable comfort. But as we lay there the wind shifted round to the north-east and blew up, directly into the entrance. It was blowing smoke very quickly. I said to chief Findlay: 'We've got to get out because she can't hold here very much longer, not with the wind in this direction.' As it was, she was bows on to the gale, so was placed to go. The wheel would need three men. Without a steering engine it was all manual, and the rudder could transmit a vicious kick to the wheel itself. It could break an arm. John Findlay was an engineer in the true tradition, proud of his calling and very careful about his machinery. The *Earl's* engines were handsome. With cylinders encased in teak, bound in brass and highly polished, all moving and stationary parts reflected the same care.

"The *Earl's* engines were in splendid working order; what was in question was the power they might generate in the face of seas surging straight into the narrow gap between Bruray and Grunay. From the bridge the welter of breaking water at the actual entrance looked formidable, swelling and bursting in thundering explosions of astonishingly white spray, then falling back in streaming light rivulets against the black rocks. And above, the fast-moving dirty grey layers of storm scud. It was an inhospitable scene. But we had to go."

A wind-torn banner of white at the safety-valve on the grey funnel indicated the head of steam as Adam Tait rang down for "Full Ahead". And all of the rather meagre 50 h.p. was brought to bear on the heaped up ridges pounding into the channel and creating creamy foam, driving hard before the sudden gale. The *Earl* dipped her straight stem into the first of the crests, throwing aside sheets of water, rose, dipped again and slammed into wave after wave, slowly, hesitatingly. If she lost way and her bow caught the wind she would be in pieces on rocks on either side, for there was no room whatever in which to manoeuvre.

Adam Tait continued: "Sure enough, Findlay opened her up for all she was worth. She staggered — I can see her yet — butted her way through, and gradually pulled out until we were clear. The sea

was just like snow drifting. For hours we battled to get through to
Mid Yell. Because the *Earl* did not have much speed she could not
hurt herself going head on. She had to be tacked in heavy seas. But
running before the wind she was lovely and would have run right
down to Australia without pooping a sea. She would just sail along
beautifully. In fact she was as good as another old ship belonging to
the North Company, the clipper bowed *St. Clair,* which was
magnificent stern-on to big seas. The *Earl,* despite the low well-deck,
did not take water to do any harm. It was never a problem, which
shows how dry she went. And that day going to Mid Yell was bad,
but she just took her own good time. We were relieved to get there,
went well in, put down both anchors, and that was us for the night.''

::   ::   ::   ::   ::   ::

If the weather continued to pose such risks, the dangers from the
war itself gradually lessened as the Allies persistently gnawed at the
Germans on various fronts throughout 1941, 1942 and 1943,
although for long months after the successive disasters which led to
the anomaly of Dunkirk — a defeat in retreat, but a victory in
survival — the Nazi monster extended its greedy maw in ever
expanding Imperialism. The submissive co-operation of the Italians
to the German Reich meant that the Mediterranean — within a few
years to be the scene of the *Earl's* final voyage — was dominated by
the Axis Powers. In June, 1941, Morocco in western North Africa,
Algeria, Tunisia and Libya on the southern shores, France, Italy,
Yugoslavia, Albania, and Greece on the northern shores, and the
islands of Corsica, Sardinia, Sicily and Crete, were all occupied by
the enemy. Tiny Malta — ultimately the George Cross island —
Cyprus, Egypt, Palestine and Transjordan were the only bastions
remaining to the beleaguered British. Little wonder the outlook
seemed bleak. However, the insatiable appetite of the monster led to
events which proved to be its undoing. Previous alliance proved a
worthless scrap of paper when in June, 1941, there was a massive
German assault on Russia over a wide front, and 120 divisions were
committed. As Poland had been caught napping in 1939, so Russia
was easily invaded from the Baltic to the Black Sea. In the first month
the Germans bit and tore their way 300 miles. Mistakenly, Hitler
sought to destroy Russian armies on the widest front, and so stretched
his resources unduly through misguided confidence. Such policy was
greeted with some relief in Britain. It eased the air attack and
diminished the threat of invasion, while the inevitable perseverence of
the Russians, coupled with vast tracts of countryside gripped by the

icy winter, eventually inflicted mortal injury on the Nazi colossus.

Meanwhile human sacrifice was immense, not least that of the Jewish inhabitants. With thousands of square miles gobbled up, the populace was over-run, and a callous enemy had no regard for life. The Jews were completely vulnerable. Only tolerated, but never accepted through the vast U.S.S.R. countryside, when the Germans came, tolerance was replaced by eradication. The city of Kiev was typical of the Nazi approach. When its defenders succumbed to the infidels, 150,000 men, women and children were killed, and another 50,000 fled. Of those who were massacred 140,000 were Jews. Their mass grave in a ravine near Kiev inspired the humanistic Yevtushenko, a Russian poet, to write in complaint that there is no memorial at Babi Yar to this tragedy: then he denounced those who "with unclean hands have often loudly taken in vain Russia's most pure name". The Babi Yar grave is thus an unmarked (but not forgotten) incidental memorial to the several hundred thousand Ukrainian and White Russian Jews who were systematically removed from the face of the earth. But then in the 1880s, and in Odessa in 1905, there were the infamous pogroms in which Jews suffered massacre — a people fated to endure injustices at the hands of those without regard for the basic tenets of human rights. Understandably they were a people desperately committed to the ultimate aim of the State of Israel, although that dream, a reality in 1948, was a nightmare of uncertainty over thousands of square miles of Europe in the early forties.

There was also repression and persecution in the Axis-occupied lands in North Africa. Jewish people in their thousands in this part of the Diaspora — the collective term used to denote all Jewish communities outside Palestine — resolved to look to the Promised Land with the silent determination of a population dominated, but not suppressed, by a hated enemy, and the idealistic incentive of seeking what was regarded as their divine right. The Nazi decision to invade Russia constituted an abomination for Russian Jews, but permitted Britain, the only remaining European bastion of freedom, to re-establish, recoup and eventually play a vital part in winning peace and democracy, creating the climate of opportunity which allowed liberation of choice.

Then, ironically, Britain proved to be a stumbling block in the ardent post-war desire in the Diaspora to flood the Land with people. The problem was the British Mandate, the trusteeship of Palestine with its restricted immigration. Navy vessels were responsible for the attempted blockade of a great and complex fleet of ships, official and unofficial, which between 1934 and 1948 brought vast numbers of aspiring immigrants to the shores of the eastern Mediterranean. Although immigrant traffic was necessarily much reduced by the fates and scale of the war, it continued spasmodically as the tide gradually turned and the spectre of defeat for Germany loomed ever larger.

In May, 1943, Britain and her Allies avenged Dunkirk when they pushed the enemy into the sea in Tunisia, and in August they repeated the feat in Sicily. Never happy with the association with the Nazis the Italians signed armistice terms which put immense pressure on the Germans as they gave ground only tenaciously up through Italy. Such successes encouraged the Allies to initiate the great invasion of France known as Operation Overlord 6th June, 1944. Apart from the glorious but abortive deeds at Arnhem and setback in the Ardennes, British, Canadian and American forces drove into Europe through the autumn of 1944 until, in March 1945, the end was clearly in sight. Hitler's Germany faced defeat. From the east the Russians commanded a wide front. The shattered countryside was recrossed revealing, stage by stage, the horrendous activities of the foe. It had been a devastation of humanity and no group suffered more than the Jews. Six million were dead, a third of the Jewish population of the world, and half of those in Europe. Gradually the evidence emerged. Allied servicemen — American, British, Canadian and Russian alike — were sickened by the confirmation of reports and rumours about the extent of the degradation and death as they opened up the concentration and extermination camps. Stick-like human frames greeted the soldiers with grimaces of pathetic delight from a living hell; others, stacked indiscriminately in grisly piles, totally emaciated and misshapen, were beyond all aid; others again were but ashes from the furnaces of a loathsome and depraved enemy. Seeing was believing. Entire families had gone: sometimes the grandparents; sometimes the parents; often the fathers; often sons and daughters. It was the attempted destruction of a race of people. There were, however, the survivors who had witnessed the crimes, frequently whose closest relatives had been murdered in cold blood. Much had been endured stoically. What choice was there and who could forget the unimagineable truth? With such a background, the great upsurge by the Jews in the Diaspora to attain unity, security and lasting peace by the creation of the State of Israel, was so entirely understandable. It was an ultimate of incentives.

:: :: :: :: :: ::

If the *Earl of Zetland's* eventual contribution to the Jewish cause was fractional, her presence in Shetland in the last few years of her career remained vital. It was Freddie Pottinger, originally a cabin boy and ultimately catering manager of the North Company in Aberdeen, before his retirement to Lerwick, who said: "The *Earl* was a lifeline." In essence this had been so often acknowledged, especially publicly when she had "retired" in 1939. Here she was, still going strong in 1943, cargo after cargo, both civilian and service; hundreds of members of the Forces introduced to her vagaries on tough days of gales, butting northwards to Unst with its most northerly garrison in the British Isles; hundreds, fascinated then seduced by the peculiar and particular atmosphere of the still days of a Shetland summer. And the leisurely-paced flitboat emerging from a silent shore as it had done for decades, rowed out gently to meet the grey-clad steamer bristling with armaments, contrasting the peace of the moment. For servicemen acutely aware of their day-to-day existence, these were hours of escape to savour and to be long remembered in nostalgic recollection. Again and again the *Earl* made her indelible impression on the memories of men like C. Birnie of Aberdeen, then in the R.A.F. on the radar station at Skaw, who recalled: "Naturally we had to travel on the *Earl* from Lerwick and we were completely enthralled by the journey, calling at all the islands en route, disposing of a couple of ponies here, bags of sugar there . . . One day when we left Unst the weather was brilliant, not a ripple on the water, no wind and blue skies all the way. We were each given a fair tot of Naval rum once we left Baltasound, then about half the lads — and we were lads, all in our early twenties — were at the rail wishing that there had been no bacon and eggs for breakfast. But the *Earl* was not blamed, only the rum! I used the steamer regularly. Sometimes the weather was very heavy, but she always got us there, bless her."

Meanwhile tremendous pressures exerted by the Allies on the European fronts greatly diluted the ability of the enemy to keep up an offensive even in terms of the U-boat war, with the result that by mid-1943 the risks in Shetland waters had been much reduced and ships like the *Earl* could move in relative security. This was to the great relief of Adam Tait and Davie Henry who had met with resignation and acceptance born of quiet courage, the grim exposure to the Germans on the east side of the islands. They had been tested and they had fought back. The risk graph had now passed its peak and was on the decline. True, the Blenheim-like JU88 and bullet-nosed Heinkel still attempted forays furtively made over the North Sea, to be met aggressively by fast-moving fighters from Sumburgh and the R.A.F. station at Scatsta bordering Sullom Voe. Radar at Skaw gave fair warning of enemy presence and interception was likely before aircraft could attack vessels like the *Earl* sailing close inshore. The likelihood of a repeat of the close shave of the 1941 bombing was remote.

In 1941 the British and Norwegians had established communications with the Resistance movements in occupied Norway, and uncompromising men had created the famous "Shetland Bus" organisation. A group of Norwegian patriots operated at first from Lunna, using a small fleet of typical fishing boats. Even the *Erkna*, salvaged by the *Earl*, was pressed into service as a reserve boat. Bard Grotle was a skipper of adventurous and near-piratical attitude. He would sail at his own convenience to anywhere between Bergen and the Lofoten Islands. With *Aksel*, Grotle's own boat, laid up with engine trouble he took the *Erkna* to Traena which lies on the Arctic Circle. She had never been fitted out with additional fuel tanks, so carried on deck spare oil in 40 gallon drums. On the return trip, with decks constantly awash, it was impossible to refuel in the heavy weather, but the intrepid Bard thought nothing of returning to enemy waters and shelter, to replenish the tanks. By mid-1942 the "Shetland Bus" activities had grown confidently to the extent that there was a Shetland-based effort to cripple the German battleship *Tirpitz* lying in a near impregnable position at the head of Trondheimfjord. This imaginative and ambitious scheme deserved a better fate, but the two-man torpedoes, known as "Chariots," were lost, along with the famous former Norwegian fishing boat *Arthur,* within a few miles of the target. Such raids were a serious thorn in the German flesh, one of many which, collectively, contrived to pin down a quarter of a million or more of the enemy in Norway. The people in Norway knew that the route to and from Shetland was kept open, and the "Shetland Bus" operators landed no fewer than 60 radio transmitters and a small army of personnel to harass the enemy and to ensure that the Allied High Command were well informed. Over the years the boats transported hundreds of tons of weapons and ammunition, of immense psychological and practical value to the Norwegian freedom fighters. By late 1943 the base, transferred to Scalloway, was equipped with three American submarine chasers, powerful and strong craft capable of 22 knots, which undertook more and more expeditions across the North Sea in ever expanding security. The *Earl's* men noted with admiration the angled prow, clean cut thrusting hull and deep bow-wave of a submarine chaser, such a remarkable contrast to the straight stem, full bows and modest wash produced by the old steamer's eight knots. They noted the ever-increasing number of voyages made, not only from Scalloway but from Lerwick, although now that Lunna had been discarded as a base, the "Shetland Bus" vessels did not pass between Fetlar and

Whalsay as they had done in earlier years when the *Earl* was playing her part in picking up the variety of refugees, a feature of German invasion which, latterly, had virtually ended. In fact there was no small satisfaction for the steamer's crew in knowing that the same *Erkna* which they had salvaged had gone on to sail to Norway against the Germans.

It could all be described as only a circumstantial contribution in the great complexity of waging a war, but, taken with the multiplicity of the *Earl's* wartime exploits, the impact made by a very small passenger/cargo steamer on a vital British garrison can be portrayed as very important. Arguably her personnel might have received more recognition, for in the booklet issued by the North of Scotland and Orkney and Shetland Steam Navigation Company Limited in 1946, the *Earl* was referred to five times. Next was the *St. Magnus* mentioned three times. The *Earl's* counterpart in Orkney, the *St. Ola,* merited two entries, one the sighting of a floating mine in the Pentland Firth and, secondly, the rescue of the occupants of a British aircraft from the sea. By contrast, up to February, 1942 the sharp-shooters on the *Earl of Zetland* had disposed of 16 allied and enemy floating mines, an aspect not mentioned in the publication. The final total was well in excess of that figure. And, of course, the steamer was involved in an impressive number of rescue and salvage operations. Of the North Company, four skippers received the M.B.E., being Captains McMillan, Dundas, Swanson and Tom Gifford. John Stewart, a chief engineer, was also awarded the M.B.E. Captain William Gifford earned the O.B.E.

Family associations had long been a characteristic of the North Company. As an example, the Gifford family had been destined to contribute remarkably and unusually to this feature. William Gifford's father was chief officer on the first *St. Rognvald.* William and Tom Gifford, so recently successor to Willie Spence, were indirectly related. Of course Tom's brother, Laurence (Lowrie), also crewed on the old and new *Earl.* Later on, in 1953, Tom's son, also Tom, joined the new vessel as a seaman before taking his mate's ticket. Subsequently, in 1972, when Captain Willie Sinclair retired from the *Earl,* his successor was Captain Michael Gray who had married a grand-daughter of William Gifford. To add to the fascinating complexity of relationships Michael Gray's father, John, was a first cousin to David Gray the purser. For many years John Gray and his wife taught on Whalsay and knew the old steamer exceptionally well. Tom Gifford jnr. had relieved as mate on the new *Earl,* skippered the *St. Clement* and *St. Rognvald,* and in 1977 Captains Gifford and Gray became joint skippers of the 4,468 ton *St. Clair,* a roll-on, roll-off vessel operating between Aberdeen and Lerwick for P&O Ferries who had bought over the old North Company. It was an impressive family connection stretching back in an unbroken sequence for 80 years.

Such continuity had certainly been a trait in the careers of men who served on the *Earl*, although Adam Tait's command was rather shorter than it might have been. After a somewhat unexpected appointment in 1940, he had proved to be an outstanding skipper, guiding ship, crew, passengers and cargoes in circumstances far more dangerous than had been experienced by any of his predecessors. Men like Nicolson, Scott, Johnson and Spence had acquitted themselves with distinction in Shetland waters without the uncertainties of a war which brought the enemy so much nearer than during the 1914-18 conflict. The 1941 JU88 bombs summed up the risk, because only providence or the Lord's guidance stood between continuing existence or eternity. At least by the dawning of 1944 the Germans were being held at bay, easing the difficulties for the crew of the aged steamer, and the spring and summer were much nearer normal.

In September, 1944, Adam Tait was appointed to the staff of Leith Nautical College based in the ship *Dolphin* at Leith Docks. His long seafaring experience and qualifications were well fitted for a task he relished, despite a reluctance to depart from a ship and crew for which he had real affection. But he took with him the goodwill of a community which had been under siege.

The natural successor was Captain David Henry, who had unswervingly supported his skipper throughout the worst and most uncertain days of the struggle. Now it was his task to pilot the *Earl of Zetland* through what were to be her last months in Shetland. He had been on her since May, 1939, was well versed in her idiosyncracies, and knew the North Isles like the back of his hand.

Over the decades few Shetland seamen have been able to swim — those who could being comfortably in a minority. Davie Henry was one of that relatively small group, and more than once he found the skill an asset. Considering the proximity of the sea in all the *Earl's* working, whether at Lerwick in manhandling cargo down planks between pier and well-deck, or at the ports with a flitboat rising and falling alongside, very few people ended up in the sea. But one chilly February day, full paraffin barrels were being eased along the planks at Lerwick by dockers and crew when Lowrie Gifford at the winch shouted: ''I tink dat Wullie has gone in the ditch''. Davie, who was at the hatch in the well-deck, never paused, but dropped over the side and managed to hold the struggling docker until a lifebelt and rope's end appeared in the dark water between the ship's belting and the
Q

piles of the pier. The two men, none the worse of the unexpected and
very icy dip, were back on the deck within seconds.

There was also the boy at Burravoe. Whether or not the anchor
went down at a port depended on the amount of cargo. If only one or
two passengers were to be put ashore the skipper rang for "Dead
Slow" and the *Earl* would have way on her and no more as a small
boat eased alongside to be briefly tied up. On this occasion at
Burravoe the flitboat came off because there was a calf to be loaded
onto the steamer. Any youthful Shetlander or visitor loved to go off to
the *Earl,* thus not surprisingly there was a lad on board the flitboat as
it closed in at the open doors of the well-deck. Like hundreds before
it, the animal was unceremoniously hoisted through space, a broad
canvas sling round its belly, eyes, legs and tail protruding
grotesquely, until it was hustled through to the cattle pens below the
bridge. Meanwhile steamer and flitboat moved gently ahead. The
boy had been balancing on the low gunwale when a gap opened up.
Caught unawares he pitched awkwardly into the water and was in
immediate trouble, drifting aft away from the *Earl's* side. Again
Davie went over for a cold douche, managed to grasp clothing, and
he hauled the lad over to the flitboat where he was bundled aboard,
limp from the immersion, but still very much alive. Such events were
unusual in that few incidents were recorded, although Davie's reflex
responses undeniably helped to preserve the *Earl's* proud record of
never having lost a human life. That the record was sustained during
the war years is of remarkable consequence when the vessel carried
such a great multitude of servicemen.

Throughout the autumn of 1944 the old grey-painted steamer
continued in her diversity of work in the war effort and domestic
circulation of the ports. Evidence of the recession in German power
showed unquestionably when the Shetland Home Guard was
officially stood down before Christmas, and the *Earl* transported units
of the Forces away from the North Isles. Now there was nothing
whatever to fear from the enemy by air or sea. The fate of Hitler's
cause was being decided by Allied successes on the Rhine and Ruhr
in the heart of Germany. Defeat was a matter of time. By the early
spring of 1945 the Allies had a stranglehold on every front. The
capitulation on 4th May of the armies facing Field-Marshal
Montgomery was followed by a general unconditional surrender to
the Allies. The surrender document for the German war was
unequivocal: "All hostilities on land, on sea, or in the air by German
forces . . . to cease at 0800 hours British Double Summer Time on
Saturday, 5th May, 1945".

The announcement in Britain came on Monday, 7th May, and

the entire country rejoiced and celebrated. On the Tuesday, in company with communities through the United Kingdom, all Shetland exulted. Bunting flew stiffly before a strong breeze along the Victoria Pier and Alexandra Wharf in Lerwick. The *Earl* appeared, the brightness of her flags contrasting with the neutral over-all battleship grey of her hull, funnel and masts. It was the final opportunity, the last time the aged steamer would be dressed overall. The termination of World War II was the virtual termination of the old *Earl of Zetland* — the war had given her a reprieve which could not last. Nevertheless there had been no abandonment by the North Company of the maintenance, care and attention which had been lavished on her over the long years. She had still gone south to Aberdeen for annual survey. She had always been well presented even during the war, temporarily grey overall, any signs of rust quickly hidden. Thus she went for her final survey with Davie Henry between 9th and 19th April, 1945. "The Shetland Times" recorded further transition on Friday, 22nd June, with a heading: "Old *Earl* Discards War Paint", and a paragraph: "People in the North Isles will be pleased to welcome the old *Earl (Earl of Zetland II)* in her peacetime paint again when she arrives today (Friday). Painting was done yesterday by the crew, with extra helpers, so that the transformation should be as complete as possible." The highly acceptable and gratefully welcomed change brought heart-felt pleasure to the outlying hamlets. It symbolised so much. Only the gun emplacements still remaining recalled the preceding six grim years. Her hull and smokestack gleamed black, contrasting the white rails and lifebelts; masts and derricks restored to the buff colour standard to the company's ships. The black section was replaced on her main-mast. So the *Earl* settled into the peace-time sailings, although clearly her end was in sight — whatever form it might take. In Aberdeen plans were made for her disposal. The directors resolved to attempt a sale rather than commit the 68 year old ship to the indignity of the breakers' hammer — at least not yet. No-one on the board could then visualise the extraordinary manner in which she outlived her time, and brought life to bear on a cause of life.

Davie Henry guided her fortunes for several more months. Still the routine. No longer the threats, apart from risks posed by the weather. In July, 1945, Captain Henry left the North Company, having achieved much as mate and skipper, and Captain William Ramsay, yet another Yell man, took over. With the conflict in Europe ended, the summer and autumn of 1945 passed peacefully, Shetland gradually returning to normal life, the lights of Lerwick and shipping again reflected in the waters of Bressay Sound.

Thomas McLaren and Company, the Glasgow shipbrokers, had been appointed agents for the sale of the *Earl of Zetland II*. A leaflet with a plan layout of the steamer on the reverse side appeared and was widely distributed in shipping circles. It announced: "Handy General Cargo and Passenger Steamer. Has always been employed in an easy regular General Cargo trade and has been kept up regardless of cost. She will be found to be in excellent condition for a vessel of her age." A description indicated, in addition to standard dimensions, that she was Class 90 A1 at Lloyd's, had a last Special Survey in October, 1931, and was examined in April, 1945. A new boiler had been fitted in October 1923 and was retubed in 1943, also a new tailshaft was attached that year. Speed was stated to be nine knots on a consumption of eight/nine tons of coal per 24 hours. Offers of around £6,000 were sought.

While the old *Earl* worked through the closing stages of her spectacular contribution to wartime Shetland, her erstwhile successor, the trim motor vessel of the same name, was still operating under Scottish Command (Army), sailing across the Pentland Firth as she had done throughout the war. Occasionally the two vessels had been seen together in Orkney waters when the first *Earl* was on replacement for her counterpart the old *St. Ola,* away for maintenance in Aberdeen, and each *Earl* had offered tremendous service to her country in both Shetland and Orkney. Many folk in Shetland, especially in the North Isles, reflected on the hand of fate and the sequence of events over the protracted and exacting months and years of the war. It would not be long before they had an opportunity to relish what had been so keenly anticipated back in August, 1939 — the services of a fast and powerful motor vessel with vastly superior facilities and accommodation. She had not had real opportunity to display her potential in the North Isles, since she had been requisitioned after only four months on the run. On the other hand the new ship had been there long enough for the folk to consider the inadequacies and limitations of her veteran predecessor. They thought of many things, especially matters of creature comforts. Below the bridge, human beings and animals shared a cramped common area open at the for'ard end; in the new *Earl* passengers were offered a large enclosed space with windows, comfortable and relatively draught free, clear of animals and the elements. No risk then of the kind of tide lump in Yell Sound which had been known to fill the old ship's well-deck to knee-level and sweep aft towards the accommodation and saloon. Even the galley had had its fire jeopardised by salt water! In the new vessel the galley, pantry and dining saloon were compactly placed on the upper deck. No difficulty then for cook or steward in transferring food.

Improvements for the crew would be even more marked. Any discomfort for passengers in the ancient Fullerton steamer was transitory — a matter of hours — but the mate, purser, chief engineer, four seamen, and two firemen and greasers had endured confined conditions right up for'ard and under the fo'c'sle. It could be a damp and draughty place in heavy weather, although there were occasions without number when the entire crew would gather round the stove in the crew's quarters for an evening of yarning at terminal ports like Baltasound and North Roe. The captain had his bunk under the bridge, the cook enjoyed the relative comfort of a minute cabin adjoining the after end of the engineroom casing, and the chief steward had accommodation next to the pantry. Lastly, the cabin boy slept on the broad shelf at the extreme after end of the dining saloon!

The navigation and working of the old *Earl* had taxed many men, exposure to the vissicitudes of Shetland weather nevertheless accepted stoically. Willie Spence had been known to come off the bridge after a bad night of roaring seas, howling gale and flying, bitterly cold spray with his lips cracked and bleeding from hours on the open bridge. And many a seaman had come off a trick at the wheel with fingers devoid of circulation despite gloves or mittens. Astonishingly, no steps were taken to ease the situation until the end was in sight. The bridge wing shelters and wheelhouse came too late to be of lasting value.

All that would be different. Good berths for the crew. No more the shouted command from bridge to wheel below, but a quiet word in the shelter and comfort of the enclosed bridge and wheelhouse of the Hall, Russell motor vessel. If folk were sorry to see the old *Earl* finally go, it had to be said that the war years had confirmed her limitations. Such comparisons had been made before the outbreak of war, and inevitably when the communities were suddenly deprived of their new-found luxury in January, 1940, to be replaced by the spartan conditions of yesteryear, the old *Earl* had been the subject of certain strong criticism. That, however, was now of the past. At least credit was given for a difficult task undertaken and accomplished in a manner so individual and characteristic. The *Earl of Zetland II* had done a good job.

Curiously, her prolonged departure into extinction coincided with the passing of two men who between them had offered and contributed yeoman service to trade and travel in Shetland. In mid-December, 1945, the intimate atmosphere of the well-used dining saloon was the setting for a retiral presentation to the long-serving purser, David Gray, who had devoted 40 years of his life to the North

Company, 30 of which had been on the veteran steamer. Davie was given a wallet of treasury notes subscribed by the *Earl's* crew, the Lerwick office staff, and the permanent staff on duty at the Victoria Pier. Only 57 years of age, this outstanding character was forced to take a shore job through ill-health and he became factor to the Garth Estate. Sadly, only months after taking leave of his beloved ship, he collapsed and died suddenly on Monday, 2nd March, 1946.

Less than a year previously it was the same Davie Gray who had penned a tribute to his former skipper, Willie Spence, who had died in April, 1945. "In the passing of Captain Spence, Shetland has lost a man of physical strength and courage. His temperament was at times a little blunt but, looking beyond that, you discovered a kindly obliging personality, ready at all times to take the heavy end of the stick and never asking his crew to do anything he could not do himself. His over-anxiousness to accommodate the public under the exposed conditions no doubt was the cause of the ill health he suffered in the years of his retirement. One thing I will always remember is that he never proffered nor cared to receive cheap praise, always minimising his accomplishments rather than magnifying them".

If the slightly built purser did not possess Willie Spence's physical strength, most of the comments would have applied to Gray himself.

In the autumn of 1945 the new *Earl* arrived in Aberdeen from Scrabster for reconditioning. By the end of November she had been suitably refurbished inside and out in peacetime garb, and headed north for Lerwick at 5 p.m. on 10th December with a full cargo, under command of Tom Gifford, with Leonard Mainland as his mate. "The Shetland Times" commented: "The *Earl of Zetland* arrived on Tuesday at 1 p.m. after a smart run from Aberdeen. The vessel is in fine condition despite the large number of passengers carried, and is a credit to Captain Gifford, his officers and crew".

Although there was lively interest in her appearance, the immaculately presented motor vessel created rather less acclaim than during her ceremonial arrival over six long years previously. She was unloaded immediately, took on a cargo for the North Isles, and sailed from Lerwick at 4 a.m. on the Wednesday. She left her predecessor lying forlornly alongside at the innermost part of Victoria Pier, until steam was raised for the old *Earl's* transference to the Pentland Firth. At 4 p.m. on 20th December she slipped almost un-noticed out of the "sooth mooth" skippered by Willie Ramsay. He was accompanied by Leonard Mainland, who had transferred as mate. About 15 hours later they took her into Stromness, her orders being to assist the *St. Ola* on the Orkney run from Scrabster.

Over the years, during relief work in the notorious and treacherous Firth, the *Earl* had been subjected to rough treatment on occasion. Wind and tide in conflict could raise mountainous waves, steeply pitched with tops torn off in seething whiteness, before a force nine or storm force ten when sailing would be impossible. Even a force eight could be bad enough and a decision about whether or not to go was never easy. Such was the situation one early morning during the month of January, 1946. The day was very bad with heavy seas driving into the mouth of Hoy Sound from the north-west. Captain Ramsay, anxious to maintain his schedule from Stromness, decided to go and as the *Earl* turned towards the west at the outermost buoy the spray was already spurting aft over her foredeck. The seas increased in size as the steamer edged out between the Kirk rocks to starboard and the Bow rocks to port, reefs which had sealed the fate of numerous old sailing vessels of another era. After an hour of hard steaming the ship was labouring, slowly, painfully, at a point of no return, for with the nature of the coastline and direction of the wind, to put her broadside on would be to invite trouble. Willie Ramsay kept a course well out from the land, taking the force of the gale on the starboard bow. This was in the nature of a "starboard tack", the essential method used by a succession of masters, although on this occasion the *Earl* was gradually being worked to seaward to keep well clear of St. John's point and Rora Head on the west side of Hoy. There was no relief and no comfort for anyone on board. Visibility was restricted in the poor January daylight, although not enough to hide the size of the onrushing masses of water. When it loomed out of the murk, the biggest sea yet looked enormous. Willie Ramsay and Leonard Mainland on the bridge saw it coming, off the starboard beam, but there was nothing they could do except hang on. They were about mid-Firth and three hours out from Stromness.

The ship staggered and came almost to a halt as a cataract of green water crashed over the bows and obliterated from sight the anchor windlass, fo'c'sle stove lum, and companionway. The torrent foamed round the cargo lights below the bell on the foremast, reached partly up the bottom end of the derrick at its mast coupling and poured down into the well-deck with a mighty roar. More of it was angled in over the starboard bulwarks at the well-deck doors and deluged the catwalk between maindeck and fo'c'sle. The top of the sea came at the teak bulwarks below the bridge and momentarily filled the deck round the tiny wheelhouse, eventually spending itself aft round engineroom casing, funnel and engineroom skylight and round the boats, and cascaded down from whence it came.

Tons of water pouring into the well-deck had no easy exit.

Initially it could only wash fore and aft until the scuppers could cope. The result was chaos — water waist-deep submerged the firmly secured main hatch in the well-deck, spilled over the bulwarks at first one side then the other as the *Earl* rolled, surged round the derrick winch, and penetrated the passageway between the crew accommodation and ladies' steerage cabin under the fo'c'sle. It swept aft through the empty animal pens, entered the purser's office and filled the galley where it extinguished the fire and ruined a meal in preparation. Freddie Pottinger had the unenviable experience of solid water washing up beyond his waist and wondering what was going to happen next. Such was the violence of the movement from that mighty sea that the bolts securing the old bogey-stove in the dining saloon gave, and the stove shifted. Seen from the bridge the forepart of the ship virtually disappeared, although solid water failed to reach captain and mate, and they were greatly relieved when the *Earl* shook herself clear. The crew then set to with any receptacles available and hurriedly baled as required. Eventually order was restored, a check revealed no undue damage, and Willie Ramsay gradually swung the ship round to the east which brought her stern to bear on the charging seas. The next exceptionally big sea did not break and her splendid sea-keeping stern lifted her up as its crest reared. Briefly her whole length pointed down into the trough, an awesome sight from the bridge, but the monster passed harmlessly below. The severe gale persisted with its dangers and difficulties until, a couple of hours later, the ship's motion eased in Scrabster Bay and her crew gave a universal sigh of relief. Such an experience was another reminder of the power of the ocean, although it proved to be the last time the old *Earl* was to be so severely battered. Any other bad weather in the Pentland Firth during the rest of January and February, 1946, never posed the same problems.

No-one in Shetland ever expected to see the old *Earl* again. People were content enough with the performance and convenience of the replacement. Her visits to the North Isles and Yell Sound ports in the first two months of 1946 proved that the new *Earl* was going to be a worthy successor. She had the right kind of speed and carrying capacity to suit all interested parties. Events elsewhere, however, decreed one ultimate change. Immediately after the war the agricultural economy of Orkney expanded fast and the North Company discovered a shortage of shipping space. A new ship, the *St. Clement,* was on the stocks, but was not likely to be available for some months, thus the management discussed which ship would best serve the Kirkwall to Aberdeen run. The answer was simple; they would bring the *Earl of Zetland* south again. At least it was appreciated that the development was very temporary when Willie Ramsay brought the old *Earl* through the "sooth mooth" at the beginning of March. This merited a brief sentence in "The Shetland Times". "The *Earl of Zetland II* arrived in Lerwick early on Sunday morning." In fact the arrangement was maintained for almost four months and met with resignation throughout the North Isles and North Mainland. Finally on 21st June, 1946, the *Earl of Zetland II* made her way towards Aberdeen to be put on view for interested parties in response to the circular which had publicised the sale. Captain William Ramsay had the privilege of taking her south. He had as his mate William Nicolson (Willie) Sinclair, grandson of William Nicolson, first skipper of the *Earl* who had watched her being built near enough 70 years before, and as his engineer Peter Johnson, son of another commander in the early years of the century. The other coincidence featured the bo'sun who was the long-serving Lowrie Gifford whose brother Tom had captained the old *Earl* and now was destined to play a significant part in the North Company.

There was little to do at Aberdeen. They had sailed empty and berthed her beside the North Company offices at Matthews Quay in the lower harbour where she remained overnight. Captain Ramsay was called away next day, thus it was left to William Sinclair to take his grandfather's ship up through the confines of the harbour to her resting place at Regent's Quay. It came about then, that a grandson and a son and a brother of former captains provided the aged steamer with a fitting touch of sentiment through a family connection, for her work in a long lifetime had been all about the family of the community. Her crew were paid off on 24th June, 1946, and the original *Earl of Zetland* was left to her fate.

As she awaited disposal throughout the months of July and August, 1946, the repercussions of the Nazi disregard for all that is right and proper were reverberating round a world seeking stability in an uneasy peace. That the old ship could conceivably have any influence on any aspect of it would seem utterly remote and any associations with strange names like, "Haganah", "Yishuv", "Yehuda Halevy" and "Mossad", highly unlikely. Nevertheless she was to become part — a tiny microcosm — of a history-making project which arose partly from a deep-seated belief in a promised land for the Jews of the world and partly from a people — a community — desperate to escape all the evidence of a ravaged Europe.

12

An Old Vision Renewed

Inexorably the Jewish peoples of Europe had been decimated, a hitherto unbelievable price paid for their nationality. Human standards had been utterly devastated in an appallingly systematic attempt at genocide, and survivors were irrevocably resolved to an escape from everything associated with the dreadful purge of the early 1940s. The urgency was proclaimed in a Haganah (the organisation for Jewish defence, founded in 1920) poster: ''They are coming. Driven by suffering they have taken the one way of light for Jews in this world — the road to Israel. The world and the nations' hearts are

Shipowners prepared to release ancient vessels . . .

S.S. EARL OF ZETLAND

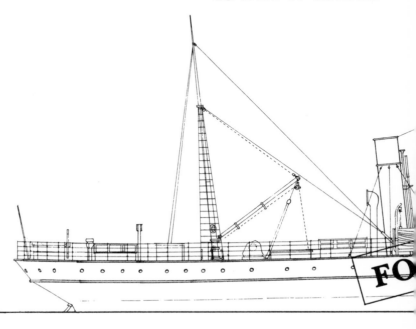

closed to them. Only one hope exists — homeland. Only one heart is open — that is of the Yishuv (The Jewish population of the land), the heart of brothers. Cruel laws will not stop them, barbed wire will not frighten nor bayonets deter them; if denied, their spirit will not break. They come and they will continue to come to their homeland, the Land of Israel''.

The ardent wish so strikingly declared was not only a product of man's inhumanity to man, but there existed the idealism of the Biblical proclamations: ''And I will plant them upon their land, and they shall no more be pulled up out of their land which I have given them saith the Lord thy God. And they shall dwell in the land that I have given unto Jacob my servant, wherein your fathers have dwelt, and they shall dwell in it even then, and their children, and their children's children for ever.'' Belief in the certainty of such statements had been an inspiration and incentive from time immemorial. Its conviction ensured that groups and individuals fought for its rights, and Palestine's position at the great cross roads

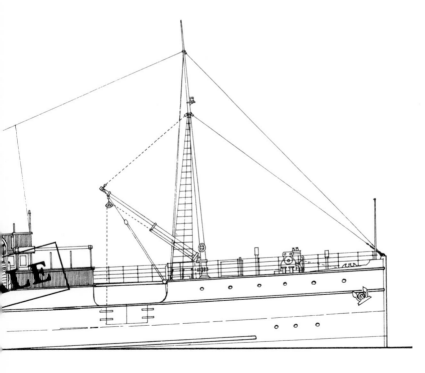

of the Middle East led to a succession of invaders who inevitably created problems which activated the idealistic fervour of the Jewish people. Philistines, Babylonians, Persians, Macedonians, Romans, Arabs, and Crusaders all had extensive forays into Palestine. The latter had been organised by the Church to counter the acts of vandalism by peoples who had attacked the Christian countries; also to colonise "a land more fruitful than any other land, like paradise in its beauties." The colonisation, however, brought such an enormous variety of invaders of different aims that continuing warfare was inevitable and the rapacious hordes murdered and robbed indiscriminately. The Jewish community was shattered. In the conquest of Jerusalem the streets were strewn with the bodies of men and women and the shattered limbs of children. Jews were assembled inside their synagogue which was set on fire. Many were taken into slavery, some drowned or beheaded on the way. People in towns and villages near Jerusalem suffered similar fates, but Samaria and Galilee were not so drastically treated. Those who fled moved to neighbouring countries or to communities which had been fortunate enough to escape the ravages of the Crusaders and, gradually, survivors began to return. The Crusaders made no attempt to prevent this, although the sacred city of Jerusalem was completely barred. Galilee was a centre of development, while Jews in coastal towns participated in overseas trade, which activity the Crusaders encouraged because of food shortages. There were commercial transactions between Jews in these coastal towns and Jews of Spain and other European countries, trade which helped to rehabilitate the Israelites.

Hardly a single Jew doubted that the persecutions and massacres were a prelude to the days of the Messiah, and none believed that the Crusaders would be permanent rulers. Such beliefs sponsored a religious dedication in communities in Palestine, Syria, Mesopotamia, Persia, the Yemen, Morocco, Spain and France. The hoped for coming of the Messiah and resultant redemption led to calls for Jews to return to the Land of Israel, calls which were eloquently expressed through the creative poetry of one Yehuda Halevi: "Doves who flock in distant lands — whose wings droop — rise up! Yours is not a place of rest. Your home is troubled."

It is likely that Halevi was born in Tudela in Northern Spain near the end of the eleventh century. Apparently from a wealthy and learned family, he had the privilege of a thorough education in Hebrew and Arabic during peaceful years for the Jewish community. At an early age he travelled and in Cordoba entered a poetry writing contest, which he won. This led to contacts with great poets in

Granada, Seville and Saragossa, and Halevi lived in Granada in an atmosphere of wealth and culture until the position of the Jews in Andalusia deteriorated and the poet began to travel again. For 20 years he journeyed through a variety of communities, adding steadily to his fame. His financial position was sound and, aside from his profession as a physician, he also engaged in trade with Jewish merchants in Egypt, North Africa and Narbonne, which connections extended his journeys.

Yehuda Halevi had always felt deeply about the concept of the Promised Land, thus it was not surprising that he eventually decided to go to Palestine. It reflected the highest aspirations of his life. It resulted from a complex of circumstances: positive and realistic political thought; disillusionment with the possibility of a secure Jewish existence in the Diaspora; intense longing for a definite and redeeming act; and the prevalent messianic climate, which so affected him that he once dreamt that the redemption would come in the year 1130 A.D. An old vision renewed! The decision was strengthened by his religious philosophy which maintained the unity, which ensues from the relationship between the God of Israel, the people of Israel to whom he chose to reveal his truth through His prophets, Eretz Israel or the Gate of Heaven, the only place where prophecy is possible, and the language of Israel, Hebrew. From this it was clear that the ideal existence for Jews was attainable only in their own land. In his philosophical work as well as in his poetry Yehuda Halevi criticised those who spoke of Zion and prayed for it, yet deceived themselves through closed hearts and no action. Yehuda, however, understood the problems of the act of immigration, but, despite the comforts of his existence, elected to realise his own aliya — the educational act of an individual who also seeks personal redemption.

Great barriers lay before him. The long journey by desert and sea was daunting. He knew that Crusader rule in Israel was oppressive, that the country had been devastated and the Jewish population attacked and scattered. Family and friends tried to prevent him. A deep struggle with his intimate attachment to Spain was a deterring factor. On the 8th September, 1140, Yehuda Halevi arrived in Alexandria in Egypt, where the scenery, pleasures, admiration and honour, attentions of friends and their hospitality all served to discourage. But his convictions were unassailable and he boarded a ship at Alexandria bound for Eretz Israel.

Prior to his voyage Yehuda lived it in his imagination and writing, overcoming deep fears in this way. He even taught himself to anticipate happily and excitedly the danger of the future. It was in his poems of dispute with others that his doctrine on Eretz Israel was developed, and he argued that there is no secure place for the Jewish people except Eretz Israel. As for its being desolate, it was also given that way to the forefathers.

Some of the poems of the voyage were actually written aboard ship. They begin with a description of the world, but the subsequent descriptions diminish in perspective: the stormy Mediterranean Sea, the weak ship at its mercy, and finally the poet in prayer. The roaring of the waves dominates the rhythm and sound patterns and his prayer is identified with Jonah's, the pounding of the sea consciously identified with the pounding of his heart.

Tragically, Yehuda Halevi's highest ideals were not realised. From elegies written in Egypt it could be concluded that he died there, the departure of his ship delayed by bad weather, yet, romantically, legend has it that he managed to reach the city of Jerusalem, but, as he kissed its stones, a passing Arab horseman trampled on him just as he was reciting his elegy ''Ziyyon ha-lo tishali''. (Zion, will thou not ask the welfare of thine prisoners?).

To large numbers of North African Jews in the immediate pre-World War II years, Yehuda Halevi was a folk hero of immense significance, embodying their highest aspirations. His philosophy and work were incentives to those who wished to chance the immigration to Israel. Their numbers came from half a million living in the Mediterranean coast countries of the continent. In Tangier in Morocco, the Sephardic Jews, so-called as Spanish Jews before their expulsion from Spain in 1492, had always been a privileged and wealthy class, although at the other extreme the Jews in the villages behind the Atlas Mountains, segregated into ghettos, lived in degredation, misery and squalor. There was no real citizenship. By contrast Tunisia proved to be a better haven, with the Jewish community of 80,000 given full nationality and status under Law, although Tunisians tended to make life uncomfortable and, again many of the persecuted turned to the alternative of immigration. In Algeria the Jewish residents had had full French citizenship since 1870, therefore the 130,000 enjoyed a stable existence until it was badly disrupted by the Axis presence during the war. Libya, hardly the richest of countries, had not provided the same security. An ugly pogrom in 1945 put pressure on whole families and very many looked to aliya. Their wishes added to a desire for ships to go out from the shores of North Africa to the Promised Land. Prior to the war there was no significant exodus of aspirants, then the Italian and German occupation and domination from 1940, until the release from bondage in May, 1943, completely nullified any thoughts of organised movement from Morocco, Algeria, Tunisia or Libya.

Admittedly the Jewish people did not suffer the extremes of degradation experienced by their counterparts in Europe, but no love was lost in the repression and persecution whenever they were identified, leading to an intensification of feeling about nationalism. There was a deep-seated desire amid sections of the Jewish population in Tunisia, and clandestinely younger members of the community indulged in fund-raising to offset their frustration in the face of confrontation by the Germans, and indifference by the French and Arabs. Jewish people were turned out into the streets in cities, towns and villages, their homes requisitioned, dispossessed of all their worldly goods, while frequently males were committed to camps and forced to assist the hated enemy in the building of fortifications or unloading of war materials. By 1942 a powerful underground Zionist movement existed, ably administered and enthusiastically led. Optimism grew by the turn of the year, when the writing was on the wall for the Germans, and, in fact, during the last days of January, 1943, the patrols of the British Eighth Army filtered over the borders of southern Tunisia. The German 10th Panzer Divison, the Potsdam grenadiers, a strong Italian force, and difficult terrain, ensured that the task for the British, and Americans advancing from the west, was not easy. Bitter fighting raged for several weeks until finally the enemy had no more holding ground and General Montgomery of Alamein fame delivered the final body blow.

In all the prevailing confusion and delirium of the victory it was easy for representatives of the Zionist movement, already members of the British forces, to contact the zealous partisans in Tunisia and establish the framework of an effective organisation. They had had ample information about the successes and failures of the tremendous efforts to attack the woefully inadequate Immigrant Quota by sending thousands of immigrants illegally by sea. Young Jewish zealots in their undercover meetings in North Africa began to look at the possibility of adding to the already vast fleet of history-making vessels taking their brethren to the eastern Mediterranean.

::   ::   ::   :   ::   ::

A system had been established in the late thirties to offer chances to European Jews, although unscrupulous agents had moved in and innumerable small craft operated by unprincipled racketeers often reached the beaches while others, less seaworthy, were frequently lost without trace. The *Velos* had been the first illegal ship to sail for Palestine in 1934. Of Greek registration she was chartered by a Zionist group in Poland, perhaps anticipating the holocaust to come.

Despite the surveillance by British warships the *Velos* escaped the net on her first voyage and 300 people were spirited into Palestine. A second trip from the Black Sea failed. The British had had information about her movement through the Bosporous, so the Royal Navy intercepted their first blockade runner. It was unfortunate in human terms that the British had no accommodation to offer. The Greek captain therefore decided to make for a Greek port, but the authorities found the illegality an embarrassment and could only offer a chance to refuel. Anything to be rid of such a controversial visitor. The protracted voyage was high-lighted by the media and the *Velos* was dubbed "The Phantom Ship" as she moved from port to port in the eastern Mediterranean, her passengers' morale sinking to a low ebb. The disastrous voyage ended at a Black Sea port, the luckless and dispirited immigrants being herded into special camps to await certificates for "legal" entry into Palestine.

Such a fate was the depths of frustration for every would-be immigrant, thwarted as each was of reaching the land which was the essence of nationality, independence and freedom. In November, 1936, Chaim Weizmann, a great leader, had spoken his mind in Jerusalem: "Today almost six million Jews are doomed to be pent up in places where they are not wanted and for whom the world is divided up into places where they cannot live and places into which they cannot enter." From this crisis there developed the Mossad l'Aliya Bet (B), the organisation for illegal immigration as distinct from L'Aliya Aleph (A), legal immigration by certificate. The Mossad devised a complex and skilful system with agents throughout Europe and the Middle East, an organisation which was to convey 100,000 illegally to Palestine.

The history of British implication in affairs of Palestine and the Jews had always been complex. In the circumstances it could never be passive yet never wholly aggressive. Attitudes in government were far from unanimous. There were sympathisers for, and outspokenly strong critics against, the principles of the Jewish cause, but one event was the inspiration — ambiguous, ill-defined, provocative though it was. Back in 1917 the British Foreign Minister, Sir Arthur Balfour, had made a declaration to Lord Rothschild (who was the "Father of the Yishuv" and the Great Benefactor whose vision was translated into the practicalities of purchase of land throughout Palestine and the creation of villages and communities): "His Majesty's Goverment view with favour the establishment in Palestine of a national home for the Jewish people, and will use their best endeavours to facilitate the achievement of this object, it being clearly understood that nothing shall be done which may prejudice the civil and religious rights of the existing non-Jewish communities in Palestine, or the rights and political status enjoyed by Jews in any other country.''

To the Arabs the Balfour Declaration was an imperialistic and self-opinionated act in which Britain had the temerity to ''sell out'' land in which the Jews had only a tenuous population claim. To the British, then still in military occupation of Palestine at the close of 1917, it was political expediency in the midst of a highly disruptive war. To the Jews of the world it was the chance of a lifetime. Move and counter move followed. At the end of the war in 1918 a British-approved Zionist Commission led by Chaim Weizmann debated the country's needs and future. A fragile alliance with Arab leaders was an outcome, but its vulnerability was exposed in Jerusalem riots in 1920 when Arab extremists visiting the Holy City for a religious celebration attacked Jewish people and property, an apparently insoluble problem which was due to continue throughout the 20th century long after the eventual establishment of the State of Israel, maintaining its pattern of triumph and defeat, sorrow and recrimination. In 1920 the League of Nations made their move and presented Britain with a 28 year-long problem. It was a request to the Westminster Parliament, to a country noted for its freedoms, fair play and democracy, to undertake the mandatory supervision of Palestine. Jewish reaction was highly optimistic and it sparked off an exciting movement of young manpower to the Land. From 1919 till 1924 almost 50,000 immigrants entered. It was a pulsating and progressive spell of terrific activity. A Zionist conference in London in 1920 ensured funds towards the purchase of land, buildings and equipment, even the education of the young. The first big kibbutz, Ein Harod, was based on the sound concepts of personal labour, mutual assistance, co-operative purchasing and marketing and assistance in sickness to members. The movement had timely stimulation in 1921 when Winston Churchill, Britain's Colonial Secretary, a confirmed supporter of Zionism, visited Jerusalem and re-affirmed the Balfour Declaration. In 1925 well over 34,000 Jewish newcomers helped to swell the population in Tel Aviv, Haifa and Jerusalem, and industry as well as agriculture began to expand as the enthusiasm and expansionism of the immigrants found expression.

Arab feeling erupted again in 1929. There was the slaughter of 59 men, women and children in Hebron. Small communities were pulverised. A British commission studied yet another problem. It was stated that the outrage was an attack by Arabs on Jews, yet the commission attributed the cause to the volume of immigration, land policy, and attempted settlement. The answer was simple with
R

complex repercussions. Well over 3,000 immigration certificates
which had just been delivered to the Jewish Agency were suspended,
causing deep misgivings in the Zionist Organisation. There were also
misgivings in the British ranks. A White Paper of 1930 proposed
severe limitations on numbers and settlement. The repercussions
came. Representations were made by Jewish agencies. What about
the Balfour Declaration? The net outcome was an annulment of the
restrictions by the British.

But other events were bringing the dark satanic shadow of
impending disaster, and with uncanny foresight David Ben Gurion
expressed his prophetic forebodings which reverberated round the
Diaspora and struck chill into the hearts of the Jewish people, many
already suffering from a repressive regime in Germany. It was in
1933 that he spoke seriously, intensely: "The disaster that has
befallen German Jewry is not limited to the terrritory of Germany
alone. Hitler's regime cannot last long without war — war against
France, Poland, Czechoslovakia and neighbouring countries, or
against Soviet Russia with its vast expanses. The world is in danger of
war during the next five years. For us here this danger is of sevenfold
gravity, and so that we shall be able to stand firm when the
catastrophe comes, we must double our numbers in this period and
consolidate our internal position to the utmost. This must be our five
year plan."

A clarion call for action was not to be ignored. Immigration
boomed to the extent that in 1935 almost 62,000 valuable people
entered Palestine bringing with them financial capital, intellect, and
industrial skills, and through the inimitable Ben Gurion's initiative
the country gained immeasurably in strength and confidence,
precarious though these were as yet. The delicate situation was
rocked again in 1936 by the intrigue of agents of the Hitler regime
when Arab militants were provoked into heated activity. In the spring
a savage mob in Jaffa killed 16 Jews. An Arab-initiated General
Strike, which ended in October, closed the port of Jaffa through
which the bulk of Jewish trade passed and the strike proclaimed three
slogans: stoppage of Jewish immigration, prohibition of the sale of
land to Jews, and the establishment of a government responsible to a
local parliament elected by the people. The inevitable British
commission which followed had brought Chaim Weizmann into the
picture with his eloquent plea: " . . . Six million . . . not
wanted . . . cannot live . . . cannot enter . . ." and its report in
1937 emphasised the historic bond between the Israelis and their
Promised Land; the distress of the Jews in the Diaspora; the
constructive achievements of the Yishuv; the eternal values which the

Jews had created in their homeland; the great heritage which they had bequeathed to humanity. It argued that the Arab community had had its share of material benefits brought to the country by immigration; that the obligations of the Mandate in this respect had been fulfilled; that the Arab economy in general had not been injured by the National Home. The report maintained that there had been Arab acceptance of the principle of the 1917 Balfour Declaration, but it concluded that the 1921 League of Nations Mandate to Britain was unworkable and a partition of Palestine was essential. The backlash was vigorous. Lloyd George, who had been in office in the British Parliament in 1917, condemned the proposal as a violation of the undertakings to the Jewish people. The 20th Zionist Congress in Zurich in 1937 severely censured the resolution. In the British camp the whole agonising problem was an ever-recurring theme of discussion and argument. Finally, on 17th May, 1939, Neville Chamberlain's government produced a White Paper which would restrict immigration and land buying. Within the next five years 75,000 would be allowed to enter by quota. After that there would be no immigration without Arab consent. This decision brought about burning wrath summed up in Chaim Weizmann's cable to the British Prime Minister: "The proposal to abolish the Mandate, freeze the Yishuv at about a third of the population and contract the area of Jewish settlement to a tiny sector is in our eyes a shattering of Jewish hopes." And an act of defiance followed at the 21st Congress in 1939 when Weizmann declared: "Fifty new settlements have been established; a Jewish port has been built almost overnight; a powerful defence organisation has been founded . . ." His determined reaction was then confirmed by David Ben Gurion's militant words: " . . . and we shall fight the White Paper as if there were no war."

But it was too late. The die had been cast. Hundreds of thousands had been denied their opportunity through political dilemma. The European gates were inexorably closing. Hitler finally turned the key. The enemy had assumed another, vastly more intolerable, form. There eventually came Belsen, Auschwitz and Ravensbruck — and despair. The "final solution". Desperation fed the desire throughout the Diaspora to sustain immigration by any means. So then began in earnest the Jewish solution — illegal immigration. Their sustained answer was "The Great Fleet". Even a world-wide conflict could not suppress it completely. It was the greatest immigrant fleet of all time. The *Velos* was the first pioneering venture in a mammoth operation which developed and continued intermittently but inexorably for 14 years — a declared war on the White Paper with ships as the weapon. Eventually the old *Earl of*

Zetland made her small though significant contribution; but much was to happen before her solitary voyage.

::   ::   ::   ::   ::   ::

The pre-war political pressures in Eastern Europe engendered a highly volatile traffic in illegals who saw in Zion the only possible solution to the ever increasing pogroms. Families and individuals were prepared to pay a high price in finance and personal sacrifice, a situation exploited by the international racketeers whose moral attitude was of the flimsiest nature. As a result outlandish sums were paid for the "privilege" of heading for the open sea on craft woefully inadequate in sea-going qualities, badly provisioned, with poor accommodation and appalling sanitation for the numbers on board. They sailed more in hope than expectancy into the unknown. No record could be kept. Had that been possible another dreadful formal statistic would have been added to the deaths on land at the grim hand of man. Instead they died in the Black Sea, or the Bosporous, or the Eastern Mediterranean at the hand of Nature; died sometimes through starvation; died often by drowning, claimed by the cruel sea. Or if they somehow came to the low beaches of Palestine they could only await nightfall and, if they were lucky, struggle through the surf to seek out the welcoming arms of compatriots. If they were unlucky there were several possible fates, even before disembarking. Boats were known to have been crewed by denizens of Mediterranean waterfronts, smugglers by occupation, whose scruples did not deter them from robbing the immigrants before allowing them to land. It was also possible to accidentally make a landfall close to an Arab village where groups of vigilantes might be roaming the coastline looking aggressively for Jewish landings; or where British troops might be deployed in their unremitting task of preventing the entry to the Promised Land. The odds were heavily stacked against success. But still they tried, undeterred, though totally disorganised, in the little ships in all their fragility. There were also the cruise liners and the freighters. Would-be immigrants who had an adequate purse could take a "tourist" passage with a visitor's visa to Egypt or Lebanon, and for suitable recompense a ship's captain would be prepared to lower a "personal" lifeboat off Palestine under cover of darkness, whereupon the initiative passed to the "tourists" to row ashore to freedom, or Arab hostility, or British captivity. And to have reached such a stage presupposed that the small boat, freighter or liner had evaded the ever expanding Royal Naval presence in the Eastern Mediterranean. Yet, despite the odds, by the end of 1938 about 1,000 illegal Jewish immigrants monthly were strengthening the population of the Land.

Necessity being the mother of invention was tellingly portrayed by the creation of the Mossad, the secret organisation which co-ordinated the frantic efforts of Jewish individuals to seek the Holy Land. It exemplified the democratic family-spirit of the kibbutz of "share and share alike". There was an absence of a hierarchy or leader and the close-knit group operated a remarkable campaign in conjunction and harmony with the Haganah, the largely part-time army, itself a product of the kibbutz. Not only did the Mossad found, develop and extend a complex business for the purchase, equipping and crewing of suitable sea-going and sea-worthy vessels, it devised schemes for departure from any number of ports in the Black, Aegean, Adriatic and Mediterranean Seas — even the North and Baltic Seas. Every ship involved demanded precise planning, preparation and hard labour. Gathering the refugees was in itself a formidable undertaking and they had to clearly understand their responsibilities. They were instructed how to climb quickly and quietly onto trucks to take them to the embarkation point, taught how to behave and react in conditions which were at the very least uncomfortable and at worst downright dangerous. Individuality and privacy were non-existent; each immigrant had to be prepared to suffer ignominy, show patience and understanding, and tolerate extremes of discomfort which would test even the strongest character. Within the environs of the small obscure ports around the geographical indentations of the northern Mediterannean which could be reasonable outlets for the endless stream of refugees, massive preparations were made by the Mossad through a splendid organisation of agents and contacts. Their aim was to move as many as possible as quickly and efficiently as possible. Immigrants were disciplined and guided into groups of thirty, trained to move silently, but swiftly, onto a waiting ship specially and carefully prepared for a load of humanity far beyond the regulations of safety at sea. Such a risk was inevitable. Numbers were of paramount importance. If possible a ship would ease alongside, customarily in darkness, so that the people, with the resignation of those who have suffered much, clutching the pathetic remains of their belongings, could creep on board along numerous planks. With nowhere for a ship to berth the other method offered a wire from vessel to shore. Large rubber dinghies were then pulled along, hand over hand, a laborious task, with each dinghy laden to the point of instability, the black surface of the sea only inches below the gunwales. And not a sound apart from the plop of water, each immigrant alone with his or her thoughts.

For each it was the end of the beginning, an old vision renewed, a long cherished dream in process of realisation. In the middle of the decade it put the hell of Europe firmly behind, if only by a few metres of sea. It would be a while before each attained that ultimate perfection of a footing in Eretz Israel; a while before the birth of the State of Israel. That would surely come. After 2,000 years one could wait a little longer. There was too much joyful anticipation, too much faith in the remarkable organisation of the Mossad, too much fervent optimism to dominate feelings and suppress concern about the pitfalls of a voyage. So there were the people, each and every one vital to the cause. And, of course, the ships.

The appearance of a vessel at a rendezvous was the result of the peerless secret procedure, nothing left to chance. Perils abounded. Finance was a major problem, but almost miraculously, week by week, month by month, indefatigable persuasion and negotiation throughout the Diaspora ensured that ships would be there in all their incredible variety, although the Mossad made strenuous efforts to ensure that they were watertight and seaworthy. Shipowners prepared to release ancient vessels had to be found, and the background story to each was often colourful — the ancient *Earl of Zetland* was to emerge from such circumstances. The fitting out of a ship was done under a cloak of concealment in an obscure corner of a port like Venice or Marseilles, each phase of reconstruction a hazard when authority was in close proximity. By fair means or otherwise, embassies, border officials, stationmasters and harbourmasters were persuaded to allow immigrants to move, eventually to the awaiting vessels. Crews were often recruited from Greece and Spain, audacious seafarers who understood the value of money and who were seeking a "quick buck". A captain took a big chance despite any financial incentives because if he had the misfortune to be apprehended by the British his days of command were over, his certificate withdrawn, his name black-listed. Any captain inevitably lived dangerously. The commander of the *Velos* had found his ship rejected by authority at several ports, doomed to sail interminably with ever increasing problems of lack of food, shortage of water and threats to the health of a host of immigrants.

Indiscretion by a captain could imperil the carefully contrived Mossad planning. There was the saga of the *Colorado*. Yugoslavia with its island-studded Adriatic coastline had proved to be appropriately screened for immigrant ship movements, although the Yugoslavs insisted on suitable visas to "legalise" travel. In this case Mexican papers had been acquired, and in the autumn of 1939 a Jewish contingent boarded the old *Colorado* at the little port of Susak at the northern end of the Adriatic. Five hundred miles to the south, off Corfu, the immigrants transferred to a faster vessel, the *Otrato*, and she was successful in landing her human cargo in Palestine. At the same time the Greek captain of the *Colorado*, ostensibly bound for Mexico, but feeling he had time with which to play, elected to put into another Yugoslavian port for personal and selfish reasons. This despite Mossad instruction to avoid the coastline. The ever alert press reporters pounced on the appearance of the now empty steamer with headlines of "Mystery Ship" and "Pirate Boat". Political and diplomatic repercussions were swift. Transit facilities from Yugoslavian ports were withdrawn and the adverse publicity was disastrous to the Zionist cause. It was with characteristic persuasion and perseverance, however, that Jewish influence prevailed to allow the *Colorado* to make a second similar trip from Yugoslavia although British warships intercepted the *Otrato* and she was towed into custody.

The story of the *Tiger Hill* has been told by the legendary member of the Mossad, Ruth Kluger (now Aliav, a Hebrew surname suggested by Ben Gurion himself). The *Tiger Hill's* arrival off Tel Aviv coincided with the German invasion of Poland followed by the British declaration of war; it also was a symbol of the reality of Ben Gurion's war on the White Paper. Her eventual commander — a Mossad man — chose the hard way of confrontation and was triumphant in a dramatic and romantic landing of immigrants.

The ship was a typical example of vessels negotiated by the Mossad. It was in a Bucharest house in an obscure back street in early 1939 that a very portly Greek announced to three Mossad members that he had found a ship after weeks of searching. A 1,500 ton cargo ship for 1,500 illegals. He was seeking to drive a hard financial bargain tempered by the diplomacy of Ruth Kluger whose restrained, quietly emotional reasoning ensured a sum well beneath the Greek's preliminary price. So the *Tiger Hill* was on offer for £30 sterling per head plus stated expenses and guarantees. A £10,000 down payment within a week was a prerequisite.

Then the practicalities. Firstly, the thorny problem of transporting the 1,500 illegal immigrants into Romania and across the country towards the embarkation port at the Black Sea. Secondly, the conversion of the accommodation and cargo space in the ship to take 1,500 human beings — in secrecy. Thirdly, supplies — fuel, cases of food, kegs of water, blankets . . . enough for a voyage normally taking three days, but possibly protracted to 14 during a game of hide and seek played out by the Mossad ships and the British Navy.

Delicate, though determined, explanation and persuasion guaranteed the provision of the £10,000. It was a personal triumph for Ruth Kluger. It was also the catalyst for meetings to be held day and night, contacts to be made, cables to be sent. Time was short with the *Tiger Hill* due to sail on 1st August, 1939. The mass of preparatory work for any sailing was daunting. There could be no logical sequence of events. In the case of the *Tiger Hill* the Mossad were contacting their agents in Palestine regarding landing plans before half the money demanded for the ship had been raised. False passports were being organised before there was confirmation about from which countries the illegals would come. No single problem could be delayed until the preceding one had been solved, because postponement could have jeopardised the vital date of 1st August. Seamen had to be hired, papers signed, contracts confirmed, insurance policies settled. And the basic incentive was fear; fear of an anticipated carnage emanating from Nazi Germany. If war came before the *Tiger Hill* sailed out of the port of Constanza she might never depart for the Promised Land.

The ship was being prepared at Braila on the River Danube, small in appearance, listing, rusted. Mossad members scrutinising her felt disappointment. 760 immigrants would be a more realistic figure. The Greek had misled them. Also he had mentioned a steamer about 15 years old. She looked nearer 50. But she had to be the deliverance of hundreds of anxious people. Polish Jews were to form the bulk of the passengers, plus Lithuanians, Latvians, Bulgarians and a number of Romanians. Panamanian visas were to be provided, at a price as always — £100 sterling per visa. And on condition that they would never be used for entry to Panama! Towards the end of July the *Tiger Hill,* now fully provisioned, moved from Braila to Constanza, where the port authorities had been bribed to turn a blind eye to her presence.

Fearful uncertainty gripped the Mossad temporarily when the Romanian Premier Calinescu ordered the impounding of the ship and an inquiry. British influence appeared to be behind the move. A trade delegation had arrived in Bucharest to discuss a loan to Romania with oil as the collateral. But other stipulations included no more illegal ships from Romanian ports. The British had been embarrassed too often. To complicate the issue further the trainload of 500 young Jews from Warsaw seemed to be at risk of being turned back. But again a financial offer of the right proportion nullified the threat and the train ground on towards Constanza where the *Tiger Hill* lay, her departure still in grave doubt. Remorselessly Ruth Kluger and her Mossad colleagues explored every avenue in the highest diplomatic circles, and, miraculously, the *Tiger Hill* was approved at the eleventh hour. Meanwhile the sealed train with its 500 young Pioneers had stood for three days and nights in a dockyard siding in the summer heat. For three days and nights excreta and urine soiled the track below the six carriages. Flies clustered in a black cloud, amid the appalling stench. Then thankfully, unbelievably, the Pioneers felt the train moving to the quayside, in a black night of rain. Stumblingly, in complete silence, the men and women moved up the gangplank, each aloof with thoughts, prospective and retrospective. About a hundred other refugees secreted in small hotels and boarding houses in Constanza were already absorbed into the *Tiger Hill's* accommodation. And there were no more to come. Gently, quietly, the ship eased out of the harbour into the night of the Black Sea.

A fortnight later the *Tiger Hill* attempted to call at the island of Rhodes, her cargo of humanity limited to half a cup of water per day. Her request for water supplies was met with a negative answer. She sailed on and another effort was made at the Turkish port of Antalya. There the police were charitable, but only to the extent of selling mouldy bread. No other food. No water. No medicines for a long passenger sick-list. Then she was ordered away like a plague ship. Further, to complicate matters, radio information revealed that a privately organised immigrant ship, the *Prosola,* was leaking badly and in danger of sinking with her 400 passengers. Either they were expendable or the *Tiger Hill* would go the rescue, overburdened though she was, with over 700 human beings — half of them ill — crammed into the accommodation and hold. And they were on their way to pick up hundreds more from the doomed *Prosola.* Reaction on the *Tiger Hill* was antipathetic and her crew threatened mutiny as the two ships closed off Cyprus, but the Mossad leader Levi Schwartz and his carefully selected group stood their ground, forced the truculent crewmen to board the *Prosola* while they organised the transfer of her passengers. Then the *Tiger Hill* her load now 1,159 people, slowly closed in on Palestine.

The Mossad had prepared for a landing on the deserted coast of Ashdad to the south of Tel Aviv, although if successful this would mean that several hundred unfit passengers might have to march five miles or more to the nearest Jewish settlement in the desert. Fate decreed otherwise. Shadowed by Royal Navy units the *Tiger Hill* seemed destined for interception like the *Velos* on her second voyage. She moved into territorial waters at night, was almost immediately challenged by a British patrol vessel whose commander chose to shoot through the searchlight beams, and machine-gun fire killed two Jews, one a Czechoslovakian doctor and the other a young Polish pioneer. Miraculously the immigrant ship evaded the navy, although other problems arose when the *Prosola's* passengers, individuals and untrained, unlike the carefully prepared group, wanted the ship given up. The captain and crew agreed with them. Why should *they* risk their lives for the sake of a thousand Jews? On the other hand the *Tiger Hill's* original people, after all they had been through, were not prepared to surrender so tamely. Mossad authority prevailed and they decided on confrontation — all or nothing. On the night of 1st September, even as the German heavy armour moved towards the brittle defences in distant Poland, the immigrant ship surged towards the long, smooth beach edging the splendid new Jewish city of Tel Aviv. It was an incredible situation! A tremendous surge of excitement swept through the ranks of the passengers as they realised that the *Tiger Hill* would be run ashore. Bold and imaginative thinking might yet succeed.

As the vessel probed the dark surface of the sea ever closer to the realisation of their dreams the people peered shore-wards with the stunning awareness that they were within a stone's throw of Eretz Israel. Two hundred yards off the beach a sandbank finally stopped the *Tiger Hill,* but the immigrants could discern that they were expected because the beach was swarming with Tel Avivians, each bent on ensuring that this would be a successful assault on that despised White Paper. Mossad representatives in the city had organised fishing and rowing boats, ropes and life buoys, anything to bring ashore those who could not swim. Like an army of ants they streamed through the final wash of surf to be met with open arms, and offered towels, blankets and, if need be, clothing. Thereafter they were spirited away in their hundreds into the streets and homes of the city. British police, alerted by the audacious approach of the *Tiger Hill,* appeared one hundred strong in an attempt to deal with the enormous belligerent concentration of Jews incensed by the news of the death of two of their fellows. Simply, the police were outnumbered by ten to one. Not only were the Tel Avivians angered by the unfortunate killings; they also knew the cramped, stinking conditions on the ship — many sensitive from personal experience — the political implications of the escape, the abrasive and heartless condemnation of Jews in much of the Diaspora; in their eyes the injustice of it all. So they fought on the beach. They fought fiercely with stones, sticks and sand, a rearguard action which enabled the newcomers to vanish through the darkness of the Mediterranean night, one more augmenting of the foundling nation of Israel.

The sagas of the *Velos, Colorado* and *Tiger Hill* were the embodiment of the problems which faced the organisers of Mossad ships. Their dedication knew no boundaries and their success was impressive in the face of colossal barriers.

Then the post-war developments brought a swelling surge of immigrants as the Mossad, freed in 1945 from the appalling bondage of European slavery, intensified the war against the 1939 White Paper — the British Government restriction which was redundant in Jewish eyes. Only 1,500 immigrants per month! What price freedom? No price was too high and the Mossad set about their task with a fleet of no fewer than 64 ships which sailed individually for Eretz Israel between August, 1945, and May, 1948. They carried 69,104 people from nine countries: from Italy 33 ships (20,480 immigrants), Romania and Bulgaria five (20,957), France 14 (15,440), Yugoslavia four (8,310), Greece four (1,249), Sweden one (1,348), Algeria two (810), and Belgium one (510). Including other methods of infiltration, the Mossad succeeded in transferring 83,000 people during that three year period. The extraordinary events surrounding the voyages of the *Velos*, *Colorado* and *Tiger Hill* were reflected in these halcyon immediate post-war years in the individuality of the voyage of each of the 64 vessels, each a unique happening in the kaleidoscope of the emergence of Israel, each ship a salvation and a realisation for a human being.

What did it matter that no immigrant knew what a ship was originally called, nor where she might have originated? What did it matter that each immigrant had to endure privation and squalor on board? It was temporary. It was worth sacrifice. These things were part of the price of seeking an Utopia. For almost 400 immigrants the former *Earl of Zetland* created her own tale in the fanciful volume of 64 chapters in the story of post-war Jewish immigration.

13

The Preparations

Foundations laid during the Axis occupation of areas of North Africa were built upon. The earnest fund-raising created by the young Jews in Tunisia, initially to send monies to Eretz Israel, had been constructive and purposeful and had helped to develop interest. By 1944 the Zionist movement was expansive and the ideas propounded had a potential for far-reaching effects. In the delirium of liberation from the invaders an active group could, in relative freedom, extend their mission of Zionism motivated by the purity of a wish to build a Nation. Authority had not yet had time to reorganise any restrictive

. . . policing the length and breadth of the Mediterranean . . .

policies and activities, thus the enthusiastic missionaries had the scope to make their presence felt in Algeria and Morocco as well as Tunisia. The upsurge of passion could not remain passive because the electrifying turmoil of motivation had reached entire families in the coastal strip, and further inland, over the expanse of North Africa at the western end of the Mediterranean. Theory and practice were, however, distinctively separate. If many hundreds of Jews domiciled there wished to emigrate, the principles of the omnipresent British White Paper effectively stifled free movement and, in fact, leaders such as Ephraim Friedman, Yani Ostrowsky and Rephael Chemel were utterly frustrated to find that only an incredibly paltry three of the much sought-after Repatriation Certificates were awarded through the Jewish Agency in June, 1944. A further award of 30 certificates in 1945 hardly mollified the mounting bafflement and anger in the cause of deliverance. Although the people knew, appreciated and sympathised with the need of the European Jews, shattered as they had been under Nazi tyranny, to receive the bulk of

the certificate allocation, this did nothing to appease the vehemence of reaction. The inevitable demands from Europe meant that the certificate supply to North Africa was likely to cease and, therefore, some drastic action was essential. If the initiative was to be maintained and a complete collapse of this eminently desirable Zionism avoided, the leaders in North Africa would require to seek illegal immigration like their counterparts elsewhere.

In 1946 the Mossad had headquarters in Paris from which the great fleet of ships was co-ordinated, and it was Ephraim Friedman who presented a case for a ship, or ships, to appear clandestinely somewhere on the long stretch of Mediterranean shore, to accept hundreds of aspiring citizens of Israel. In the early stages Friedman saw a problem in convincing the Mossad that the movement had enough impetus to succeed, because there were serious doubts in Paris about the numbers. Dedication and perseverence brought their fair reward. Jewish authority, anxious to make the utmost use of shipping space, yet sympathetic to any just cause in expanding numbers in Palestine, looked carefully at the proposition and eventually decided to comply. The decision was hailed as a victory for common sense, and immediately Ephraim Friedman received the glad news he acted.

Ordinarily, in a peaceful situation, it would have been relatively uncomplicated to gather several hundred people for shipment, but there was likely to be hostility no matter what shoreline was selected, whether it was that of Morocco, Algeria or Tunisia. Once again theory and practice were polarised. Secrecy was to be vitally important in contacting very many individuals in towns and communities in three countries, a vulnerable undertaking which could so easily break down. Support from the Jewish communities had been a tremendous incentive to Friedman, Ostrowsky and Chemel, although the task of informing and preparing and transporting would be taxing in the extreme. In Algeria the people resided in towns like Mostaganem, Sétif, Médéa, Tizi Ouzou, Mansoura, and Batna amid the inland mountains; in Morocco, in communities such as Casablanca, Marrakech, Fez, Sefrou and Tangier; in Tunisia, in places like Tebourba, Grombalia, Gabès, Sousse, Sfax, Beja, Djerba and Tunis. They lived in the main cities as well as the towns, the villages and the hamlets. They were widespread and frequently isolated, but united in a spirit of patriotism which could overcome barriers. The co-ordinating committee, co-opting the young Tunisian Jew, Nadia Franco, then brought in active members of the Zionist movement and began to plan.

Morocco and Tunisia were regarded as impracticable for bringing the people to a central point. The Arab influence would inevitably be very antagonistic towards the merest suggestion of a gathering of Jewish nationality. Algeria was under French control, with less likelihood of active repression. The committee settled for Algeria. It would not be easy there, but the members sensed goodwill from Jewish sympathisers in influential positions. A reconaissance revealed a suitable shoreline for boarding a ship lying offshore, a shallow bay near a town called Ténès, 200 kilometres west of Algiers. It had the added advantage of a craggy, well-wooded hillside above the coast road to Morocco, terrain where tents and any small buildings could be distributed unobtrusively. And providentially the land was owned by a Jewish supporter of the North African movement who gladly and unconditionally offered the ground for a camp which would ostensibly be titled "Calm and Health", proclaimed by a large sign at the roadside. With such basic planning achieved and, as a result, information to impart, the committee set about the exacting task of communicating with the people in the places named and, in fact, in every conceivable area containing potential migrants. It was an immense undertaking done with tireless zeal.

In parallel with the construction of the camp. Ephraim, Nadia and the others travelled extensively. In the absence of any specific addresses, the Synagogue proved to be a meeting point in each of a multitude of small Jewish groups spread throughout the three countries. At the end of a prayer meeting, Nadia and Ephraim, working together in Algeria, would informally approach a worshipper with an enquiry about any known Zionist. Once identified he would be requested to gather about him, normally at home, a group of sympathisers and possibly immigrants. In the privacy and security of a house the plan was described, secrecy emphasised, inspiration given, instructions offered and an address taken in good faith, yet with no assurance that any self-confessed Zionist would co-operate in the cold light of reality. It was all a calculated risk on the part of the missionaries, who repeated their pleas, times without number, in the best Zionist tradition. And in Morocco and Tunisia the call to action was equally exhorted.

Furtive though the meetings had to be, the concepts of Zionism divulged raised the highest aspirations in the minds of the people, thoughts of idealism in the best tradition of the perfectionist Yehuda Halevi with his timeless evocation: "Doves who flock in distant lands — whose wings droop — rise up! Yours is not a place of rest. Your home is troubled." Such a zealous call appealed to large numbers of young Jews who elected to support the cause and they awaited an order to make their way to an establishment named the "Alliance School" in Algiers. Such an educational institution helped to allay suspicion on the part of the French authorities of any illegal group activity. Those in Algiers had no difficulty with free movement, but many others from Morocco and Tunisia ran risks as they crossed borders in groups, often on foot and clad in the uniform of a suitable youth organisation like the Boy Scouts. They proved to be acceptable to authority, so people began to converge on Algiers and then Ténès from east, west and south with a common purpose and a smile on their lips and the traditional blessing "Shalom", which means "Peace be with you". If Nadia Franco and Ephraim Friedman had had doubts about support, these were speedily dispelled as the "Alliance School" was invaded by not only young men and women, but entire families, in a striking response of faith in that spring of 1947. Behind them they left relatives and property, reasonable living conditions and security, creature comforts and individuality, though not the kind of freedom they might attain in a cherished National Home. They hoped that any inconvenience in transit would be of short duration and not unduly severe. It could be only a hope, not an expectancy. And awaiting them as an immediate destination was the camp "Calm and Health".

Four hundred people were expected; six hundred and fifty appeared. They came on foot or by vehicle throughout the first fortnight of March, carrying the rather pathetic remnants of worldly goods, for the immigrant ship would have little space for luggage. The committee organising the camp had planned for the short term. It was only a rallying point. This expected ship would not be long in coming. Conditions were spartan. Nevertheless it had been an impressive feat of ingenuity in gathering tents enough for the numbers, sufficient water and food, cooking utensils and necessities for existence from sources where suspicion or antagonism prevailed. A small building was to serve as a kitchen, and latrines had been carefully prepared in the hard ground.

Gradually the camp filled up. People from Morocco and Tunisia, who had succeeded in crossing borders without legal papers, were distributed in the tents throughout the heavily wooded upper part of the hillside, while those with Algerian passports were accommodated on the lower slopes above the coast road. The exceptionally big response to the missionary visits to Synagogues and subsequent meetings in private homes through Algeria, Morocco and Tunisia proved an embarrassment to the committee; enough water and food, mats on which to sleep — no such thing as the "luxury" of a bed — became almost immediate problems in the camp which proclaimed "Calm and Health". It became a testing time for the discipline and patience within the committee, a sacrifice for hundreds who began to feel the food restrictions. Drinking water was rationed. All personal washing of self and clothing, cleaning of dishes and cooking equipment had to be done in the sea, kneeling on the rocky foreshore down the slopes and across the coast road. Food was cut back to a barely sufficient and inevitably monotonous diet. Tea, jam and bread for breakfast; soup, dates and bread for lunch. Sardines sometimes supplemented the scanty evening meal.

No attempt had been made to screen the camp from prying eyes — it would not have been possible to do so — and an Arab village a mere kilometre and a half along the coast was of concern to the committee. It was deliberate policy to make the inhabitants aware of the camping community on their doorstep with movements of groups of people often heard singing as they marched, in keeping with the spirit of youth and family. Each night they sang and danced by the light of a large bonfire; each night they marched on the periphery of the Arab village and passed on in the direction of the sea so that when the ship arrived under cover of darkness her commander would see the arranged signal of a fire and the leaders could respond to the prearranged acknowledgment from the vessel and begin the transit. The villagers would not be suspicious of what was a regular daily feature of the life of the camp, but, again, theory and practice proved to have widely differing effects.

The people had been briefed to make their own way to the "Alliance School" in Algiers three weeks before the ship was due, on receiving letters from the committee. Allow a full week for everyone to reach the camp "Calm and Health". Allow a fortnight for people to be trained in ship behaviour when they would be closely confined on board. Allow time for the morale of the immigrants to be sustained. Allow for a settled spell to allay suspicions of the local Arabs. Accordingly, budget for three weeks at the most, for about four hundred. Such a programme was neat and compact and was immediately put in hand when the message arrived from Paris early in March that the ship would come as planned. The theory was good. But two hundred and fifty extra mouths to feed posed a major setback with food supplies. A form of rationing would be essential, even for only three weeks.

When the time passed with no sign of the promised vessel the discomfiture of the campers became a nagging doubt. This was emphasised when the immigrants, feeling the shortages in their diet as the days dragged on into April, began to barter some remaining
S

belongings and personal effects for food, in the Arab community. To the villagers this was a strange manifestation of a camp proclaiming "Calm and Health" and they saw fit to inform the French police. Thus the practice brought problems.

When the police arrived by car and truck they were met by committee members who attempted to explain the poor material conditions by describing the poverty of the campers and how this was the only way they could have the benefits of the sea. The slim and rather weak description appeared to satisfy the gendarmes, who then sought identity cards. Providentially they did not move up the hillside to seek out the large numbers of Jews who were dispersed among the heavily wooded slopes and who had no Algerian papers. Finally, a request was made that the "campers" should not attempt to trade with the Arab villagers and the police departed. The committee stated the request to the people. For a week the instruction was obeyed, until some irresponsible individuals tried to renew the commerce and placed the entire operation in further jeopardy. A full month had passed since the six hundred and fifty had gathered, with the arrangements made for food for four hundred for a fortnight. Yet, despite an offer by the committee that people who wished to leave the camp and return from whence they came could do so, no one elected to withdraw in the face of ever increasing difficulties. It was a tribute to the conviction of the people that they persevered in the full knowledge that any voyage would entail frightening prospects, if, indeed, it came about at all.

::   ::   ::   ::   ::   ::

Five hundred and forty miles distant, in Marseilles, lay the promised ship. She had arrived there on 24th February and was being fitted out by Haganah personnel at a quay at the far side of the port, and well away from regular traffic, owned by a French Jew, Mr Joe, a ship-chandler. The two foremen in charge of a difficult task were members of a kibbutz, sent specially from Palestine. The work was time-consuming and hard and they knew the urgency as they supervised, sawed and hammered, joined and fitted. They knew the ship as the *Anal* and they understood from various sources that she had been an inter-island steamer for a remote community off the North of Scotland and had come from Aberdeen to the Mediterranean, with a stormy passage in the Bay of Biscay. What they did not know was the background to her purchase.

The *Earl of Zetland II,* now *Anal,* had been widely advertised by the Glasgow ship-broking firm but she attracted only a few interested parties. In September, 1946, she was scrutinised, co-incidentally, by a representative of Palestine Marine and Commercial Agency, Tel Aviv, which at that time was involved mainly in the importation of British goods. The old steamer was considered suitable for local trade in the Mediterranean, but any possible deal fell through and the way was left open for an interest on the part of a Mr Pilides who, reputedly, had formed a company entitled the Anal Compania Provential S.A., of Panama. Mr Pilides, a dapper and somewhat elderly Greek, of short and stout build, negotiated the transfer of the ship with the managers of the North of Scotland and Orkney and Shetland Steam Navigation Company Limited, through the ship brokers, Thomas McLaren and Company. ". . . as she is now lying at Aberdeen with all gear belonging to her on board, and on shore, including spare propeller and chronometer (if any) for the sum of £2,650 . . ." (She had been on offer for £6,000 and had cost £7,060.13.11½ when built). "The vessel having been already examined and approved, is now purchased as and where she presently lies at Aberdeen, and conditional only that the Ministry of Transport sanctions the transfer of the vessel to the Purchaser for operating under the Panamanian flag. Should sanction to transfer be declined, this contract shall become null and void, and deposit returned to the Purchaser without deduction. Any fittings, gear, outfit or such materials that may be the property of the Admiralty or other Government Department are not included in the sale of this vessel. Sellers shall deliver the vessel to the Purchaser at Aberdeen in the same condition as examined by him on the 16th October, 1946, fair wear and tear excepted." The signature of James L. Smith, manager of the North Company was witnessed by Robert C. Mackie and that of Simon Pilides witnessed by W. H. Cunningham of T. W. Tamplin and Company, Limited, ship brokers, London. The date of the agreement was 25th October, 1946.

There was no question about the future of the ship. After Ephraim Friedman's request for an immigrant vessel capable of absorbing several hundred people, the Mossad headquarters in Paris already had notification about her suitability, and negotiated arrangements which would still comply with the requirements of Lloyd's. Specifically she was now the *Anal* and registered at the port of Panama. Ostensibly she was on a voyage to the Mediterranean for unspecified trading purposes and, accordingly, she was duly recorded at Lloyd's as having sailed from Aberdeen on 19th December, 1946. Until steam was raised two days before, the old *Earl* had lain silent and untenanted, apart from the supervision of a watchman and official visits, amid sundry vessels at the Regent's Quay below

Aberdeen's bustling Market Street. Few people gave her more than a glance, knowing nothing of the pulsating life aboard for all the halcyon days of her existence in Shetland. Within six months she was destined to lie similarly abandoned amongst a motley collection of ships in the distant Palestine port of Haifa, finally discarded and fated to suffer the ignominy of the breaker's hammer. There would be no more reprieves.

As Freddie Pottinger of the *Earl's* crew, and Willie Keir of the North Company's office staff in Aberdeen, took an inventory of fittings and equipment in the July of 1946 they could only speculate on the future and that was not an easy exercise. No one was certain about any arrangements, although rumour had it that the ship might go to the Mediterranean. The inventory and distribution proved to be an unenviable undertaking for Freddie Pottinger. He had originally joined the *Earl* as cabin boy in 1932, and now there was the realisation that the beat of engines and propeller below the saloon, would no longer set the crested crockery rattling on the dining tables; that the lilt of Shetland voices mingling with the bleating of sheep and lowing of cattle would no longer fill the air; that the clank and rattle of the winch beside the open doors of the well-deck at a port would no longer be heard. Sentiment and sadness abounded. They removed clocks and barometers, sheets, pillows and blankets, table cloths, crockery and cutlery, pots and pans — all taken to store, although the old, somewhat stained photographs of Shetland scenes in the dining saloon, and fitted into the wooden panelling, were left. The ship gradually took on an anonymous quality as evidence of the North Company disappeared, but unmistakably, and proudly, there was the clearly carved name *Earl of Zetland* in the teak casing of her rudder quadrant at the stern. It was to remain her identification, as if refusing to lose all of her original character, right through to her demolition. Freddie Pottinger had the privilege of being the last Shetlander to stay on board the lifeless ship. Her engines were powerless without steam and even the generator was not in use. He elected to use the familiar Shetland form of light and warmth in the shape of a Tilley lamp and, since there was a wide choice of accommodation, he settled for a small cabin which had been constructed for the gunners on the starboard side and beside the afterhatch on the lower deck. There he found a modicum of comfort in an awkward situation which fortunately was only temporary.

By late November appropriate freshening up had been done, with her new name *Anal* on bow and stern, and "Panama" had replaced "Aberdeen" as the port of registry on her counter. Her new owner had appeared satisfied with progress and events, had appointed a mysterious Greek captain and an ad hoc crew, and six days before Christmas the steamer, laden with bunker coal, slipped unobtrusively down the harbour at Aberdeen, past the North Company offices at Matthews Quay, and the *St. Clair* lying alongside prior to her normal Thursday run to Lerwick. The *St. Rognvald* had arrived in Aberdeen two days previously for winter lay-up. Both ships were mute witnesses of the *Earl's* departure. She steamed out through the breakwaters and turned south.

Her arrival in the River Tyne on 20th December, and her departure the next day, had been recorded. Three days later, on Christmas Eve, she was noted in the Port of London where she lay until 10th January, 1947. By the 18th she had reached Brest for a week's stay and some provisioning. The Bay of Biscay then proved to be a major obstacle in the voyage to Gibraltar when a severe gale generated heavy seas which damaged the mainmast. The 1,150 miles from Brest to Gibraltar took her a week of hard steaming which greatly reduced her supply of bunker coal. She had reached the sheltered harbour under the towering rock looking rather the worse for wear and showing signs of the battering taken in the notorious Bay of Biscay. Another nondescript tramping coastal vessel caused little stir in an international port. There were no suspicions about her use or destination as she lay in Gibraltar for almost three weeks from 1st February. On the 20th of the month the former *Earl of Zetland* had entered the waters of the Mediterranean, bunkered and provisioned further. It was the last lap of her voyage from Scotland prior to arrival in Marseilles and fitting-out. The coastal trip up the eastern seaboard of Spain had proved to be much less exacting than the open Atlantic and the ship covered 800 miles in under five days, with the Spanish landmarks clearly seen to port at regular intervals. Almeria, Cartagena and Alicante all appeared, followed by low-lying Formentera and Ibiza close to starboard after 48 hours of steaming. Inconspicuously the *Anal* had slipped quietly through the harbour entrance at Marseilles to berth at the ship-chandler's quay set aside from the normal shipping berths of the ancient seaport. And there she was destined to lie until the end of April, undergoing what was a near-transformation externally and internally, the biggest change in appearance since the ancient steamship had been lengthened in Aberdeen 63 years before.

Mossad representatives in Paris had been encouraged by the deal done with Pilides, the Greek, although it was general knowledge that he had not lost on the transaction. The vital factor was the acquisition of a ship which was well-found, seaworthy and with proven reliable machinery. The Haganah men had set about their

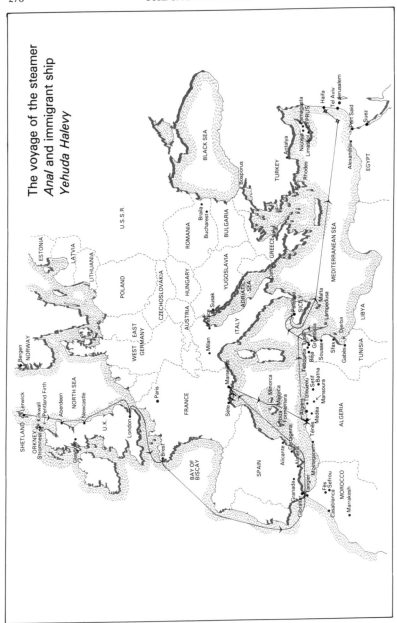

The voyage of the steamer
Anal and immigrant ship
Yehuda Halevy

task with zest and purpose, although it became obvious that the work would probably take longer than expected, despite the fact that the call had already gone out to the people, the Zionists, from Morocco, Algeria and Tunisia who would be gathering expectantly at a camp on the Algerian coast to anxiously await the arrival of the immigrant ship. Nothing could be speeded up with limited resources available, so by the end of March, when the occupants of the camp "Calm and Health" were feeling the deprivations, their ship was still under refit.

The well-deck, so familiar to Shetlanders as a focal point in the life and events of the northern islands, disappeared as the shipworkers moved in, sealed off the doors to port and starboard and roughly welded plating above them to form a continuous, unbroken hull. Between the wing-shelters the bridge remained open, but a large deckhouse engulfed the wheelhouse and incorporated a group of three latrines on each side. Two large cowled ventilators sprouted through the roof of the deckhouse for'ard of the teak boarding on the front of the bridge. They would be badly needed when the hold and deck spaces below were crowded with human beings in the sometimes windless heat of the Mediterranean. Close attention was paid to safety. The Mossad committee were painfully aware of the disasters of unseaworthy vessels sent to sea by the unscrupulous racketeers. They also remembered cases like the immigrant ship *Salvador* which had sunk in the autumn of 1940, taking 250 lives, and the *Struma* with 769 men, women and children, driven out of Istanbul to blow up, leaving a solitary survivor. That had been in February, 1942. They therefore asked for life-rafts in abundance. The two boats which had served the ship for so long, the adequacy of which had been questioned away back in 1912 when she ran ashore on Lunna Holm in far-off Shetland, were augmented by two more, one on top of each of the originals, with extended davits. Life-rafts were stacked on available deck or roof space. Each measured roughly two by three metres. Six were stored on the foredeck, another six on the for'ard deckhouse and three more at the stern abaft another new deckhouse. The immigrants would be able to board their ship with confidence.

Below, in every available space, wooden three-tiered bunks were cut and hammered into place. Ladders were firmly fixed through the former fore-hatch, leading to the cramped and claustrophobic tiers of bunks in the hold. The Haganah men supervised the placing of a large fresh-water tank under the foredeck near the chain locker. It would be vital for creature comforts. Space also had to be found to take additional bunker coal, for, although the *Anal* would formally be bound for Port Said with "labourers" for the Suez Company, there could well be an emergency. Perhaps no port would be prepared to

bunker a suspicious looking vessel. Further, there could be delays
caused by bad weather. Even in April and May a Mediterranean
storm could be vicious. Such eventualities had to be considered by the
Haganah team, two of whom, Palestinian Jews, Israel Kharkovsky
and Eytan Sapodznikov, were key figures in the negotiations with Mr
Joe; indeed, Kharkovsky was to command the *Anal* on her
forthcoming mission.

The prolonged reconstruction was at the finishing stage by the
end of the third week in April. Provisioning and bunkering were
organised, a mainly Spanish-exiles crew recruited, the engines run
after steam was raised. The well-worn power unit so carefully tended
and nursed along over the decades by a succession of engineers still
sounded healthy in the throbbing vibration throughout the frame of
the ship. When in Shetland waters such solicitous men as John
Robertson, Sammy Harrison and John Findlay had been fastidious
in their attentions, thus maintaining mechanical reliability. It was
unlikely that the engines would fail the expected passengers. The hull
was as strong and secure as the best of the immigrant fleet. She was
still a well-found steamer, now ready for sea. At break of day on 28th
April, Israel Kharkovsky ordered the warps away and the *Anal*
probed out into the Mediterranean. The following day she was in the
little port of Sete further to the west where she lay for a few days while
final preparations were made; then back to Marseilles for more
victualling and crew completion. Subsequently, her sailing lights
bright in the early morning darkness, the ship headed south.

::   ::   ::   ::   ::   ::

The presence of immigrant vessels like the *Anal* was the serious
problem in the implementation by the British of that despised White
Paper, and Ben Gurion's vociferous threat to attack it found
aggressive expression in the sailing of the Zionist Armada,
fragmented though it was. Persistent forays by immigrant ships from
a huge variety of Mediterranean and, indeed, European ports
ensured that the British Admiralty was forced to commit large
numbers of personnel and ships in maintaining a vigil and keeping a
blockade throughout the area. Once again the British found
themselves in a situation of embarrassment in the action, and
discomfiture in political and diplomatic circles in those post-war
years.

The Zionist leaders had abandoned faith — even hope — in the
British Government as a means of relief, and had looked to
Washington for real support. Initially they sought to pressurise the

British through American influence but later, sensing a decline in authority of the Mandatory power, they began to seek direct help from Americans for the developing mass immigration. Paradoxically the two wartime allies, generally in sympathy over Europe, differed profoundly over Palestine. Their conflict was complicated by disagreement about that controversial country within Britain and the United States. For long, differences had been aired in the London Parliament, while some of President Truman's close advisers in the White House were Zionists and not always in tune with men in the State Department. Initially Truman attempted to work with Foreign Secretary, Ernest Bevin, stalwart of the Labour Party and strong supporter and articulator of the working class, but one who had little sympathy with the Jewish cause. Bevin was angered by Truman's recommendations that Jews be given carte blanche as if the matter were merely one of cash and carry and had no political connotations. He resented the extent to which White House policy was under Jewish influence and the pro-Zionist bias of some important American newspapers. Also, he was annoyed by the apparent reaction in the United States that they were the only people to be moved by the extreme plight of Jewry. Conversely the American President considered Ernest Bevin so obstinate that he was led back to the Zionist contention that Palestine was the only feasible haven for Jews from the Diaspora. To the British the Americans seemed utterly insensitive to the burden this policy placed on the power that had to carry it out.

The Arab factor was the other provocative problem area. The Arabs had for long been placed in a dilemma. That highly controversial White Paper had taken the sting out of their natural acute sense of grievance at the disruption of their life and lands by Jewish aspirations. Antipathy towards Britain diminished and anti-British agitation eased-off temporarily. Arab leadership was, however, not consistent. On the one hand a section had demanded adherence to the White Paper while on the other the Arab Palestine Party had insisted on the drastic policy of the "dissolution of the Jewish National Home". The result was an odd paradox; the Arab states outside were united in the Arab cause in Palestine, while the nationalists within Palestine were so disunited that there was no chance of a strong Arab leadership from Jeruselem. The Arab aims were not helped by the fact that their former vigorous leader Haj Amin El Husseini, the ex-Mufti of Jerusalem, had spent most of the war in Berlin broadcasting in Arabic from Hitler's capital. Sadly, he had also been closely identified with the Nazi cause of "final solution", with an ironic involvement in protestation to Hitler at some small alleviations in regard to children. He was, therefore, not a reliable figure to follow to success and prosperity.

With such a background of political fragments the British Labour government, and its Foreign Secretary Bevin, followed a path fraught with disenchantment and exasperation in what seemed to them Arab obstinacy and Jewish perversity, exacerbated by American involvement.

Before the war the large Jewish population of New York had kept America informed about the atrocities of the Nazi regime then, later, at the news of the "final solution" American opinion reacted with that typical spontaneous generosity. Zionism became a fashionable cult. In November, 1942, an American Palestine Committee composed of 68 Senators and 200 Representatives had issued a statement denouncing the White Paper. Later, in 1944, confirmation had come in the shape of a statement: "Resolved that the United States shall use its good offices to the end that the doors of Palestine shall be opened for free entry of Jews to that country, and that there shall be full opportunity for colonisation so that the Jewish people may ultimately reconstitute Palestine as a free and democratic Jewish commonwealth." The issue had ostensibly been deferred because of the war, but the American Executive looked with concern on the rising tide of Zionism. Another factor had been the great political and commercial aspects of oil in which there had to be no risk of antagonising the Arab oil producers, thus the United States was obliged to follow a pro-Arab policy. Like the British, the American Government had found that Zionism became a thorny problem in formulating an approach to the Middle East. Truman's predecessor President Roosevelt had taken a simple approach: he gave positive encouragement to both sides. At a convention of American Zionists in 1944 he commented: "I know how long and ardently the Jewish people have worked and prayed for the establishment of Israel . . ." Yet in 1945 he reaffirmed — a few days before his death — in a personal letter to Arabian King Ibn Sa'ud: "Your Majesty will doubtless recall . . . I assured you that I would take no action, in my capacity as Chief of the Executive Branch of this Government, which might prove hostile to the Arab people."

Such a two-faced approach proved to be a serious embarrassment to the straightforward Truman who was inevitably committed to continue Roosevelt's ploy of encouraging both sides, but from 1945 till 15th May, 1948, when the State of Israel was formally established, he pursued two simple principles: that the United States must not be involved in Palestinian strife (not difficult when the British were already there with the thankless task), and that action must be taken with the object of giving a chance of new life to as many as possible of the survivors of Nazi barbarism. The second principle caused deep misgivings in Westminster and to Ernest Bevin, as Foreign Secretary, in particular. His views were deeply entrenched. There would be no retreat from the concept of the White Paper, no relaxation of the Mandatory responsibility. The American support for Zionism in principle, and financial practice, fanned the flames of uprising against all that Britain stood for in Palestine. In the Jewish view the gloves were off. The British could have no feeling for the spiritual depth of the European disaster to Jewry. It was a depth expressed through Ben Gurion when he warned against optimism and urged "passive and active resistance . . ." The methods were referred to by different names: "resistance", "defence", "activism". Common to all of them was the conviction of the need to fight against British authority in Palestine. They never wavered from their ultimate goal of complete control of immigration. In August, 1945, Ben Gurion put forward a demand to the British Colonial Office that 100,000 immigration certificates should be issued immediately for European Jews. The Americans gave the proposal support and President Truman wrote to Prime Minister Attlee whose response was not cordial. He pointed out that the 100,000 demand was not an isolated attempt to rescue deserving cases of hardship, but part of a drive for the total abrogation of the White Paper without any thought for consequences in the Middle East. Further, he reminded the President of assurances to the Arabs that before any radiacal action was taken they would be consulted. He added that he would endeavour to obtain facilities for immigration, but asked that nothing should be initiated before "the United Nations could assume charge of the situation." Even at that early stage the disenchantment, frustration and exasperation were finding expression in the British Government's comment involving the United Nations (as the successor of the League of Nations).

Never happy with the post-war problems of the Mandate, the British now became victims of an extensive onslaught which had profound effects on public opinion in the United Kingdom. Originally the Jewish Agency had not approved of extremist groups, and the Haganah represented moderation which had then been splintered by the formation of the "Irgun Tsva'i Leumi" (The National Military Organisation). Next the formation of the Stern Gang put a different complexion on events, because in their view there was no radical distinction between German Nazis or the British; they were both opposed to the total realisation of the Jewish State and there were no degrees in mortal sin. They believed that the only way to achievement lay in absolute and dedicated ruthlessness, an attitude which added insult to injury in the British camp. War conditions create intolerance generated by violence and in the early 1940s extreme views ensured extremely provocative actions in an all-out guerilla warfare which featured unprincipled acts of killing, terrorism and indiscriminate sabotage. These involved Israelis and British alike in extensive and expensive preparations, the Israelis aided by monies and arms-trafficking from abroad, and the Mandatory forces obliged to maintain a large troop presence in Palestine in addition to the British sponsored Palestine Police and an augmented fleet of warships in the Mediterranean to compete in the undeclared war at sea. A complex period of frenetic activity evolved.

In effect the White Paper was under serious siege. The atmosphere was likely to induce further atrocity and Irgun had publicly called off any suggestion of truce by a widely distributed declaration in January, 1944. "Four years have passed since war began and all the hopes that beat in our hearts then, have evaporated without a trace. We have not been accorded international status; no Jewish Army has been set up; the gates of the country have not been opened. The British regime has sealed its shameful betrayal of Jewish people and there is no moral basis whatever for its presence in Eretz Israel. We shall fearlessly draw our own conclusions. There is no longer any armistice between the Jewish people and the British Administration which hands our brothers over to Hitler. Our people is at war with this regime, war to the end. This then is our demand: immediate transfer of power: Eretz Israel to have a provisional Hebrew Government. We shall fight. Every Jew in the Homeland will fight. The God of Israel, the Lord of Hosts, will aid us. There will be no retreat. Freedom or death." Curiously enough, in September, only months after the Irgun declaration, a Jewish Brigade was formed — political machinations had frustrated its desirability until then. The British War Office gave formal approval which enabled a purposeful fighting force to battle in the Italian campaign from March to May, 1945. It spent six weeks in the front line commanded by Brigadier E. F. Benjamin, and its services won the commendation of Field Marshal Alexander. The unit was mainly Palestinian, although members could be traced to 37 countries of origin. Its sign was the Star of David.

It was ironic that by the early autumn of 1944 the Stern Gang had killed — murdered — fifteen men and made an attempt to assassinate the British High Commissioner, Sir Harold MacMichael. He escaped, but Lord Moyne, Minister of State in Cairo, was shot by a Stern Gang bullet in his car in a Cairo street, an outrage which united the Haganah and British Army against the gunmen for a short time. By contrast to the Stern group the Irgun followed what they considered to be a policy of self-restraint initiated by their leader Menachem Begin, destined to play such a vital part in Israel in later years. They recognised Britain's sacrificial role in the war against Hitler by concentrating their destructive energies on civilian installations related to the Mandatory authority. It was Begin's belief that they then managed the double aim of fighting the war and the White Paper simultaneously without detriment to either cause. The three levels of attitude seemed irreconcilable, yet paradoxically the principles, aims and purposes were identical — a National Home. Jewish Agency approaches were more balanced and moderate, akin to awarding itself the powers and status of an independent Jewish Government. The statesmanlike Ben Gurion felt that a descent into the nightmare of terrorism was impolitic. He reminded Begin that the Jewish Agency officially represented the people, but the two men of common purpose had to agree to differ on application. Irgun and Stern extremes dominated the scene for many months with painful consequences.

The resistance forces struck often and hard. Railways were popular and easy targets. A military express was blown up and five soldiers and three civilians killed; the track was repeatedly destroyed; nine bridges were demolished; Lydda railway station was attacked. Haifa oil refinery also received the attention of the terrorists, while a bomb destroyed the main hall of the railway station in September, 1946. Two months previously a load of milk churns had been delivered to the service door of the King David Hotel, Jerusalem, headquarters for the Military Command and the High Commission. Irgun terrorists disguised as milkmen in Arab garb placed the churns, each packed with high explosives, inside the building. All Jerusalem was shaken by a tremendous explosion which tore apart a wing of the hotel and killed over 90 people inside — some Arabs, some Jews but mostly British.

Public reaction in the United Kingdom was strong. Such an outrage was totally unacceptable, and reminded the British of the cost in lives and in retaining the armed services in every facet of the Palestine problem. In fact the British taxpayer was faced with a bill for £100 million for maintaining the Mandate between January, 1945 and November, 1947. It was a poor return for money at a time when the Westminister Government was finding if financially necessary to ration bread at home and to make troop withdrawals from all over southern Europe. There was also the cost of the Cyprus camps, to which the *Anal* passengers would add their price. It was yet another factor in the great British mortification. The camps in the British Colony of Cyprus had been set up after the quota laws of the White Paper before the German War and it was standard practice to deport illegal immigrants, to await their turn in the monthly allocation of certificates of entry to Palestine. Immigrant vessels intercepted by Royal Navy warships were towed into Haifa where the passengers stepped briefly ashore on their cherished Promised Land for a few hours before they found themselves yet again in internment.

Several British troopships, heavily guarded, operated a transport service from Haifa to Famagusta or Limassol, each port about 150 miles distant. Such troopships were also targets for the committed terrorists. The *Empire Rival* was blasted by limpet mines in Haifa harbour and another transport, the *Empire Lifeguard,* was sabotaged. Even as she was preparing to leave Haifa for Cyprus with her load of illegal immigrants bound for custody, the *Empire Haywood* was damaged below the waterline, apparently by individuals amongst her passengers. The *Ocean Vigour,* destined to carry the *Anal's* load of Zionists to internment, was twice temporarily disabled, once in Cypriot waters, illustrating the tenacity of the Jewish zealots. Naval

HMS Talybont at sea.

vessels were frequent targets for terrorists in Haifa port. Daytime surveillance of the waters in harbour was a straightforward matter, but as a deterrent to Israeli frogmen at night crewmen on warships tossed 1¼ lb. charges of explosive overboard at irregular intervals during the hours of darkness. Nevertheless damage was not unknown, and the risks caused further tension with up to ten guards nightly on each destroyer, sloop or minesweeper based in Haifa. Even the suppressed immigrants indulged in aggression or, at the very least, passive resistance to British boarding parties, another encumbrance for the hard-pressed services personnel.

Surveillance of illegal shipping by units of the Royal Navy committed a wide variety of vessels to policing the length and breadth of the Mediterranean. Based at ports such as Gibralter, Malta and Haifa the ships, from cruisers to minesweepers and launches, played cat and mouse with the astonishing range of illegals. The *Anal* incident was a typical situation and her interception involved four ships at very considerable, although unspecified, expense to the British taxpayer. His Majesty's Ship *Whitesand Bay* was the first to be involved. A "Bay" class escort sloop, she had been completed after the end of the war, in July, 1945, and was assigned to the Mediterranean Fleet. Of 1,600 tons she was capable of about 20 knots and carried a crew of 157.

A destroyer of the Hunt class, H.M.S. *Talybont,* and an escort sloop of the modified Black Swan type, H.M.S. *Peacock,* acted in concert when the *Anal* was ultimately intercepted, boarded and impounded. *Talybont* was a unit of the 3rd Destroyer Flotilla. She had been launched in February, 1943, displaced 1,087 tons, could raise 25 knots and required a crew of 158. *Peacock* was attached to the 5th Escort Flotilla. Launched in December, 1943 with a tonnage of 1,350, she had a speed of 20 knots and was manned by 192 men. The fourth vessel due to be assigned to the interception was H.M.S. *Skipjack,* a minesweeping sloop of the Algerine class. Commissioned in April, 1943 *Skipjack* was formerly H.M.S. *Scorpion,* then had been seconded to the Canadian Navy as *Solebay.* She displaced 850 tons, had a moderate capacity of 16½ knots and carried 85 of a crew.

Towards the end of May, 1947, *Whitesand Bay* was patrolling south of Sicily while *Talybont* and *Peacock* were at sea in the Eastern Mediterranean. *Skipjack* lay moored in Haifa after assisting the big troopships in transporting immigrants to Cyprus.

14

The End of the Beginning —
An Old Vision Realised

The facade and pretence of the camp "Calm and Health", so precariously set up on the slopes adjoining Ténès and bordering the sea, were under strain. Water and food were even more strictly apportioned, while the illegal bartering with Arab villagers had taxed relationships throughout the assembled, anxiously waiting, six hundred and fifty. By the end of April frustration was having a detrimental effect on morale, although the people tried desperately to

The *Anal* took another knock.

maintain spirits with the nightly ritual of song in the firelight and march on the fringes of the village and in the direction of the Mediterranean, the potential highway to Eretz Israel. Despite the now acute hardship of material conditions and undermining of attitudes by the seemingly interminable delay, still no-one elected to withdraw and return to abandoned homes throughout the three countries.

Nadia Franco, Ephraim Friedman and committee members worked indefatigably to sustain the drooping spirits of so many and by the first days of May, 1947, they could at least reassure the despondent people that a ship would come — and soon. With flagging enthusiasm and zeal restored, the immigrants looked for further solace from the inspired creations of the nationalistic poet Yehuda Halevi. His 800 poems had the heady qualities of religion and love alternating with the down-to-earth practicalities of human existence, a combination so essential to the North African Zionists. Their elation found visual expression during the long days of waiting

T

in the making of two 20-feet long banners of white material each with lettering about two feet high. One proclaimed in Hebrew, the other in English, "Haganah Ship Yehuda Halevy" (choosing to spell the surname with a "y" instead of an "i"). It was of no consequence what the vessel had been called. To the people she would be the *Yehuda Halevy*. What better name to grace their ship? When they might be able to use the banner was a matter of conjecture. Hopefully it might be when they drove ashore like the *Tiger Hill*. Certainly it would be done close inshore when any need for pretence had been abandoned. As the narrow block capitals were placed on the banners there was speculation and discussion about the ship herself, the chances of success, the possibility of failure, the dangers of interception by blockading ships. What size would this steamer be? Would the accommodation cope with the numbers? What about catering and sanitation? No one could be certain, although Nadia and Ephraim assured questioners that the Haganah would have done a good job on preparations. So they waited.

Arab suspicions had resulted in the fleeting visit of the French gendarmes, curious to check on the unusual nature of this camp "Calm and Health", yet superficially apparently satisfied with their rather desultory scrutiny. They had not returned, much to the relief of the immigrants' committee.

As the first week of May dragged past, there were those who thought that plans and arrangements had gone adrift and something had happened to the promised ship. Optimism was again abating in the day-to-day incessant discussion. The evening of the 9th followed the routine of the now very meagre meal, half-hearted song beside the customary bonfire and a dispirited walk round the all-too-familiar route. Dawn on the 10th looked like most North African sunrises, heralding another day of steadily beating sun, with heat and discomfort for the campers. There was little point in looking seawards when the ship was not expected before darkness. Passing vessels were few and far between in any case.

Around noon that day a group of immigrants on the rocky foreshore suddenly became aware of a speck on the otherwise wide and uninterrupted expanse of the horizon to seaward. A stirring of interest and speculation brought an excited flutter to conversation and several young men ran back up the slopes towards the camp as the tiny dark shape slowly acquired definition. The news brought an immense surge of excitement throughout the entire camp. This must be the ship coming directly shorewards right out of the north. Committee members, anticipating a night arrival, warned the people to avoid any show of preoccupation. Such a reaction could, conceivably, arouse suspicion amid the Arab population, their curiosity possibly sparked off by the appearance of the strange vessel. It continued to close in until, unmistakably, all observers saw a flush-decked, single-funnelled, black-painted coastal-type steamer slowly moving, perhaps just outwith the three miles. A fire by night and smoke by day were the intended signals for Israel Kharkovsky and his ad hoc crew. Confirmation came from Nadia, who had visited Marseilles during fitting out, that this was indeed the expected steamer and, accordingly, a burning of brushwood at the site of the daily bonfire produced a suitable smear of smoke against the tree-clad hillside. Without any apparent acknowledgement the little ship cruised, only just under way, on a sea's surface stirred by an easterly breeze. The former *Earl of Zetland* had arrived, lying offshore at a stretch of coast devoid of piers as she had done on so many occasions in distant Shetland. For the remaining hours of daylight the *Anal* lingered there. Onshore the immigrants were instructed to wear as much clothing as possible, leaving little to be carried. There would be no room for personal effects or trivialities of baggage. Only people mattered. Final guidance was given on how to behave on the boats and rubber dinghies during embarkation. It had all been spelled out previously in training.

While the Jews prepared, the Arabs were not idle. Such a vessel with its unusual collection of boats and life rafts seemed dubious and aroused mistrust. Their community leaders were concerned enough to meet and discuss the mystery ship which was still hovering near the shore as the daylight faded. They worried about the security of their own village. For a second time they decided unanimously to seek the help of the French police.

The heightened sense of elation throughout the Jewish immigrant fraternity raised morale immeasurably. Eretz Israel was a mere sea-trip away for men, women and children, old and young alike. The protracted delay had been hard, but here was opportunity, and the waiting over the tedious days and weeks was at an end. A move at long last. It was a heady prospect!

In keeping with the studied preliminaries vehicles had been arranged to transport the older Jews to the embarkation point. All the younger and fitter people would go on foot. The night proved to be suitably dark, moonless and windless, and as stealthily as possible the movement of the 650 began. A long, silent column marched purposefully along the dusty, winding road towards the rock-bound foreshore; three borrowed trucks with screened headlights operated a shuttle service for older men and women and small children. Nadia Franco organised and supervised loading at the camp; Ephraim

Friedman and Shimshon Sarfati, a committee member, checked the vehicles on each run; Yani Ostrowsky and Rephael Chemel were at the embarkation place. More than two thirds of the immigrants had reached the shore when the feared police activity erupted. Car headlights heralded their arrival, coming from behind the short convoy of trucks. The first car swerved narrowly past the convoy on the rough road, halted with a screech of brakes and out leapt six French gendarmes. Ephraim Friedman was quickly out of the cab of the leading truck ready to meet them. His French was more than adequate. "What are you doing here?" came from the sergeant of gendarmes. "Just driving and looking around." "And what are you looking around for in such a deserted place? Papers please!" As Ephraim fumbled for papers the immigrants in the trucks were discovered and ordered out to be searched. They complied, but immediately lay down round the police vehicles in passive resistance; anything to delay the police in driving down to the sea. To add to the confusion Shimshon and several others charged into scrubland bordering the road, taking different directions away from the coast. The gendarmes gave chase. Sarfati himself zigzagged wildly through the thick bushes and dived into hiding where he held his breath as the torch-flashing police searched the immediate area. He remained undiscovered. Back at the camp "Calm and Health" the remaining Jews heard the commotion in the still darkness and realised that something had gone wrong, then saw the evidence as the trucks returned to disgorge their disconsolate occupants whose luck had run out. Their wait would have to go on.

Israel Kharkovsky had brought his ship as close in as he dared, a mere stone's throw from the rocks under the craggy slopes containing the bay, and there he had anchored in the gloom of the night, a welcome cloak of secrecy. Even as the *Anal* came to rest the first of the immigrants signalled readiness for embarkation. The Spanish crew had boats and life-rafts down into the black water and paddled them ashore within minutes. Time was vital. Here was the outcome of months of scheming and planning, arranging and executing — patience, tact, perseverance and courage. Each craft was loaded to near-instability again and again; each immigrant scaled the vertical wall of the *Anal's* hull aided by ladders, ropes, cargo nets, and willing hands. Well over 300 had been absorbed into the accommodation on board before a breathless Shimshon Sarfati ran onto the shore with the alarming news that the French police had intercepted the trucks, although the people had taken delaying action.

In the confusion, due partly to the dark night, and haste because of the disconcerting information, children arrived on board without their parents, parents without their children. Belongings were left on the shore and large numbers of immigrants possessed only what they wore. Despite the urgency there were no accidents and no casualties.

With the threat of the gendarmes in mind Kharkovsky was forced into a quick decision. He had to go. As he rang down for "full ahead" he glanced back to the land-mass to starboard, aware of the misfortune of committee members and immigrants alike, concerned and anxious about their future. But his thoughts reverted to the responsibilities of the moment and the daunting prospects of the voyage beginning. The *Anal,* completely blacked out, moved away from the coast of North Africa to turn east towards Israel. At the embarkation point the French found only the remnants of possessions. It had been a narrow escape for the steamer and her complement, but any relief was nullified by the thought of relatives and colleagues left behind. They could not then know that another vessel *Shivat Zion* (Return to Zion) would call for the forsaken in mid-July, 1947. Theirs is another episode.

By noon on 11th May the *Anal* was well to the seaward off Algiers, with her passengers settling in for the 2,000 miles voyage to Israel. What they discovered on board was primitive and basic, especially felt when Israel Kharkovsky made it clear that only a limited number of people could be on deck at one time. The ship had to appear to be sailing legally. This requirement was unexpectedly highlighted when, only hours out, a fast French patrol launch swept alongside the slow-moving steamer with questions about origin, destination and cargo. Her crew appeared satisfied with the answers which were given: "Panamanian ship *Anal* proceeding to Port Said with labourers for the Suez Company." This was a heart-felt relief to all on board the *Anal* when it was thought that the launch had probably come as a result of the gendarmes' visit at the time of embarkation. Relief was complete and universal as the police launch moved off.

Shipboard life began to develop a pattern. As commander, Israel Kharkovsky called a meeting of key figures amid the immigrants so that watches could be organised. A close-knit discipline would be essential in the overcrowded hold and 'tween-decks. Help was allocated to engine-room staff, stoking duties, cleaning of living quarters and sanitary facilities, preparing and cooking food, keeping watch. Men, women and the elder of 26 children on board were all co-operative. The incentive was too great for selfish attitudes to prevail. The assistance was invaluable to other leaders on board like Moshe Amir and Jacob Melnitzer, radio operator, who had dubbed the old vessel "The Grandmother", such was her apparent vintage.

A radio transmitter and receiver, also vintage, maintained contact with Mossad centres in Europe throughout the voyage. Of limited frequency the radio was at its best at night and Melnitzer preferred the evening for communication since distortion was minimal then.

With 550 miles logged and the *Anal* north of Tunis there was a threatening change in the wind. It rose and lifted the sea, which put the ancient hull through all manner of gyrations, much to the discomfiture of the great majority of passengers. Conditions below rapidly became chaotic. Ventilation was inadequate and the overpowering stench of vomit permeated the ship, the overcrowded and claustrophobic bunks draped with the prostrate forms of seasick immigrants, hardly keeping body and soul together and wishing they were anywhere but on this old tub at this time. Israel Kharkovsky discovered that the *Anal* did not have the power to face the strength of the gale and resorted to "tacking" the ship, a gambit so often employed over bygone years by former captains in Shetland — Nicolson, Scott, Johnson, Spence, Gifford and Tait. There was nothing else to do short of running. Unable to make any more than 1½ knots into the northerly storm, Kharkovsky elected to head for the island of Lampedusa off the east coast of Tunisia where there might be a degree of shelter. He reported: "We looked for shelter at Lampedusa which we sighted at dawn. We tried to anchor, but owing to the depth we could not reach bottom and we used a 'floating anchor' to avoid being smashed on the rocks." The sea anchor made little difference to the dreadful rolling and pitching, violent movement which sapped the resources of the people until the commander considered an unscheduled call at Tunis. The gale seemed endless, and after several days the fuel factor became a nagging doubt. Fate seemed cruel. More than a week had gone, yet they had covered only a quarter of the distance. A brief respite in Tunis brought relief to the sorely tried ship's complement, but it had to be short. All the immigrants were obliged to remain in the soursmelling confinement out of sight of port authorities, and without a bill of loading the *Anal* had to sail or be arrested.

Thankfully they put to sea in greatly improved weather, steaming north-east towards the western tip of Sicily and Palermo, the capital of the island. Jacob Melnitzer had had radio communication with Mossad agents in Milan to the effect that 40 tons of coal could be purchased in Palermo, enough to see them to Haifa. What had not been anticipated was British influence. The *Anal* lay in the coaling berth taking on the much needed fuel through the circular, narrow scuttles in the 'tween-decks, a lengthy and laborious process involving hard manual work. At least there was no shortage of labour or volunteers, but the task was irksome in the heat of the day accompanied by the all-encroaching coal-dust which was inescapable. The stuff crept through the accommodation, an added insult to injury after the trauma of seasickness. Then, as further bitter insult, the Italian coal-suppliers had a directive from British sources to unload the coal already supplied, an order which caused great dismay in the Jewish camp. Curses were directed at the White Paper, Bevin, the British Government and British Intelligence agents presumed to be responsible for informing the authorities that the *Anal* was a Jewish illegal immigrant ship. And without coal she was nothing but a lifeless hulk. Suddenly the prospect seemed bleak. It was Kharkovsky himself who salvaged the situation by using his "emergency fund" to bribe the suppliers to leave 20 tons secreted away and, hopefully, enough to see them through to Palestine at much reduced speed. On 19th May, fuelled, although only just, and provisioned, the venerable vessel moved slowly away from Palermo on her last voyage between ports. It was the beginning of her end, yet, blessedly, for her people merely the end of the beginning.

Meanwhile His Majesty's Ship *Whitesand Bay* was patrolling on "immigrant interception" in the eastern approaches of the Malta Channel around 36°N by 16°E and her communications had had information from intelligence about a possible illegal vessel in her area. Prolonged sunshine by day and clear skies at night made surveillance easy, but the build up of heat in near windless conditions made life uncomfortable on board. Some action would not come amiss. On the morning of the 21st a ship was sighted to the west, her funnel smoke creating a long smear on the horizon. *Whitesand Bay* headed towards the unknown vessel, her lookouts training binoculars at the stranger, curious to pick out detail. What they saw was what the immigrants had seen as the *Anal* approached their bay. Their immediate official interest stopped short at the likelihood that she was an illegal, although there was no particular evidence that she carried any more than a reasonable number on board. Movement of human beings on deck suggested no more than the possibility of a moderate group of passengers. A smoke-blackened Panamanian ensign at her mainmast was the only suggestion as to nationality or origin. Being "a flag of convenience" it would not necessarily be authentic. The flag lifted with the wind only occasionally since the vessel could be making little more than four knots, with a barely perceptible bow wave and negligible wake astern. Although the hull had obviously been black, it was now discoloured and rust-streaked. On board the warship the crew speculated on the ship's origin. Common opinion was that the steamer had been British and had been built around the turn of the century, if not before. The tall smoke-stack, straight stem and rather stylish counter stern all pointed towards a ship of considerable age.

For the moment the brief for *Whitesand Bay* was to shadow the stranger. At four knots the Panamanian ship, which also carried no trace of any name, provided the 157 crew of the escort sloop with a monotonous task. Steering a consistent course slightly south of east, the direction appeared to be towards the south-east corner of the Mediterranean, maybe Port Said. The wind and sea remained quiet, hardly a swell on the surface; while the sun glared down impassively on the ships by day, welcome darkness brought relief in coolness by night. For over three days *Whitesand Bay* remained a couple of miles off, then on the morning of the 24th she closed the distance and dipped her large White Ensign in salute. The steamer responded with the barely recognisable Panamanian flag, performing the niceties of acknowledgement at sea. A hiss and crackle heralded a megaphone greeting from the sloop — "Good morning." The disembodied voice wafted across the intervening space. There was a lapse of ten seconds before there was a thin response through a loudspeaker. "Good morning." The reply in English sounded convincing enough. "Are you under full power?" came next. "No, but we are saving fuel." Then the inevitable query, "What ship are you, where bound and why?" "Panamanian ship *Anal* bound for Port Said with labourers for the Suez Company." "Thank you, *Anal*." The conversation over, *Whitesand Bay* pulled away from the now identified *Anal* and resumed station a mile away from the little steamer.

Israel Kharkovsky had little real doubt about the outcome of the interview at sea. The rather transparent explanation was unlikely to convince the commanding officer of the warship. Israel suspected that arrangements would already be in hand for an "official reception" by the British. As day gave way to night on the 24th many immigrants thankfully climbed out of the stifling, polluted atmosphere below deck. Content to maintain close observation throughout the hours of daylight, at least the British C.O. had not used searchlights to further embarrass the *Anal's* people. Even so the Haganah men did not permit everyone on deck simultaneously. But living conditions on board could not improve and the exceptionally close confinement had led to a gradual deterioration. The claustrophobic atmosphere, especially in the hold where the bunks were tiered three-deep, was a dreadful reality for men, women and children herded like sheep in the far off days of the ship steaming direct from Lerwick to Scottish ports with the season's lambs. At least the animals suffered only a matter of hours. The immigrants had already been subjected to the privations for a full fortnight in an ever-worsening situation. If the fo'c'sle, tween decks, cabins aft and saloon had a modicum of air circulating through portholes, the hold was a cesspit of perspiring bodies and reek of inadequate sanitation plus the effects of the prolonged seasickness of so many during the long gale off Tunis. To those coming on deck from the shadowy depths — literally coming up for air — the purity of the sea air was a revelation. But the ship sailed in an invisible shroud of pollution which was inescapable and the people had to suffer resignedly. As had been inevitable in the erstwhile camp "Calm and Health", food and water were doled out on a strict ration, barely enough to keep body and soul together, a problem faced by the people for all the long weeks from early March until the end of May. Loss of weight was a common problem amid all the Zionists, which made them less resistant to infection and, sadly, the hazard was stressed when the youngest Jewish child on board, a two year old, fell sick and died. The formal burial at sea performed at the side of the *Anal* away from the prying eyes on board HMS *Whitesand Bay,* cast gloom and despondency throughout the Jewish fraternity. Perhaps a death was inescapable, a symbol of the sacrifice of the immigrants in striving to attain their national home.

For another four days the two ships gradually closed the distance towards Port Said; still the *Anal* wallowed along at her half speed; still there was the pretence of passengers who were labourers for the Suez Company; still the people operated a shift system of being on deck. Excitement and uncertainty grew in parallel amid the Jewish group on board. Kharkovsky, Melnitzer, Amir, Sarfati and others met in conference and discussed plans. Radio contact with Europe had been switched to Mossad headquarters in Israel, and Jacob Melnitzer was, in regular evening communication. The radio equipment was in a small shack on the deck behind the bridge and, although very limited in its frequency range, it served its purpose. Another factor was its value as a morale booster in helping to convince the immigrants that there was an organisation behind the whole venture. Guidance by the Mossad to the Haganah men was clear. Ideally the ship would be run ashore during the hours of darkness. Alternatively, should she be intercepted, the main valve of the engine would be ditched in the sea to ensure that the *Anal* could not be turned about from whence she came, a move which would be unthinkable to each man, woman and child at this stage. There was no way that could be allowed to happen. Common to both possibilities was the destruction of all the ship's papers and records and the necessary disappearance of the steamer's commander into the anonymous throng above and below decks. At a given signal the national flag, the Star of David, would be hoisted at the masthead to proclaim identity, but there would be no apparent authority remaining on the *Anal*. Immigrants were given instructions to resist British boarding parties at discretion and Israel Kharkovsky gave orders for the banners "Haganah Ship Yehuda Halevy" to be hoisted between the ratlines, the Hebrew version at the foremast and English at the mainmast. But only when the fates had decreed what might happen — before running aground or before interception, and only when he had decided to declare their true colours.

Meanwhile the destroyer *Talybont* and sloop *Peacock* had returned to Haifa just before the end of May to await further orders. On the 28th, *Whitesand Bay* communicated with Naval Command in Haifa to the effect that she had continued to shadow the suspect, and there was now confirmation that the claim of labourers being transported to Port Said was bogus. The Suez Company was not relevant. Therefore it was assumed that the vessel had on board Jewish illegal immigrants and, indeed, had apparently altered course away from Port Said.

At 0001 hours on the 30th, HMS *Peacock* sailed from Haifa towards the position given by *Whitesand Bay*. She worked up to her full speed of 20 knots heading 155° for a point about 150 miles out. By 0730 the commander of *Peacock* had the two ships in his binoculars and an hour later he had taken up station to starboard of the *Anal*. The log of *Peacock* recorded: "Rendezvoused with *Whitesand Bay* 0832 on 30/5 in position 32°01′ N and 33°25′ E." A fresh north-westerly breeze gave the ships a set to the south-east on the *Anal's* steered course of 065°, and with *Peacock* on her starboard beam and downwind, the crew of the sloop on deck were frequently subjected to the pungent smell emanating from the immigrant vessel. During the late afternoon the destroyer HMS *Talybont* was attached to the little fleet. She took up station to port, while *Whitesand Bay* covered astern. The fate of the *Anal* and her 392 people could well be sealed. Now interception seemed inevitable.

About 1800 *Peacock* closed in on the slow-moving steamer and her C.O. addressed a message to her commander. "Good evening. You must understand that it will be futile for you to attempt to enter harbour or to run your vessel ashore. If you try either of these I have instructions to board your ship. It will be in the interests of the safety of your passengers if you stop when I require you to do so. You should now steer 042° towards Haifa. Please acknowledge." Once again the remote metallic voice boomed across the gap and Israel Kharkovsky picked up his loud hailer, well screened amid the crowd on the *Anal*. His anonymity was of paramount importance. He responded by agreeing to aim for Haifa, but was non-committal about stopping at any given time. He wished to keep his options open.

Conservation of coal was still important because the supply, so drastically curtailed at Palermo by British interference, was dangerously low — a matter of maybe two days' steaming. Therefore the victim set the pace and continued at only four knots. Night came again — the 21st of the voyage — and at 2040 HMS *Skipjack* arrived to increase the remarkable convoy. She took up station ahead of the *Anal.*

At 2110 the commanding officer of *Peacock* radioed all skippers to the effect that he had spoken to the commander of the illegal, and he hoped that she would stop when ordered to do so in daylight in territorial waters. When way was off her *Talybont* would provide a boarding party to subdue any resistance, take over the bridge, engine room and deck, and organise towing facilities. It would then be up to *Skipjack* to tow the *Anal* into the harbour entrance at Haifa. If the immigrants were adversely inclined and refused to stop, then *Peacock* to starboard and *Talybont* to port would intercept by the "line abreast" method. This was the "sandwich" way of tackling illegal immigrant vessels and it had proved to be effective in a variety of situations, although sensitive handling was required, especially when the escort sloop proved to be unwieldy. As a type she was slow to accelerate and decelerate, clumsy in engine reversal in an emergency, and was ponderous in steering.

After the illegal had been secured and stopped by any means required, HMS *Skipjack* would still be available for towing. Whatever developed the next day *Whitesand Bay* would remain astern in reserve and be prepared to pick up any swimmers. Each immigrant ship tended to have its quota of Jews who, in their highly motivated and emotional state, were desperate enough to leap overboard into the sea and strike out wildly for the shore — to them so near, and yet in the restrictive finality of the White Paper, so far.

For the *Anal's* people darkness was again welcome, although the starlight was augmented by the sailing and other lights of the four British warships. To the 392 they were not friendly lights, but served only to remind them of all the associated frustrations of the Mandate and their own precarious position when daylight would dawn on 31st May. The hours passed painfully slowly as the host of immigrants, sleepless in their tremendous excitement, talked and sang the night away in a strange mixture of anticipation and apprehension; and 592 British sailors heard the noise drifting over the dark face of the sea, the sounds sometimes recognisable as the immigrants occasionally burst into the words of Hatikva, the Zionist anthem, when the waves of emotion prevailed. The British had heard them before, from other illegal vessels.

An agonising moment came for Kharkovsky's people as the cloak of darkness lifted to reveal the Palestinian coast south of Haifa, the sweep of the low-lying beaches with the Plain of Sharon behind them; the hills rising afar off in which nestled the hallowed places like Nazareth and the Sea of Galilee. To the south-east lay the sacred city of Jerusalem with all its implications, the centre of the Jewish universe, embodying all the Biblical proclamations. "And I will plant them upon their land and they shall no more be pulled up out of their land which I have given them said the Lord thy God . . . And they shall dwell in the land that I have given unto Jacob my servant . . ." The Bible was the incentive and the reality. It had all been stated and written so often before. And there was before them Halevi's inspiration, "Doves who flock in distant lands — whose wings droop — rise up! Yours is not a place of rest. Your home is troubled."

On board that microcosm of Israeli desires feeling ran high in the first hours of daylight on 31st May. Clearly submissive surrender was unacceptable to the great majority of people on the now-declared *Yehuda Halevy* and Israel Kharkovsky had decided that they must at least show their hand with a token resistance. The spirit of the immigrants came back with a tremendous surge of optimism; they would meet the obvious aggressive intent of the British with a display of hostility. If the Navy wanted to board their ship they would have to fight. Now that all pretence had been abandoned the immigrants massed on deck, although if boarding became a reality women and children would remain below. Weapons in the form of guns and knives were non-existent, but the young men acquired whatever they could lay hands on, objects like sticks, plates and corned beef tins.

The morning sunlight lit the group of ships with warmth, and on the coast the town of Haifa was only five miles distant, the buildings sharply etched white against the slopes of Mount Carmel behind. At 0845 the log of HMS *Peacock* noted: "Closing on territorial waters. Illegal vessel *Anal* warned of futility of resistance. Informed immigrants that they will be ordered to stop." In anticipation of some opposition a boarding party had been made ready on *Peacock* as well as *Talybont*. Fifteen minutes later, at 0900, the megaphone was again used to warn the illegals. There was no reply and the *Anal* sailed on placidly at her four knots. Within ten minutes she entered the three mile limit and her people raised a great noise of acclaim. Shimshon Sarfati went to the foremast with the blue and white flag of the Star of David. Momentarily the assembled multitude fell silent, anticipating the poignancy of what was about to happen. Jewish hearts beat faster,

HMS *Peacock* directs powerful water jets at the stern of the former *Earl of Zetland,* as her consort HMS *Talybont* awaits developments. It is a fine clear morning off Haifa.

H. G. Fuller

The warships close in to prepare for boarding by the "sandwich" method. A solitary Jewish passenger has defiantly survived the water blast, but the way is clear for the British Navy.

H. G. Fuller

Sailors advance from Ramp Number 1 in depth and width as if from a rugby scrum. *Peacock's* commander observes from the bridge.   *H. G. Fuller*

An unusual view showing the steamer under the warship's port bow. The protective wire mesh against sundry missiles can be seen clearly and beyond it another banner with Hebrew lettering depicting *Haganah Ship Yehuda Halevy*.   *H. G. Fuller*

Peacock's men are in charge of the stern and now *Talybont's* boarding party go on at the *Yehuda Halevy's* bridge. The smoke-blackened Panamanian flag still flies at the mainmast.

H. G. Fuller

The occupation of the foredeck, and the sailors adopt a commanding attitude. Bemused and resigned acceptance shows on the faces of the immigrants. *C. A. Thompson*

The bridge of *Talybont* off her port quarter appears to be part of the *Yehuda Halevy*. As a striking contrast to former days the hull of the old *Earl* is badly stained and discoloured.   C. A. Thompson

HMS *Skipjack*, outside Haifa harbour, passes a hawser and prepares to tow the illegal. Sailors in the foreground observe the old steamer under tow. HMS *Skipjack's* White Ensign fluttering in the breeze is defiantly matched by the distant "Star of David" flag at the *Yehuda Halevy's* foremast. HMS *Talybont* stands off.   C. A. Thompson

the pulses raced, lips were bitten as tears sprang into eyes. Sarfati shouted ''The Hope'' (Hatikva) and as he hauled the foremast bunting halliard, the striking white flag with its linear blue star and horizontal blue bands lifted, stiff in the breeze, up to the yardarm. ''Hatikva'' carried in the wind to the ears of the British and it was followed by another patriotic song, during which the long, lettered banners were defiantly slung at the rigging fore and aft.

Another broadcast from *Peacock* penetrated the volume of sound and its significance was unmistakeable. The crackle of the loudspeaker checked the cheering, then *''Anal,* you are ordered to stop now,'' came over loud and clear. This was greeted by bedlam among the massed Jews, a crescendo of noise and wild gesticulations. An angry crowd awaited developments as *Peacock* to starboard and *Talybont* to port closed to within 30 yards and water jets suddenly arched across the intervening spaces to drench the steamer's stern. As the destroyer and sloop slowed, the steamer suddenly increased speed, then cut across *Peacock's* bows, doing her maximum nine knots. The archaic engines had responded well enough in their ultimate flurry and for a few minutes the old frame of the former *Earl of Zetland* pulsated with the rhythm and life of a bygone era. It also almost came to an end on the sea bed for, as she altered course to starboard, she came under the warship's port bow. Full helm and full astern on the starboard engine made little difference to the unwieldy sloop's progress over the short distance; the sailors gathered on her bow watched apprehensively as the weight of the *Peacock* pushed the *Anal* over to an alarming 40°, and fear showed on the faces of immigrants packed on the angled deck some 15 feet below the sloop's foredeck. The stench of packed humanity from the three-week close confinement wafted up. It was sickening in its pungency. Swinging away from the sloop the *Anal* then crossed the bows of the destroyer and took another knock which led *Peacock's* commander to write prosaically in his later report: ''Her (*Anal's*) tactics of increasing speed and altering course into the approaching ships were extremely hazardous and both *Peacock* and *Talybont* struck her fairly hard and listed the ship over considerably.''

Israel Kharkovsky's resistance with his ship could be only token, although in a lost cause he had tried to make his point. Having had a foray at each of the flanking British warships he rang down ''Stop Engines'' and the *Anal* drifted to a halt about 2½ miles offshore. Reality faced all of them now. The game was up. His next task was to immobilise the vessel by removing the main valve from the engine-room, a matter he found distasteful because he had built up a certain affection for his charge as her last captain. *Talybont's* personnel were U aware of the splash roughly amidships along the illegal's hull. An object had fallen or been pushed out from between the two boats and the deckhouse on the port side. It could have been done by anyone in the milling throng, but they supposed that a piece of the engines had been jettisoned. Sadly the hapless old steamer now lay completely at the mercy of her adversaries.

Although confronting the illegals offered British personnel variety and excitement, few found significant satisfaction in a task which was at times dangerous and mostly frustrating, a problem with negative results in human terms. It was one thing taking on an enemy who could retaliate — the terms were equal — but another to batter unarmed civilians into submission with water jets then subdue them further with tear gas and cudgels in the event of resistance.

The approach to intercepting and boarding an illegal required proficiency. Warships and men were specially prepared. Each destroyer or escort sloop was fitted with heavy metal mesh screens on the fo'c'sle as a protection against missiles hurled by irate immigrants — and these could fly thick and fast on occasion. Stout coir and rubber fenders were suspended over the bows and along the forepart of the hull, invaluable when there was a severe dunt as happened when the *Anal* cut across *Peacock's* course. Through experience it was discovered that the most effective way of boarding was by means of specially fitted numbered ramps, each projecting about 15 feet, at different levels, hinged at the hull and lowered depending on the height of the stern of an illegal vessel. This avoided the very real risk of a man falling into the sea between the ships and gave more scope for strength of numbers across the width of an illegal's stern, an area cleared of immigrants by the powerful fire hose jets of sea water. Invariably the technique worked, enabling a boarding party to move forward in width and depth as if from a rugby scrum. For a time navy men likely to be involved in boarding were given a week's preparation at a Royal Marine training base in Malta, an exercise not without its hazards as described by Petty Officer G. A. Neale of the HMS *Talybont*. "The idea was mainly to keep us fit. The only trouble was it worked in reverse and by the end of the week we had so many with injuries like sprained ankles that sometimes a ship left short of some of its crew. Of one boarding party on the last day of training — I can see them now — coming back from their last exercise singing 'We Three are Alone', I remember only three escaped injury out of twenty".

There was a standard dress for boarding parties. Each man had a deep helmet, shirt, web-belt and gaiters, all white for clear identification. Gas masks when needed, dark overalls, rubber-soled

There was a standard dress for boarding parties. Two of *Peacock's* men pause for the camera.   *H. G. Fuller*

HMS *Peacock* berthed in a Metiterranean port.

At the entrance to Haifa harbour a tug prepares to take over from *Skipjack*. The banner in English, *Haganah Ship Yehuda Halevy* still billows in the wind at the mainmast. All the Jewish immigrants crowd the deck. *T. Anderson*

Her passengers now taken to Cyprus to await the official quota of entry into Palestine, the former *Earl of Zetland's* fate is finally sealed. Moored at Haifa breakwater amid a ghost fleet of illegal immigrant vessels she awaits the ignominy of the breakers hammer. *T. Anderson*

boots and life-jackets completed the uniform. A strong leather pad guarded the left or right forearm, to ward off blows. Specially padded under-garments protected the area of the groin against another method of resistance in which knitting needles were used indiscriminately with painful consequences. Some personnel carried automatic guns or holstered pistols, others small tear-smoke canisters and Chinese crackers, both of which helped to clear deck space. Most were equipped with truncheons. All were reluctant to use force when they were challenged by people who were so much victims of circumstances. But some element of violence was inescapable.

As the two ships had closed on their victim the fire pumps had pressured six powerful jets of water at the truculent crowd clustered on the *Anal's* stern. From 30 yards the force of the water was devastating. The water blasted everything movable. It exploded in stark whiteness off the liferafts, steering-wheel casing still embellished with the carved *Earl of Zetland,* old dining-saloon skylight of former decades in Shetland, deckhouse and the deck itself. It cascaded down the hull into the sea in rushing torrents. And it achieved its purpose. The immigrants were in disarray, bowled over, forced into an ignominious retreat until they reassembled by the main mast, a dripping rebellious group. For a few minutes a solitary saturated Jew mustered brave defiance until he was caught squarely by a jet from *Peacock's* fire pumps, knocked down and forced to retreat to his colleagues. With the after-deck cleared and the escort sloop's bows alongside the *Anal* the way was open for the first boarding party. The time was 0914 on 31st May. Two officers and 19 men went over from ramp number one as it moved slowly over the top of the illegal's stern rails six feet above the deck. As *Peacock's* men edged forward, weapons ready, to port and starboard and over the top of the after deck-house, *Talybont* crept in to the port side of the stationary victim. She progressed along the stained and discoloured hull until her bows nudged the deck-houses in front of the open bridge itself. This discouraged the minor bombardment of tins, plates and pieces of wood and allowed *Talybont's* boarding party to establish a foothold in a vital area. The bridge was cleared within minutes, physical resistance quickly abandoned by the immigrants and the people crammed on the foredeck resorted to desultory verbal abuse which gave vent to their feelings but was endured impassively by the British. Further aft *Peacock's* men had similar success. A couple of tear-smoke canisters had subdued opposition as the boarding party edged past the funnel through spasmodic skirmishing to make contact with *Talybont's* group in the wheelhouse and on the bridge itself.

For Israel Kharkovsky, Jacob Melnitzer, Moshe Amir and

Shimshon Sarfati the nature of the end of the voyage was not unexpected, although it was still a bitter blow when the hopes and aspirations had been so idealistic. Sarfati wrote in his diary: "On the decks of another two destroyers we could see British soldiers armed with guns, sticks and gas masks. The time was eight o'clock in the morning. With grief, and tears in our eyes we could see the coast of our Land behind us. We had all looked with loving eyes towards this Land, the Land of our Fathers about which we had dreamt with all our families . . ."

For the individual immigrants, including the 53 women and 25 children, most of whom were below deck, the sight of the warships looming large on each side made an indelible impression, frightening and awe-inspiring. Through the *Yehuda Halevy's* portholes the grey hull of one coming ever closer was seen to carry the letter and number "U 96". They were aware of the extra and unaccustomed vibration when their ship had increased speed, then the plating of the warship closed in. Since they had no idea what was going to happen, when the collision with HMS *Peacock* came and their ship rolled 40°, there was a chaos of rolling and falling bodies, shouts and screams of alarm. A near panic arose in the murk of the hold and dimly lit 'tween decks subdued only by reassuring shouts from others on deck as the ancient steamer assumed an even keel again. Momentarily many had thought death was staring them in the face. To be trapped in a capsizing ship was an appalling vision. Minutes afterwards the women and children realised that the commotion on deck was the result of British sailors boarding, and their contrasting vision of Eretz Israel faded. They knew that the prospect would be Cyprus and internment. The white-helmeted sailors appeared at every companionway and invaded the lower decks, sought out the engineroom and stokehold and looked for the crew. Clearly the engines would never again operate. A long life of service had ended. No one was to be found who could be identified as crew. Engineroom and stokehold were abandoned. Kharkovsky and Melnitzer had melted into the mass of immigrants, although the radio operator had maintained contact with the Mossad headquarters until the last moment, even as the British began to break open the sealed-up door of the windowless radio shack. He altered the wavelength on the set and squeezed through an escape hole cut in the deck to mingle with the crowd underneath. His task was completed. The immigrants below deck regarded the invaders with a silent hatred eloquent in its glowering, smouldering stare. Such reaction was inevitable when each Jew saw in each British sailor or soldier the ultimate deprivation — a denial of stepping ashore freely onto their own soil by Divine Right.

Few, if any, British servicemen regarded the immigrants with animosity. Authority encouraged them to see the pathetic crowd on each ship as a group of political detainees guilty of attempting illegal entry, but the vast majority, many of them young National Servicemen in the immediate post war years, not unaware of the European disaster to Jewry, often appreciated the extreme

. . . yet we had still arrived.

circumstances. There were many recorded incidents of sympathy and understanding in dire contrast to the heart-rending treatment of the same people by the Nazis. Petty Officer Neale confirmed such attitudes, " . . . you could not help feeling sorry for these people. They had suffered so much and were huddled on board like cattle, and when they finally did reach Haifa, only to be shipped to Cyprus to be interned, you could understand their determination to make a bid for freedom . . . There was no feeling of hate, in fact we had more a feeling of pity for them." Chief Petty Officer Cyril Martin of HMS *Peacock* commented on the physical hardship of the *Yehuda Halevy's* people, ". . . a complete shambles. The middle deck below

was in such a state of filth and the stench beyond description that it
left me bewildered as to how any human being could survive such a
horrifying voyage . . .''

Such an assault on the senses made the *Talybont* and *Peacock's*
men reel as they probed through the cramped and claustrophobic,
tightly packed mass of crudely formed bunks and humanity. At least
there was little baggage to check. The great majority of the people
appeared to have little more than the clothes they already were
wearing. No sailor spent any longer below than was essential, and
when the searchers emerged from the hellish murk of the interior they
rejoiced in the purity of sun and sea air. They arrived on deck to see
the destroyer and escort sloop lying off and the minesweeper HMS
Skipjack close alongside. The white-helmeted men at the bow were
taking up the slack of a light line attached to a towing rope as *Skipjack*
prepared to get under way with the immobilised steamer. The
subsequent report from HMS *Peacock* was a travesty of the human
situation: "At 0922 *Skipjack* was ordered to take *Anal* in tow and by
0930 the tow had been passed and the ships were going ahead. A very
prompt and able evolution. *Skipjack* towed *Anal* to the harbour
entrance where she was taken over by tugs and berthed. Boarding
took place in position 32° 50' 15'' N. 34° 54' 06'' E.''

As if in deference to the impassioned desires of the North African
Jews no one had thought to remove the bunting so proudly displayed
when Shimshon Sarfati had broken the Star of David at the foremast
and the banners ''Haganah Ship Yehuda Halevy'' which had been
raised fore and aft, thus the Israeli flag stood stiff in the breeze as the
two ships neared the Haifa breakwaters, the immigrants shouting and
singing their defiance. At the harbour entrance *Skipjack* transferred
the tow to tugs which eased the aged hull through the still waters
towards the quay. Sarfati chronicled the subsequent events through
Jewish eyes: ''. . . suddenly we could see Mount Carmel and
beneath it the harbour of Haifa. There was great excitement. At last
we approached, but we were told that we must leave the *Yehuda Halevy*
when it went alongside and transfer to a British ship which, according
to what they said, would take us to camps in Cyprus. Our protest did
not help. We began to sing loudly, 'We shall build our Land; we shall
be the first . . .'' As we sang we lay down on the deck, refusing
instructions to disembark. It seemed to me that the whole city of
Haifa would hear us. The soldiers who had come aboard became
excited and carried off people bodily onto the quay. Only the elderly
and women walked down without offering passive resistance,
although they cursed the soldiers. We all wept when our feet touched
our beloved Land and we kissed the quay . . . After we had been

sprayed with disinfectant like some diseased animals we were directed to a large and broad ship. Around the deck there was a very high fence and barbed wire to prevent escape. After we had boarded this prison ship we were told in Hebrew that in keeping with British Law we would be transferred to Cyprus. The voyage of the ship *Yehuda Halevy* which had brought with it the first people to go to Israel from North Africa ended not as had been hoped, yet we had still arrived. During the sailing, youngsters and adults, women and children, had shown the same spirit in volunteering and kept up a dedication during the voyage bringing all their hearts together.''

Epilogue

The next day, 1st June, 1947, the English language newspaper "Palestine Post" carried the story of the Former *Earl of Zetland's* epic voyage. It was headlined "*Yehuda Halevy* Dodged Warships for Ten Days". A slightly inaccurate account followed: "Haifa, Saturday. The latest prize of the Royal Navy, 399 ragged Oriental Jews on a 300 ton tramp steamer, whom four warships had dogged for ten days before finally preventing them from entering Palestine, was handed over to the Army at Haifa Port late this Sabbath morning. Their number would have been around 400, but a two-year-old child had died at sea during the 21-day journey from an unknown port.

"The immigrants had proudly named their dingy little boat after the great Hebrew poet of the 12th century, Yehuda Halevy, described as 'the foremost Hebrew poet since the Bible,' whose Songs of Zion were nostalgic with longing for the ancient homeland ('My heart is in the East and I am in the uttermost West') and who himself set out from Spain through Egypt to Palestine. The steamer, originally the *Anal* and before that the *Earl of Zetland,* flew a smoke-blackened Panama flag and bright, clean Zionist colours — the banners proclaimed that she was a Haganah ship.

"It did not take the military long to complete their part of the joint operation and transfer the people to the *Ocean Vigour,* which has resumed its deportation task after having been out of the running since a hole was blown into it by a limpet mine off Famagusta on April 2.

"The newcomers said after being followed for ten days by four warships their boat was boarded yesterday morning while still far south of Haifa, and tear gas was used by the Navy as a 'preventive measure' although there was no indication of resistance. The majority of them are young men, very pale and thin faced, dark with curly hair. The children looked undernourished. Few of the people had more than just the clothes on their backs and such things as they had would have to be discarded as soon as possible as sanitary conditions on the boat were bad. The soldiers detailed to searching bundles had little work to do.

"Now and then one of the men would resent being moved

around by a soldier as they were hastened down the gangplank, but altogether the routine went off without incident and in silence.

"The official figures report 392 persons — 314 men, 53 women and 25 children — were sent to Cyprus this afternoon and that three, including a baby, have been transferred to Athlit hospital, with four relatives to accompany them."

On 3rd June the same newspaper printed a brief statement by their reporter, Shahe Guebenlian: "Nicosia, Sunday. The *Ocean Vigour* carrying the *Yehuda Halevy* immigrants anchored off Cyprus at 1.30 this afternoon and disembarkation began at 3 o'clock.

"The 387 immigrants were landed without incident although the last group was caught in a heavy shower during the afternoon. Five stretcher cases were transferred to the Nicosia Military Hospital. The other immigrants were taken to the Caraolos camp."

For all the erstwhile crew and passengers on the now abandoned old *Earl* it had been a love/hate relationship. She could not have been ignored. They felt a deep appreciation for the fact that she had been available at all, a well-found and seaworthy vessel, old, but with all the evidence of maintenance and care. They sensed a profoundly deep dislike of the primitive layout and makeshift sanitation which had become desperately bad, and a hatred of close confinement which had seemed endless in its acute discomfort. For these and many reasons the ship would never be forgotten. In time perhaps she would be remembered with affection since, above all else, she had provided them with an opportunity. It had been of their own choosing. Now, however, they became victims and prisoners of a system featuring another type of confinement, one of barbed wire and guns, albeit under a more tolerant and humane enemy than had been the tragic fate of millions of their fellow Jews in Europe. Israel Kharkovsky had had the satisfaction of seeing his people step ashore onto the Promised Land if only for a few precious hours, but he could now rejoice in the assurance that they would eventually return to play their part in the institution of the forthcoming State of Israel. That would be merely a matter of time — again weeks, months, even a year or two were as nothing compared to hundreds of decades of waiting by their forebears. Then they could combine with the great host of fundamentalists, idealists, opportunists, socialists, capitalists, those dedicated people of the Yishuv uniting with their counterparts from the Diaspora, in the great common aim and purpose of creating a country for themselves and generations to come. Their very presence in the Cyprus camps was the end of their beginning, the realisation of an old vision.

::   ::   ::   ::   ::   ::

And so it was. Collectively they did it. Those thousands already on the precious soil of Palestine; those who came despite the White Paper, ship by ship, also in their thousands, having responded to Ben Gurion's compelling call. They schemed and planned, debated and implemented, fought, and experienced the elation of victory. A year later on 14th May, 1948, Ben Gurion, like a 20th century Moses, delivered his oration in Tel Aviv, the primal Jewish city. He spoke for Moses and Amos, for those who had opposed the Romans, and the escapers from the ravages of the Crusaders, for Yehuda Halevi, for the fugitives of pogroms in Russia and Africa, for the recent survivors of the German death camps, for Israel Kharkovsky's people (now in Palestine), for the builders of Tel Aviv itself, for the man and woman and child in the street . . . The Land of Israel was the birth place of the Jewish people. Here, their spiritual, religious and national identity was formed. In their exile from the land of Israel the Jews remained faithful to it in the countries of their dispersal, never ceasing to hope and pray for the restoration of their national freedom . . . ''Therefore by virtue of the natural and historic right of the Jewish people to be a nation as other nations and of the Resolution of the General Assembly of the United Nations, we hereby proclaim the establishment of the Jewish nation in Palestine to be called the Medinat Yisrael: the State of Israel.''

He outlined freedom with responsibility, social and political equality for all citizens, opportunity in religion and education, a life in a country based on the rights of a people rather than on the sufferance of others. He appealed to the United Nations for co-operation and to accept Israel into their structure. He offered peace and friendship to all neighbouring states and people . . . In his own charismatic and unique manner he finally declared: ''With trust in God, we set our hand to this declaration, at this session of the Provisional State Council, on the soil of the Homeland, in the city of Tel Aviv, on this Sabbath eve, the fifth of Lyar 5708, the fourteenth day of May, 1948.''

::   ::   ::   ::   ::   ::

For all the immigrants on board the *Yehuda Halevy* there was a future. They were integrated; they were welcomed with open arms into Israel to live in the chequered and precarious existence of all nations in the second half of the 20th century. For the vessel which had been fated to provide them with that chance there was no future. In the nature of things her time had run out.

A glimpse of the crudely formed and tightly packed bunks below deck at the after hatch. The immigrants were forced to endure privation and squalor in such cramped and claustrophobic conditions.

T. Anderson

As if to maintain her identity to the bitter end, the carved teak lettering *Earl of Zetland* is clearly defined. The wheel shows signs of wear and tear. For her passengers it is the end of their beginning; for the old steamer — the end.

T. Anderson

After the disembarkation of her people on 1st June, 1947, she had been taken by the harbour tugs to the main breakwater of Haifa harbour and there she was finally moored stern on, abandoned, silent, alone with the ghosts of the past. No more the flamboyant, bluff figure of Willie Spence on the bridge, with his utterances; no more Sammy Harrison faithfully tending his beloved engines; no more the slight figure of purser Davie Gray with his cheerful personality. Gone were Colin Henry, John Fraser and Ogilvy Gray. Gone were the generations of Shetlanders who crowded her decks on a Victoria Day jaunt or trip to the Agricultural Show at Fetlar. Gone was the welcome and familiar sight of the black hull appearing round headlands, through sounds and into voes, carrying people, animals and the victuals and goods of the sequestered island communities. The ship had moved out of the ken of Shetlanders. More recent crew members such as Tom Gifford, Adam Tait, David Henry, Robbie Robertson, Lowrie Gifford and Magnie Fraser, all so familiar with the idiosyncracies of the old *Earl,* had no factual knowledge of her whereabouts. Rumour suggested that she had gone to the Mediterranean under the Panamanian flag, but no one could be certain about her use there. Remarkably it was an islander, Tom Anderson, nephew of Captain Adam Tait, who saw her in Haifa. As a member of the 6th Airborne Division, so closely involved in the Palestine Mandate in its final desperate writhings, he had the extra-ordinary experience of recognising the familiar profile. Despite the disappearance of the well-deck, the addition of deck houses, boats and life-rafts, the line and proportions were unmistakable. That large gap between foremast and funnel where she had been lengthened away back in 1884, the way her stern "sat down" into the water, the rake of her mainmast, left him in no doubt as he observed the great mass of immigrants on board from a harbour tug that momentous day, 31st May, 1947.

Then he saw her taken to the breakwater after the disembarkation, tied up finally amid the fragments of the Great Immigrant Armada, lying close alongside the famous immigrant ship the *Hatiquva,* formerly the United States Coastguard vessel *Trade Winds,* which had brought 1,414 immigrants, landed on 8th May, three weeks before the *Earl's* contingent. On board the timeworn steamer the sole remaining evidence of the Shetland connection was the carved lettering on the teak casing of the steering gear aft, still clearly decipherable on the stained and discoloured wood. Fashioned by a Paisley craftsman from a bygone era, the words Earl of Zetland had survived the tempests of the seas over seven decades only to be faced by the inevitable unthinking stroke of the breaker's hammer.

For some ships there was a stay of execution. Several were patched up and incorporated into the Israel Navy, others were refitted and utilised to carry legal immigrants after the end of the tiresome Mandate; others were unfit for any practical purpose, too small to be of value, of insufficient power and slow and of inadequate bunker capacity. Into the last category came the *Yehuda Halevy*. She was relegated and, as if convicted, a large number "28" was crudely painted on her starboard bow immediately abaft the chain of the lowered anchor. The Port Authority of the Mandatory Government had sealed her fate. Only the "Haogen" co-operative boatyard maintained an interest by checking moorings and keeping a watch on the discarded vessels arrayed along the sea wall. The fugitive steamer finally faded into obscurity and eventual oblivion when, months later, she was towed to the Shemen beach of Haifa, driven ashore, and lay in shallow water as an ad hoc breakers' firm took apart the craftsmanship of John Fullerton and Company.

> *"So goodbye old ship o' mine,*
> *And for the sake of auld lang syne,*
> *Your name will live on till the day is gone,*
> *Goodbye auld ship o' mine."*

Acknowledgments

Acknowledgment is made to: Ranald J. Allan, Norma C. Anderson, Danny Anderson, Margaret Bowen, Christopher Cannon, Erling J. F. Clausen, Howard Gee (Public Record Office Researcher), Captain Thomas Gifford (Jnr.), Captain Michael Gray, Douglas Grierson, Richard Hargreave, John Harvey, the late Mackie Hughson, Jim Jamieson, Graham Langmuir, the late George Longmuir (formerly Shetland Librarian), Captain Leonard Mainland, Dr. T. M. Y. Manson, the late Ann Moar, Kitty Moar, David Nisbet, Douglas Paul, Rev. Clem Robb, Gracie Robertson, Herbert Scott, Carol Smith, Hance Smith, Bruce Spence, John Spence, Andrew Williamson, Jonathan Wills, Robert Wishart, Basil Wishart, the late James Wyllie.

Also to: Moshe Amir, Rev. A. Graeme Auld, Shaul Avigur, Yizhak Avrahami, Arie Ben-Eli, Professor G. Elkoshi, Carol Elliot, Ephraim Ben Haimi, Shmuel Hatzor, Ivor Wynn Jones, Jon Kimche, Commodore H. Kimchy, Joseph Kopilov, Moshe Lootsky, David Maimon, A. J. McMillan (Public Record Office Researcher), T. Pelz, J. H. S. Portsmouth, L. Teog, Eva and Dov Tzidony. William Wilson very kindly checked the proofs and, finally, grateful acknowledgment is made to Netta, my wife, for countless hours of transcribing tape recordings and typing the draft and final manuscripts.

Sources

1. *BOOKS (a)*

BLAKE, George: Down to the Sea (Collins, London. 1937).

BROWN, George Mackay: Letters from Hamnavoe (Gordon Wright, Edinburgh. 1975).

CHURCHILL, Winston S.: The Second World War, Volume 1 (Cassell and Co. Ltd., London. 1948).

CLUNESS, A. T.: The Shetland Isles (Robert Hale Ltd., London. 1951).

CLUNESS, A. T.: Told Round the Peat Fire (Robert Hale Ltd., London. 1955).

CLUNESS, A. T.: The Shetland Book (Shetland Times Ltd., Lerwick. 1967).

CORMACK, Alastair and Anne: Days of Orkney Steam (Kirkwall Press, Orkney, 1971).

DONALDSON, Gordon: Northwards by Sea (Second Edition) (Paul Harris, Edinburgh. 1978).

DUCKWORTH and LANGMUIR: Clyde River and Other Steamers (Brown and Ferguson Ltd., Glasgow. 1946).

GOODLAD, C. A.: Shetland Fishing Saga (Shetland Times Ltd., Lerwick. 1971).

GRANT, Roderick: The Lone Voyage of Betty Mouat (Impulse Books, Aberdeen. 1973).

HALCROW, A.: Deep Sea Plunderings (Oliver and Boyd Ltd., Edinburgh. 1938).

HOGG, Gary: The Far Flung Isles (Robert Hale Ltd., London. 1961).

HOWARTH, David: The Shetland Bus.

HUME, Crawford W.: A Hundred Years of Howden Engineering (John Bellows, Gloucester. 1954).

IRVINE, Fred: Pictures from Shetland's Past (The Shetland Times Ltd., Lerwick).

LIVINGSTONE, W. P.: Shetland and the Shetlanders (Thomas Nelson, Edinburgh. 1947).

LORD, Walter: A Night to Remember (Longmans Green & Co. 1957).

McLEAN, Charles: Island on the Edge of the World (Tom Stacey Ltd., London. 1972).

NICOLSON, James R.: Lerwick Harbour (Lerwick Harbour Trust. The Shetland Times Ltd., Lerwick. 1976).

NICOLSON, James R.: Shetland (David and Charles, Newton Abbot. 1972).

SANDISON, Charles: Unst My Island Home and Its Story (The Shetland Times Ltd., Lerwick. 1968).

TAYLOR, Harry P.: A Shetland Parish Doctor (T. & J. Manson, Shetland News, Lerwick. 1948).

TUDOR, John R.: The Orkneys and Shetland. Their Past and Present State (Edward Stanford, London. 1883).

BOOKS (b)

ALIAV, Ruth and MANN, Peggy: The Last Escape (Hodder and Stoughton, London. 1973).

AVRIEL, Ehud: Open the Gates (George Weidenfeld and Nicolson Ltd., London).

BEN-GURION, David: The Jews in Their Land (Aldus Books — Jupiter Books, London).

CAMERON, James: The Making of Israel (Secker and Warburg, London. 1976).

GUNTHER, John: Inside Russia Today (Hamish Hamilton, London. Revised Edition. 1962).

HAMMERTON, Sir John, and GWYNN, Major General Sir Charles: The Second Great War (Volumes 7 and 9) (The Waverley Book Company Ltd., in association with the Amalgamated Press, London).

KIMCHE, Jon and David: The Secret Roads (Secker and Warburg, London. 1955).

MONROE, Elizabeth: Britain's Moment in the Middle East (Chatto and Windus, London. 1964).

MONTGOMERY, Field Marshal Sir Bernard: Memoirs of Field Marshal Montgomery (Collins, London. 1958).

SYKES, Christopher: Cross Roads to Israel (Collins, London. 1965).

2. *ORGANISATIONS*

Aberdeen Harbour Board.
B.B.C. Radio Shetland.
British Embassy Information Department, Oslo, Norway.
Corporation of Glasgow Libraries Department.
Corporation of Lloyd's, London.
Dollar Academy Library.
Edinburgh Corporation Libraries Department.
Embassy of Israel, London.
Imperial War Museum, London.
Jewish Museum, London.
Ministry of Defence, London.
Mitchell Library, Glasgow.
Lloyds' Register of Shipping, London.
National Maritime Museum, Haifa.
National Maritime Museum, London.
Norval, Photographers, Stirling.
Paisley Library.
P. and O. Ferries.
Public Record Office: ADMIN. 11201 — Subject: Salvage of s.s. *Vahva* by H.M. Tug *St. Mellons* Feb. 1940. Report by Master.
    ADMIN. 20661 — Subject: Boarding of s.s. *Anal* 31.5.47 by H.M.S. *Peacock*.
Royal Norwegian Embassy, London.
Scottish Television.
Shetland Library and Museum.
State of Israel, Department of Shipping and Ports, Haifa.
World Ship Society.
Zionist Federation of Great Britain and Ireland, London.

3. *NEWSPAPERS AND MAGAZINES*

Davar, (Tel Aviv, Israel) Hebrew Language Newspaper.
The Jerusalem Post.
The Palestine Post.
Marine News (World Ship Society).
Navy News.
The New Shetlander.
The Portsmouth Evening News.
The Scotsman.
Sea Breezes.
The Shetland News.
The Shetland Times.

Index